Mastering OpenStack

Second Edition

Discover your complete guide to designing, deploying, and managing OpenStack-based clouds in mid-to-large IT infrastructures with best practices, expert understanding, and more

Omar Khedher

Chandan Dutta Chowdhury

BIRMINGHAM - MUMBAI

Mastering OpenStack

Second Edition

First published: July 2015

Second edition: April 2017

Production reference: 1240417

Published by Packt Publishing Ltd.
Livery Place
35 Livery Street
Birmingham
B3 2PB, UK.
ISBN 978-1-78646-398-2

www.packtpub.com

Credits

Authors

Omar Khedher

Chandan Dutta Chowdhury

Reviewer

Mohamed Jarraya

Commissioning Editor

Kartikey Pandey

Acquisition Editor

Rahul Nair

Content Development Editor

Trusha Shriyan

Technical Editor

Naveenkumar Jain

Copy Editor

Safis Editing

Project Coordinator

Kinjal Bari

Proofreader

Safis Editing

Indexer

Pratik Shirodkar

Graphics

Kirk D'Penha

Production Coordinator

Arvindkumar Gupta

About the Authors

Omar Khedher is a systems and network engineer who has worked for a few years in cloud computing environment and has been involved in several private cloud projects based on OpenStack. He has also worked on projects targeting public cloud AWS.

Leveraging his skills as a system administrator in virtualization, storage, and networking, Omar works as a cloud system engineer for a leading advertising technology company, Fyber, based in Berlin. He is part of a highly skilled team working on several projects which include building and migrating infrastructure to the cloud using latest open source tools and DevOps philosophy.

He is also the author of the first edition of *Mastering OpenStack and OpenStack Sahara Essentials*, Packt Publishing. He has also authored a few academic publications based on a new research for cloud performance improvement.

Chandan Dutta Chowdhury is a tech lead at Juniper Networks Pvt. Ltd, working on OpenStack Neutron plugins. He has over 11 years of experience in the deployment of Linux-based solutions. In the past, he has been involved in developing Linux-based clustering and deployment solutions. He has contributed to setting up and maintaining a private cloud solution in Juniper Networks.

He was a speaker at the OpenStack Tokyo summit, where he presented the idea of adding firewall logs and other Neutron enhancements. He is speaker at the Austin summit where he talks about making enhancements to the Nova scheduler. He loves to explore technology and he blogs at `https://chandanduttachowdhury.wordpress.com`.

About the Reviewer

Mohamed Jarraya received his PhD and Master's degrees in Computer Science, LAAS-CNRS, Paul Sabatier University of Toulouse in 2000 and 1997, respectively. Mohamed have obtained an Engineering Diploma in Computer Science from ENIT, Tunisia. He is currently assistant professor at the College of Computation and Informatics, Saudi Electronic University, Saudi Arabia. His research interests include cloud computing, performance evaluation, modeling computing systems, and security.

www.Packtpub.com

For support files and downloads related to your book, please visit www.PacktPub.com.

Did you know that Packt offers eBook versions of every book published, with PDF and ePub files available? You can upgrade to the eBook version at www.PacktPub.com and as a print book customer, you are entitled to a discount on the eBook copy. Get in touch with us at service@packtpub.com for more details.

At www.PacktPub.com, you can also read a collection of free technical articles, sign up for a range of free newsletters and receive exclusive discounts and offers on Packt books and eBooks.

https://www.packtpub.com/mapt

Get the most in-demand software skills with Mapt. Mapt gives you full access to all Packt books and video courses, as well as industry-leading tools to help you plan your personal development and advance your career.

Why subscribe?

- Fully searchable across every book published by Packt
- Copy and paste, print, and bookmark content
- On demand and accessible via a web browser

Customer Feedback

Thanks for purchasing this Packt book. At Packt, quality is at the heart of our editorial process. To help us improve, please leave us an honest review on this book's Amazon page at `https://www.amazon.com/dp/1786463989`.

If you'd like to join our team of regular reviewers, you can e-mail us at `customerreviews@packtpub.com`. We award our regular reviewers with free eBooks and videos in exchange for their valuable feedback. Help us be relentless in improving our products!

Table of Contents

Preface

Today, OpenStack becomes a massive project increasingly extended with new features and subprojects. As hundreds of large array of enterprises are adopting and continuously contributing to the OpenStack ecosystem, it becomes the ultimate next generation private cloud solution. The range of services supported by OpenStack has grown naturally with the integration of new projects. This was a result of the innate stability of the core components of OpenStack and its great modular architecture. OpenStack has proved to be a mature private cloud platform for providing Infrastructure as a Service (IaaS) capabilities. With the emergence of new projects, the OpenStack ecosystem is trending to provide cloud services associated with Platform as a Service (PaaS). Why you should consider adopting OpenStack? There are many use cases and approaches that justify the adoption of OpenStack in any infrastructure based on various requirements and development needs. Still to think about how a private setup could rule the enterprise infrastructure, more specifically with OpenStack. The fundamental approach of such modular cloud platform is to provide more flexibility to manage the underlying infrastructure. Turning a traditional data center to a private cloud setup leverages the power of automation and increase the responsiveness for service delivery. You may notice while operating an OpenStack setup how easy it is to spin up new components. Its modular architecture unleashes the power of OpenStack as a pluggable cloud software solution. Another advantageous reason is its REST APIs exposure for each service. This embraces automation and easily facilitates the integration within the existing system setup. OpenStack can point you to the right path to overcome issues with legacy IT and vendor lock in. Within the latest releases of OpenStack, more modules and plugins have been developed to support third-party software services, including compute, storage, and network components.

In this new edition, we will be moving to a new learning path that will cover the novelty in OpenStack within the latest releases. Ideally, we will continue our journey by revisiting the OpenStack components and design patterns. We keep updating what is new in the core services architecture of OpenStack. That will cover new compute segregation and supported capabilities, including containerization, new network service shape, which includes Software Defined Network (SDN) and extends storage layout in OpenStack with the new incubated project. In each part of this edition, we keep sharing the experience in forms of best practices inspired from deployed OpenStack projects. We take a different method in this edition for automating the OpenStack deployment using system management tools on containers for the lab setup to mimic a real-production environment. This will give you a deep insight on the novelty of the OpenStack ecosystem and how to adopt it to meet your business needs.

The final section of this book will provide a complementary part in an OpenStack-ready production setup that includes administration, troubleshooting, monitoring, and benchmarking tool sets.

What this book covers

Chapter 1, *Designing OpenStack Cloud Architectural Consideration*, revisits the main architectural core services of OpenStack and highlights various updates on each architectural design. The chapter will be a starting stage for the first logical design of OpenStack that ends with a first physical model design framed with basic calculation for storage, compute, and network services. This will help choosing the right hardware to start building a private cloud ready for production deployment.

Chapter 2, *Deploying OpenStack - The DevOps Way*, introduces the trend of the philosophy of DevOps and how to exploit its benefits when deploying and managing the OpenStack environment. The chapter will introduce Ansible as a chosen system management tool to automate and manage the deployment of an OpenStack environment.

A succinct overview of the concept of Infrastructure as Code (IaC) will be taken under scope to enhance the OpenStack infrastructure management and operation. The first deployment will be based on containers for better isolation of OpenStack services and to mimic a real production setup.

Chapter 3, *OpenStack Compute - Choice of Hypervisor and Node Segregation*, presents deeper insights on the new updates of different services running in a cloud controller node and how to design for high availability and fault tolerant OpenStack services at an early stage. This will be covering the basic OpenStack core components, database, and message bus system. The chapter will decompose Ansible roles and playbooks in more detail for different OpenStack core components and common services.

Chapter 4, *OpenStack Compute – Choice of Hypervisor and Node Segregation*, covers the compute service in OpenStack and exposes the newly supported different hypervisors. A special fast growing virtualization technology supported lately by OpenStack will be introduced by covering Docker and the Magnum project. The chapter will introduce newly adopted concepts for large OpenStack setup including compute and host segregation, availability zones, regions, and the concept of cells in Nova. Compute scheduling will take a good part of the chapter by getting the grips of instance life cycle details. Ansible playbook of the compute service will be detailed to automate the installation of a new compute node in an existing OpenStack environment. The chapter will also explore few alternatives to backup an entire cluster in OpenStack.

Chapter 5, *OpenStack Storage - Block, Object, and File Share*, enlarges the scope of different storage types and alternatives supported by OpenStack. The chapter will give succinct updates on object and block storage in the latest releases of OpenStack. A new stable project supported by OpenStack Manilla will be covered in detail by going through its architecture layout within the OpenStack ecosystem. The chapter will explore different roles and Ansible playbooks for block and object storage, including an updated part for Ceph.

Chapter 6, *Openstack Networking – Choice of Connectivity Type and Other Networking Services*, focuses on presenting the current state of art in networking in OpenStack. This includes the new and updated Neutron plugins and different tunneling implementations developed in the latest OpenStack releases. The chapter describes different network implementations using Neutron. It details different network components and terminologies to simplify the management of virtual networks in OpenStack. A good part of the chapter is reserved to simplify the complexity of setting up virtual networks and routers by discovering how traffic flows under the hood. By the end of the chapter, Firewall as a Service (FWaaS) and VPN as a Service (VPNaaS) will be covered armed with examples.

Chapter 7, *Advanced Networking - A Look at SDN and NFV*, illustrates a new advanced networking topic in OpenStack. The chapter is dedicated to present the concepts of Software Defined Network (SDN) and NVF (Network Function Virtualization) and discuss their integration in OpenStack. The end of the chapter will explore the new implementation of Load Balancer as a Service in OpenStack.

Chapter 8, *Operating the OpenStack Infrastructure – The User Perspective*, discusses the usage of the readily deployed OpenStack platform. It will guide operators on how to manage users and projects and define how the underlying resources will be consumed. The chapter also gives a special insight on helping users to automate launching demanded stacks using the OpenStack orchestration service Heat. It will expose the need of adopting the concept of Infrastructure of Code and how it fulfills the new modern infrastructure requirements. As Heat will be introduced as the built-in tool to define resources from the template in OpenStack, the chapter will open the curtains for a new promising tool that supports multiple cloud providers: Terraform.

Chapter 9, *OpenStack HA and Failover*, speculates on the different high availability design patterns in OpenStack for each component. This will include a complete cluster setup for active and passive OpenStack services. The chapter will leverage not only the power of external tools to achieve high availability for message bus, database and other services, but will also explore the native relevant high available setups in OpenStack including network service.

Chapter 10, *Monitoring and Troubleshooting - Running a Healthy OpenStack Cluster*, explores the novelty of the telemetry service in OpenStack. More architectural discussions will be elaborated regarding the composition of the telemetry service within the latest releases, including alarms, events, and metrics in the ecosystem of OpenStack. It will show how to embrace the monitoring of the platform using external and popular tools such as Nagios. The chapter will help to get readers acquainted with how to diagnose common possible issues in OpenStack using different troubleshooting tools and methodologies.

Chapter 11, *Keeping Track for Logs – ELK and OpenStack*, goes through the available log files in OpenStack and how to use them for deep investigation when troubleshooting issues in OpenStack. The chapter will help you understand how to efficiently parse log files in OpenStack per service using modern and great log pipeline tools such as ELK (ElasticSearch, LogStash, and Kibana) stack. An updated and mature version of the ELK stack will be presented. The chapter will illustrate how to identify the root cause of the possible issues using effective ELK queries.

Chapter 12, *OpenStack Benchmarking and Performance Tuning - Maintaining Cloud Performance*, navigates through an advanced topic in the OpenStack journey: OpenStack performance boosting and benchmarking. By the means of one of the greatest benchmarking tools developed for OpenStack, Rally, you will gain a deeper understanding on how the OpenStack platform would behave. This would help to adjust the platform capacity and its architecture. Another novel topic will be elaborated to evaluate the OpenStack data plane. This will include benchmarking the network capabilities using Shaker tool.

What you need for this book

This book assumes a moderate level of the Linux operating system and cloud computing concepts. While this edition has been enhanced with richer content based on the latest updates in OpenStack, being familiar with the OpenStack ecosystem is very important. A basic knowledge and understanding of the network jargon, system management tools, and architecture design patters is required. Unlike the first edition, this book uses Ansible as the main system management tool for the OpenStack infrastructure management. It uses the OpenStack-Ansible official project, which is available in github `https://github.com/opens tack/openstack-ansible`. Thus, a good understanding of the YAML syntax is a big plus.

Feel free to use any tool for the test environment such as Oracle's VirtualBox, Vagrant, or VMware workstation. The lab setup can run OpenStack-Ansible using All-In-One build(OSA) found in the OpenStack-Ansible github repository. The book recommends installing the OpenStack environment on physical hardware to accomplish a production ready environment. Thus, a physical network infrastructure should be in place. On the other hand, running OpenStack in a virtual environment for testing purposes is possible if virtual network configuration is properly configured.

In this book, the following software list is required:

- Operating System: CentOS 7 or Ubuntu 14.04
- OpenStack – Mitaka or later release
- VirtualBox 4.5 or newer
- Vagrant 1.7 or newer
- Ansible server 2.2 or newer

As you run the OpenStack installation in a development environment, the following minimum hardware resources are required:

- A host machine with CPU hardware virtualization support
- 8 CPU cores
- 12 GB RAM
- 60 GB free disk space
- Two network interface cards

Internet connectivity is required to download the necessary packages for OpenStack and other tools. Additionally, refer to the `http://docs.openstack.org` guide for detailed instructions on installing the latest versions of OpenStack or to update the package that no longer exists in the older versions.

Who this book is for

This book is essentially geared towards the novice cloud operators, architects, and DevOps engineers who are looking to deploy a private cloud setup based on OpenStack. The book is also for those who are following up the trend of the novelty of OpenStack, willing to expand their knowledge and enlarge their current OpenStack setup based on the new features and projects recently added to the OpenStack ecosystem. The book does not provide detailed steps on installing or running OpenStack services, so the reader can focus on understanding advanced features and methodologies that treat the topic at hand. This edition gives more options to deploy and run an OpenStack environment, so the reader should be able to follow the examples included in each chapter of this book.

Conventions

In this book, you will find a number of text styles that distinguish between different kinds of information. Here are some examples of these styles and an explanation of their meaning.

Code words in text, database table names, folder names, filenames, file extensions, pathnames, dummy URLs, user input, and Twitter handles are shown as follows: "The configuration files of OSA are stored at /etc/openstack_ansible/ on the deployment host."

A block of code is set as follows:

```
[computes]
compute1.example.com
compute2.example.com
compute3.example.com
compute[20:30].example.com
```

Any command-line input or output is written as follows:

```
# vagrant up --provider virtualbox
# vagrant ssh
```

New terms and **important words** are shown in bold. Words that you see on the screen, for example, in menus or dialog boxes, appear in the text like this: "To manage security groups, navigate to **Compute|Access & Security| Security Group**."

Warnings or important notes appear in a box like this.

Tips and tricks appear like this.

Reader feedback

Feedback from our readers is always welcome. Let us know what you think about this book-what you liked or disliked. Reader feedback is important for us as it helps us develop titles that you will really get the most out of.

To send us general feedback, simply e-mail feedback@packtpub.com, and mention the book's title in the subject of your message.

If there is a topic that you have expertise in and you are interested in either writing or contributing to a book, see our author guide at www.packtpub.com/authors.

Customer support

Now that you are the proud owner of a Packt book, we have a number of things to help you to get the most from your purchase.

Downloading the example code

You can download the example code files for this book from your account at http://www.packtpub.com. If you purchased this book elsewhere, you can visit http://www.packtpub.com/support and register to have the files e-mailed directly to you.

You can download the code files by following these steps:

1. Log in or register to our website using your e-mail address and password.
2. Hover the mouse pointer on the **SUPPORT** tab at the top.
3. Click on **Code Downloads & Errata**.
4. Enter the name of the book in the **Search** box.
5. Select the book for which you're looking to download the code files.
6. Choose from the drop-down menu where you purchased this book from.
7. Click on **Code Download**.

Once the file is downloaded, please make sure that you unzip or extract the folder using the latest version of:

- WinRAR / 7-Zip for Windows
- Zipeg / iZip / UnRarX for Mac
- 7-Zip / PeaZip for Linux

The code bundle for the book is also hosted on GitHub at `https://github.com/PacktPubl ishing/Mastering-OpenStack-SecondEdition`. We also have other code bundles from our rich catalog of books and videos available at `https://github.com/PacktPublishing/`. Check them out!

Errata

Although we have taken every care to ensure the accuracy of our content, mistakes do happen. If you find a mistake in one of our books-maybe a mistake in the text or the code- we would be grateful if you could report this to us. By doing so, you can save other readers from frustration and help us improve subsequent versions of this book. If you find any errata, please report them by visiting `http://www.packtpub.com/submit-errata`, selecting your book, clicking on the **Errata Submission Form** link, and entering the details of your errata. Once your errata are verified, your submission will be accepted and the errata will be uploaded to our website or added to any list of existing errata under the Errata section of that title.

To view the previously submitted errata, go to `https://www.packtpub.com/books/conten t/support` and enter the name of the book in the search field. The required information will appear under the **Errata** section.

Piracy

Piracy of copyrighted material on the Internet is an ongoing problem across all media. At Packt, we take the protection of our copyright and licenses very seriously. If you come across any illegal copies of our works in any form on the Internet, please provide us with the location address or website name immediately so that we can pursue a remedy.

Please contact us at `copyright@packtpub.com` with a link to the suspected pirated material.

We appreciate your help in protecting our authors and our ability to bring you valuable content.

Questions

If you have a problem with any aspect of this book, you can contact us at `questions@packtpub.com`, and we will do our best to address the problem.

1
Designing OpenStack Cloud Architectural Consideration

The adoption of cloud technology has changed the way enterprises run their IT services. By leveraging new approaches on how resources are being used, several cloud solutions came into play with different categories: private, public, hybrid, and community. Whatever cloud category is used, this trend was felt by many organizations, which needs to introduce an orchestration engine to their infrastructure to embrace elasticity, scalability, and achieve a unique user experience to a certain extent. Nowadays, a remarkable orchestration solution, which falls into the private cloud category, has brought thousands of enterprises to the next era of data center generation: **OpenStack**. At the time of writing, OpenStack has been deployed in several large to medium enterprise infrastructures, running different types of production workload. The maturity of this cloud platform has been boosted due to the joint effort of several large organizations and its vast developer community around the globe. Within every new release, OpenStack brings more great features, which makes it a glorious solution for organizations seeking to invest in it, with returns in operational workloads and flexible infrastructure.

In this edition, we will keep explaining the novelties of OpenStack within the latest releases and discuss the great opportunities, which OpenStack can offer for an amazing cloud experience.

Deploying OpenStack is still a challenging step, which needs a good understanding of its beneficial returns to a given organization in terms of automation, orchestration, and flexibility. If expectations are set properly, this challenge will turn into a valuable opportunity, which deserves an investment.

After collecting infrastructure requirements, starting an OpenStack journey will need a good design and consistent deployment plan with different architectural assets.

The Japanese military leader, Miyamoto Musashi, wrote the following, very impressive thought on *perception and sight*, in *The Book of Five Rings, Start Publishing LLC*:

> *"In strategy, it is important to see distant things as if they were close and to take a distanced view of close things."*

Our OpenStack journey will start by going through the following points:

- Getting acquainted with the logical architecture of the OpenStack ecosystem by revisiting its components
- Learning how to design an OpenStack environment by choosing the right core services for the right environment
- Enlarging the OpenStack ecosystem by joining new projects within the latest stable releases
- Designing the first OpenStack architecture for a large-scale environment
- Planning for growth by going through first-deployment best practices and capacity planning

OpenStack - The new data center paradigm

Cloud computing is about providing various types of infrastructural services, such as **Software as a Service** (**SaaS**), **Platform as a Service** (**PaaS**), and **Infrastructure as a Service** (**IaaS**). The challenge, which has been set by the public cloud is about agility, speed, and self-service. Most companies have expensive IT systems, which they have developed and deployed over the years, but they are siloed and need human intervention. In many cases, IT systems are struggling to respond to the agility and speed of the public cloud services. The traditional data center model and siloed infrastructure might become unsustainable in today's agile service delivery environment. In fact, today's enterprise data center must focus on speed, flexibility, and automation for delivering services to get to the level of next-generation data center efficiency.

The big move to a software infrastructure has allowed administrators and operators to deliver a fully automated infrastructure within a minute. The next-generation data center reduces the infrastructure to a single, big, agile, scalable, and automated unit. The end result is a programmable, scalable, and multi-tenant-aware infrastructure. This is where OpenStack comes into the picture: it promises the features of a next-generation data center operating system. The ubiquitous influence of OpenStack was felt by many big global cloud enterprises such as VMware, Cisco, Juniper, IBM, Red Hat, Rackspace, PayPal, and eBay, to name but a few. Today, many of them are running a very large scalable private cloud based on OpenStack in their production environment. If you intend to be a part of a winning, innovative cloud enterprise, you should jump to the next-generation data center and gain valuable experience by adopting OpenStack in your IT infrastructure.

To read more about the success stories of many companies, visit `https ://www.openstack.org/user-stories`.

Introducing the OpenStack logical architecture

Before delving into the OpenStack architecture , we need to refresh or fill gaps and learn more about the basic concepts and usage of each core component.

In order to get a better understanding on how it works, it will be beneficial to first briefly parse the things, which make it work. In the following sections, we will look at various OpenStack services, which work together to provide the cloud experience to the end user. Despite the different services catering to different needs, they follow a common theme in their design that can be summarized as follows:

- Most OpenStack services are developed in Python, which aids rapid development.
- All OpenStack services provide REST APIs. These APIs are the main external communication interfaces for services and are used by the other services or end users.
- The OpenStack service itself may be implemented as different components. The components of a service communicate with each other over the message queue. The message queue provides various advantages such as queuing of requests, loose coupling, and load distribution among the worker daemons.

With this common theme in mind, let's now put the essential core components under the microscope and go a bit further by asking the question: What is the purpose of such component?

Keystone - identity management

From an architectural perspective, **Keystone** presents the simplest service in the OpenStack composition. It is the core component and provides an identity service comprising authentication and authorization of tenants in OpenStack. Communications between different OpenStack services are authorized by Keystone to ensure that the right user or service is able to utilize the requested OpenStack service. Keystone integrates with numerous authentication mechanisms such as username/password and token/authentication-based systems. Additionally, it is possible to integrate it with an existing backend such as the **Lightweight Directory Access Protocol** (**LDAP**) and the **Pluggable Authentication Module** (**PAM**).

 Keystone also provides a service catalog as a registry of all the OpenStack services.

With the evolution of Keystone, many features have been implemented within recent OpenStack releases leveraging a centralized and federated identity solution. This will allow users to use their credentials in an existing, centralized, sign-on backend and decouples the authentication mechanism from Keystone.

The federation identity solution becomes more stable within the OpenStack **Juno** release, which engages Keystone as a **Service Provider** (**SP**), and uses and consumes from a trusted **Provider of Identity** (**IdP**), user identity information in **SAML** assertions, or **OpenID Connect** claims. An IdP can be backed by LDAP, Active Directory, or SQL.

Swift - object storage

Swift is one of the storage services available to OpenStack users. It provides an object-based storage service and is accessible through REST APIs. Compared to traditional storage solutions, file shares, or block-based access, an Object-Storage takes the approach of dealing with stored data as objects that can be stored and retrieved from the Object-Store. A very high-level overview of Object Storage goes like this. To store the data, the Object-Store splits it into smaller chunks and stores it in separate containers. These containers are maintained in redundant copies spread across a cluster of storage nodes to provide high availability, auto-recovery, and horizontal scalability.

We will leave the details of the Swift architecture for later. Briefly, it has a number of benefits:

- It has no central brain, and indicates no **Single Point Of Failure** (**SPOF**)
- It is curative, and indicates auto-recovery in the case of failure
- It is highly scalable for large petabytes of storage access by scaling horizontally
- It has a better performance, which is achieved by spreading the load over the storage nodes
- It has inexpensive hardware that can be used for redundant storage clusters

Cinder - block storage

You may wonder whether there is another way to provide storage to OpenStack users. Indeed, the management of the persistent block storage is available in OpenStack by using the **Cinder** service. Its main capability is to provide block-level storage to the virtual machine. Cinder provides raw volumes that can be used as hard disks in virtual machines.

Some of the features that Cinder offers are as follows:

- **Volume management**: This allows the creation or deletion of a volume
- **Snapshot management**: This allows the creation or deletion of a snapshot of volumes
- Attaching or detaching volumes from instances
- Cloning volumes
- Creating volumes from snapshots
- Copy of images to volumes and vice versa

It is very important to keep in mind that like Keystone services, Cinder features can be delivered by orchestrating various backend volume providers through configurable drivers for the vendor's storage products such as from IBM, NetApp, Nexenta, and VMware.

Cinder is proven as an ideal solution or a replacement of the old **nova-volume** service that existed before the **Folsom** release on an architectural level. It is important to know that Cinder has organized and created a catalog of block-based storage devices with several differing characteristics. However, we must obviously consider the limitation of commodity storage such as redundancy and auto-scaling.

When Cinder was introduced in the OpenStack **Grizzly** release, a joint feature was implemented to allow creating backups for Cinder volumes. A common use case has seen Swift evolves as a storage backup solution. Within the next few releases, Cinder was enriched with more backup target stores such as NFS, Ceph, GlusterFS, POSIX file systems, and the property IBM solution, *Tivoli Storage Manager*. This great backup extensible feature is defined by the means of Cinder backup drivers that have become richer in every new release. Within the OpenStack Mitaka release, Cinder has shown its vast number of backup options by marrying two different cloud computing environments, bringing an additional backup driver targeting *Google Cloud Platform*. This exciting opportunity allows OpenStack operators to leverage an hybrid cloud backup solution that empowers , a disaster recovery strategy for persistent data. What about security? This latent issue has been resolved since the **Kilo** release so Cinder volumes can be encrypted before starting any backup operations.

Manila - File share

Apart from the block and object we discussed in the previous section, since the **Juno** release, OpenStack has also had a file-share-based storage service called **Manila**. It provides storage as a remote file system. In operation, it resembles the **Network File System (NFS)** or **SAMBA** storage service that we are used on Linux while, in contrast to Cinder, it resembles the **Storage Area Network (SAN)** service. In fact, NFS and SAMBA or the **Common Internet File System (CIFS)** are supported as backend drivers to the Manila service. The Manila service provides the orchestration of shares on the share servers.

More details on storage services will be covered in `Chapter 5`, *OpenStack Storage - Block, Object, and File Share*.

Each storage solution in OpenStack has been designed for a specific set of purposes and implemented for different targets. Before taking any architectural design decisions, it is crucial to understand the difference between existing storage options in OpenStack today, as outlined in the following table:

Specification	Storage Type		
	Swift	**Cinder**	**Manila**
Access mode	Objects through REST API	As block devices.	File-based access
Multi-access	OK	No, can only be used by one client	OK
Persistence	OK	OK	OK
Accessibility	Anywhere	Within single VM	Within multiple VMs
Performance	OK	OK	OK

Glance - Image registry

The Glance service provides a registry of images and metadata that the OpenStack user can launch as a virtual machine. Various image formats are supported and can be used based on the choice of hypervisor. Glance supports images for KVM/Qemu, XEN, VMware, Docker, and so on.

As a new user of OpenStack, one might often wonder, What is the difference between Glance and Swift? Both handle storage. What is the difference between them? Why do I need to integrate such a solution?

Swift is a storage system, whereas Glance is an image registry. The difference between the two is that Glance is a service that keeps track of virtual machine images and metadata associated with the images. Metadata can be information such as a kernel, disk images, disk format, and so on. Glance makes this information available to OpenStack users over REST APIs. Glance can use a variety of backends for storing images. The default is to use directories, but in a massive production environment it can use other approaches such as NFS and even Swift.

Swift, on the other hand, is a storage system. It is designed for object-storage where you can keep data such as virtual disks, images, backup archiving, and so on.

The mission of Glance is to be an image registry. From an architectural point of view, the goal of Glance is to focus on advanced ways to store and query image information via the Image Service API. A typical use case for Glance is to allow a client (which can be a user or an external service) to register a new virtual disk image, while a storage system focuses on providing a highly scalable and redundant data store. At this level, as a technical operator, your challenge is to provide the right storage solution to meet cost and performance requirements. This will be discussed at the end of the book.

Nova-Compute service

As you may already know, **Nova** is the original core component of OpenStack. From an architectural level, it is considered one of the most complicated components of OpenStack. Nova provides the compute service in OpenStack and manages virtual machines in response to service requests made by OpenStack users.

What makes Nova complex is its interaction with a large number of other OpenStack services and internal components, which it must collaborate with to respond to user requests for running a VM.

Let's break down the Nova service itself and look at its architecture as a distributed application that needs orchestration between different components to carry out tasks.

nova-api

The **nova-api** component accepts and responds to the end user and computes API calls. The end users or other components communicate with the OpenStack nova-api interface to create instances via the OpenStack API or EC2 API.

> The nova-api initiates most orchestrating activities such as the running of an instance or the enforcement of some particular policies.

nova-compute

The **nova-compute** component is primarily a worker daemon that creates and terminates VM instances via the hypervisor's APIs (XenAPI for XenServer, Libvirt KVM, and the VMware API for VMware).

nova-network

The **nova-network** component accepts networking tasks from the queue and then performs these tasks to manipulate the network (such as setting up bridging interfaces or changing IP table rules).

 Neutron is a replacement for the nova-network service.

nova-scheduler

The **nova-scheduler** component takes a VM instance's request from the queue and determines where it should run (specifically which compute host it should run on). At an application architecture level, the term scheduling or scheduler invokes a systematic search for the best outfit for a given infrastructure to improve its performance.

nova-conductor

The **nova-conductor** service provides database access to compute nodes. The idea behind this service is to prevent direct database access from the compute nodes, thus enhancing database security in case one of the compute nodes gets compromised.

By zooming out of the general components of OpenStack, we find that Nova interacts with several services such as Keystone for authentication, Glance for images, and Horizon for the web interface. For example, the Glance interaction is central; the API process can upload any query to Glance, while nova-compute will download images to launch instances.

 Nova also provides console services that allow end users to access the console of the virtual instance through a proxy such as **nova-console**, **nova-novncproxy,** and **nova-consoleauth**.

Neutron - Networking services

Neutron provides a real **Network as a Service** (**NaaS**) capability between interface devices that are managed by OpenStack services such as Nova. There are various characteristics that should be considered for Neutron:

- It allows users to create their own networks and then attaches server interfaces to them
- Its pluggable backend architecture lets users take advantage of commodity gear or vendor-supported equipment
- It provides extensions to allow additional network services to be integrated

Neutron has many core network features that are constantly growing and maturing. Some of these features are useful for routers, virtual switches, and SDN networking controllers.

Neutron introduces the following core resources:

- **Ports**: Ports in Neutron refer to the virtual switch connections. These connections are where instances and network services are attached to networks. When attached to subnets, the defined MAC and IP addresses of the interfaces are plugged into them.
- **Networks**: Neutron defines networks as isolated Layer 2 network segments. Operators will see networks as logical switches that are implemented by the Linux bridging tools, Open vSwitch, or some other virtual switch software. Unlike physical networks, either the operators or users in OpenStack can define this.
- **Subnet**: Subnets in Neutron represent a block of IP addresses associated with a network. IP addresses from this block are allocated to the ports.

Neutron provides additional resources as extensions. The following are some of the commonly used extensions:

- **Routers**: Routers provide gateways between various networks.
- **Private IPs**: Neutron defines two types of networks. They are as follows:
    - **Tenant networks**: Tenant networks use private IP addresses. Private IP addresses are visible within the instance and this allows the tenant's instances to communicate while maintaining isolation from the other tenant's traffic. Private IP addresses are not visible to the Internet.

- **External networks**: External networks are visible and routable from the Internet. They must use routable subnet blocks.
- **Floating IPs:** A floating IP is an IP address allocated on an external network that Neutron maps to the private IP of an instance. Floating IP addresses are assigned to an instance so that they can connect to external networks and access the Internet. Neutron achieves the mapping of floating IPs to the private IP of the instance by using **Network Address Translation (NAT)**.

Neutron also provides advanced services to rule additional network OpenStack capabilities as follows:

- **Load Balancing as a Service (LBaaS)** to distribute the traffic among multiple compute node instances.
- **Firewall as a Service (FWaaS)** to secure layer 3 and 4 network perimeter access.
- **Virtual Private Network as a Service (VPNaaS)** to build secured tunnels between instances or hosts.

> You can refer to the latest updated Mitaka release documentation for more information on networking in OpenStack at `http://docs.openstack.org/mitaka/networking-guide/`.

The Neutron architecture

The three main components of the Neutron architecture are:

- **Neutron server**: It accepts API requests and routes them to the appropriate Neutron plugin for action.
- **Neutron plugins**: They perform the actual work for the orchestration of backend devices such as the plugging in or unplugging ports, creating networks and subnets, or IP addressing.

> Agents and plugins differ depending on the vendor technology of a particular cloud for the virtual and physical Cisco switches, NEC, OpenFlow, OpenSwitch, Linux bridging, and so on.

- **Neutron agents**: Neutron agents run on the compute and network nodes. The agents receive commands from the plugins on the Neutron server and bring the changes into effect on the individual compute or network nodes. Different types of Neutron agents implement different functionality. For example, the Open vSwitch agent implements L2 connectivity by plugging and unplugging ports onto **Open vSwitch** (**OVS**) bridges and they run on both compute and network nodes, whereas L3 agents run only on network nodes and provide routing and NAT services.

Neutron is a service that manages network connectivity between the OpenStack instances. It ensures that the network will not be turned into a bottleneck or limiting factor in a cloud deployment and gives users real self-service, even over their network configurations.

Another advantage of Neutron is its ability to provide a way to integrate vendor networking solutions and a flexible way to extend network services. It is designed to provide a plugin and extension mechanism that presents an option for network operators to enable different technologies via the Neutron API. More details about this will be covered in Chapter 6, *OpenStack Networking - Choice of Connectivity Types and Networking Services* and `Chapter 7`, *Advances Networking - A Look SDN and NFV*.

 Keep in mind that Neutron allows users to manage and create networks or connect servers and nodes to various networks.

The scalability advantage will be discussed in a later topic in the context of the **Software Defined Network** (**SDN**) and **Network Function Virtualization** (**NFV**) technology, which is attractive to many networks and administrators who seek a high-level network multi-tenancy.

Ceilometer, Aodh, and Gnocchi - Telemetry

Ceilometer provides a metering service in OpenStack. In a shared, multi-tenant environment such as OpenStack, metering resource utilization is of prime importance.

Ceilometer collects data associated with resources. Resources can be any entity in the OpenStack cloud such as VMs, disks, networks, routers, and so on. Resources are associated with meters. The utilization data is stored in the form of samples in units defined by the associated meter. Ceilometer has an inbuilt summarization capability.

Ceilometer allows data collection from various sources, such as the message bus, polling resources, centralized agents, and so on.

As an additional design change in the Telemetry service in OpenStack since the **Liberty** release, the **Alarming** service has been decoupled from the Ceilometer project to make use of a new incubated project code-named **Aodh**. The Telemetry Alarming service will be dedicated to managing alarms and triggering them based on collected metering and scheduled events

More Telemetry service enhancements have been proposed to adopt a **Time Series Database as a Service** project code-named **Gnoochi**. This architectural change will tackle the challenge of metrics and event storage at scale in the OpenStack Telemetry service and improve its performance.

Telemetry and system monitoring are covered in more detail in `Chapter 10`, *Monitoring and Troubleshooting - Running a Healthy OpenStack Cluster*.

Heat - Orchestration

Debuting in the **Havana** release is the OpenStack Orchestration project **Heat**. Initial development for Heat was limited to a few OpenStack resources including compute, image, block storage, and network services. Heat has boosted the emergence of resource management in OpenStack by orchestrating different cloud resources resulting in the creation of stacks to run applications with a few pushes of a button. From simple template engine text files referred to as **HOT** templates (**Heat Orchestration Template**), users are able to provision the desired resources and run applications in no time. Heat is becoming an attractive OpenStack project due to its maturity and extended support resources catalog within the latest OpenStack releases. Other incubated OpenStack projects such as Sahara (Big Data as a Service) have been implemented to use the Heat engine to orchestrate the creation of the underlying resources stack. It is becoming a mature component in OpenStack and can be integrated with some system configuration management tools such as **Chef** for full stack automation and configuration setup.

Heat uses templates files in YAML or JSON format; indentation is important!

 The Orchestration project in OpenStack is covered in more detail in `Chapter 8`, *Operating the OpenStack Infrastructure- The User Perspective*.

Horizon - Dashboard

Horizon is the web dashboard that pulls all the different pieces together from the OpenStack ecosystem.

Horizon provides a web frontend for OpenStack services. Currently, it includes all the OpenStack services as well as some incubated projects. It was designed as a stateless and data-less web application. It does nothing more than initiate actions in the OpenStack services via API calls and display information that OpenStack returns to Horizon. It does not keep any data except the session information in its own data store. It is designed to be a reference implementation that can be customized and extended by operators for a particular cloud. It forms the basis of several public clouds, most notably the HP Public Cloud, and at its heart is its extensible modular approach to construction.

Horizon is based on a series of modules called **panels** that define the interaction of each service. Its modules can be enabled or disabled, depending on the service availability of the particular cloud. In addition to this functional flexibility, Horizon is easy to style with **Cascading Style Sheets** (**CSS**).

Message Queue

Message Queue provides a central hub to pass messages between different components of a service. This is where information is shared between different daemons by facilitating the communication between discrete processes in an asynchronous way.

One major advantage of the queuing system is that it can buffer requests and provide unicast and group-based communication services to subscribers.

The database

Its database stores most of the build-time and run-time states for the cloud infrastructure, including instance types that are available for use, instances in use, available networks, and projects. It provides a persistent storage for preserving the state of the cloud infrastructure. It is the second essential piece of sharing information in all OpenStack components.

Gathering the pieces and building a picture

Let's try to see how OpenStack works by chaining all the service cores covered in the previous sections in a series of steps:

1. Authentication is the first action performed. This is where Keystone comes into the picture. Keystone authenticates the user based on credentials such as the username and password.
2. The service catalog is then provided by Keystone. This contains information about the OpenStack services and the API endpoints.
3. You can use the Openstack CLI to get the catalog:

```
$ openstack catalog list
```

 The service catalog is a JSON structure that exposes the resources available on a token request.

4. Typically, once authenticated, you can talk to an API node. There are different APIs in the OpenStack ecosystem (the OpenStack API and EC2 API):

The following figure shows a high-level view of how OpenStack works:

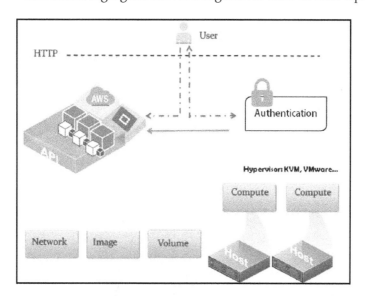

5. Another element in the architecture is the instance scheduler. Schedulers are implemented by OpenStack services that are architected around worker daemons. The worker daemons manage the launching of instances on individual nodes and keep track of resources available to the physical nodes on which they run. The scheduler in an OpenStack service looks at the state of the resources on a physical node (provided by the worker daemons) and decides the best candidate node to launch a virtual instance on. An example of this architecture is nova-scheduler. This selects the compute node to run a virtual machine or Neutron L3 scheduler, which decides which L3 network node will host a virtual router.

 The scheduling process in OpenStack Nova can perform different algorithms such as simple, chance, and zone. An advanced way to do this is by deploying weights and filters by ranking servers as its available resources.

Provisioning a VM under the hood

It is important to understand how different services in OpenStack work together, leading to a running virtual machine. We have already seen how a request is processed in OpenStack via APIs.

Let's figure out how things work by referring to the following simple architecture diagram:

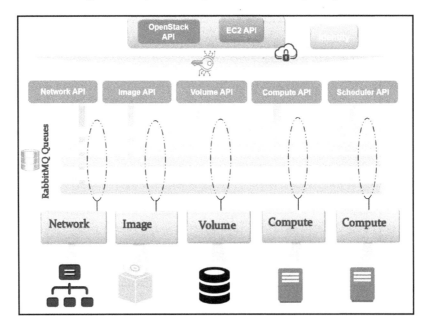

The process of launching a virtual machine involves the interaction of the main OpenStack services that form the building blocks of an instance including compute, network, storage, and the base image. As shown in the previous diagram, OpenStack services interact with each other via a message bus to submit and retrieve RPC calls. The information of each step of the provisioning process is verified and passed by different OpenStack services via the message bus. From an architecture perspective, sub system calls are defined and treated in OpenStack API endpoints involving: Nova, Glance, Cinder, and Neutron.

On the other hand, the inter-communication of APIs within OpenStack requires an authentication mechanism to be trusted, which involves Keystone.

Starting with the identity service, the following steps summarize briefly the provisioning workflow based on API calls in OpenStack:

- Calling the identity service for authentication
- Generating a token to be used for subsequent calls
- Contacting the image service to list and retrieve a base image
- Processing the request to the compute service API
- Processing compute service calls to determine security groups and keys
- Calling the network service API to determine available networks
- Choosing the hypervisor node by the compute scheduler service
- Calling the block storage service API to allocate volume to the instance
- Spinning up the instance in the hypervisor via the compute service API call
- Calling the network service API to allocate network resources to the instance

It is important to keep in mind that handling tokens in OpenStack on every API call and service request is a time limited operation. One of the major causes of a failed provisioning operation in OpenStack is the expiration of the token during subsequent API calls. Additionally, the management of tokens has faced a few changes within different OpenStack releases. This includes two different approaches used in OpenStack prior to the **Liberty** release including:

- **Universally Unique Identifier (UUID)**: Within Keystone version 2, an UUID token will be generated and passed along every API call between client services and back to Keystone for validation. This version has proven performance degradation of the identity service.
- **Public Key Infrastructure (PKI)**: Within Keystone version 3, tokens are no longer validated at each API call by Keystone. API endpoints can verify the token by checking the Keystone signature added when initially generating the token.

Starting from the Kilo release, handling tokens in Keystone has progressed by introducing more sophisticated cryptographic authentication token methods, such as Fernet. The new implementation will help to tackle the token performance issue noticed in UUID and PKI tokens. Fernet is fully supported in the Mitaka release and the community is pushing to adopt it as the default. On the other hand, PKI tokens are deprecated in favor of Fernet tokens in further releases of Kilo OpenStack.

 More advanced topics regarding additions introduced in Keystone are covered briefly in `Chapter 3`, *OpenStack Cluster – The Cloud Controller and Common Services*.

A sample architecture setup

Let us first go through the architecture that can be deployed.

OpenStack deployment

Deployment of OpenStack depends on the components were covered previously. It confirms your understanding of how to start designing a complete OpenStack environment. Of course, assuming the versatility and flexibility of such a cloud management platform, OpenStack offers several possibilities that can be considered an advantage. However, owing to such flexibility, it's a challenge to come with the right design decision that suits your needs.

At the end of the day, it all comes down to the use cases that your cloud is designed to service.

Many enterprises have successfully designed their OpenStack environments by going through three phases of design: designing a conceptual model, designing a logical model, and finally, realizing the physical design. It's obvious that complexity increases from the conceptual to the logical design and from the logical to the physical design.

The conceptual model design

As the first conceptual phase, we will have our high-level reflection on what we will need from certain generic classes from the OpenStack architecture:

Class	Role
Compute	Stores virtual machine images Provides a user interface
Image	Stores disk files Provides a user interface
Object storage	Stores objects Provides a user interface
Block storage	Provides volumes Provides a user interface
Network	Provides network connectivity Provides a user interface
Telemetry	Provides measurements, metrics, and alerts Provides a user interface
File Share	Provides a scale-out file share system for OpenStack Provides a user interface
Identity	Provides authentication
Dashboard	Provides a graphical user interface
Orchestration	Provides orchestration engine for stack creation Provides a user interface

Let's map the generic basic classes in the following simplified diagram:

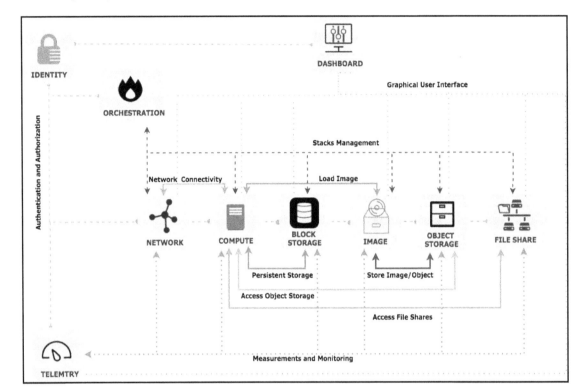

Keep in mind that the illustrated diagram will be refined over and over again since we will aim to integrate more services within our first basic design. In other words, we are following an *incremental* design approach, within which we should exploit the flexibility of the OpenStack architecture.

At this level, we can have a vision and direction of the main goal without worrying about the details.

The logical model design

Based on the conceptual reflection design, most probably you will have a good idea about different OpenStack core components, which will lay the formulation of the logical design.

We will start by outlining the relationships and dependencies between the service core of OpenStack. In this section we will look at the deployment architecture of OpenStack. We will start by identifying nodes to run an OpenStack service: the cloud controller, network nodes, and the compute node. You may wonder why such a consideration goes through a physical design classification. However, seeing the cloud controller and compute nodes as simple packages that encapsulate a bunch of OpenStack services will help you refine your design at an early stage. Furthermore, this approach will help plan in advance further high availability and scalability requirements, and will allow you to introduce them later in more detail.

 Chapter 3, *OpenStack Cluster – The Cloud Controller and Common Services* describes in depth how to distribute OpenStack services between cloud controllers and compute nodes.

Thus, the physical model design will be elaborated based on the previous theoretical phases by assigning parameters and values to our design. Let's start with our first logical iteration:

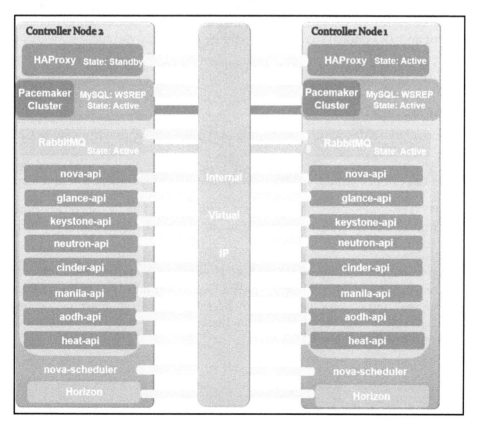

Obviously, in a highly available setup, we should achieve a degree of redundancy in each service within OpenStack. You may wonder about the critical OpenStack services claimed in the first part of this chapter: the database and message queue. Why can't they be separately clustered or packaged on their own? This is a pertinent question. Remember that we are still in the second logical phase where we try to dive slowly into the infrastructure without getting into the details. Besides, we keep on going from a generic and simple design to targeting specific use-cases. Decoupling infrastructure components such as RabbitMQ or MySQL from now on may lead to skipping the requirements of a simple design.

What about high availability?

The previous figure includes several essential solutions for a highly-scalable and redundant OpenStack environment such as **virtual IP** (**VIP**), HAProxy, and Pacemaker. The aforementioned technologies will be discussed in more detail in `Chapter 9`, *Openstack HA and Failover*.

Compute nodes are relatively simple as they are intended just to run the virtual machine's workload. In order to manage the VMs, the nova-compute service can be assigned for each compute node. Besides, we should not forget that the compute nodes will not be isolated; a Neutron agent and an optional Ceilometer compute agent may run these nodes.

Network nodes will run Neutron agents for DHCP, and L3 connectivity.

What about storage?

You should now have a deeper understanding of the storage types within Swift, Cinder, and Manila.

However, we have not covered third-party software-defined storage, Swift and Cinder.

More details will be covered in Chapter 5, *OpenStack Storage , and File Share*. For now, we will design from a basis where we have to decide how Cinder, Manila, and/or Swift will be a part of our logical design.

You will have to ask yourself questions such as: How much data do I need to store? Will my future use cases result in a wide range of applications that run heavy-analysis data? What are my storage requirements for incrementally backing up a virtual machine's snapshots? Do I really need control over the filesystem on the storage or is just a file share enough? Do I need a shared storage between VMs?

Many will ask the following question: If one can be satisfied by ephemeral storage, why offer block/share storage? To answer this question, you can think about ephemeral storage as the place where the end user will not be able to access the virtual disk associated with its VM when it is terminated. Ephemeral storage should mainly be used in production when the VM state is non-critical, where users or application don't store data on the VM. If you need your data to be persistent, you must plan for a storage service such as Cinder or Manila.

Remember that the current design applies for medium to large infrastructures. Ephemeral storage can also be a choice for certain users; for example, when they consider building a test environment. Considering the same case for Swift, we claimed previously that object storage might be used to store machine images, but when do we use such a solution? Simply put, when you have a sufficient volume of critical data in your cloud environment and start to feel the need for replication and redundancy.

Networking needs

One of the most complicated services defined previously should be connected.

The logical networking design

OpenStack allows a wide ranging of configurations that variation, and tunneled networks such as GRE, VXLAN, and so on, with Neutron are not intuitively obvious from their appearance to be able to be implemented without fetching their use case in our design. Thus, this important step implies that you may differ between different network topologies because of the reasons behind why every choice was made and why it may work for a given use case.

OpenStack has moved from simplistic network features to more complicated ones, but of course the reason is that it offers more flexibility! This is why OpenStack is here. It brings as much flexibility as it can! Without taking any random network-related decisions, let's see which network modes are available. We will keep on filtering until we hit the first correct target topology:

Network mode	Network Characteristics	Implementation
nova-network	Flat network design without tenant traffic isolation	nova-network Flat DHCP
	Isolated tenants traffic and predefined fixed private IP space size Limited number of tenant networks (4K VLANs limit)	nova-network VLANManager
Neutron	Isolated tenants traffic Limited number of tenant networks (4K VLANs limit)	Neutron VLAN
	Increased number of tenant networks Increased packet size Lower performance	Neutron tunneled networking (GRE, VXLAN, and so on)

The preceding table shows a simple differentiation between two different logical network designs for OpenStack. Every mode shows its own requirements: this is very important and should be taken into consideration before the deployment.

Arguing about our example choice, since we aim to deploy a very flexible, large-scale environment we will toggle the Neutron choice for networking management instead of nova-network.

Note that it is also possible to keep on going with nova-network, but you have to worry about any **Single Point Of Failure** (**SPOF**) in the infrastructure. The choice was made for Neutron, since we started from a basic network deployment. We will cover more advanced features in the subsequent chapters of this book.

We would like to exploit a major advantage of Neutron compared to nova-network, which is the virtualization of Layers 2 and 3 of the OSI network model.

Let's see how we can expose our logical network design. For performance reasons; it is highly recommended to implement a topology that can handle different types of traffic by using separated logical networks.

In this way, as your network grows, it will still be manageable in case a sudden bottleneck or an unexpected failure affects a segment.

Let us look at the different rate the OpenStack environment the OpenStack environment

Physical network layout

We will start by looking at the physical networking requirements of the cloud.

The tenant data network

The main feature of a data network that it provides the physical path for the virtual networks created by the OpenStack tenants. It separates the tenant data traffic from the infrastructure communication path required for the communication between the OpenStack component itself.

Management and the API network

In a smaller deployment, the traffic for management and communication between the OpenStack components can be on the same physical link. This physical network provides a path for communication between the various OpenStack components such as REST API access and DB traffic, as well as for managing the OpenStack nodes.
For a production environment, the network can be further subdivided to provide better isolation of traffic and contain the load on the individual networks.

The Storage network

The storage network provides physical connectivity and isolation for storage-related traffic between the VMs and the storage servers. As the traffic load for the storage network is quite high, it is a good idea to isolate the storage network load from the management and tenant traffic.

Virtual Network types

Let's now look at the virtual network types and their features.

The external network

The features of an external or a public network are as follows:

- It provides global connectivity and uses routable IP addressing
- It is used by the virtual router to perform SNAT from the VM instances and provide external access to traffic originating from the VM and going to the Internet

SNAT refers to **Source Network Address Translation**. It allows traffic from a private network to go out to the Internet. OpenStack supports SNAT through its Neutron APIs for routers. More information can be found at `http://en.wikipedia.org/wiki/Network_address_translati on`.

- It is used to provide a DNAT service for traffic from the Internet to reach a service running on the VM instance

While using VLANs, by tagging networks and combining multiple networks into one **Network Interface Card** (**NIC**), you can optionally leave the public network untagged for that NIC, to make the access to the OpenStack dashboard and the public OpenStack API endpoints simple.

The tenant networks

The features of the tenant network are as follows:

- It provides a private network between virtual machines
- It uses private IP space
- It provides isolation of tenant traffic and allows multi-tenancy requirements for networking services

The next step is to validate our network design in a simple diagram:

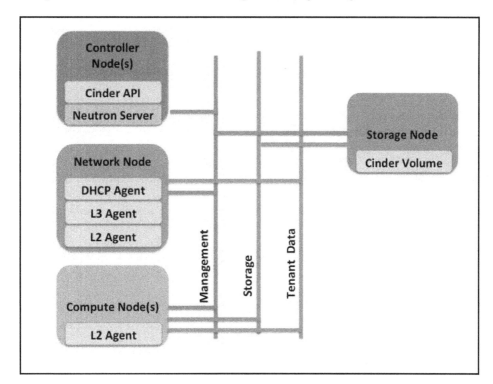

The physical model design

Finally, we will bring our logical design to life in the form of a physical design.

We can start with a limited number of servers just to setup the first deployment of our environment effectively.

You have to consider the fact that hardware commodity selection will accomplish the mission of our *massive scalable architecture*.

Estimating the hardware capabilities

Since the architecture is being designed to scale horizontally, we can add more servers to the setup. We will start by using commodity class, cost-effective hardware.

In order to expect our infrastructure economy, it would be great to make some basic hardware calculations for the first estimation of our exact requirements.

Considering the possibility of experiencing contentions for resources such as CPU, RAM, network, and disk, you cannot wait for a particular physical component to fail before you take corrective action, which might be more complicated.

Let's inspect a real-life example of the impact of underestimating capacity planning. A cloud-hosting company set up two medium servers, one for an e-mail server and the other to host the official website. The company, which is one of our several clients, grew in a few months and eventually ran out of disk space. The expected time to resolve such an issue is a few hours, but it took days. The problem was that all the parties did not make proper use of the cloud, due to the on demand nature of the service. This led to **Mean Time To Repair** (**MTTR**) increasing exponentially. The cloud provider did not expect this!

Incidents like this highlight the importance of proper capacity planning for your cloud infrastructure. Capacity management is considered a day-to-day responsibility where you have to stay updated with regard to software or hardware upgrades.

Through a continuous monitoring process of service consumption, you will be able to reduce the IT risk and provide a quick response to the customer's needs.

From your first hardware deployment, keep running your capacity management processes by looping through tuning, monitoring, and analysis.

The next stop will take into account your tuned parameters and introduce, within your hardware/software, the right change, which involves a synergy of the change management process.

Let's make our first calculation based on certain requirements. For example, let's say we aim to run 200 VMs in our OpenStack environment.

CPU calculations

The following are the calculation-related assumptions:

- 200 virtual machines
- No CPU oversubscribing

Processor over subscription is defined as the total number of CPUs that are assigned to all the powered-on virtual machines multiplied by the hardware CPU core. If this number is greater than the GHz purchased, the environment is oversubscribed.

- GHz per physical core = 2.6 GHz
- Physical core hyper-threading support = use factor 2
- GHz per VM (AVG compute units) = 2 GHz
- GHz per VM (MAX compute units) = 16 GHz
- Intel Xeon E5-2648L v2 core CPU = 10
- CPU sockets per server = 2

The formula for calculating the total number of CPU cores is as follows:

(number of VMs x number of GHz per VM) / number of GHz per core

*(200 * 2) / 2.6 = 153.846*

We have 153 CPU cores for 200 VMs.

The formula for calculating the number of core CPU sockets is as follows:

Total number of sockets / number of sockets per server

153 / 10 = 15.3

We will need 15 sockets

The formula for calculating the number of socket servers is as follows:

Total number of sockets / Number of sockets per server

15 / 2 = 7.5

You will need around seven to eight dual socket servers.

The number of virtual machines per server with eight dual socket servers is calculated as follows:

We can deploy 25 virtual machines per server

200 / 8 = 25

Number of virtual machines / number of servers

Memory calculations

Based on the previous example, 25 VMs can be deployed per compute node. Memory sizing is also important to avoid making unreasonable resource allocations.

Let's make an assumption list (keep in mind that it always depends on your budget and needs):

- 2 GB RAM per VM
- 8 GB RAM maximum dynamic allocations per VM
- Compute nodes supporting slots of: 2, 4, 8, and 16 GB sticks
- RAM available per compute node:

    8 * 25 = 200 GB

Considering the number of sticks supported by your server, you will need around 256 GB installed. Therefore, the total number of RAM sticks installed can be calculated in the following way:

    Total available RAM / MAX Available RAM-Stick size
    256 / 16 = 16

Network calculations

To fulfill the plans that were drawn for reference, let's have a look at our assumptions:

- 200 Mbits/second is needed per VM
- Minimum network latency

To do this, it might be possible to serve our VMs by using a 10 GB link for each server, which will give:

10,000 Mbits/second / 25VMs = 400 Mbits/second

This is a very satisfying value. We need to consider another factor: highly available network architecture. Thus, an alternative is using two data switches with a minimum of 24 ports for data.

Thinking about growth from now, two 48-port switches will be in place.

What about the growth of the rack size? In this case, you should think about the example of switch aggregation that uses the **Multi-Chassis Link Aggregation** (**MCLAG/MLAG**) technology between the switches in the aggregation. This feature allows each server rack to divide its links between the pair of switches to achieve a powerful active-active forwarding while using the full bandwidth capability with no requirement for a spanning tree.

 MCLAG is a Layer 2 link aggregation protocol between the servers that are connected to the switches, offering a redundant, load-balancing connection to the core network and replacing the spanning-tree protocol.

The network configuration also depends heavily on the chosen network topology. As shown in the previous example network diagram, you should be aware that all nodes in the OpenStack environment must communicate with each other. Based on this requirement, administrators will need to standardize the units will be planned to use and count the needed number of public and floating IP addresses. This calculation depends on which network type the OpenStack environment will run including the usage of Neutron or former nova-network service. It is crucial to separate which OpenStack units will need an attribution of Public and floating IPs. Our first basic example assumes the usage of the Public IPs for the following units:

- Cloud Controller Nodes: 3
- Compute Nodes: 15
- Storage Nodes: 5

In this case, we will initially need at least 18 public IP addresses. Moreover, when implementing a high available setup using virtual IPs fronted by load balancers, these will be considered as additional public IP addresses.

The use of Neutron for our OpenStack network design will involve a preparation for the number of virtual devices and interfaces interacting with the network node and the rest of the private cloud environment including:

- Virtual routers for 20 tenants: 20
- Virtual machines in 15 Compute Nodes: 375

In this case, we will initially need at least 395 floating IP addresses given that every virtual router is capable of connecting to the public network.

Additionally, increasing the available bandwidth should be taken into consideration in advance. For this purpose, we will need to consider the use of NIC bonding, therefore multiplying the number of NICs by 2. Bonding will empower cloud network high availability and achieve boosted bandwidth performance.

Storage calculations

Considering the previous example, you need to plan for an initial storage capacity per server that will serve 25 VMs each.

A simple calculation, assuming 100 GB ephemeral storage per VM, will require a space of *25*100 = 2.5 TB* of local storage on each compute node.

You can assign 250 GB of persistent storage per VM to have *25*250 = 5 TB* of persistent storage per compute node.

Most probably, you have an idea about the replication of object storage in OpenStack, which implies the usage of three times the required space for replication.

In other words, if you are planning for *X* TB for object storage, your storage requirement will be 3X.

Other considerations, such as the best storage performance using SSD, can be useful for a better throughput where you can invest more boxes to get an increased IOPS.

For example, working with SSD with 20K IOPS installed in a server with eight slot drives will bring you:

(20K * 8) / 25 = 6.4 K Read IOPS and 3.2K Write IOPS

That is not bad for a production starter!

Best practices

Well, let's bring some best practices under the microscope by exposing the OpenStack design flavor.

In a typical OpenStack production environment, the minimum requirement for disk space per compute node is 300 GB with a minimum RAM of 128 GB and a dual 8-core CPU.

Let's imagine a scenario where, due to budget limitations, you start your first compute node with costly hardware that has 600 GB disk space, 16-core CPUs, and 256 GB of RAM.

Assuming that your OpenStack environment continues to grow, you may decide to purchase more hardware: large, and at an incredible price! A second compute instance is placed to scale up.

Shortly after this, you may find out that demand is increasing. You may start splitting requests into different compute nodes but keep on continuing scaling up with the hardware. At some point, you will be alerted about reaching your budget limit!

There are certainly times when the best practices aren't in fact the best for your design. The previous example illustrated a commonly overlooked requirement for the OpenStack deployment.

If the minimal hardware requirement is strictly followed, it may result in an exponential cost with regards to hardware expenses, especially for new project starters.

Thus, you should choose exactly what works for you and consider the constraints that exist in your environment.

Keep in mind that best practices are a guideline; apply them when you find what you need to be deployed and how it should be set up.

On the other hand, do not stick to values, but stick to the spirit of the rules. Let's bring the previous example under the microscope again: scaling up shows more risk and may lead to failure than scaling out or horizontally. The reason behind such a design is to allow for a fast scale of transactions at the cost of duplicated compute functionality and smaller systems at a lower cost. That is how OpenStack was designed: degraded units can be discarded and failed workloads can be replaced.

Transactions and requests in the compute node may grow tremendously in a short time to a point where a single *big* compute node with 16 core CPUs starts failing performance-wise, while a few *small* compute nodes with 4 core CPUs can proceed to complete the job successfully.

As we have shown in the previous section, planning for capacity is a quite intensive exercise but very crucial to setting up an initial, successful OpenStack cloud strategy.

Planning for growth should be driven by the natural design of OpenStack and how it is implemented. We should consider that growth is based on demand where workloads in OpenStack take an *elastic* form and not a linear one. Although the previous resource's computation example can be helpful to estimate a few initial requirements for our designed OpenStack layout, reaching acceptable capacity planning still needs more action. This includes a detailed analysis of cloud performance in terms of growth of workload. In addition, by using more sophisticated monitoring tools, operators should be consistent in tracking the usage of each unit running in the OpenStack environment, which includes, for example, its overall resource consumption over time and cases of unit overutilization resulting in performance degradation. As we have conducted a rough estimation of our future hardware capabilities, this calculation model can be hardened by sizing the instance *flavor* for each compute host after first deployment and can be adjusted on demand if resources are carefully monitored.

Summary

This chapter has revisited the basic components of OpenStack and exposed new features such as Telemetry, Orchestration, and File Share projects.

We continued refining our logical design for future deployment by completing a first design layout. As an introductory chapter, we have rekindled the flames on each OpenStack component by discussing briefly each use case and role in its ecosystem. We have also covered a few tactical tips to plan and mitigate the future growth of the OpenStack setup in a production environment.

As a main reference for the rest of the book, we will be breaking down each component and new functionality in OpenStack by extending the basic layout covered in this chapter.

We will continue the OpenStack journey to deploy what was planned in a robust and effective way: the *DevOps* style.

2
Deploying OpenStack - The DevOps Way

"Besides black art, there is only automation and mechanization."
- Federico Garcia Lorca

Deploying an OpenStack environment based on the profiled design, as shown in the previous chapter, is not simple. Although we created our design by taking care of several aspects related to scalability and performance, we still have to make it real. If you are still looking at OpenStack as a single block system, you should take a step back and recheck what was explained in `Chapter 1`, *Designing OpenStack Cloud Architectural Consideration*. Furthermore, in the introductory section of this book, we covered the role of OpenStack in the next generation of data centers. A large-scale infrastructure used by cloud providers with a few thousand servers needs a very different approach to setup.

In our case, deploying and operating the OpenStack cloud is not as simple as you might think. Thus, you need to make the operational task easier or, in other words, **automated**.

In this chapter, we will cover new topics about the ways to deploy OpenStack. The next part will cover the following points:

- Learning what the DevOps movement is and how it can be adopted in the cloud
- Knowing how to see your infrastructure as code and how to maintain it
- Getting closer to the DevOps way by including configuration management aspects in your cloud
- Making your OpenStack environment design deployable via automation
- Starting your first OpenStack environment deployment using Ansible

DevOps in a nutshell

The term DevOps is a conjunction of development (software developers) and operations (manage and put software into production). Many IT organizations have started to adopt such a *concept*, but the question is how and why? Is it a job? Is it a process or a practice?

DevOps is *development and operations compounded*, which basically defines a methodology of software development. It describes practices that streamline the software delivery process. It is about raising communication and integration between developers, operators (including administrators), and quality assurance teams. The essence of the DevOps movement lies in leveraging the benefits of collaboration. Different disciplines can relate to DevOps in different ways, and bring their experiences and skills together under the DevOps banner to gain **shared values**.

So, DevOps is a methodology that integrates the efforts of several disciplines, as shown in the following figure:

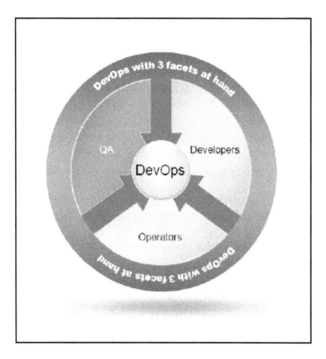

This new movement is intended to resolve the conflict between developers and operators. Delivering a new release affects production systems. It puts different teams in conflicting positions by setting different goals for them, for example, the development team wants their latest code to go live, while the operations team wants more time to test and stage the changes before going to production. DevOps fills the gap and streamlines the process of bringing in change by encouraging collaboration between the developers and operators.

 DevOps is neither a toolkit nor a job; it is the synergy that streamlines the process of change.

Let's see how DevOps can incubate a cloud project.

DevOps and cloud - everything is code

Let's look at the architecture of cloud computing. While discussing a cloud infrastructure, we must remember that we are talking about a large, scalable environment! The amazing switch to bigger environments requires us to simplify everything as much as possible. System architecture and software design are becoming more and more complicated. Every new release of software affords new functions and new configurations.

Administrating and deploying a large infrastructure would not be possible without adopting a new philosophy, **Infrastructure as code**.

When infrastructure is seen as code, the components of a given infrastructure are modeled as modules of code. What you need to do is to abstract the functionality of the infrastructure into discrete reusable components, design the services provided by the infrastructure as modules of code, and finally implement them as blocks of automation.

Furthermore, in such a paradigm, it will be essential to adhere to the same well-established discipline of software development as an infrastructure developer.

The essence of DevOps mandates that developers, network engineers, and operators must work alongside each other to deploy, operate, and maintain cloud infrastructure which will power our next-generation data center.

DevOps and OpenStack

As mentioned in the previous section, deploying complex software on a large-scale infrastructure requires adopting a new strategy. The ever-increasing complexity of software such as OpenStack and the deployment of huge cloud infrastructure must be simplified. Everything in a given infrastructure must be automated! This is where OpenStack meets DevOps.

Breaking down OpenStack into pieces

Let's gather what we covered previously and signal a few steps towards our first OpenStack deployment:

- Break down the OpenStack infrastructure into independent and reusable services.
- Integrate the services in such a way that you can provide the expected functionalities in the OpenStack environment.

It is obvious that OpenStack includes many services, as discussed in `Chapter 1`, *Designing OpenStack Cloud Architectural Consideration*. What we need to do is see these services as packages of code in our infrastructure as code experience. The next step will investigate how to integrate the services and deploy them via automation.

Deploying service as code is similar to writing a software application. Here are some important points you should remember during the entire deployment process:

- Simplify and modularize the OpenStack services
- Develop OpenStack services as building blocks that integrate with other components to provide a complete system
- Facilitate the customization and improvement of services without impacting the complete system.
- Use the right tool to build the services
- Be sure that the services provide the same results with the same input
- Switch your service vision from how to do it to what we want to do

Automation is the essence of DevOps. In fact, many system management tools are intensely used nowadays due to their efficiency of deployment. In other words, there is a need for automation!

You have probably used some of available the automation tools, such as Ansible, Chef, Puppet, and many more. Before we go through them, we need to create a succinct, professional code management step.

Working with the infrastructure deployment code

While dealing with infrastructure as code, the code that abstracts, models, and builds the OpenStack infrastructure must be committed to source code management. This is required for tracking changes in our automation code and reproducible of results. Eventually, we must reach a point where we shift our OpenStack infrastructure from a code base to a deployed system while following the latest software development best practices.

At this stage, you should be aware of the quality of your OpenStack infrastructure deployment, which roughly depends on the quality of the code that describes it.

It is important to highlight a critical point that you should keep in mind during all deployment stages: Automated systems are not able to understand human error. You'll have to go through an ensemble of phases and cycles using agile methodologies to end up with a release that is *largely* bug free and then promoted to the production environment.

On the other hand, if mistakes cannot be totally eradicated, you should plan for the continuous development and testing of code. The code's life cycle management is shown in the following figure:

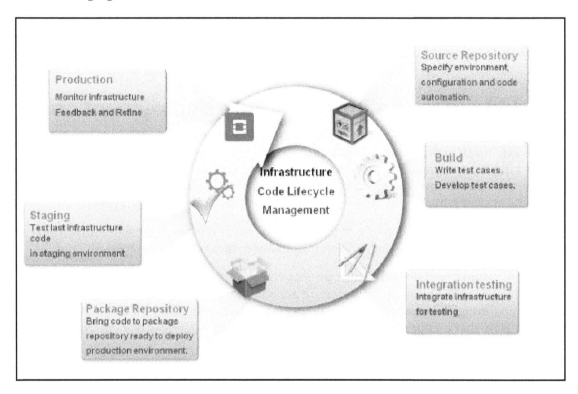

Changes can be scary! To handle changes, it is recommended that you do the following:

- Keep track of and monitor the changes at every stage
- Build flexibility into the code and make it easy to change
- Refactor the code when it becomes difficult to manage
- Test, test, and retest your code

Keep checking every point that has been described previously till you start to get more confident that your OpenStack infrastructure is being managed by code that won't break. By treating the infrastructure as code, operators will be able to overcome the challenges presented by any dynamic infrastructure. Systems can be redeployed at ease by ensuring the consistency throughout the entire fleet of servers or the same infrastructure elements. Bear in mind that system design also keeps changing as new package release comes to an update with different configuration requirements. A streamlined change management process will facilitate to deliver an anti-fragile infrastructure that can be changed safely with minimum degree of complexity.

Integrating OpenStack into infrastructure code

To keep the OpenStack environment working with a minimum rate of surprises and ensure that the code delivers the functionalities that are required, we must continuously track the development of our infrastructure code.

We will connect the OpenStack deployment code to a tool chain, where it will be constantly monitored and tested as we continue to develop and refine our code. This tool chain is composed of a pipeline of tracking, monitoring, testing, and reporting phases and is well known as a **continuous integration** and **continuous development** (**CI-CD**) process.

Continuous integration and delivery

Let's see how continuous integration (**CI**) and life cycle of our automation code will be managed by the following categories of tools:

- **System Management Tool Artifact** (**SMTA**): This can be any IT automation tool such as Chef cookbook, Puppet manifest, Ansible playbook, or juju charms.
- **Version Control System** (**VCS**): This tracks changes to our infrastructure deployment code. Any version control system, such as CVS, Subversion, or Bazaar, that you are most familiar with can be used for this purpose. **Git** can be a good outfit for our VCS.
- **Jenkins**: This is a perfect tool that monitors to changes in version control system and does the continuous integration testing and reporting of results.
- **Gerrit**: This is a Git review system designed to review code changes at every Git push. It creates patch sets for each change and allows the review of code lines based on rating score.

Take a look at the model in the following figure:

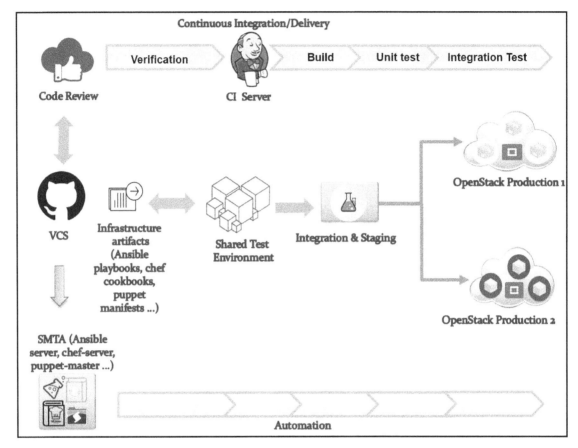

The life cycle for infrastructure as code consists of infrastructure configuration files (for example, Ansible playbooks and Vagrant files) that are recorded in a **VCS** and are built continuously by the means of a continuous integration (CI) server (Jenkins, in our case).

Infrastructure configuration files can be used to set up a unit test environment (a virtual environment using Vagrant, for example) and makes use of any system management tool to provision the infrastructure (Ansible, Chef, Puppet, and so on).

Within every added patch, **Gerrit** triggers an event in the CI server to perform test and build before publishing results for reviewing.

The CI server keeps listening to changes in version control and automatically propagates any new versions to be tested, and then it listens to target environments in production.

Vagrant allows you to build a virtual environment very easily; it is available at `https://www.virtualbox.org/` and can run virtual machines, so you will need these before moving on with the installation in your test environment.

The proposed life cycle for infrastructure code highlights the importance of a test environment before moving on to production. You should give a lot of importance to the testing stage, although this might be a very time-consuming task.

Especially in our case, with infrastructure code for deploying OpenStack that are complicated and have multiple dependencies on other systems the importance of testing cannot be overemphasized. This makes it imperative to ensure effort is made for an automated and consistent testing of the infrastructure code.an automated and consistent testing of the infrastructure code.

The best way to do this is to keep testing thoroughly in a repeated way till you gain confidence in your code.

Choosing the automation tool

At first sight, you may wonder which automation tool is the most useful for our OpenStack production day. We have already chosen Git and Jenkins to handle our continuous integration and testing. It is time to choose the right tool for automation.

It might be difficult to select the right tool. Most likely, you'll have to choose between several of them. Covering all the existing IT automation tools could fill an entire book or even books. Therefore, giving succinct hints on different tools might be helpful in order to distinguish the best outfit for certain particular setups. Of course, we are still talking about large infrastructures, a lot of networking, and distributed services.

As Ansible becomes a very mature tool and well integrated within the cloud automation world, we will use it for the next deployment phase.

Introducing Ansible

We have chosen Ansible to automate our cloud infrastructure. Ansible is an infrastructure automation engine. It is simple to get started with, and yet is flexible enough to handle complex, interdependent systems.

The architecture of Ansible consists of the deployment system where Ansible itself is installed and the target systems that are managed by Ansible. It uses an agentless architecture to push changes to the target systems. This is due to the use of SSH protocol as its transport mechanism to push changes to the target systems. This also means that there is no extra software installation required on the target system. The agentless architecture makes setting up Ansible very simple.

Ansible works by copying modules over SSH to the target systems. It then executes them to change the state of the target systems. Once executed, the Ansible modules are cleaned up, leaving no trail on the target system.

Although the default mechanism for making changes to the client system is an SSH-based push model, if you feel the push-based model for delivering changes is not scalable enough for your infrastructure, Ansible also supports an agent-based pull-model.

Ansible is developed in Python and comes with a huge collection of core automation modules.

The configuration files for Ansible are called playbooks and they are written in YAML, which is just a markup language. YAML is easier to understand; it's custom-made for writing configuration files. This makes learning Ansible automation much easier.

The Ansible Galaxy is a collection of reusable Ansible modules that can be used for your project.

 To read more about Ansible, please refer to the official website that contains great wiki documentation: `http://docs.ansible.com/ansible/intro.html`

Modules

Ansible modules are constructs that encapsulate a system resource or action. A module models the resource and its attributes. Ansible comes with packages with a wide range of core modules to represent various system resources; for example, the **file** module encapsulates a file on the system and has attributes such as owner, group, mode, and so on. These attributes represent the state of a file in the system; by changing the attributes of the resources, we can describe the required final state of the system.

Ansible also provides great and stable modules designated for multiple cloud providers and virtualization engines, including OpenStack. Take a look at the official website for the supported OpenStack modules found at: `http://docs.ansible.com/ansible/list_of_cloud_modules.html#ope nstack`

Variables

While modules can represent the resources and actions on a system, the variables represent the dynamic part of the change. Variables can be used to modify the behavior of the modules.

Variables can be defined from the environment of the host, for example, the hostname, IP address, version of software and hardware installed on a host, and so on.

They can also be user-defined or provided as part of a module. User-defined variables can represent the classification of a host resource or its attribute.

Inventory

An inventory is a list of hosts that are managed by Ansible. The inventory list supports classifying hosts into groups. In its simplest form, an inventory can be an **INI** file. The groups are represented as sections on the INI file. The classification can be based on the role of the hosts or any other system management need. It is possible to have a host appearing in multiple groups in an inventory file. The following example shows a simple inventory of hosts:

```
logserver1.example.com

[controllers]
ctl1.example.com
ctl2.example.com

[computes]
compute1.example.com
compute2.example.com
compute3.example.com
compute[20:30].example.com
```

The inventory file supports special patterns to represent large groups of hosts.

Ansible expects to find the inventory file at `/etc/ansible/hosts`, but a custom location can be passed directly to the Ansible command line.

Ansible also supports dynamic inventories that can be generated by executing scripts or retrieved from another management system, such as a cloud platform.

Roles

Roles are the building blocks of an Ansible-based deployment. They represent a collection of tasks that must be performed to configure a service on a group of hosts. The Role encapsulates tasks, variable, handlers, and other related functions required to deploy a service on a host. For example, to deploy a multinode web server cluster, the hosts in the infrastructure can be assigned roles such as web server, database server, load balancer, and so on.

Playbooks

Playbooks are the main configuration files in Ansible. They describe the complete system deployment plan. Playbooks are composed of a series of tasks and are executed from top to bottom. The tasks themselves refer to group of hosts that must be deployed with roles. Ansible playbooks are written in YAML.

The following is an example of a simple Ansible playbook:

```
---
- hosts: webservers
  vars:
    http_port: 8080
  remote_user: root
  tasks:
  - name: ensure apache is at the latest version
    yum: name=httpd state=latest
  - name: write the apache config file
    template: src=/srv/httpd.j2 dest=/etc/httpd.conf
    notify:
  - restart apache
  handlers:
  - name: restart apache
    service: name=httpd state=restarted
```

Ansible for OpenStack

OpenStack Ansible (**OSA**) is an official OpenStack big tent project. It focuses on providing roles and playbooks for deploying a scalable, production-ready OpenStack setup. It has a very active community of developers and users collaborating to stabilize and bring new features to OpenStack deployment.

The official OpenStack-Ansible repository and documentation can be found at GitHub: `https://github.com/openstack/openstack-ansible`

One of the unique features of the OSA project is the use of containers to isolate and manage OpenStack services. OSA installs OpenStack services in **LXC** containers to provide each service with an isolated environment.

LXC is an OS-level container, and it encompasses a complete OS environment that includes a separate filesystem, networking stack, and resource isolation using **cgroups**.

Containerization technology enhanced the chroot concept within the Linux operating system. LXC is a very popular implementation of containers in Linux, allowing the isolation of resources, including filesystems, to run multiple applications and group of processes without interfering with each other.

OpenStack services are spawned in separate LXC containers and communicate to each other using the REST APIs. The *microservice-based* architecture of OpenStack complements the use of containers to isolate services. It also decouples the services from the physical hardware and provides encapsulation of the service environment that forms the foundation for providing portability, high availability, and redundancy.

Microservice architecture has become a highly-adopted approach for developing applications at a fast and efficient pace. The foundation of the microservice model has become more solid with the rise of cloud technology. Microservice patterns help developers to overcome the challenge of a monolithic application by converting it to a suite of modular services easy to deploy, fast to go to production, being scalable, and reusable. Using containers in a based microservice architectural setup enables developers to gain more granularity and much more flexibility during testing and deployment.

The **OSA** deployment is initiated from a deployment host. The deployment host is installed with Ansible and it runs the OSA playbooks to orchestrate the installation of OpenStack on the target hosts:

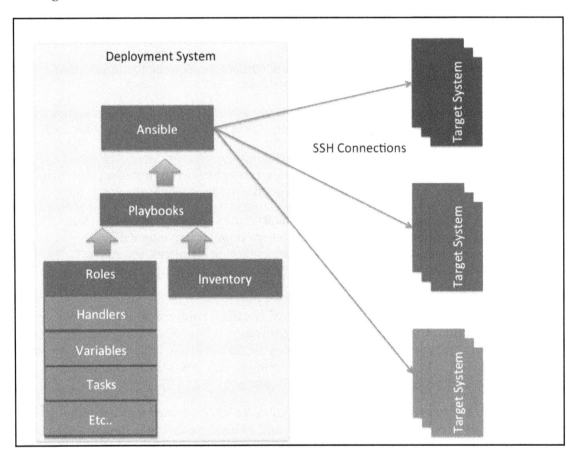

The Ansible target hosts are the ones that will run the OpenStack services. The target nodes can be installed with Ubuntu 14.04 LTS and configured with SSH-key-based authentication to allow login from the deployment host.

The development and production environments

One of the requirements of deploying OpenStack in a production environment is to continuously test and improve the setup. This means we need to have a test environment that closely resembles the deployment architecture of the production environment and yet is not too complex to be easily implemented by individual developers. OpenStack Ansible provides a developer mode with **All-in-One** (**AIO**) node installation. We will look into the details of setting up a development environment later in this chapter.

The production environment, on the other hand, needs to be very robust, provide redundancy of services and service isolation, and be extensible. OSA's recommended architecture groups the target hosts into the following:

- Infrastructure and control plane host
- Logging host
- Compute hosts
- Optional storage hosts

The recommended architecture recommends at least three infrastructure and control plane hosts for providing service redundancy. We will also need a deployment host that will run the OSA playbooks.

The infrastructure hosts are installed with common services such as the following:

- Database server with MySQL Galera cluster
- RabbitMQ messaging server
- Memcached
- Repository servers

They also host the OpenStack control plane services, such as the following:

- Identity server (Keystone)
- Image server (Glance)
- Compute management service (Nova)
- Networking (Neutron)
- Other API services such as Heat, Ceilometer, and so on

The logging server hosts a centralized log server, such as rsyslog, and a log analyzer using **Logstash** and **Elasticsearch**. The compute hosts run the Nova compute service, along with the networking and logging agents:

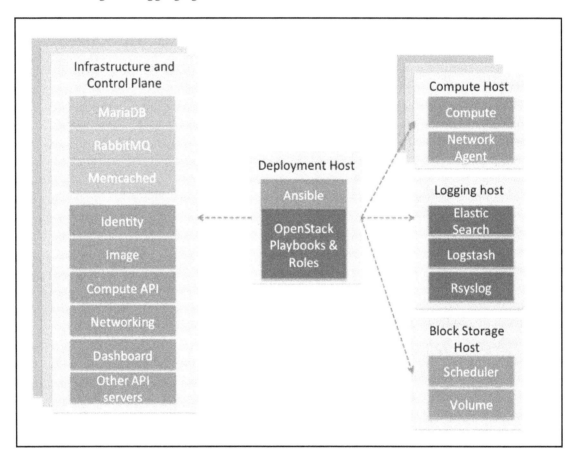

For the production environment, separate storage hosts that run the Cinder scheduler and the Cinder volume services must provide storage services.

The hardware and software requirements

The recommended hardware and software requirements for the target nodes are as follows:

	Deployment hosts	Compute hosts	Storage hosts	Infrastructure hosts	Logging hosts
Disk size	100 GB	100 GB SSD disks	1 TB	100 GB	50 GB
Network	Multiple bonded NICs	Multiple bonded NICs	Multiple bonded NICs	Multiple bonded NICs	Multiple bonded NICs
Software	Ubuntu 14.04 LTS, OpenSSH, Python 2.7	Ubuntu 14.04 LTS, OpenSSH, Python 2.7	Ubuntu 14.04 LTS, OpenSSH, Python 2.7	Ubuntu 14.04 LTS, OpenSSH, Python 2.7	Ubuntu 14.04 LTS, OpenSSH, Python 2.7
CPU		Virtualization extensions		Multicore with hyperthreading	

Although OpenStack can be installed with a much lower hardware specification, in a production environment, you would likely need more redundancy and isolation of services so that the failure of one service will have very minimal impact on the cloud infrastructure. The figures mentioned in the table are the recommendation from the OpenStack Ansible project but we must also take into account the physical model design and the hardware sizing and hardware requirement estimation as discussed in `Chapter 1`, *Designing OpenStack Cloud Architectural Consideration*.

Networking requirements

Due to the use of containers to isolate the OpenStack services, the deployment needs special networking configuration. OSA uses various bridges to provide network connectivity to the LXC containers. The following is a list of bridges created for connectivity of OpenStack nodes:

- **br_mgmt** provides management access to the containers
- **br_storage** provides access to the storage services
- **br_vxlan** provides tunneled networking using vxlan
- **br_vlan** is used to provide vlan-based tenant networks

The following table summarizes the network connectivity for OpenStack nodes:

Bridge name	Configured on
br-mgmt	Every node
br-storage	Every storage node
	Every compute node
br-vxlan	Every network node
	Every compute node
br-vlan	Every network node
	Every compute node

The OpenStack nodes are configured with bonded network links to provide redundancy of network connectivity. Each node is installed with four physical NIC cards. The following figure shows the configuration of the bonded interfaces and connectivity using Linux bridges:

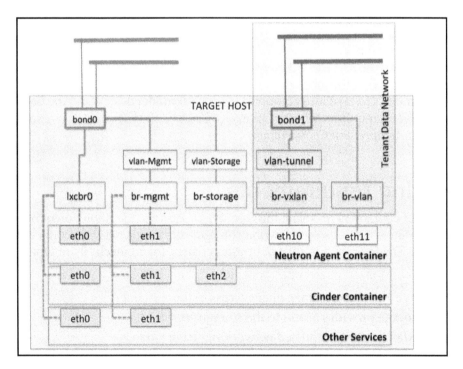

We will look at each of the OpenStack services in subsequent chapters, but if you need to immediately install a production-ready OpenStack environment, follow the documentation at `https://docs.openstack.org/developer/openstack-ansible/`.

In the next section, we will start discussing a test environment that closely resembles the production setup.

The development environment

OpenStack Ansible provides an AIO mode that caters to the develop-and-test environment. Even in the AIO mode, the installation process uses the containerize services approach and brings up OpenStack services in multiple LXC containers. This is done to mimic the production environment.

As all the services have their private container, the AIO environment is quite heavy on system requirements. At the time of writing, the AIO development environment requires an absolute minimum of 60 GB of disk space with 8 GB of RAM and eight CPUs. The AIO environment can be installed within a VM. The AIO installation is supported on Ubuntu 14.04 LTS or later and requires a kernel version 3.13.0-34-generic or higher. At the time of writing, the support for Red Hat/CentOS7 is in progress.

 To follow the progress of the OpenStack Ansible project and AIO setup, please refer to the official OpenStack website: `http://docs.openstack.org/developer/openstack-ansible/`

Setting up the development machine

Although OpenStack Ansible automates the complete process of setting up a dev and test OpenStack environment, it requires a machine with the correct hardware and software installed to start with. That leaves getting the development machine up and running with basic software such as the correct operating system and hardware still a manual job.

This is where tools such as Vagrant comes in handy. Vagrant helps automate the process of creating a reproducible development environment. Vagrant does this by launching virtual machines with the right operating system image. It also sets up SSH access to the virtual machine. With Vagrant, it is easy to quickly bring up a development and test environment on your laptop.

Vagrant uses VirtualBox as the default hypervisor, but can also work with other providers such as VMware and HyperV to launch virtual machines.

To start a development machine, all we need is an image for the operating system. Other hardware configuration and customization of the development machine can be described in the Vagrant configuration file. With this, Vagrant can start a development environment in a virtual machine.

Let's look at the process of creating the development machine:

1. To start using Vagrant, we need the Vagrant installer, which can be downloaded from the Vagrant website at: https://www.vagrantup.com/downloads.html
2. Install Vagrant on your host machine.
3. Vagrant starts the virtual machines based on images of the operating system, which it calls boxes. So next we will find the suitable operating system image for our development machine and add it to Vagrant:

```
# vagrant init ubuntu/trusty64
```

4. The preceding command will download Ubuntu Trusty 14.04 for amd64 architecture and create a Vagrant file with default values. An example of the Vagrant file is shown here:

```
# -*- mode: ruby -*-
# vi: set ft=ruby :

# All Vagrant configuration is done below. The "2" in Vagrant.configure
# configures the configuration version (we support older styles for
# backwards compatibility). Please don't change it unless you know what
# you're doing.
Vagrant.configure(2) do |config|
  # The most common configuration options are documented and commented below.
  # For a complete reference, please see the online documentation at
  # https://docs.vagrantup.com.

  # Every Vagrant development environment requires a box. You can search for
  # boxes at https://atlas.hashicorp.com/search.
  config.vm.box = "ubuntu/trusty64"

  # Disable automatic box update checking. If you disable this, then
  # boxes will only be checked for updates when the user runs
  # `vagrant box outdated`. This is not recommended.
  # config.vm.box_check_update = false

  # Create a forwarded port mapping which allows access to a specific port
  # within the machine from a port on the host machine. In the example below,
  # accessing "localhost:8080" will access port 80 on the guest machine.
  # config.vm.network "forwarded_port", guest: 80, host: 8080

  # Create a private network, which allows host-only access to the machine
  # using a specific IP.
  # config.vm.network "private_network", ip: "192.168.33.10"

  # Create a public network, which generally matched to bridged network.
  # Bridged networks make the machine appear as another physical device on
  # your network.
  # config.vm.network "public_network"

  # Share an additional folder to the guest VM. The first argument is
  # the path on the host to the actual folder. The second argument is
  # the path on the guest to mount the folder. And the optional third
  # argument is a set of non-required options.
  # config.vm.synced_folder "../data", "/vagrant_data"

  # Provider-specific configuration so you can fine-tune various
  # backing providers for Vagrant. These expose provider-specific options.
  # Example for VirtualBox:
  #
  # config.vm.provider "virtualbox" do |vb|
  #   # Display the VirtualBox GUI when booting the machine
  #   vb.gui = true
  #
```

5. Vagrant provides various other customization features through the Vagrantfile; the defaults for those configuration options are provided in the generated file.

6. Next, we have to customize the hardware for our development machine using the Vagrantfile. Edit the Vagrantfile and add the following settings:

```
config.vm.provider "virtualbox" do |v|
  v.memory = 8192
  v.cpus = 8
end
```

The preceding settings will set up root access to the development virtual machine and set the memory and CPU requirements.

7. Finally, you can start and log in to the development machine using the following Vagrant commands:

```
# vagrant up --provider virtualbox
# vagrant ssh
```

With the above, you should be able to log in as a Vagrant user. Use **sudo -I** to become root and proceed with the next steps to create the Ansible OpenStack All-In-One development setup as described in the next section.

 Due to the large disk requirement of the development environment, you will have to extend the size of the virtual machine started by Vagrant. You can always generate your own Vagrant image with a bigger disk size to fit the requirements of the development machine. The steps to create a Vagrant box are detailed at https://www.vagrantup.com/docs/virtualbox/boxes.html.

Preparing the infrastructure code environment

We have chosen Git to be our version control system. Let's go ahead and install the Git package on our development system.

Install Git:

```
$ sudo apt-get install git
```

Check the correctness of the Git installation:

```
$ git --version
```

> If you decide to use an IDE such as eclipse for your development, it might be easier to install a Git plugin to integrate Git to your IDE. For example, the EGit plugin can be used to develop with Git in Eclipse. We do this by navigating to the **Help | Install New Software** menu entry. You will need to add the following URL: `http://download.eclipse.org/egit/update`.

Preparing the development setup

The installation process is divided into the following steps:

1. Check out the OSA repository
2. Install and bootstrap Ansible
3. Initialize host bootstrap
4. Run playbooks

To start the installation, check out the OSA Git repository:

```
# git clone https://github.com/openstack/openstack-ansible
/opt/openstack-ansible
# cd /opt/openstack-ansible
```

Check out the required branch you want to install:

```
# git branch -r
# git checkout BRANCH_NAME
```

Check out the latest tag on the branch:

```
# git describe --abbrev=0 -tags
# git checkout TAG_NAME
```

Configuring your setup

The AIO development environment uses the configuration files in `test/roles/bootstrap-host/defaults/main.yml`.

This file describes the default values for the host configuration. In addition to the configuration file, the configuration options can be passed through shell environment variables.

The BOOTSTRAP_OPTS variable is read by the bootstrap script as a space-separated key value pair. It can be used to pass values to override the default ones in the configuration file:

```
# export BOOTSTRAP_OPTS="${BOOTSTRAP_OPTS}
bootstrap_host_loopback_cinder_size=512"
```

OSA also allows overriding default values for service configuration. These override values are provided in the /etc/openstack_deploy/user_variables.yml file.

The following is an example of overriding the values in nova.conf using the override file:

```
nova_nova_conf_overrides:
  DEFAULT:
    remove_unused_original_minimum_age_seconds: 43200
  libvirt:
    cpu_mode: host-model
    disk_cachemodes: file=directsync,block=none
  database:
    idle_timeout: 300
    max_pool_size: 10
```

This override file will populate the nova.conf file with the following options:

```
[DEFAULT]
remove_unused_original_minimum_age_seconds = 43200

[libvirt]
cpu_mode = host-model
disk_cachemodes = file=directsync,block=none

[database]
idle_timeout = 300
max_pool_size = 10
```

The override variables can also be passed using a per host configuration stanza in /etc/openstack_deploy/openstack_user_config.yml.

 The complete set of configuration options are described in the OpenStack Ansible documentation at http://docs.openstack.org/developer/open stack-ansible/install-guide/configure-openstack.html

Building the development setup

To start the installation process, execute the Ansible bootstrap script. This script will download and install the correct Ansible version. It also creates a wrapper script around `ansible-playbook` called `openstack-ansible` that always loads the OpenStack user variable files:

```
# scripts/bootstrap-ansible.sh
```

The next step is to configure the system for the All-In-One setup. Executing the following script does this:

```
# scripts/bootstrap-aio.sh
```

This script does the following tasks:

- Applies Ansible roles to install the basic software requirements, such as openssh and pip
- Applies the `bootstrap_host` role to check the hard disk and swap space
- Creates various loopback volumes for use with Cinder, Swift, and Nova
- Prepares networking

Finally, run the playbooks to bring up the AIO development environment:

```
# scripts/run-playbooks.sh
```

This script will execute the following tasks:

- Create the LXC containers
- Apply security hardening to the host
- Reinitiate the network bridges
- Install the infrastructure services such as MySQL, RabbitMQ, and Memcached
- Finally, it installs the various OpenStack services

Running the playbooks takes a long time to build the containers and start the OpenStack services. Once finished, you will have all the OpenStack services running in their private containers. The following command line output shows the AIO server deployed using containerized OpenStack services:

```
root@os-aio1:~# lxc-ls --fancy
NAME                                          STATE    IPV4                                              IPV6  AUTOSTART
----------------------------------------------------------------------------------------------------------------------
aio1_aodh_container-23d40fcb                  RUNNING  10.255.255.143, 172.29.239.138                     -    YES (onboot, openstack)
aio1_ceilometer_api_container-16d5c4ac        RUNNING  10.255.255.41, 172.29.237.191                      -    YES (onboot, openstack)
aio1_ceilometer_collector_container-b8a6b87c  RUNNING  10.255.255.131, 172.29.238.75                      -    YES (onboot, openstack)
aio1_cinder_api_container-fb2b1757            RUNNING  10.255.255.246, 172.29.238.250, 172.29.244.84      -    YES (onboot, openstack)
aio1_cinder_scheduler_container-687e8178      RUNNING  10.255.255.28, 172.29.239.168                      -    YES (onboot, openstack)
aio1_galera_container-00db0032                RUNNING  10.255.255.173, 172.29.239.87                      -    YES (onboot, openstack)
aio1_galera_container-54bd128c                RUNNING  10.255.255.139, 172.29.238.66                      -    YES (onboot, openstack)
aio1_galera_container-d16bd93f                RUNNING  10.255.255.211, 172.29.236.136                     -    YES (onboot, openstack)
aio1_glance_container-82b3c4c5                RUNNING  10.255.255.42, 172.29.239.250, 172.29.245.51       -    YES (onboot, openstack)
aio1_heat_apis_container-e531e4fe             RUNNING  10.255.255.109, 172.29.237.12                      -    YES (onboot, openstack)
aio1_heat_engine_container-56984b7e           RUNNING  10.255.255.247, 172.29.239.103                     -    YES (onboot, openstack)
aio1_horizon_container-4a52b4ab               RUNNING  10.255.255.62, 172.29.236.189                      -    YES (onboot, openstack)
aio1_horizon_container-b23effb5               RUNNING  10.255.255.251, 172.29.238.222                     -    YES (onboot, openstack)
aio1_keystone_container-b79ecc7d              RUNNING  10.255.255.220, 172.29.237.218                     -    YES (onboot, openstack)
aio1_keystone_container-e29d298d              RUNNING  10.255.255.64, 172.29.237.197                      -    YES (onboot, openstack)
aio1_memcached_container-3d69da4a             RUNNING  10.255.255.175, 172.29.238.10                      -    YES (onboot, openstack)
aio1_neutron_agents_container-bcbf8a14        RUNNING  10.255.255.149, 172.29.236.236, 172.29.241.144     -    YES (onboot, openstack)
aio1_neutron_server_container-ad2cc458        RUNNING  10.255.255.144, 172.29.239.222                     -    YES (onboot, openstack)
aio1_nova_api_metadata_container-fa462c7e     RUNNING  10.255.255.88, 172.29.238.139                      -    YES (onboot, openstack)
aio1_nova_api_os_compute_container-6f39acb3   RUNNING  10.255.255.24, 172.29.239.93                       -    YES (onboot, openstack)
aio1_nova_cert_container-222c4ebe             RUNNING  10.255.255.240, 172.29.236.167                     -    YES (onboot, openstack)
aio1_nova_conductor_container-01c0347b        RUNNING  10.255.255.114, 172.29.239.73                      -    YES (onboot, openstack)
aio1_nova_console_container-475ecfd5          RUNNING  10.255.255.250, 172.29.238.194                     -    YES (onboot, openstack)
aio1_nova_scheduler_container-006e779a        RUNNING  10.255.255.190, 172.29.238.52                      -    YES (onboot, openstack)
aio1_rabbit_mq_container-3466f631             RUNNING  10.255.255.44, 172.29.237.64                       -    YES (onboot, openstack)
aio1_rabbit_mq_container-4c722c96             RUNNING  10.255.255.162, 172.29.237.108                     -    YES (onboot, openstack)
aio1_rabbit_mq_container-a54fc4d2             RUNNING  10.255.255.43, 172.29.239.171                      -    YES (onboot, openstack)
aio1_repo_container-2d6f82c0                  RUNNING  10.255.255.197, 172.29.239.52                      -    YES (onboot, openstack)
aio1_repo_container-7b1c3dd3                  RUNNING  10.255.255.230, 172.29.236.230                     -    YES (onboot, openstack)
aio1_rsyslog_container-bfb9264d               RUNNING  10.255.255.142, 172.29.237.44                      -    YES (onboot, openstack)
aio1_swift_proxy_container-127e077e           RUNNING  10.255.255.53, 172.29.238.39, 172.29.247.246       -    YES (onboot, openstack)
aio1_utility_container-962c9996               RUNNING  10.255.255.238, 172.29.238.160                     -    YES (onboot, openstack)
```

You can use the `lxc-ls` command to list the service containers on the development machine:

```
# lxc-ls --fancy
```

Use the `lxc-attach` command to connect to any container, as shown here:

```
# lxc-attach --name <name_of_container>
```

Use the name of the container from the output of `lxc-ls` to attach to the container. LXC commands can be used to start and stop the service containers.

 The AIO environment brings a MySQL cluster. Take special care when starting the MySQL cluster if the development machine is rebooted. Details of operating the AIO environment are available in the OpenStack Ansible QuickStart guide at http://docs.openstack.org/developer/openstack-ansible/developer-docs/quickstart-aio.html.

Although our setup is not considered a ready staging environment yet, it is important to consider forking the host files in Ansible into more units with different OpenStack nodes. The OSA deployment empowers the isolation of the various OpenStack services and keeps maintaining each service separately easy and safe. The current development environment is crucial to run functional tests of the OpenStack playbooks and generate a first feedback about the consistency of the Ansible code. More iterations will be performed during subsequent phases before pushing to staging and then deploying into production by considering a multinode setup running in a containerized environment.

Tracking your changes

The OSA project itself maintains its code under version control at the OpenStack Git server: `http://git.openstack.org/cgit/openstack/openstack-ansible/tree/`

The configuration files of OSA are stored at `/etc/openstack_ansible/` on the deployment host. These files define the deployment environment and the user override variables. To make sure that you control the deployment environment, it is important that the changes to these configuration files are tracked in a version control system.

To make sure that you track the development environment, make sure that the Vagrant configuration files are also tracked in a version control system.

Summary

In this chapter, we covered several topics and terminologies on how to develop and maintain a code infrastructure using the DevOps style.

Viewing your OpenStack infrastructure deployment as code will not only simplify node configuration, but also improve the automation process.

You should keep in mind that DevOps is neither a project nor a goal, but a methodology that will make your deployment successfully empowered by using team synergy with different departments.

Despite the existence of numerous system management tools to bring our OpenStack up and running in an automated way, we have chosen Ansible for the automation of our infrastructure.

Puppet, Chef, Salt, and others can do the job, but in different ways. You should know that there isn't one way to perform automation. Both Puppet and Chef have their own OpenStack deployment projects under the OpenStack Big Tent.

At the end of the day, you can choose to use any automation tools that fit your production needs; the key point to keep in mind is that to manage a big production environment, you must simplify the operation by doing the following:

- Automating deployment and operation as much as possible
- Tracking your changes in a version control system
- Continuously integratining code to keep your infrastructure updated and bug free
- Monitoring and testing your infrastructure code to make it robust

Although we deployed a basic AIO setup of OpenStack in this chapter, the successive chapters will take you through the process of extending our design by using clustering, defining the various infrastructure nodes, the controller, and compute hosts.

3
OpenStack Cluster – The Cloud Controller and Common Services

"If you want to go quickly, go alone. If you want to go far, go together."
- African proverb

Now that you have good knowledge of the approaches taken to deploy a large OpenStack infrastructure in an automated way, it is time to dive deeper and cover more specific conceptual designs within OpenStack.

In a large infrastructure, especially if you are looking to keep all your services up and running, it is essential that you ensure the OpenStack infrastructure is reliable and guarantees business continuity.

We already discussed several design aspects and highlighted some best practices of scalable architecture models within OpenStack in `Chapter 1`, *Designing OpenStack Cloud Architectural Consideration*.

Soon after, we discovered the efficiency of automation, where we resumed a basic setup of an all-in-one cloud controller and compute node using the OpenStack Ansible deployment tool.

This chapter begins by covering some clustering aspects. It soon guides you to discover more OpenStack design patterns based on breaking down functionality into different services while focusing on the cloud controller. Bear in mind that this chapter will not treat high availability in detail and will not touch on all OpenStack service layers. Instead, it will aim to give a generic overview of several possibilities of the OpenStack clustering design. The art of clustering is the key to providing a solution that fits into a methodology that stresses standardized, consistent IT build-out OpenStack operations.

In this chapter, we will cover the following topics:

- Covering, briefly, the art of clustering
- Defining the use case of cloud controllers and common services in an OpenStack environment
- Introducing other OpenStack clustering models based on the distribution of functionality based on services on the cloud controller
- Understanding common infrastructure services
- Learning the OpenStack services that compose the controller nodes
- Getting to grips with the automation of infrastructure deployment using Ansible in OpenStack

Understanding the art of clustering

Do not be afraid to claim that clustering actually provides high availability in a given infrastructure. The aggregation of the capacity of two or more servers is meant to be a server cluster. This aggregation will be performed by means of the accumulation of several machines.

 Do not get confused between **scaling up**, which is also called **vertical scaling**, and **scaling down**, which is also known as **horizontal scaling**. The horizontal scaling option refers to adding more commodity servers, unlike the vertical scaling option, which refers to adding more expensive and robust servers with more CPU and RAM.

This makes it imperative to differ between the terminologies of high availability, load balancing, and failing over, which will be detailed in `Chapter 9`, *OpenStack HA and Failover*.

Keep this in mind that for any of the previously mentioned terms, their configuration results always start from the clustering concept. You will discover how to differentiate between them in the next section.

Asymmetric clustering

Asymmetric clustering is mostly used for high availability purposes as well as for the scalability of read/write operations in databases, messaging systems, or files.

In such systems, a standby server is involved to take over only if the other server is facing an event of failure. We may call the passive server, the *sleepy watcher*, where it can include the configuration of a failover.

Symmetric clustering

In symmetric clustering, all nodes are active and all participators handle the process of requests. This setup might be cost-effective by serving active applications and users.

A failed node can be discarded from the cluster, while others take over its workload and continue to handle transactions.

Symmetric clustering can be thought of as being similar to a load-balancing cluster situation, where all nodes share the workload by increasing the performance and scalability of services running in the cloud infrastructure.

Divide and conquer

OpenStack was designed to be horizontally scalable; we have already seen how its functions have been widely distributed into multiple services. The services themselves are composed of the API server, schedulers, workers, and agents. While the OpenStack controller runs the API services, the compute, storage, and network nodes run the agents and workers.

The cloud controller

The concept of cloud controllers aims to provide central management and control over your OpenStack deployments. We can, for example, consider that the cloud controller is managing all API calls and messaging transactions.

Considering a medium- or large-scale infrastructure, we will need, with no doubt, more than a single node. For an OpenStack cloud operator, controllers can be thought of as service aggregators, where the majority of management services needed to operate OpenStack are running.

Let's see what a cloud controller mainly handles:

- It presents a gateway for access to cloud management and services consumption
- It provides the API services in order to make different OpenStack components talk to each other and provides a service interface to the end user
- It provides mechanisms for highly available integrated services by the means of clustering and load-balancing utilities
- It provides critical infrastructure services, such as a database and message queue
- It exposes the persistent storage, which might be backed onto separate storage nodes

Most probably, you have already noticed the main services of the cloud controller in Chapter 1, *Designing OpenStack Cloud Architectural Consideration*, but we did not take a deep look at why such services should run in the controller node in the first place.

In this chapter, we will examine the cloud controller as a node in detail. The controller node aggregates the most critical services for OpenStack. Let's look at the services on the controller node:

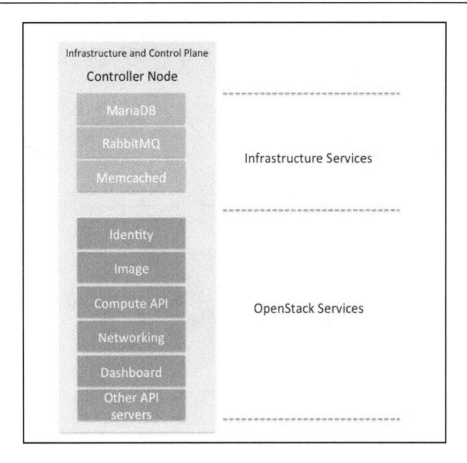

The Keystone service

The Keystone service provides identity and service cataloging in OpenStack. All other services in OpenStack must register with Keystone with their API endpoints. Keystone thus keeps a catalog of various services running in your OpenStack cloud that can be queried using the Keystone REST APIs.

Keystone also maintains a policy engine which provides rule-based access and authorization of services.

The Keystone service itself is composed of multiple providers that work in conjunction with each other. Each of these providers implements a concept in the Keystone architecture:

- Identity
- Resource
- Authorization
- Token
- Catalog
- Policy

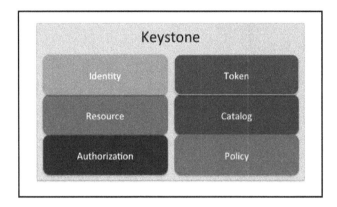

The identity provider

The identity provider validates user and group credentials. OpenStack Keystone provides a built-in identity provider that can be used to create and manage user and group credentials.

Keystone can also integrate with external identity providers such as LDAP. The OpenStack Ansible project provides the playbooks to integrate the LDAP service with Keystone as an external identity provider.

Keystone supports various user types to manage access levels to OpenStack services. The user can be one of the following:

- A service user who is associated with a service running in OpenStack
- An administrative user who has administrative access to services and resources created
- An end user who has no extra access rights and is a consumer of OpenStack resources

The resource provider

The resource provider implements the concept of projects and a domain in Keystone. The concept of a domain in Keystone provides a container for Keystone entities such as users, groups, and projects. Think of a domain as a company or a service provider.

The authorization provider

The concept of authorization provides a relationship between OpenStack users and groups to a list of roles. The roles are used to manage access to services running in OpenStack. The Keystone policy provider enforces rules based on the group and role a user belongs to.

The token provider

To access the services in OpenStack, the user must authenticate with the identity provider. Once the authentication of the user is established, the token provider generates a token that provides the user with authorization to access the OpenStack services. The token is valid for a limited period of time before it expires. A valid token is required to access the OpenStack services.

The catalog provider

As mentioned earlier, all the OpenStack services must register with the Keystone service. The catalog provider maintains a registry of services and associated endpoints running in the OpenStack cloud. In a way, Keystone provides an entry point for discovering services running in your OpenStack cluster.

The policy provider

The policy provider associates rules to allow access to the Keystone resources. The policies are composed of individual rules that define which users and roles are allowed to access which resources. For example, the ability to add users to a group is provided only to users with an admin role.

Now that we have looked at the main concepts in the identity service, let's look at some of the advanced features provided by the Keystone service:

- Federated Keystone
- Fernet tokens

Federated Keystone

Federated Identity is a mechanism to use the identity service provided by an external **Identity Provider** (**IdP**) to access resources available with the **Service Providers** (**SP**).

In the case of OpenStack, the identity provider can be a third party while OpenStack acts as the SP with resources such as virtual storage, network, and compute instances.

Using Federated Identity has some advantages over maintaining an authentication system in OpenStack:

- An organization can use an already existing identity source, such as LDAP or Active Directory, to provide user authentication in OpenStack. It removes the need to manage separate identity sources for OpenStack users.
- Using an identity service can help in integrating with different cloud services.
- It provides a single source of truth and user management. So, if a user is part of the identity service, he can be very easily provided access to the OpenStack cloud infrastructure.
- It lowers the security risk by not running yet another identity system for OpenStack users.
- It helps in providing better security to OpenStack users and a single sign on.

So, the obvious question to ask is: How does Federated Identity work? To understand this, let's look at how the user interacts with the SP and the Identity Provider services.

In a nutshell, the steps involved in authenticating users using Federated Identity are as follows:

- The user tries to access a resource available with the SP.
- The SP checks to see whether the user already has an authenticated session. If the user does not have a session, he is redirected to the authentication URL of the Identity Provider.
- The Identity Provider prompts the user for the identity credentials such as username and password, which it validates, and issues an unscoped token. The unscoped token contains, among other information, the list of groups the authenticated user belongs to.
- The user then uses the unscoped token to determine a list of accessible domains and projects in the Service Provider's cloud.
- The user then uses the unscoped token to get a scoped token for the project and domain of his interest and can start using resources on the cloud.

An interesting use case of Federated Identity is the use of the Keystone service from two different cloud infrastructures that act as a Service Provider and Identity Provider (also known as the K2K or Keystone to Keystone use case), thus allowing the user from the first Keystone instance acting as the Identity Provider to access the resources on the other cloud infrastructure that is acting as the Service Provider.

> The OpenStack Ansible project we discussed in `Chapter 2`, *Deploying OpenStack - The DevOps Way*, provides extensive configuration options for the Keystone federation service. The details for the configuration options for, Mitaka release, for example, are available at `https://docs.openstack .org/developer/openstack-ansible/mitaka/install-guide/configur e-federation.html`.

Fernet tokens

Traditionally, Keystone issues **Public Key Infrastructure** (**PKI**) -based tokens to authenticated users. The user accesses various OpenStack services using these tokens. The PKI tokens encapsulate the user's identity and the authorization context in JSON format. This makes the PKI tokens large in size. In addition, these tokens need to be stored in the database to allow token revocation.

PKIZ tokens are an enhancement to the PKI tokens in that they use compression to reduce the size of the tokens but still create considerable stress on the database for holding all the issued tokens.

Fernet tokens were introduced in Keystone to counter the shortcomings of size and database load and are on the way to becoming the default token format. The Fernet tokens are comparatively smaller in size. The major advantage of using Fernet tokens is that they need not be stored in the database and they are considerably faster in token creation as there is no database interaction involved. The Fernet token contains the user identity, scope of authorization over a project, and an expiration time. Encrypting the identity and authorization with keys generates Fernet tokens. They are considerably smaller and faster than the PKI tokens.

To enable Fernet tokens in Keystone, change the token provider as follows:

```
keystone.token.providers.fernet.Provider
```

The OpenStack Ansible project provides Fernet tokens by default, although they can be configured using the user variable, `keystone_token_provider`.

As Fernet uses encryption keys to generate new tokens, to maintain security of the system these keys need to be rotated from time to time. A Keystone service using the Fernet provider will have multiple Fernet keys active at the same time. The key rotation mechanism is configurable and it determines the number of active keys and frequency of rotation.

There are a few variables that are worth mentioning for configuring the Fernet key rotation. They are the key repository location, number of active keys, and the rotation mechanism. The following are the defaults provided by the OpenStack Ansible tool:

```
keystone_fernet_tokens_key_repository: "/etc/keystone/fernet-keys"
keystone_fernet_tokens_max_active_keys: 7
keystone_fernet_rotation: daily
keystone_fernet_auto_rotation_script: /opt/keystone-fernet-
rotate.sh
```

Default configuration settings using Ansible Keystone playbook can be found here:
https://github.com/openstack/openstack-ansible-os_keystone/blob/master/defaults/main.yml

The nova-conductor service

If you have tried to install OpenStack from the Grizzly release onward, while checking Nova services running in your OpenStack node, you may have noticed a new service called nova-conductor. Do not panic! This amazing new service has changed the way the nova-compute service accesses the database. It was added to provide security by decoupling direct database access from the compute nodes. A vulnerable compute node running the nova-compute service may be attacked and compromised. You can imagine how attacking a virtual machine can bring the compute node under the control of the attacker. Even worse, it can compromise the database. Then, you can guess the rest: your entire OpenStack cluster is under attack! The job of nova-conductor is to carry out database operations on behalf of compute nodes and provide a layer of database access segregation.

So, you can assume that nova-conductor compiles a new layer on top of nova-compute. Furthermore, instead of resolving the complexity of the database requests bottleneck, nova-conductor parallelizes the requests from compute nodes.

 If you are using nova-network and multihost networking in your OpenStack environment, nova-compute will still require direct access to the database, but again with every new release of OpenStack, operators are migrating to Neutron for their networking needs.

The nova-scheduler service

Several workflow scheduling studies and implementations have been recently conducted in cloud computing, generally in order to define the best placement of a resource provisioning.

In our case, we will decide which compute node will host the virtual machine. It's important to note that there are bunches of scheduling algorithms in OpenStack.

Nova-scheduler may also influence the performance of the virtual machines. Therefore, OpenStack supports a set of filters that implement a resource availability check on the compute nodes and then runs the filtered list of compute nodes through a weighting mechanism to arrive at the best node to start a virtual machine. The scheduler gives you the choice to configure its options based on a certain number of metrics and policy considerations. Additionally, nova-scheduler can be thought of as the *decision-maker box* in a cloud controller node that applies complex algorithms for the efficient usage and placement of virtual machines.

Eventually, the scheduler in OpenStack, as you may understand at this stage, will be running in the cloud controller node. A point here that needs to be investigated is: what about different schedulers in a high-availability environment? In this case, we exploit the openness of the OpenStack architecture by running multiple instances of each scheduler, as all of them are listening to the same queue for the scheduling requests.

It is important to know that other OpenStack services also implement schedulers. For example, cinder-scheduler is a scheduling service for block storage volumes in OpenStack. Similarly, Neutron implements a scheduler to distribute network elements such as routers and DHCP servers among the network nodes.

 The scheduler can be configured in a variety of options. Different scheduler settings can be found at `/etc/nova/nova.conf`. To read more about scheduling in OpenStack, refer to the following link: `https://docs.openstack.org/mitaka/config-reference/compute/scheduler.html`.

The API services

In a nutshell, we have already covered the nova-api service in `Chapter 1`, *Designing OpenStack Cloud Architectural Consideration*. It might be important to step forward and learn that nova-api is considered the *orchestrator engine* component in cloud controller specifications. Without any doubt, nova-api is assembled in the controller node.

The nova-api service may also fulfill more complicated requests by passing messages within other daemons by means of writing to the databases and queuing messages. As this service is based on the endpoint concept where all API queries are initiated, nova-api provides two different APIs using either the OpenStack API or EC2 API. This makes it imperative to decide which API will be used before deploying a cloud controller node that may conduct a real issue, as you may decide to take over both APIs. The reason behind this is the *heterogeneity* of the information presentation used by each API; for example, OpenStack uses names and numbers to refer to instances, whereas the EC2 API uses identifiers based on hexadecimal values.

Additionally, we have brought compute, identity, image, network, and storage APIs to be placed in the controller node, which can also be chosen to run other API services.

For instance, we satisfy our deployment by gathering the majority of the API services to run in the cloud controller node.

 An **Application Programming Interface** (**API**) enables public access to the OpenStack services and offers a way to interact with them. The API access can be performed either through a command line or through the Web. To read more about APIs in OpenStack, refer to the following link: `http://de veloper.openstack.org/#api`.

Image management

The cloud controller will also be hosting the Glance service for image management that is responsible for the storage, listing, and retrieval of images using the `glance-api` and `glance-registry`. The Glance API provides an external REST interface to query virtual machine images and associated metadata. The Glance registry stores the image metadata in the database while the storage backend stores the actual image. While designing the image, a store decision can be made about which backend will be used to launch the controller in the cloud.

 The `glance-api` supports several backend options to store images. Swift is a good alternative and allows storing images as objects, providing a scalable placement for image storage. Other alternatives are also possible such as filesystem backend, Amazon S3, and HTTP. `Chapter 5`, *OpenStack Storage - Block, Object, and File Share*, covers different storage models in OpenStack in more detail.

The network service

Just like OpenStack's Nova service provides an API for dynamic requests to compute resources, we adopt the same concept for the network by allowing its API to reside in the cloud controller, which supports extensions to provide advanced network capabilities, such as firewall, routing, load balancing, and so on. As was discussed earlier, separating most of the network workers is highly recommended.

On the other hand, you must also think about the huge amount of traffic that hits a cloud controller with regards to its running multiple services; therefore, you should bear in mind the performance challenges that you may face. In this case, clustering best practices come in to help your deployment be more scalable and increase its performance. The previous mentioned techniques are essential but not sufficient. They need basic hardware support with at least 10 GB of **bonded** NICs, for example.

The NIC bonding technique is used to increase the available bandwidth. Two or more bonded NICs appear to be the same physical device.

You can always refer to `Chapter 1`, *Designing OpenStack Cloud Architectural Consideration*, to use some calculation in order to make your cloud controller capable of responding to all requests smoothly without a bottleneck.

Complicating your performance metrics at such an early stage will not help to satisfy your topology resiliency. To do so, scalability features are always there to refine your deployment. Remember that we tend to scale horizontally when required.

The Horizon dashboard

As the OpenStack dashboard runs behind an Apache web server and is based on the Python Django web application framework, you might consider providing a separate node that is able to reach the API endpoints to run the Horizon dashboard to decrease the load on your cloud controller node. Several OpenStack deployments in production run Horizon in the controller node but still leave it up to you to monitor it and take separate decisions.

The telemetry services

Prior to the **Liberty** release, the telemetry service was composed initially of one component, known as Ceilometer, providing metering of resource utilization in OpenStack. In a multi-user shared infrastructure, keeping track of resource usage is of prime importance. Resource utilization data can be used for multiple purposes such as billing, capacity planning, and auto scaling of virtual infrastructure based on demand and throughput.

Ceilometer was originally designed to be part of the billing solution for OpenStack but, later, numerous other use cases were discovered for its independent existence.

Since the Liberty release, the telemetry service has been decomposed in two additional projects where it can be optionally enabled to function alongside Ceilometer:

- **Aodh**: a sub-project which takes care of generating alarms when resources utilization crosses a certain predefined threshold.
- **Gnocchi**: a sub-project for metrics and events storage at scale

Ceilometer uses agent-based architecture. The service itself is composed of an API server, multiple data collection agents, and the data store. Ceilometer collects data through the REST APIs, listening to notifications, and directly polling resources.

The following are the data collection agents and their roles:

- The Ceilometer polling agent provides a plugin framework to collect various resource utilization data. It runs on the controller nodes and provides a flexible means to add data collection agents by implementing them as plugins.
- The Ceilometer central agent runs on the controller node and uses the REST APIs exposed by other OpenStack services to poll for virtual resources created by tenants. The Central agent can poll for object and block storage, network, and physical hardware using SNMP.
- The Ceilometer compute agent runs on the compute node and its main purpose is to collect hypervisor statistics.
- The Ceilometer IPMI agent runs on the monitored compute node. It polls data by using the **Intelligent Platform Management Interface** (**IPMI**) on the servers to collect physical resource utilization data. The monitored servers must be equipped with IPMI sensors and installed with the `ipmitool` utility. It uses the message bus to send the collected data.
- The Ceilometer notification agent consumes notification data from various OpenStack components on the message bus. It also runs on the controller node.

Alarms

Apart from the various agents for data collection, Ceilometer also contains alarm notification and evaluation agents. The alarm evaluation agent checks for resource utilization parameters crossing a threshold value and uses the notification agent to emit the corresponding notification. The alarm system can be used to build auto-scaling infrastructure or take other corrective actions. The Aodh sub-project has been designed to decouple the alarming from Ceilometer and can be enabled when deploying a fresh installation of OpenStack.

Events

Events describe the state change of a resource in OpenStack; for example, the creation of a volume, starting a virtual machine instance, and so on. Events can be used to provide data to the billing systems. Ceilometer listens to the notification emitted from various OpenStack services and converts them to events.

More details and updates of the telemetry services and monitoring in OpenStack will be covered in `Chapter 10`, *Monitoring and Troubleshooting - Running a Healthy OpenStack Cluster*.

Infrastructure services

The infrastructure services are non-OpenStack common services that are used by multiple OpenStack components, such as the database servers, the message queue, and the caching server.

Let's look at the performance and reliability requirements of these services.

Planning for the message queue

The queuing message system should definitely be clustered. This is another critical subsystem. If the message queue fails, the whole OpenStack cluster will come to a halt.

OpenStack supports multiple queue solutions, such as the following:

- RabbitMQ
- ZeroMQ
- Qpid

We have chosen RabbitMQ to handle our queuing system as it has its native clustering support. To provide a highly available message queue in an OpenStack environment, RabbitMQ messaging servers must run in cluster. Keep in mind, by default, clustering the message queue servers only replicates the state data required for running the message servers in a highly available mode but does not replicate the queues. The queues reside on a single node where they are originally created. To provide a robust messaging service, we should also enable mirrored queues.

It should be noted that even in a cluster with mirrored queues, the clients always connect to the master node to send and consume messages, although the slave nodes replicate the messages. The slaves hold the messages only till the master node acknowledges receiving the message.

To provide a fully clustered active-active message, queues require integration with clustering solutions such as Pacemaker and DRBD.

Another aspect of a production - quality message queue is security of communication. RabbitMQ provides transport - level security using TLS. Using TLS, the clients can gain protection from the tampering of messages in transit. TLS uses the SSL certificate to encrypt and secure communication. SSL certificates can be either self-signed or provided by a CA.

In addition, RabbitMQ provides authentication and authorization based on username and password.

A good practice is to keep in mind such complex challenges that have to be undertaken when we start a simple cloud controller holding a RabbitMQ service.

It is a good thing that our design is very elastic and we can scale the cluster by adding controller nodes; where in RabbitMQ clusters can be installed. We also have the option of keeping controller nodes simple and separating the RabbitMQ node cluster relatively easily.

 Refer to the OpenStack Ansible documentation for configuring RabbitMQ for Mitaka release, for example: `https://docs.openstack.org/develope r/openstack-ansible/mitaka/install-guide/configure-rabbitmq.ht ml`.

We will discuss the high availability of RabbitMQ in detail in *Chapter 9, OpenStack HA and Failover*.

Consolidating the database

The majority of disasters that happen in any IT infrastructure can result in the loss, not only of data in production, but also historical data. Such critical points may lead to non-operational and even non-recoverable OpenStack environments. Thus, we need to start working with MySQL clustering and high availability solutions at an early stage.

We can start adapting MySQL using Galera running in the cloud controller. More details about setting up the MySQL cluster will be covered in `Chapter 9`, *OpenStack HA and Failover*.

With telemetry services enabled in OpenStack, we also need to install a No-SQL database for storing metering information. We will use MongoDB as our No-SQL database.

Cloud controller clustering

Being a proponent of the physical cloud controller, efforts made towards clustering machines are considered a step in the right direction of achieving high availability. Several HA topologies will be discussed in *Chapter 9, OpenStack HA and Failover*.

As we have seen the use cases of several services at this point, which can be separated and clustered, we will extend our logical design of the cloud controller described in `Chapter 1`, *Designing OpenStack Cloud Architectural Consideration*. Keep in mind that OpenStack is a highly configurable platform and the rest of the description is an example that suits a certain requirement and specific conditions.

The next step is to confirm the first logical design. Questions such as the following may come up: Does it satisfy certain requirements? Are all services in the safe HA zone?

Well, note that we include the MySQL Galera cluster to ensure HA for the database. Eventually, this means at least a third cloud controller has to join the cloud controller team to satisfy the quorum-based consensus system of Galera.

The questions that arise from this are: Should I add an extra cloud controller to achieve the replication and database HA? What about a fourth or fifth controller?

Great! Keep this mindset for later. At this level, you assume that, logically, your design is on the right path and you already know that some changes have to be made to fulfill some physical constraints.

At this point, we ensure that our design is deployed in HA at an early stage. Remember, there should be no single point of failure in any layer!

Redundancy is implemented by means of virtual IP and Pacemaker. Then, HAProxy will ensure load balancing. Databases and messaging queue servers have been implemented in active-active HA mode when MySQL uses Galera for replication, while RabbitMQ is built in a cluster - capable mode. Other choices can be made for our current design by integrating, for example, with Corosync, Heartbeat, or Keepalived instead. Aspects of load balancing, high availability, and failover with relative solutions will be explained in detail in *Chapter 9, OpenStack HA and Failover*.

It is important to prepare how the cloud controllers should be clustered in advance. You can refer to *Chapter 9, OpenStack HA and Failover*, to check out more details and practical examples. For instance, the overall OpenStack cloud should expand easily by joining new nodes running several services that require more care. We continue later by adumbrating an automated approach to facilitating the horizontal expansion of the cloud.

Starting deployment with OpenStack Ansible

Now that we have discussed the services running on the controller node, let's start the deployment of our controller nodes using OpenStack Ansible (OSA). The suggested configuration for a production - grade controller consists of at least three controller nodes which run the OpenStack API services and also host the infrastructural services, such as the MySQL server, memcached, the RabbitMQ server, and so on. This is in line with our clustering needs.

Also, in addition to the OpenStack controller nodes, we need to have a node to run the OpenStack Ansible tool from the called the deployment node:

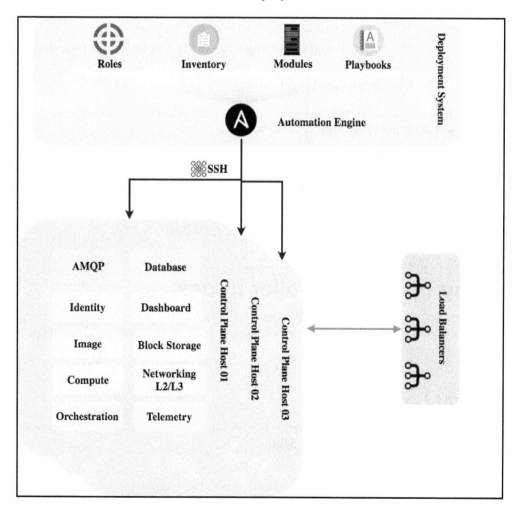

The deployment node

The deployment node is the one that hosts the Ansible OpenStack tools and will orchestrate the OpenStack cloud nodes on the target nodes. The deployment node can be installed with Ubuntu 14.04 LTS 64bit. The following steps are needed to bring up a working OpenStack Ansible on the deployment host:

1. Install essential packages on the deployment host. This includes `Git`, `ntp`, `sudo`, and `openssh-server`:

    ```
    # apt-get install aptitude build-essential git ntp ntpdate
    openssh-server python-dev sudo
    ```

2. Configure NTP to synchronize the time over the network.
3. Configure the network so that the target hosts are accessible from the deployment host.
4. Clone the OpenStack Ansible repository:

    ```
    # git clone -b TAG https://github.com/openstack/openstack-
    ansible.git /opt/openstack-ansible
    ```

5. Bring up Ansible for OpenStack:

    ```
    # cd /opt/openstack-ansible
    # scripts/bootstrap-ansible.sh
    ```

6. Generate SSH keys on the Ansible deployment host.

Bringing up the controller nodes

Let's now look at the controller nodes. We need to install all the API servers, common, and infrastructure services. In this section, we will look at the playbooks from OpenStack Ansible to deploy our controller node.

The target hosts

The controller nodes are among the target hosts for OpenStack Ansible. All target nodes can be installed with Ubuntu 14.04 LTS 64bit.

CentOS 7 has been supported since the OpenStack **Ocata** release.

The nodes need to be installed with the latest package updates:

```
# apt-get dist-upgrade
```

The packages for bonding, VLAN, and bridging should be installed on the target nodes:

```
# apt-get install bridge-utils debootstrap ifenslave
ifenslave-2.6 lsof lvm2 ntp ntpdate openssh-server sudo
tcpdump vlan
```

Configure the target nodes to synchronize with an NTP server. At the time of writing, OpenStack Ansible also requires a minimal kernel version of 3.13.0-34-generic.

Next, deploy SSH keys from the OpenStack Ansible deployment host. This can be done by adding the public key from the deployment host to the `authorized_keys` file on each of the target hosts.

The target hosts can optionally be configured with the LVM volume group named `lxc`. If the LVM volume group, `lxc`, exists on the target host, the `lxc` filesystem is created on the volume group or else it is created under `/var/lib/lxc`.

Configuring the network

The networking setup for the target nodes must provide communication paths for the following services:

- Management access
- Storage management
- Tenant networks

OpenStack Ansible uses bridges to provide the above communication paths on the target nodes. The tenant networks can be implemented either as VLAN - based segments or using tunneled networks such as VXLAN. The physical link to the bridges can be provided by creating sub-interfaces from a single NIC or multiple bonded interfaces. The management access is provided by the **br-mgmt** bridge, the storage access is provided over the bridge **br-storage**, while the tenant networks are provided over the **br-vlan** and **br-vxlan** bridges.

The following figure shows a detailed bridge configuration with bonding and multiple NICs:

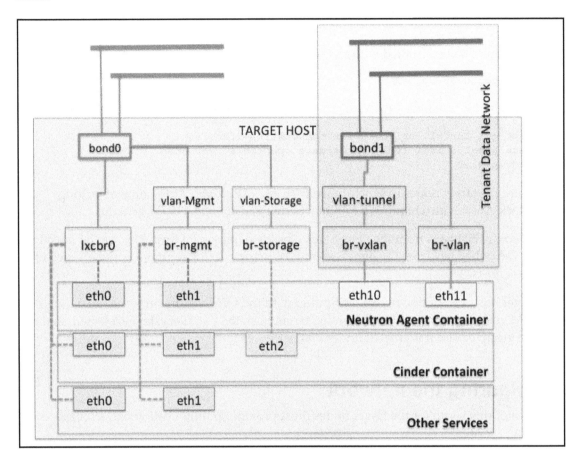

Although the multiple NICs and bonding interfaces are not mandatory requirements, it is suggested as the production architecture.

 A more detailed description of a reference network setup can be found at
`https://docs.openstack.org/developer/openstack-ansible/`.

Running the OpenStack playbooks

OSA provides playbooks to configure the different OpenStack services. The playbooks will be used to run tasks to bring up OpenStack services on the target hosts.

Configuring OpenStack Ansible

Deploying OpenStack using OSA is controlled through a number of configuration files. The configuration files must be present at /etc/openstack_deploy. A sample directory structure is included in the AIO repository. We can start by copying the sample configuration files from the repository and then adapting them to our needs:

```
#cp /opt/openstack-ansible/etc/openstack_deploy /etc/openstack_deploy
#cd /etc/openstack_deploy
#cp openstack_user_config.yml.example openstack_user_config.yml
```

We can now start customizing the user configuration file for our deployment. The openstack_user_config.yml uses host groups to define the target hosts that run a particular service.

Network configuration

The next step is to configure network addresses for the different network paths we mentioned earlier in our discussion. This includes the CIDRs used for the management access to the service container, the storage, and the tunnel networks. Here is an example from the openstack_user_config.yaml file in the AIO repository:

```
cidr_networks:
   container: 172.47.36.0/22
   tunnel: 172.47.40.0/22
   storage: 172.47.44.0/22
```

The CIDR used for containers should be the same as your lab management network. These CIDR addresses are mapped to the management, storage, and tunnel bridges.

Use the used_ips group to exclude any IP addresses in the CIDR range that are already used in your infrastructure.

Use the provider network level to define various network paths such as the br-mgmt, br-storage, br-vxlan, and br-vlan. The example config file in the OSA repository, openstack_user_config.yml.example, is well commented with example configurations.

Configuring Host Groups

The following table lists the host groups used by OpenStack Ansible and their purposes. The hosts can be part of more than one host group mapping. The hosts are identified using their management IP addresses. By referring to the same `openstack_user_config.yml` file, new sections can be added to describe our OpenStack infrastructure, including controller nodes. In a multi-node setup environment, each section describes a group of target hosts organized by role, summarized as follows:

OpenStack Ansible Host Groups	Role
repo-infra_hosts	Used for the hosting package repository. The **shared-infra_hosts** can be assigned a **repo-infra_hosts** role.
shared-infra_hosts	Runs the shared infrastructure services such as MySQL, RabbitMQ and memcached.
os-infra_hosts	Runs OpenStack API services such as the Glance API, Nova API, Ceilometer API, and so on.
identity_hosts	Runs the identity service.
network_hosts	Runs the network service.
compute_hosts	Lists hosts running the `nova-compute` service.
storage-infra_hosts	Runs the Cinder API service.
storage_hosts	Runs the Cinder volume service.
log_hosts	Lists hosts running logging services.
haproxy_hosts	Lists hosts running HAProxy service. For production setup, target hosts can point to hardware load balancers.

As discussed in `Chapter 1`, *Designing OpenStack Cloud - Architectural Consideration*, we will be using three controller nodes to run common OpenStack services including native API services. This can be implemented and deployed easily from one single file by pointing which host group will be assigned to the controller node. In the `openstack_user_config.yml` file, start by adjusting the `shared-infra_hosts` for shared services such as database and message queue:

```
shared-infra_hosts:
cc-01:
  ip: 172.47.0.10
cc-02:
  ip: 172.47.0.11
cc-03:
  ip: 172.47.0.12
```

The next `os-infra_hosts` section will point Ansible to install OpenStack API services in the controller nodes:

```
os-infra_hosts:
cc-01:
  ip: 172.47.0.10
cc-02:
  ip: 172.47.0.11
cc-03:
  ip: 172.47.0.12
```

We can also address our block storage API service to run in the same OpenStack control plane by adding the list of controller nodes in the `storage-infra_hosts` section:

```
storage-infra_hosts:
cc-01:
  ip: 172.47.0.10
cc-02:
  ip: 172.47.0.11
cc-03:
  ip: 172.47.0.12
```

Keystone will be deployed in the controller plane by adjusting the `identity_hosts` section:

```
identity_hosts:
cc-01:
  ip: 172.47.0.10
ccr-02:
  ip: 172.47.0.11
cc-03:
  ip: 172.47.0.12
```

Optionally, controller nodes can host the installation packages repository described in the `repo-infra_hosts` section:

```
repo-infra_hosts:
cc-01:
  ip: 172.47.0.10
ccr-02:
  ip: 172.47.0.11
cc-03:
  ip: 172.47.0.12
```

To load balance the APIs, Ansible can be set to install HAProxy as a virtual load balance in each controller node in the `haproxy_hosts` section:

```
haproxy_hosts:
cc-01:
  ip: 172.47.0.10
cc-02:
  ip: 172.47.0.11
cc-03:
  ip: 172.47.0.12
```

 Depending on the HA setup of the controller nodes, it is recommended to use hardware load balancers in a production environment. Ansible user configuration will differ between both load balancing configurations.

Installing HAProxy per controller node requires additional configuration in the `/etc/openstack_deploy/user_variables.yml` Ansible configuration file by setting the following Keepalived directives:

- Configure the CIDR virtual IP to be shared between all HAProxy instances for both external and internal network interfaces:

  ```
  haproxy_keepalived_external_vip_cidr
  haproxy_keepalived_internal_vip_cidr
  ```

- Define virtual network devices for each external and internal interface for all HAProxy instances:

  ```
  haproxy_keepalived_external_interface
  haproxy_keepalived_internal_interface
  ```

HA setup for controller nodes and API services are discussed in more detail in *Chapter 9, OpenStack HA and Failover.*

Ansible OpenStack approaches the way of handling secrets and keys for the service configuration, such as the database root password and compute service passphrase, differently.

Secrets are stored in a different file: `/etc/openstack_deploy/user_secrets.yml`.

Exposing secret passwords and passphrases in a repository in plain text presents a high security issue and must be addressed by using encryption mechanisms. Ansible provides more advanced features to protect password data and keys in encrypted files using **Vaults**. To read more about **Vaults** in Ansible, refer to the official Ansible web page found here: `http://docs.ansible.com/ansible/playbooks_vault.html`.

After revisiting our network setup and host services setup for the control plane in Ansible, we can move on and detail briefly which playbooks will be used to deploy control nodes and common OpenStack services.

The playbooks

OpenStack Ansible playbooks are the blueprints that describe how the services are deployed on the target systems. They are composed of tasks, which Ansible must perform to bring up the OpenStack services. The tasks, on the other hand, refer to the specific roles that encapsulate all the details of a service deployment.

The following table lists the individual playbooks. The playbooks run using the `openstack-ansible` command. This is a wrapper script that provides the OpenStack configuration to the `ansible-playbook` command:

```
# openstack-ansible playbook-name.yaml
```

Replace the playbook-name with the playbook that you want to run.

Playbook Name	OpenStack Service
os-keystone-install.yml	Identity Service
os-glance-install.yml	Image Service
os-cinder-install.yml	Block Storage Service

`os-nova-install.yml`	Compute Service
`os-neutron-install.yml`	Network Service
`os-heat-install.yml`	Orchestration Service
`os-horizon-install.yml`	OpenStack Dashboard

`os-ceilometer-install.yml`
`os-aodh-install.yml`
`os-gnocchi-install.yml`
	Telemetry Service

Each of the playbooks provide configuration options using Ansible variables. The playbooks apply roles to the target hosts. OpenStack Ansible maintains the OpenStack services as an external role repository. For example, the Keystone deployment is handled with the `os_keystone` role that can be found in the playbook code source:

```
...
roles:
- role: "os_keystone"
...
```

The Git repository for the role is maintained at `https://github.com/openstack/openstack-ansible-os_keystone`

Deploying the controller nodes is achieved just by running the playbooks which Ansible will take care of orchestrating the installation of each service as described in the user and variable configuration files. This requires first installing and configuring the containers across the target controller hosts by running the `setup-hosts.yml` playbook under `/etc/openstack_deploy/`:

 # openstack-ansible setup-hosts.yml

For our control plane, we will need to install infrastructure services including Galera, MariaDB, memcached and RabbitMQ. This can be achieved by running the `setup-infrastructure.yml` playbook under `/etc/openstack_deploy/`:

 # openstack-ansible setup-infrastructure.yml

The OpenStack API services, including image, network, identity, dashboard, compute API, telemetry, and orchestration services, can be installed by firing the `setup-openstack.yml` playbook under `/etc/openstack_deploy/`:

```
# openstack-ansible setup-openstack.yml
```

Since our compute and network target hosts have not been defined yet, the Ansible configuration for the OpenStack environment is still incomplete. Before proceeding to cover them in more detail in the next chapters, it is crucial to understand how OpenStack-Ansible playbooks are organized by role.

To allow the installation of a virtual load balancer by deploying HAProxy in each controller node, use the `haproxy-install.yml` playbook under `/etc/openstack_deploy/` as follows:

```
# openstack-ansible haproxy-install.yml
```

 More details about HA setup using HAProxy will be discussed in more detail in `Chapter 9`, *OpenStack HA and Failover*.

Additionally, operators could have more flexibility by setting several options for each playbook configuration file before running the Ansible wrapper command-line interface. Customizing the OpenStack configuration control plane can be performed via each OpenStack playbook role found at `https://github.com/openstack/openstack-ansible-os_Service/blob/master/defaults/main.yml`. Where *Service* is the name of any OpenStack service you need to customize the configuration of before deployment using Ansible. Each `main.yml` file located under the `defaults` directory exposes an extensive list of options and directives that can be applied to target nodes when applying roles. For example, the Horizon playbook can be customized to enable Neutron features such as **Load Balancer as a Service** (**LBaaS**) by default so can be exposed in the dashboard tab by setting in the `/openstack-ansible-os-horizon/defaults/main.yml` file the directive `horizon_enable_neutron_lbaas` to **true.**

The `user_variables.yml` can be used with higher precedence level when applying Ansible OpenStack playbooks. Additional directives adjusted in the `user_variables` file will be loaded and applied in the target hosts as default.

Summary

In this chapter, we looked at the OpenStack controller node. We briefly discussed the need for high availability and the significance of clustering. We will discuss HA and clustering in detail in *Chapter 9, OpenStack HA and Failover*.

We discussed the services that run on the controller nodes and the common services that are required for running the OpenStack cluster. We looked at the Keystone service and its support of a variety of backends that can be used to provide identity and authentication. We also discussed the new trend of Keystone identity support by the means of federated authentication.

Later, we checked the OpenStack Ansible tools and the different playbooks involved in bringing up the controller nodes.

We also looked at the basic configuration of the target servers that will be used to bring up OpenStack services. We discussed network configuration and looked at some of the customization options provided by the OpenStack Ansible automation tool.

The next chapter will discuss setting up the compute nodes and the various configuration options.

4
OpenStack Compute - Choice of Hypervisor and Node Segregation

"Be sure you put your feet in the right place, then stand firm."
Abraham Lincoln

Once the orchestrator has evaluated the instruments that should be integrated on the stage, we still need the *players* to accomplish the song. All we need are *worker horses* that do the job of hosting our virtual machines.

The compute nodes should be separately deployed in the cluster, as it forms the resources part of the OpenStack infrastructure. The compute servers are the heart of the cloud computing service, as they provide the resources that are directly used by the end users; it becomes imperative, then, to give attention to the fact that compute node resources should not be overlooked in terms of processing power, memory, network, and storage capability.

From a deployment perspective, an OpenStack compute node might not be complicated to install, as it will basically run nova-compute and the network agent for Neutron. However, its hardware and specification choice might not be obvious. The cloud controller presents a wide range of services, so we have agreed to use HA clusters and a separate deployment scheme for the controller to crystallize the cloud controller setup. This way, we suffer less from the issue of service downtime. On the other hand, a compute node will be the *space* where the virtual machine will run; in other words, the space on which the end user will focus. The end user only wants to push the button and get the application running on the top of your IaaS layer. It is your mission to guarantee a satisfactory amount of resources to enable your end user to do this.

A good design of cloud controller is needed but is not enough; we need to take care over compute nodes as well. In the previous chapters, we have already discussed the Nova API service. In this chapter, we will concentrate on the nova compute service in detail.

We will look at the following topics:

- Iterating through different supported hypervisors
- Defining a strategy for scaling and segregation of the compute cluster
- Covering different hardware requirements for the compute nodes
- Understanding the details of launching a new virtual machine
- Learning about adding a new compute node to the OpenStack cluster using Ansible
- Setting a disaster recovery plan in case the OpenStack deployment suffers a node failure

The compute service components

The compute service is composed of multiple components that take care of receiving the request, and launching and managing the virtual machines. Here is a summary of the various building blocks of the compute service:

- The **nova-api** service interacts with the user API calls that manage the compute instances. It communicates with the other components of the compute service over the message bus.
- The **nova-scheduler** is the service that listens to the new instance request on the message bus. The job of this service is to select the best compute node for the new instance.
- The **nova-compute** service is the process responsible for starting and terminating the virtual machines. This service runs on the compute nodes and listens for new requests over the message bus.

The compute nodes are not provided direct access to the database. This design limits the risk of a compromised compute node providing the attacker complete access to the database. The database access calls from the compute nodes are handled by the **nova-conductor** service.

Nova uses the **metadata service** to provide the virtual machines with configuration data used to initialize and configure the instance.

Apart from these, the **nova-consoleauth** daemon provides authentication for the VNC proxy, such as **novncproxy** and **xvncproxy**, access to the console of instances over the VNC protocol.

Deciding on the hypervisor

The hypervisor is the heart of your OpenStack compute node. This is called the **virtual machine monitor** (**VMM**), which provides a set of manageability functions for virtual machines to access the hardware layer. The amazing part about hypervisors in OpenStack is the wide range of VMMs that it can offer, including KVM, VMware ESXi, QEMU, UML, Xen, Hyper-V, LXC, bare metal, and lately, Docker.

If you already have some experience with one or more of these, it will be better to take a look at how they differ at an architectural level. Currently, the latest OpenStack release at the time of writing this book is **Ocata**, which has many hypervisor features added or extended. Keep in mind that not all of these support the same features. The Hypervisor Support Matrix (`https://wiki.openstack.org/wiki/HypervisorSupportMatrix`) is a good reference that can help you to choose what fits your needs.

Obviously, all the hypervisors are not supported the same in OpenStack. For example, **Quick EMUlator** (**QEMU**) and **User Mode Linux** (**UML**) might be used for general development purposes, while Xen requires a nova-compute installation on a para-virtualized platform.

Para-virtualization is an improvement of virtualization technology in which the guest operating system needs to be modified to run on the hypervisor. In contrast to complete virtualization, in which the hypervisor simulates a hardware platform and is able to run an operating system unmodified, a para-virtualization hypervisor provides enhanced performance by doing away with some of the costly hardware emulation, but requires the guest operating system to be specially compiled. Xen and IBM have adopted this technology, keeping in mind the high-performance deliverance that it can provide. The operating system and the hypervisor work efficiently in tandem, which helps avoid the overheads imposed by the native system resource emulation.

On the other hand, most of the OpenStack nova-compute deployments run KVM as the main hypervisor. The fact is that KVM is best suited for workloads that are natively stateless using `libvirt`.

KVM is the default hypervisor for OpenStack compute. You can check out your compute node from `/etc/nova/nova.conf` in the following lines:

```
compute_driver=libvirt.LibvirtDriver
libvirt_type=kvm
```

For proper, error-free hypervisor usage, it is required to first check whether KVM modules are loaded from your compute node:

```
# lsmod | grep kvm
kvm_intel or kvm_amd
```

Otherwise, you may load the required modules via the following:

```
# modprobe -a kvm
```

To make your modules persistent at reboot, which is obviously needed, you can add the following lines to the `/etc/modules` file when your compute node is an Intel-based processor:

```
kvm
kvm-intel
```

 That `kvm-intel` can be replaced by `kvm-amd` in the case of an AMD-based processor. Our further compute deployments will be based on KVM.

The Docker containers

Most probably, you have heard about most of these previously mentioned hypervisors, but what do you think Docker could be?

It is interesting to discover another attractive point about OpenStack, which has steadily grown and can include any virtualization technology in its ecosystem, such as the Docker driver for OpenStack nova-compute.

While a virtual machine provides a complete virtual hardware platform on which an operating system can be installed in a conventional way and applications can be deployed, a container, on the other hand, provides an isolated user space to host an application. The containers use the same underlying kernel of the host operating system. In a way, containers are providing an encapsulation mechanism that captures the user space configuration and dependencies of an application. This encapsulated application runtime environment can be packaged into portable images. The advantage of this approach is that an application can be delivered along with its dependency and configuration as a self-contained image:

Out of the box, Docker helps enterprises deploy their applications in highly portable and self-sufficient containers, independent of the hardware and hosting provider. It brings the software deployment into a secure, automated, and repeatable environment. What makes Docker special is its usage of a large number of containers, which can be managed on a single machine. Additionally, it becomes more powerful when it is used alongside Nova. Therefore, it would be possible to manage hundreds and even thousands of containers, which makes it the cat's meow. You may wonder about the use cases of Docker, especially in an OpenStack environment. Well, as mentioned previously, Docker is based on containers that are not a replacement for virtual machines, but which are very specific to certain deployments. Containers are very lightweight and fast, which may be a good option for the development of new applications and even to port older applications faster. Imagine an abstraction that can be shared with any application along with its own specific environment and configuration requirements without them interfering with each other. This is what Docker brings to the table. Docker can save the state of a container as an image that can be shared through a central image registry. This makes Docker awesome, as it creates a portable image that can be shared across different cloud environments.

OpenStack Magnum project

There has been a bit of confusion with container support in OpenStack, especially with implementations such as the Docker driver for Nova and the **Magnum** project. The OpenStack Magnum project provides **Container-as-a-Service** capability. So what is the difference between the two approaches? Well, the aim of the Nova Docker driver was to add Docker to be a supported hypervisor for Nova. This enables OpenStack Nova to launch and manage the lifecycle of a Docker container in a fashion similar to other virtual machine instances.

However, it quickly becomes evident that containers, especially the application containers, are not like virtual machines. Hosting an application in containers very often means deploying multiple containers, each running just a single process; these containerized processes then collaborate with each other to provide the complete features of the application. This means that, unlike virtual machines, containers running a single process would most likely need to be spawned in groups, would require network connectivity for communication between collaborating processes, and have storage requirements too. This is the idea behind the OpenStack Magnum project. Magnum is built to support orchestration of groups of connected containers using a **Container Orchestration Engine** (**COE**) such as Kubernetes, Apache Mesos, Docker Swamp, and so on.

In contrast to the Nova Docker driver, Magnum works by first deploying the COE nodes and then launching groups of containers for deploying applications on these nodes. The COE system acts as an orchestrator to launch applications across multiple containers.

Magnum leverages OpenStack services to provide the COE infrastructure. COE Nodes are deployed as Nova instances. It uses the Neutrons networking service to provide network connectivity between the COE nodes, although the connectivity between the application containers is handled by the COE itself. Each of the COE nodes is connected to a Cinder volume that is used to host the application containers. Heat is used to orchestrate the virtual infrastructure for COE. The following figure shows a typical Magnum installation hosting a containerized application:

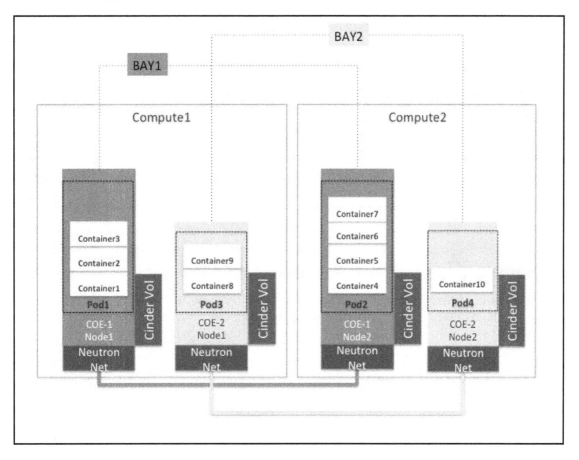

Let's drill down into the concept of Magnum and how it fits into the container orchestration picture. As shown in the previous diagram, Magnum defines the following components:

- A **Bay** is a group of nodes that run COE software. The nodes can run an API server or minions. The COE architecture consists of an API server that receives the orchestration requests from the user. The API server then interacts with the minion server where the **Containers** are launched.
- A **Pod** is a group of containers running on the same node and the concept of **Service** that consists of one or more Bays that provide to a consumable service. The Service abstraction is required as the bays providing the service may get created and deleted while the service is still available.
- A **BayModel** is a template that can be used to create a Bay; it is similar to the concept of Nova flavor that is used to create a virtual machine instance.

 A `ReplicationController` is the process that is responsible for making sure that multiple replicas of pods are running to provide redundancy. It is also responsible for re-spawning a container if it fails.

The Magnum project is still maturing and is undergoing a lot of change. It is worth tracking the development of this project as it brings robust support for the evolving Containers technology and orchestration engines. To follow the development of the Magnum project, please refer to the official developer OpenStack web page found at: `https://docs.opensta ck.org/developer/magnum/`.

Segregating the compute cloud

As your cloud infrastructure grows in size, you need to devise strategies to maintain low latency in the API services and redundancy of your service. To cope with unplanned downtime due to natural forces or based on the hypervisor capability itself, the operator must plan for service continuity.

OpenStack Nova provides several concepts that help you segregate the cloud resources. Each segregation strategy brings in its own advantages and shortcomings. We must have a discussion to understand the tools available with an OpenStack cloud operator to manage the need for scale and availability of compute servers.

Availability zones

The concept of **Availability Zones** (**AZ**) in Nova is to group together compute nodes based on fault domains: for example, all compute nodes hosted on a rack in the lab. All the nodes connect to the same **Top-of-Rack** (**ToR**) switch or are fed from the same **Power Distribution Unit** (**PDU**), and can form a fault domain as they depend on a single infrastructure resource. The idea of Availability Zones maps to the concept of hardware failure domains. Think of a situation when you lost network connectivity to a ToR switch or lost power to the rack of compute nodes due to the failure of a PDU.

With Availability Zones configured, the end users can still continue to launch instances just by choosing a different Availability Zone. One important thing to keep in mind is that a compute node cannot be part of multiple Availability Zones.

To configure an Availability Zone for a compute node, edit the `/etc/nova.conf` file on that node and update the `default_availability_zone` value. Once updated, the Nova compute service on the node should be restarted.

Host Aggregates

The Host Aggregate is a strategy of grouping together compute nodes that provides compute resources with specialized features. Let's say you have some compute nodes with better processors or better networking capability. Then you can make sure that virtual machines of a certain kind that require better physical hardware support are always scheduled on these compute nodes.

Attaching a set of metadata to the group of hosts can create the Host Aggregates. To use a Host Aggregate, the end user needs to use a flavor that has the same metadata attached. We will discuss Host Aggregates in detail in the following section and demonstrate how this concept can be used to launch virtual machines in a multi-hypervisor environment.

Nova cells

In a conventional OpenStack setup, all the compute nodes need to speak to the message queue and the database server (using nova-conductor). This approach creates a heavy load on the message queues and databases. As your cloud grows, a lot of compute servers try to connect to the same infrastructure resources, which can cause a bottleneck. This is where the concept of cells in Nova helps scale your compute resources. Nova cells are a way of scaling your compute workload by distributing the load on infrastructure resources, such as databases and message queues, to multiple instances.

The Nova cell architecture creates groups of compute nodes that are arranged as trees, called cells. Each cell has its own database and message queue. The strategy is to constrain the database and message queue communication to be within the individual cells.

So how does the cell architecture work? Let's look at the components involved in the cells' architecture and their interaction. As mentioned earlier, the cells are arranged as trees. The root of the tree is the API cell and it runs the Nova API service but not the Nova compute service, while the other nodes, called the compute cells, run all Nova services.

The cells' architecture works by decoupling the Nova API service that receives the user input from all other components of Nova compute. The interaction between the Nova API and other Nova components is replaced by message-queue-based RPC calls. Once the Nova API receives a call to start a new instance, it uses the cell RPC calls to schedule the instance on one of the available compute cells. The compute cells run their own database, message queue, and a complete set of Nova services except the Nova API. The compute cell then launches the instance by scheduling it on a compute node:

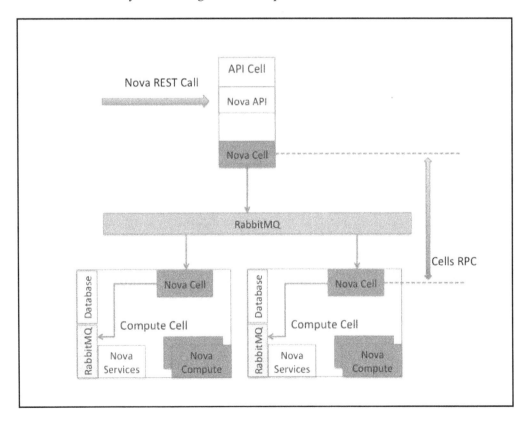

Although cells have been implemented in Nova for quite some time, they have not seen widespread deployment and have been marked as experimental. As of today, the cells are an optional feature, but the Nova project is working on a newer implementation of cell architecture with the vision to make cells the default architecture to implement the compute cloud. In the current cell architecture, scheduling of an instance requires two levels of scheduling. The first level of scheduling is done to select the cell that should host the new virtual machine. Once a cell is selected, the second level of scheduling selects the compute node to host the virtual machine. Among other improvements, the new implementation (V2 API) will remove the need for two levels of scheduling.

Regions

The concept of cells allows extending the compute cloud by segregating compute nodes into groups but maintaining a single Nova API endpoint. Nova regions take an orthogonal approach and allow multiple Nova API endpoints to be used to launch virtual machines. Each Nova region has a complete Nova installation, with its own set of compute nodes its and own Nova API endpoint. Different Nova regions of an OpenStack cloud share the same Keystone service for authentication and advertising the Nova API endpoints. The end user will have to select the region where he wants the virtual machines to be launched. Another way of thinking about the contrast between cells and regions is that Nova - cells implementation uses RPC calls, while regions use REST APIs to provide segregation.

Workload segregation

Although the workload segregation is more of a usability feature of OpenStack cloud, it is worth mentioning in a discussion on cloud segregation. In the previous sections, we discussed Availability Zones and Host Aggregates that impact the way virtual machine instances are placed in an OpenStack cloud. The approach discussed till now handled the instance scheduling by handling a single virtual machine at a time, but what happens if you need to place your instances relative to each other? This use case is handled with workload segregation with affinity policy.

To make the situation a bit clearer, let's take the example of when you have two virtual machines and you want them to be placed on the same compute node. Another example is when you want to have virtual machines running your application in a high-availability mode. Obviously, you don't want to place the instances providing the HA application on the same compute node.

To use workload segregation, the Nova filter scheduler must be configured with Affinity filters. Add `ServerGroupAffinityFilter` and `ServerGroupAntiAffinityFilter` to the list of scheduler filters:

```
scheduler_default_filters = ServerGroupAffinityFilter,
ServerGroupAntiAffinityFilter
```

Use the Nova client to create server groups. The server group can be created with an affinity or anti-affinity-based policy as shown here:

```
# nova server-group svr-grp1 affinity
# nova server-group svr-grp2 anti-affinity
```

The affinity policy places the virtual machines on the same compute node while the anti-affinity policy forces the virtual machines onto different compute nodes.

To start the virtual machines associated with a server group, use the `--hint group=svr-grp1-uuid` command with the Nova client:

```
# nova boot --image image1 --hint group=svr-grp1-uuid --flavor "Standard 1"
vm1
# nova boot --image image1 --hint group=svr-grp1-uuid --flavor "Standard 1"
vm2
```

This will make sure that the virtual machines, vm1 and vm2, are placed in the same compute node.

Changing the color of the hypervisor

While we have decided to use KVM for nova-compute, it would be great to learn how OpenStack could support a wide range of hypervisors by means of nova-compute drivers. You might be suggested to run your OpenStack environment with two or more hypervisors. It can be a user requirement to provide a choice of more than one hypervisor. This will help the end user resolve the challenge of native platform compatibility for their application, and then we can calibrate the performance of the virtual machine between different hypervisor environments. This could be a common topic in a hybrid cloud environment.

The following figure depicts the integration between nova-compute and KVM, QEMU, and LXC by means of libvirt tools and XCP through APIs, while vSphere, Xen, or Hyper-V can be managed directly via nova-compute:

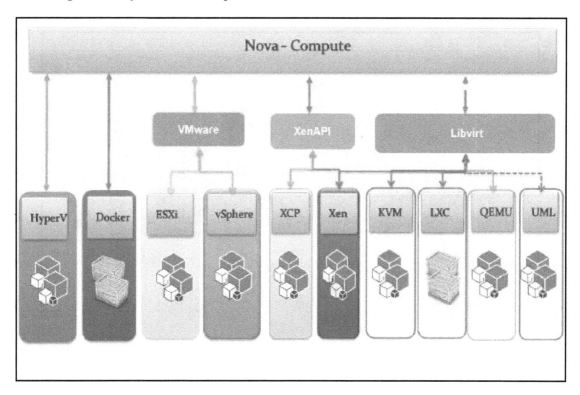

Let's take an example and see how such multi-hypervisor capability can be factored in the OpenStack environment. If you already have a VMware vSphere running in your infrastructure, this example will be suitable for you if you plan to integrate vSphere with OpenStack. Practically, the term **integration** on the hypervisor level refers to the OpenStack driver that will be provided to manage vSphere by nova-compute. Eventually, OpenStack exposes two compute drivers that have been coded:

- `vmwareapi.VMwareESXDriver`: This allows nova-compute to reach the ESXi host by means of the vSphere SDK
- `vmwareapi.VMwareVCDriver`: This allows nova-compute to manage multiple clusters by means of a single VMware vCenter server

Imagine the several functions we will gain from such an integration using the OpenStack driver with which we attempt to harness advanced capabilities, such as vMotion, high availability, and **Dynamic Resource Scheduler** (**DRS**). It is important to understand how such integration can offers more flexibility:

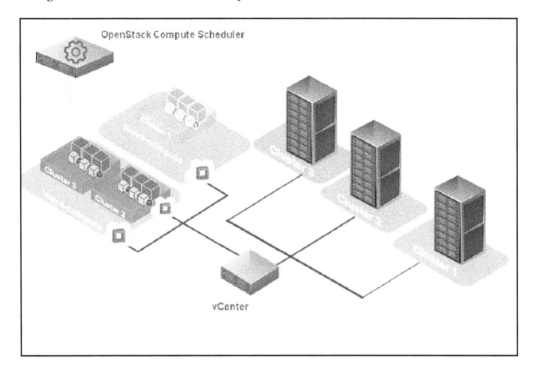

 vMotion is a component of VMware vSphere that allows the live migration of a running virtual machine from one host to another with no downtime. VMware's vSphere virtualization suite also provides a load-balancing utility called DRS, which moves computing workloads to available hardware resources.

In a vSphere implementation coupled with OpenStack, nova-scheduler will assume each cluster as a single compute node that has the aggregate of resources of all ESXi hosts managed by that cluster, as shown in the previous figure.

A good practice retrieved from this layout implementation is to place the compute node in a separate management vSphere cluster so that nodes that run nova-compute can take advantage of vSphere HA and DRS. vCenter can be managed by the OpenStack compute nodes only if a management vSphere cluster is created outside the OpenStack cluster.

 One common use case for Host Aggregates is when you want to support scheduling instances to a subset of compute hosts because they have a specific capability.

Our previous example can be thought of as the following if we seek a heterogeneous hypervisor deployment in an OpenStack installation using KVM and vSphere ESXi.

It is important to guarantee that particular VMs are spun up on their specific vSphere cluster, which exposes more hardware requirements. To do this, OpenStack facilitates such requirements by means of **Host Aggregates**. They are used with nova-scheduler in order to place VMs on a subset of compute nodes based on their rank capabilities in an automated fashion.

A brief example can be conducted with the following steps:

1. Create a new host aggregate; this can be done through Horizon.
2. Select **Admin project**. Point to the **Admin** tab and open **System Panel**. Click on the **Host Aggregates** category and create new host named vSphere-Cluster_01.
3. Assign the compute nodes managing the vSphere clusters within the newly created host aggregate.
4. Create a new instance flavor and name it vSphere.extra, with particular VM resource specifications.
5. Map the new flavor to the vSphere host aggregate.

This is amazing because any user requesting an instance with the vSphere.extra flavor will be forwarded only to the compute nodes in the vSphere-Cluster_01 host aggregate.

Therefore, it will be up to vCenter to decide which ESXi server should host the virtual machine:

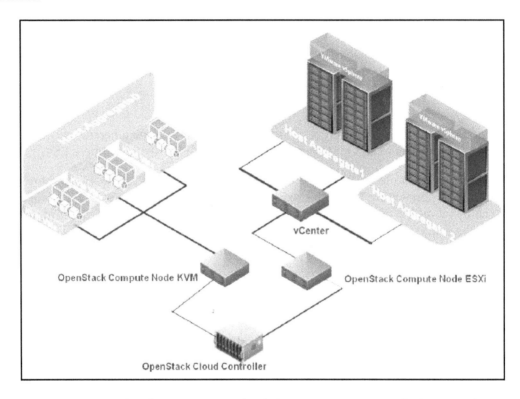

At this point, we consider that running multiple hypervisors in a single OpenStack installation is possible using Host Aggregates or using Nova cells. If you factor in hypervisors' varieties, do not get confused by the fact that an individual compute node always runs a single hypervisor.

Finally, in the previous figure, the VM instance is running on KVM that is hosted directly on a nova-compute node, whereas the vSphere with vCenter on OpenStack requires a separate vCenter server host where the VM instances will be hosted on ESXi.

Overcommitment considerations

We have already taken into consideration the need for CPU-supporting virtualization in Chapter 1, *Designing OpenStack Cloud Architectural Consideration*. What we need to understand now is the number of cores needed, which might affect the CPU power. Remember, for example, that *hyper-threading* is a highly recommended option for your CPU per compute node in order to double the number of existing cores.

It would be great if you could afford such powerful technology, which is common nowadays. On the other hand, in many cases, the physical compute nodes you purchase might be more powerful than is needed. To avoid such waste, you should keep in mind that sizing your compute nodes is important.

However, this catch-all formula that is applicable in all cases won't be easy to find. You will need to work through three main steps:

1. Estimate a sample calculation for the CPU and RAM size.
2. Use OpenStack resources' overcommitment without overlooking.
3. As much as possible, gather resources' usage statistics periodically.

In Chapter 1, *Designing OpenStack Cloud Architectural Consideration*, we covered how to estimate such resources. The next step is to extend your assumption by introducing the power of over commitment in OpenStack.

The art of memory or CPU overcommitment is a hypervisor feature, allowing the usage of more resource power by the virtual machine than the compute host has.

For example, it allows a host server with 4 GB of physical memory to run eight virtual machines, each with 1 GB of memory space allocated.

Well, there is no secrecy in this case! You should think about the hypervisor; just calculate the portion of physical memory not used per virtual machine and assign it to one that may need more RAM at certain moments. This is a technique based on the dynamic relocation of unused resources that are being held in an idle state. On the other hand, it might be a nice feature but must be used without exaggeration!

It might be dangerous if resources are exhausted and can lead to a server crash. Therefore, we need to dive into overcommitment use cases.

In OpenStack, you will be able to overcommit CPU and RAM resources by changing the default limit by their local configuration. Compute nodes use the *ratio* to determine how many VMs you can run per hardware thread or core and how much memory can be associated with the instance. By default, OpenStack uses 16:1 for CPU allocation and 1.5:1 for RAM allocation ratios.

Before setting any ratio value per compute node, it is recommended to collect a few measurement results for a specific hardware vendor. The `spec.org` website publishes performance benchmark results, and is available at `http://spec.org/benchmarks.html#virtual`.

The CPU allocation ratio

The default 16:1 CPU allocation ratio means that you can run a maximum of 16 virtual CPU cores for every physical CPU core within all running virtual machines. If you choose a physical node that has 24 cores, scheduling CPU resources will consider *24*16* available virtual cores. Thus, defining four virtual cores per instance, for example, will provide 96 instances on each compute node. Ensure that overcommitting the CPU only makes sense when running workloads are not extremely CPU-intensive. Otherwise, you should limit its ratio value.

Some values of the CPU ratio commitment can be misused by changing it to 1:1, and then you will not be able to overcommit CPU anymore. Therefore, you will be limited to running no more vCPUs than there are physical CPU cores in your hardware. On the other hand, one virtual machine cannot have more virtual CPUs than the existing physical CPUs, whereas it is still possible to run more virtual machines than the number of existing physical CPU cores in the compute node.

Keep in mind that planning for CPU power per compute node would require additional power of around 20% for the virtual CPU overhead, as well as the operating system itself, to keep handling processes when overloaded. Assuming that one compute node capacity is estimated to have 100 vCPUs for hosting X virtual machines, including the operating system overhead, will update the calculation by multiplying 100 vCPUs **1.2** times:
100 * (100% + 20%) = 120 vCPUs required for the compute node

Additionally, the new ratio value exposes a new way to refine resources' estimations. Let's add a new formula that might accomplish the resources cited in `Chapter 1`, *Designing OpenStack Cloud Architectural Consideration*.

The calculation formula to determine how many virtual instances can run on a compute node is as follows:

*(CPU overcommitment ratio * Number of physical cores)/Number of virtual cores per instance*

The RAM allocation ratio

The default 1.5:1 memory allocation ratio means that allocating instances to compute nodes is still possible if the total instance memory usage is less than 1.5 times the amount of physical memory available. For example, a compute node with 96 GB of memory can run a number of instances that reach the value of the sum of RAM associated with 144 GB. In this case, this refers to a total of 36 virtual machines with 4 GB of RAM each.

Use the `cpu_allocation_ratio` and `ram_allocation_ratio` directives in `/etc/nova/nova.conf` to change the default settings.

What about surprises? You have done the required resource computation for your compute nodes and already estimated how many virtual machines within specific flavors can run for each.

Flavors in OpenStack are a set of hardware templates that define the amount of RAM, disk space, and the number of cores per CPU.

Remember that we only use overcommitment when it is needed. To make it more valuable, you should keep an eye on your servers. Bear in mind that collecting resource utilization statistics is essential and will eventually conduct a better ratio update when needed. Overcommitting is the starting point for performance improvement of your compute nodes; when you think about adjusting such a value, you will need to know exactly what you need! To answer this question, you will need to actively monitor the hardware usage at certain periods. For example, you might miss a sudden huge increase in resources' utilization requirements during the first or the last days of the month for certain user machines, whereas you were satisfied by their performance in the middle part of the month.

We are talking about peak times, which can differ from one physical machine to another. Users who use virtual instances, for example, in accounting systems, cannot hold the same requirements all the time. You may face a trade-off between big resource assignments to fulfill peak times and performance issues when committing resources. Remember that it is important to have a strong understanding of what your system is virtualizing. Furthermore, the more information you gather, the better prepared and the more ready you will be to face surprises. Besides, it becomes your mission to find the best-optimized way of handling those requirements dynamically. Then, you will need to pick the right hypervisor(s).

Storing instances' alternatives

Compute nodes have been sized with the total CPU and RAM capacity, but we did not cover the disk space capacity. Basically, there are many approaches to doing this, but it might expose other trade-offs: capacity and performance.

External shared file storage

The disks of running instances are hosted externally and do not reside in compute nodes. This will have many advantages, such as the following:

- Ease of instance recovery in the case of compute - node failure
- Shared external storage for other installation purposes

On the other hand, it might present a few drawbacks, such as the following:

- Heavy I/O disk usage affecting the neighboring VM
- Performance degradation due to network latency

Internal non-shared file storage

In this case, compute nodes can satisfy each instance with enough disk space. This has two main advantages:

- Unlike the first approach, heavy I/O won't affect other instances running in different compute nodes
- Performance increase due to direct access to the disk I/O

However, some further disadvantages can be seen, such as the following:

- Inability to scale when additional storage is needed
- Difficulties in migrating instances from one compute node to another
- Failure of compute nodes automatically leading to instance loss

In all cases, we might have more concerns for reliability and scalability. Thus, adopting the external shared file storage would be more convenient for our OpenStack deployment. Although there are some caveats to the external instances' disk storage that must be considered, performance can be improved by reducing network latency.

Understanding instance booting

Launching an instance on your OpenStack cloud requires interaction with multiple services. When a user requests a new virtual machine, behind the scenes, the user request must be authenticated, a compute node with adequate resources to host the virtual machine must be selected, requests must be made to the image store to get the correct image for the virtual machine, and all the resources required to launch the virtual machine must be allocated. These resources include network connectivity and storage volume allocation.

Understanding the Nova scheduling process

Nova scheduling is one of the critical steps in the process of launching the virtual machine. It involves the process of selecting the best candidate compute node to host a virtual machine. The default scheduler used for placing the virtual machine is the filter scheduler that uses a scheme of filtering and weighting to find the right compute node for the virtual machine. The scheduling process consists of going through the following steps:

1. The virtual machine flavor itself describes the kind of resources that must be provided by the hosting compute node.
2. All the candidates must pass through a filtering process to make sure they provide adequate physical resources to host the new virtual machine. Any compute node not meeting the resource requirements is filtered out.
3. Once the compute nodes pass the filtering process, they go through a process of weighting that ranks the compute nodes according to the resource availability.

The filter scheduler uses a pluggable list of filters and weights to calculate the best compute node to host an instance. Changing the list of filters or weights can change the scheduler behavior. Setting the value of `scheduler_default_filters` can do this.

Booting from image

Let's discuss the booting of a virtual machine instance in more detail. To launch a virtual machine, the user must select the image that will be loaded on the virtual machine and the hardware characteristics of the instance, such as the memory, processor, and disk space. The hardware requirements can be selected by choosing the correct machine flavor. Flavors provide the hardware definition of a virtual machine. New flavors can be added to provide custom hardware definitions.

To boot the virtual machine, the compute node must download the image that needs to be loaded on the instance. It should be noted that the same image could be used to launch multiple virtual machines. The image is always copied to the hypervisor. Any changes made to the image are local to the virtual machine and are lost once the instance is terminated. The compute nodes cache images that are frequently used.

The virtual machine image forms the first hard drive of the instance. Additional hard drives can be added to the instances by using the block storage service.

Getting the instance metadata

As virtual machines are launched on the OpenStack environment, it must be provided with initialization data that will be used to configure the instance. This early initialization data configures the instance with information such as hostname, local language, user SSH keys, and so on. It can be used to write out files such as repository configuration or set up automation tools such as Puppet, Chef, or keys for Ansible-based deployment. This initialization data can be metadata associated with the instance or user-provided configuration options.

The cloud images are packaged with an instance initialization daemon called **cloud-init**. The cloud-init daemon looks at various data sources to get configuration data associated with a virtual machine. The most commonly used data sources are the EC2 and Config Drive.

The EC2 source is the most widely used data source. It provides metadata service over an HTTP server running at a special IP address of **169.256.169.254**. To retrieve the metadata, the instances must already have networking configured and be able to reach the metadata web server. The metadata and user data can be retrieved on the virtual machine by sending a GET request to the metadata IP address using the `curl` or `wget` command line as follows:

```
# curl http://169.254.169.254/latest/meta-data/
reservation-id
public-keys/
security-groups
public-ipv4
ami-manifest-path
instance-type
instance-id
local-ipv4
local-hostname
placement/
ami-launch-index
public-hostname
hostname
ami-id
instance-action
```

The previous list exposes possible instance information hierarchically organized and can be requested by sending a GET request to the metadata endpoint. For example, downloading the SSH public key injected in the instance during the boot sequence can be performed as follows:

```
# curl http://169.254.169.254/latest/meta-data/public-keys/0/openssh-key -O
% Total % Received % Xferd Average Speed Time Time Time Current
Dload Upload Total Spent Left Speed
100 228 100 228 0 0 1434 0 --:--:-- --:--:-- --:--:-- 1447
```

> The metadata itself is provided in various formats. In the preceding example, we used the latest format of metadata. You can query the metadata format by using the following **GET** query: GET `http://169.254.169.254/`.

On the other hand, `user-data` is customized user information that can be injected to an instance during boot time. Typically, `user-data` can take the form of the script shell or userdata file containing, for example, a set of environment variables. This is assuming that a user requires the sourcing of custom environment variables on boot and will not require additional manual steps when accessing the instance once launched. A file named `custom_userdata_var` can be created and injected when creating the instance using the Nova command line:

```
# nova boot --user-data /root/custom_userdata_var --image some_image
cool_instance
```

Once the instance is launched successfully, retrieving the user data can be performed by querying the metadata service endpoint through the OpenStack metadata API:

```
# curl http://169.254.169.254/openstack/2012-08-10/user-data
export VAR1=var1
export VAR2=var2
export VAR3=var3
```

The original Config Drive implementation was not considered as a complete data source but rather as a source of network configuration. Once the network setup is configured, the initialization proceeded to contact the metadata HTTPs server. The later version of cloud-init allows using Config Drives as a complete data source.

Add a compute node

Using **OpenStack Ansible** (**OSA**), adding a compute node is much simpler than understanding the resource requirements needed for a node. Basically, the compute node will run nova-compute together with the networking plugin agent. What you should understand at this stage of automated deployment is how to make the new compute node communicate with the controller and network nodes:

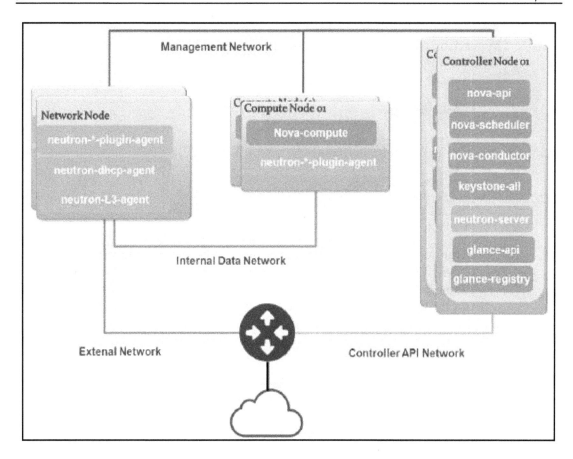

As performed in the previous chapter, `Chapter 3`, *OpenStack Cluster - The Cloud Controller and Common Services*, deploying compute nodes using Ansible can be achieved by revisiting the same Ansible configuration files as follows:

1. Adjust the `/etc/openstack_deploy/openstack_user_config.yml` file by adding a new `compute_hosts` stanza pointing to the new compute node:

```
compute_hosts:
cn-01:
ip: 172.47.0.20
```

2. Additional settings can be added to our compute node, including the type of hypervisor, CPU, RAM allocation ratio, and the maximum number of instances that can be spawned per host. This can be defined in the `/etc/openstack_deploy/user_variables.yml` file:

```
## Nova options
# Hypervisor type for Nova
nova_virt_type: kvm
# CPU overcommitment ratio
nova_cpu_allocation_ratio: 2.0
# RAM overcommitment ratio
nova_ram_allocation_ratio: 1.5
# Maximum number of virtual machines per compute node
nova_max_instances_per_host: 100
```

3. Install the containers in the target compute node by running the `setup-hosts.yml` Playbook under `/etc/openstack_deploy/`. If an OpenStack environment is fully running, we can instruct Ansible to limit the deployment only for the new host using the `--limit` option followed by the new hostname in the Ansible wrapper command line as follows:

```
# openstack-ansible setup-hosts.yml --limit cn-01
```

4. Optionally, it is possible to monitor the new compute node using the telemetry service by including a new `metering-compute_hosts` stanza in the `/etc/openstack_deploy/conf.d/ceilometer.yml` file:

```
...
metering-compute_hosts:
cn-01:
ip: 172.47.0.20
...
```

5. For a more refined update of the OpenStack infrastructure, we can instruct Ansible to deploy the new service only in the `compute_hosts` group added previously in the `openstack_user_config.yml` file :

```
# openstack-ansible setup-openstack.yml --limit compute_hosts
--skip-tags nova-key-distribute
# openstack-ansible setup-openstack.yml --limit compute_hosts
--tags nova-key
```

The new compute node should join the OpenStack environment and be ready to host instances. This can be verified in different ways by accessing the compute container. To identify the newly deployed host, use the **ssh** command line to access the compute node by filtering the utility container in the deployment machine. All deployed hosts should be listed in the /etc/hosts file.

Planning for service recovery

One of the most critical tasks for a system administrator or cloud operator is to plan a backup. Building an infrastructure and starting in production without a disaster recovery background is considered highly risky and you will need to start taking immediate action. We may find a bunch of property software in the cloud computing area that does the job, such as the VMware backup solution.

However, backing up open source clouds will not be that easy. OpenStack does not, for instance, support any special tool for backup. As it is merely a collection of components combined to deliver services, an OpenStack operator should think how to map the components used in its infrastructure and prepare a backup strategy for each; the strategy should be easy, efficient, and auto-recovery enabled.

Thus, you should not miss the first question: what do we need to back up and how do we perform such a mission?

At first glance, you might be tempted to think that backing up the cloud controller will be centered on configuration files and databases.

Backup with backup-manager

Considering that there are many backup methods, you may wonder how to choose the right tool for your system.

One of these methods involves using the backup-manager tool, a simple command-line backup that is available for most Linux distributions. You can install it on your nodes and configure it easily from one central file. If you are using CentOS 7, you will need to enable your EPEL repository:

```
$ sudo rpm -Uvh
https://dl.fedoraproject.org/pub/epel/epel-release-latest-7.noarch.rpm
```

Import the GPG key, as follows:

```
$ sudo rpm --import http://dl.fedoraproject.org/pub/epel/RPM-GPG-KEY-EPEL-7
```

Install the backup-manager package:

```
$ sudo yum install backup-manager
```

On an Ubuntu server, use apt to install backup-manager and make sure to update the package repository.

The main configuration file for backup-manager is `/etc/backup-manager.conf`. You can edit the file by defining each section by the backup methods and their associated variables. We can start by listing the directories and files that we want to back up:

```
$ export BM_TARBALL_DIRECTORIES="/var/lib/nova /etc/keystone /etc/cinder
/etc/glance /var/lib/glance /var/lib/glance/images /etc/mysql"
```

Note that we have excluded the `/var/lib/nova/instances` file from the backup folder list, as it contains running KVM instances. It might result in corrupted bootable images once you have restored them from the backup. For safety reasons, it is possible to save the image states first by means of snapshots, and backing up the generated image files in the next step.

Then, we specify the backup methods, such as `mysql`, using `mysqldump` and tarball to define the list of directories of corresponding tarballs:

```
$ export BM_ARCHIVE_METHOD="tarball mysql"
```

The next line will point to where you can store the backups:

```
$ export BM_REPOSITORY_ROOT="/var/backups/"
```

You may consider a redundancy plan by uploading the archived backup to a secondary server using `rsync`. You can use your Swift cluster to provide more data redundancy across the SWIFT rings.

Backing up your nodes' configuration files locally needs continuous monitoring, especially for disk space consumption. Try to keep an eye on your monitoring system to prevent a full disk space state in your nodes.

Next, we will explain how files will be compressed using `gzip`. For example:

```
$ export BM_MYSQL_FILETYPE="gzip"
```

Optionally, you can define the SSH account to upload your archives remotely:

```
$ export BM_UPLOAD_SSH_USER="root"
```

Next, we move to backing up our SQL databases. You can use the traditional method using `mysqldump`. We can continue with backup-manager and add the following sections to `/etc/backup-manager.conf`:

```
$ export BM_MYSQL_DATABASES="nova glance keystone dash mysql cinder"
$ export BM_MYSQL_ADMINPASS="Provide the root password in /root/.my.cnf"
```

The downside of this approach is the plaintext presentation of the password of the databases. Thus, if you intend to secure the database, ensure that the permissions are restricted for `/etc/backup-manager.conf`, including the root user.

What about compute nodes? In fact, it employs the same folder, `/var/lib/nova/`, and excludes the subdirectory instances where the live KVM resides. Backing up the instances themselves is also possible, by either creating a snapshot from Horizon or by installing a backup tool in the instance itself.

Simple recovery steps

For a safe and successful recovery process, you can follow the next set of simple steps:

1. Stop all the services that you intend to recover. For example, for a full Glance recovery in the cloud controller, run these commands:

```
$ stop glance-api
$ stop glance-registry
```

2. Import the Glance backed-up database:

```
$ mysql glance < glance.sql
```

3. Restore the Glance directories:

```
$ cp -a /var/backups/glance /glance/
```

4. Start all Glance services:

```
$ service start mysql
$ glance-api start
$ glance-registry start
```

Data protection as a service

Some third-party solutions have been used to support tenants to easily back up entire clusters in OpenStack by means of external storage such as NetApp SolidFire. Other implementations consider using object storage as a backup location for files and archives. That will require regular snapshots of the instances, which will be uploaded to the image store, whereas block storage volumes can be snapshoted and uploaded to the object storage. This sort of backup implementation does not provide a seamless and efficient backup solution, considering not only the absence of performing incremental backup but also the complexity of managing different storage backup workloads.

The OpenStack community

It has started recently to include a data protection service to handle backup tasks destined to the OpenStack environment. Behind all this, a proposed project named **Raksha** aims to provide a non-disruptive, flexible, and application-aware backup solution destined to OpenStack. This solution includes the possibilities to perform full and incremental backup of instances to an object storage endpoint. It uses the native snapshot mechanisms from OpenStack and leverages a task scheduler for periodic and regular backups. Users will have more flexibility to manage their own backups and instances running their applications, regardless of the type of the hypervisor. At the time of writing, Raksha is a standalone project and not yet integrated officially in the OpenStack ecosystem. To read more about Raksha, refer to the development wiki page at `https://wiki.openstack.org/wiki/Raksha`. Another new incubated project in OpenStack for backup and disaster recovery services is a project code named Freezer. To follow the development of the Freezer project, refer to the official wiki page at `https://wiki.openstack.org/wiki/Freezer`.

Summary

In this chapter, we have learned about the various scaling and segregation techniques for building a scalable and responsive compute cluster. We understood the instance scheduling, bootup, and initial configuration process.

We discussed containers and container orchestration systems, and the various concepts of the Magnum project. That should give you a clear idea about the variety of hypervisor technologies supported recently by OpenStack.

We also looked at the requirements from a hardware perspective by refining the decision related to hypervisor selection and how to conduct the best storage outfit for your compute nodes. The chapter detailed how to deploy a new compute node in an existing OpenStack cluster using Ansible that should be a complement to the initiated Ansible setup discussed in Chapter 3, *OpenStack Cluster - The Cloud Controller and Common Services*.

Another important topic was highlighted, which investigates how to back up your OpenStack environment. This is not something to ignore; as your OpenStack installation grows, the size of disk usage per node may increase dramatically and can bring it down quite easily. In this case, we have to look at the storage approaches existing in OpenStack and how to harness them to be useful for different purposes, which will be covered in the next chapter.

5
OpenStack Storage - Block, Object, and File Share

"As is our confidence, so is our capacity."
- William Hazlitt

A large cloud deployment requires a reliable, scalable, and robust storage solution. The next generation of data centers aims to leverage the power of cloud storage. The storage infrastructure in the data center has been simplified by the means of software-defined storage. With OpenStack, managing storage through the software stack in the data center becomes easier. Additionally, OpenStack provides several storage types that need more understanding in order to make the right choice with regard to which storage solution will suffice for our workload requirements.

The mission of this chapter is to make the readers self-confident about the design of their storage in the OpenStack environment. In this chapter, we will learn how to use **Swift**, **Cinder**, and **Manila**. Additionally, we will introduce **Ceph**, a cloud storage solution that seamlessly integrates with OpenStack.

In this chapter, we will go through the following topics:

- Understanding the different storage types in OpenStack
- A few best practices under the umbrella of storage systems
- Understanding the Swift architecture and explaining how to do it
- Bringing Cinder under the microscope and demonstrating its use case
- Discuss about Manila, a file share based storage project
- Getting to know Ceph and ways to integrate it within OpenStack

Understanding the storage types

Which storage technology will fit into your OpenStack cloud implementation? To answer this question, it is necessary to differentiate between different storage types. The fact that OpenStack clouds can work in tandem with many other open source storage solutions might be an advantage, but it can be overwhelming at the same time.

Thus, you are faced with the question, what storage solution do you need - persistent or ephemeral storage?

Ephemeral storage

For the sake of simplicity, we will start with non-persistent storage, also known as ephemeral storage. As its name suggests, a user who actively uses a virtual machine in the OpenStack environment will lose the associated disks once the VM is terminated. When a tenant boots a virtual machine on an OpenStack cluster, a copy of the glance image is downloaded on the compute node. This image is used as the first disk for the Nova instance, which provides the ephemeral storage. Anything stored on this disk will be lost once the Nova instance is terminated.

 Ephemeral disks can be created and attached either locally on the storage of the hypervisor host or hosted on external storage by the means of NFS mount. Using the last option, it is possible to migrate virtual machines between multiple compute nodes since the instance root disk sits on a shared storage accessible by more than one hypervisor host.

Persistent storage

Persistent storage means that the storage resource is always available. Powering off the virtual machine does not affect the data on a persistent storage disk. We can divide persistent storage in OpenStack into three options: object storage, file share storage, and block storage with the code names Swift, Manila, and Cinder, respectively. We did talk about Swift, Manila and Cinder in `Chapter 1`, *Designing OpenStack Cloud Architectural Consideration*, in a nutshell.

Let's dive into each of the storage options for OpenStack and see how the different storage concepts are used by OpenStack for different purposes.

Object storage is not NAS/SAN

Object storage allows a user to store data in the form of objects by using the RESTful HTTP APIs. If you compare an object storage system to traditional NAS or SAN storage, it might be claimed that object storage can scale infinitely and can better handle node failure without data loss. Let's take a closer look at how object storage differs from a traditional NAS/SAN based storage:

- The data are stored as **binary large objects** (**blobs**) with multiple replicas on the object storage servers.
- The objects are stored in a flat namespace. Unlike a traditional storage system, they do not preserve any specific structure or a particular hierarchy.
- Accessing the object storage is done using an API such as REST or SOAP. Object storage cannot be directly accessed via file protocol such as BFS, SMB, or CIFS.
- Object storages are not suitable for high-performance requirements or structured data that is frequently changed, such as databases.

A spotlight on Swift

Swift was one of the first two OpenStack projects. It was a joint effort of NASA and Rackspace's contribution to the OpenStack project. The development of object based storage systems are fueled by a few major changes to the ways in which storage systems are used.

Firstly, the emergence of web and mobile applications fundamentally changed data consumption. Secondly, a major change was introduced with the concept of **software-defined storage** (**SDS**), which decoupled storage solutions from underlying hardware and enables a large distributed storage system to be built using commodity storage.

The object storage service named Swift is analogous to the **service storage service** (**S3**) provided by Amazon web services.

By adopting Swift as a cloud storage solution, you can enjoy several benefits, some of which are as follows:

- **Scalability**: Swift is designed as a distributed architecture that provides performance and scalability
- **On-demand**: Swift offers provisioning storage on demand with a entralized management endpoint
- **Elasticity**: The dynamic ways to increase or decrease storage resources as needed

The Swift architecture

By relying on Swift for management of data instead of specialized vendor hardware, you gain incredible flexibility and features related to scaling your storage system. This is what SDS is all about. Swift is fundamentally a new type of storage system that scales out and tolerates failures without compromising the data availability. Swift does not attempt to be like other storage systems; it doesn't mimic their interfaces. Instead, it changes how the storage works.

The Swift architecture is very distributed, which prevents any **single point of failure** (**SPOF**). It is also designed to scale horizontally.

The components of Swift consist of the following:

- **The Swift proxy server**: This accepts the incoming requests via either the OpenStack object API, or just the raw HTTP. It accepts requests for file uploads, modifications to metadata, or container creation and so on.
- **The proxy server**: This may optionally rely on caching, which is usually deployed with memcached to improve performance.
- **The account server**: This manages the account that is defined with the object storage service. Its main purpose is to maintain a list of containers associated with the account. A Swift account is equivalent to a tenant on OpenStack.
- **The container server**: A container refers to the user-defined storage area within a Swift account. It maintains a list of objects stored in the container. A container can be conceptually similar to a folder in a traditional filesystem.
- **The object server**: It manages an actual object within a container. The object storage defines where the actual data and its metadata are stored. Note that every object must belong to a container.

 Metadata provides descriptive information about the object. It is stored as key-value pairs. For example, a database backup can contain information about the backup time and backup tool. Swift uses **extended attributes** (**xattr**) of the underlying filesystem to store metadata.

Also, there are more processes that perform the housekeeping task on the large data stores. The most important of these are the replication services, which ensure consistency and availability through the cluster. Other post-processing processes include auditors, updaters, and reapers.

Auditors, updaters, replicators, and reapers are background daemons that are run by Swift. Note that these processes can be high resource consumers, which can be noticed by the increase in the disk I/O traffic. It is recommended to adjust a few settings in every object and container configuration file. For example, it is possible to limit the number of background processes running simultaneously on each node by adding a concurrency value in each background daemon. To see more about the Swift object, container, and server configurations, check out link: `http://d ocs.openstack.org/mitaka/config-reference/object-storage.html`.

Indexing the data

Searching, retrieving, and indexing the data in an **object storage device (OSD)** is done via the extensive usage of metadata. Although a typical NAS storage uses the metadata, you should consider the fact that the metadata in OSD are stored with the object itself in key-value pairs. What makes it simpler is that the OSD keeps tagging the object even if it is sliced or chunked with its metadata for storage efficiency reasons.

A rich API access

The Swift proxy process is the only one that can communicate outside a storage cluster, and what it does is listen and speak to a specific REST API.

Thanks to the Swift proxy, we will be able to access the OSDs. On the other hand, Swift provides language-specific libraries for PHP, Java, Python, and so on for ease of integration with applications. The libraries use HTTP calls to speak to the Swift proxy.

An object request always requires an authentication token. Therefore, an authentication can be configured through the WSGI middleware, which is typically keystone.

A complete reference to the object storage APIs can be found at `http://de veloper.openstack.org/api-ref-objectstorage-v1.html`.

Swift gateways

Although the object store does not provide interfaces for traditional access to data such as CIFS or NFS, this can be achieved using an additional layer to interact with the storage interfaces called Swift filesystem gateways. This enables the integration of Swift with traditional applications.

Physical design considerations

The hallmark of Swift usage is that it needs to look after the data durability and availability. By default, a Swift cluster storage design considers a replica of three.

Therefore, once the data is written, it is spread across two other redundant replicas, which increases the availability of the data. On the other hand, this means you will need more storage capacity. In addition, referring to the first logical design in `Chapter 1`, *Designing OpenStack Cloud Architectural Consideration*, we have selected a dedicated network for storage.

This was on purpose, firstly for logical network design organization and secondly, to mitigate the load on the network by dedicating a separate storage handler. Imagine a situation where one of the storage nodes with 50 TB fails when you need to transfer this huge blob of data remotely to accomplish the required three-replica design. It can take a few hours, but we need it immediately! Thus, we should consider the bandwidth usage between the storage servers and proxies. This is a good reason to put the spotlight on the physical design and the way of data are organized in Swift.

In the first stage, we saw that the accounts, containers, and objects form the term data in Swift, which will need physical storage. In this stage, the storage node will be constructed first. Remember that Swift aims to isolate failures, which makes the cluster wider in terms of grouping according to the nodes. Thus, Swift defines a new hierarchy that helps abstract the logical organization of data from the physical one:

- **Region**: Being in a geographically distributed environment, data can be held in multiple nodes that are placed in different regions. This is the case with a **multi-region cluster** (**MRC**). A user can suffer due to higher latency that comes with the different servers being placed away from each other in each region. To do so, Swift supports a performance read/write function called read/write affinity. Based on the latency measurements between the connections, Swift will favor the data that is closer to read. On the other hand, it will try to write data locally and transfer the data to the rest of the regions asynchronously.
- **Zone**: Regions encapsulate zones, which define the availability level that Swift aims to provide. A grouping or a set of hardware items, such as a rack or storage node, can refer to a zone. You can guess the rest-zoning to isolate hardware failure from the other neighbors.

 It is recommended to use as many zones as your data replica and start with at least one zone in a cluster.

- **Storage nodes**: The logical organization continues the storage abstraction from the region, which is the highest level and zones within the region, until we find the storage servers, which define the zone. A set of storage nodes forms a cluster that runs the Swift processes and stores an account, a container, the object data, and its associated metadata.
- **Storage device**: This is the smallest unit of the Swift data stack. The storage device can be the internal storage node's device or connected via an external stack of a collection of disks in a drive enclosure.

> The drives that are used in Swift can be set in a **just a bunch of disks** (**JBOD**) regardless of the configuration and can be accessed from the host computer as a separate drive, unlike RAID, which treats a collection of drives as a single storage unit.

The following figure shows the hierarchy in Swift:

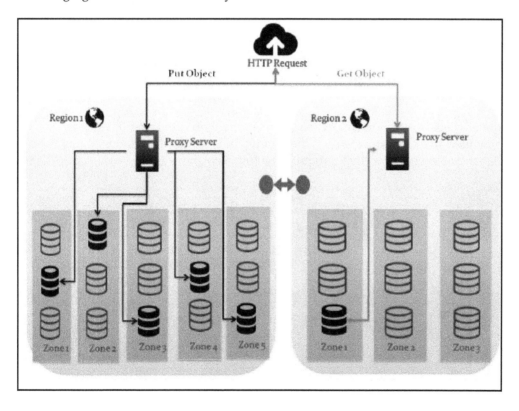

The Swift ring

Swift rings define the way Swift handles data in the cluster. Untill now, we have discussed the various constructs in Swift such as regions, zones, nodes, and devices, but how does Swift actually store data on the disk? How can replicas be maintained and stored? Understanding the concept of rings in Swift will help to answer the previous questions.

In Swift the logical layout of object data is mapped to a path based on the account, container and object hierarchy. In the context of OpenStack, the account maps to the tenant. Each tenant can have multiple containers, which are like folders in the filesystem, and finally the object belongs to a container just like a file belongs to a folder in convention filesystem based storage.

The Swift, ring maps the logical layout of data from account, container, and object to a physical location on the cluster. Swift maintains one ring per storage construct, that is there are separate rings maintained for account, container, and object. The Swift proxy finds the appropriate ring to determine the location of the storage construct, for example, to determine the location of a container, the Swift proxy locates the container ring.

The rings are built by using an external tool called the **swift-ring-builder**. The ring builder tool performs the inventory of Swift storage cluster and divides them into slots called partitions.

A frequently asked question is how many partitions should the ring have? It is recommended that each storage drive be divided into 100 partitions. For example, using 50 disks for the object storage cluster requires having 5000 partitions:

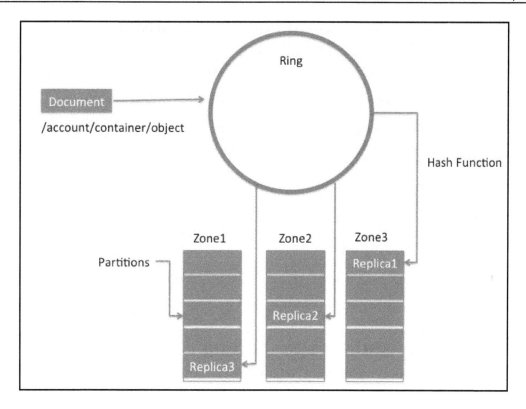

The following is the generic format of the ring builder command:

```
#swift-ring-builder <builder_file> create <part_power> <replicas>
<min_part_hours>
```

The `<builder_file>` can be one of `account.builder`, `container.builder`, or `object.builder`. The number of partitions is approximated to the closest power of 2 to get the part power of the cluster. If we have, for example, 50 disks with 100 partitions, we approximate the part power to be 13, which gives a value of 8192. It is recommended that the approximation be rounded to the higher side.

It is recommended to have 3 replicas of each partition in the cluster. The `<min_part_hours>` determines the time in an hour during which only one replica of a partition can be moved. the following is an example of the account file command line build:

```
#swift-ring-builder account.builder create 13 3 1
```

Once the ring is built, the devices must be added to the ring and initiate a rebalance using the following Swift command line tools:

```
# swift-ring-builder <builder_file> add z<zone>-
<ip>:<port>/<device_name>_<meta> <weight>
# swift-ring-builder <builder_file> rebalance
```

The data stored in Swift is mapped into these partitions. The full path of the data itself determines the partition to which the data belongs. This is done by determining the MD5 hash of the object path as follows:

```
md5("/account/container/object")
```

Only a certain part of this hash is used as an index to place the object into a partition. Swift maintains replicas of partitions and disperses them in to different zones.

At a high level, the Swift object, stores functions like a giant hash data structure where all the available space is divided into slots. Then a hash function is used to map the data to be stored into these slots.

Storage policy and erasure coding

The traditional way of providing high availability of data in Swift is to maintain multiple copies of it and disperse them on different regions, zones, nodes, and disks. This strategy works well from a redundancy perspective but the storage cost associated with this approach is quite high. With a default replication level of three copies for each object stored, the amount of available storage is reduced to a third of the actual available capacity.

Depending of the criticality of the data, you may be willing to invest in maintaining data in triplicate for redundancy. This presents a challenge to afford an expensive Swift object storage system to fulfill data availability and performance requirements. The Swift storage policy is targeted towards solving the cost of providing redundancy by using differential data replication strategy.

Which sort of policies can be defined in Swift apart replication? This is where the erasure coding comes into play to set a redundancy policy. Erasure coding uses parity to recreate lost data. When the user uploads a document to the object storage configured with erasure coding, the Swift proxy breaks the uploaded data into segments. It then calls `PyECLib` to encode the data into erasure-coded fragments. The fragments are then streamed to the storage nodes.

Erasure coding presents a novel concept targeting storage systems to tackle the tradeoff of performance and cost by leveraging coding theories. Several erasure coding theories have been implemented using different approaches for different storage variations. Since Kilo release, erasure coding has been added to the Swift project. To support encoding and decoding objects with erasure codes, Swift uses `PyECLib`, a backend library which provides a Python interface to several erasure coding libraries such as `liberasurecode`. `PyECLib` also exposes an extensibility feature by implementing custom erasure codes and integrating them as plugins. To read more about the integration of `PyECLib` in Swift, refer to the developer OpenStack website at `https://docs.openstack.org/devel oper/swift/overview_erasure_code.html#pyeclib-external-erasure -code-library`.

To retrieve the data, the proxy server simultaneously requests the participating storage nodes to get the encoded fragments of data, which are decoded to reconstruct the object and send them back to the client. The actual library used to generate the erasure coding is configurable as a plugin to `PyECLib`. Erasure coding mechanism has an overhead of around 40% of data size, which is much smaller than a replication based scheme.

This approach can be compared to the RAID levels with the default Swift policy of replication analogous to RAID level 1 also known as mirroring, where the data are replicated across the drives in the array. Then erasure coding is similar to RAID level 5 where data is broken down into strips and parity strips are generated to recover from drive failure.

Swift now allows creation of containers with different storage policies. The complete documentation about storage policies and how to enable them on the Swift cluster is available on the official OpenStack Swift developer website at `http://docs.openstack.org /developer/swift/overview_policies.html`.

Swift hardware

Basically, we want to know how many proxy and storage nodes (containers, accounts, and objects) we will need. Note that we can logically group containers, accounts and/or objects in a node to form a storage tier. Note that the racks formed by a set of storage tiers that are logically sharing a physical point of failure, such as a connection to a standalone switch, will be grouped into the same zone. The following is an example of the deployment that we intend to have:

- For 50 TB of object storage
- Cluster replica of 3
- The Swift filesystem is XFS
- A hard drive of 2.5 TB
- 30 hard drive slots per chassis

With a few basic calculations, we can conclude how many storage nodes we will need. Assuming a cluster of 3 replicas, the total storage capacity can be calculated in the following way:

```
50 * 3 replicas = 150 TB
```

 It is important to bring into the calculation the factor of the XFS filesystem metadata overhead with a value of `1.0526` for filesystem size over 50 TB. A great post for filesystem overhead comparison can be found at `https://rwmj.wordpress.com/2009/11/08/filesystem-metadata-overhead/`.

Considering the factor of metadata overhead, the total raw storage capacity can be calculated by rounding to the nearest decimal number as follows:

```
150 * 1.0526 = 158 TB
```

Now, we need to determine the number of hard drives that are required, as follows:

```
[158 / 2.5]  => 64 drives
```

Finally, the total number of storage nodes will be calculated in the following way:

```
64/30 = 2.1333 -> 3 nodes
```

Where to place what

The proxy server in the Swift cluster will forward the client's request and send back the responses across the storage nodes, which might increase the CPU utilization.

Storage nodes will perform intensive disk I/O operations, while providing more CPUs is highly recommended with regards to the Swift process handler for the replication and auditing of data.

Thus, with more drives per node, more CPUs are needed. Assuming the using a CPU of 2 GHz processors with a ratio of cores GHz to drives of 3:4, we can calculate the number of cores that we will need, as follows:

```
(30 drives * 3/4)/2 GHz = 11.25 cores
```

The CPU cores can be obtained by using the following formula: *(Total_Number_Drives * (core:drive ration)) / GHz_Cores*

Swift recommends the use of the XFS filesystem, where it caches its nodes into the RAM. More RAM implies more caching, and therefore, faster object access. On the other hand, it might cache all nodes into the RAM, because of the necessity of keeping the network without bottlenecks. We will start with 2 GB RAM per server.

Finally, we need to find a cost/performance fit for the storage nodes. The account and container servers can be deployed with the use of SSDs, which will boost the speed during the localization of the data. On the other hand, utilizing the 6 TB SATA/ATA disks, for example, can satisfy the object storage servers. Note that if the object storage server is complaining of a low IOPS, you should add more disks till you get an acceptable value of IOPS.

The Swift network

Our first network design assumes that an additional network is dedicated for the storage system. In fact, we should remind ourselves that we are talking about a large infrastructure. More precisely, Swift is becoming a big house with small rooms in our OpenStack deployment.

For this reason, we will extend the Swift network as follows:

- **The front-cluster network**: Proxy servers handle communication with the external clients over this network. Besides, it forwards the traffic for the external API access of the cluster.
- **The storage cluster network**: It allows communication between the storage nodes and proxies as well as inter-node communication across several racks in the same region.
- **The replication network**: We do care about the development of our infrastructure size, right? Therefore, we will plan for the same for the multi-region clusters, where we dedicate a network segment for replication-related communication between the storage nodes.

The Swift network is shown in the following figure:

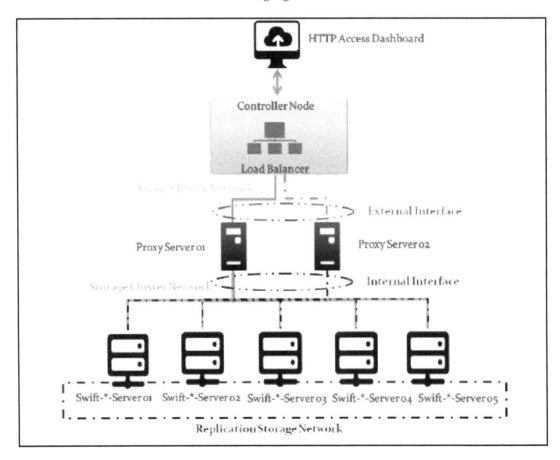

Deploying Swift service

We will use OpenStack Ansible to deploy Swift service. The following files control the process of deploying Swift with Ansible: `/etc/openstack_deploy/conf.d/swift.yml`

and `/etc/openstack_deploy/user_variables.yml` files.

The OpenStack Ansible project recommends at least three storage nodes with five disk drives. The first step is to add a filesystem to the drives. We will use `xfs` as our filesystem as recommended by Swift project as it supports caching and extended attributes used for storing metadata associated with the objects. Replace `x` with the appropriate drive letter:

```
# apt-get install xfsprogs
# mkfs.xfs -f -i size=1024 -L sdX /dev/sdX
```

The filesystem must be created for all five attached drives. Next make an entry in `/etc/fstab` to mount the drives on boot:

```
LABEL=sdX /srv/node/sdX xfs
noatime,nodiratime,nobarrier,logbufs=8,noauto 0 0
```

Make sure that you don't forget to create the directory for the mount point:

```
# mkdir -p /srv/node/sdX
```

Finally mount the drives with `mount /srv/node/sdX` command. The mount points are referenced in the /etc/openstack_deploy/conf.d/swift.yml file.

The /etc/openstack_deploy/conf.d/swift.yml provides many variables to customize the Swift deployment. Some of them are the `storage_network` and `replication_network` as described earlier. The number of replicas of object that Swift must maintain. The drives list references the disks we prepared for data storage in the previous steps. You can also configure the storage policy and policy type, which could be either replication or `erasure_coding`.

The configuration variables are provided at various levels; the cluster level values can be adjusted using the Swift level. Here is an example from the sample file:

```
swift:
  storage_network: 'br-storage'
  replication_network: 'br-repl'
  part_power: 8
  repl_number: 3
  min_part_hours: 1
  region: 1
  zone: 0
```

This section also configures the storage policies for the cluster:

```
storage_policies:
  - policy:
  name: standard
  index: 0
  default: True
  policy_type: replication
```

More specific configuration can be overridden in the `swift-proxy_hosts` and `swift_hosts` sections. Options such as read and write affinity can be set in the `swift-proxy_hosts` stanza. The `swift_hosts` stanza lists the per node Swift variable overrides like the region and zone to which the Swift node belongs to . It also gives a hand to adjust the drives which will be used and the weight of a disk.

 Default configuration settings using Ansible Swift playbook can be found at `https://github.com/openstack/openstack-ansible-os_swift/blob /master/defaults/main.yml`.

A reference configuration file is provided in the source of OpenStack Ansible.

Copy the file to `/etc/openstack_deploy/conf.d/swift.yml` and make the appropriate changes as follows:

```
# cp /etc/openstack_deploy/conf.d/swift.yml.example
/etc/openstack_deploy/conf.d/swift.yml
```

The `swift-proxy_hosts` section defines the target hosts in the OpenStack environment to deploy the Swift proxy service. For the sake of simplicity, the Swift proxy service can be delegated to the cloud controller nodes with additional options including write affinity in favor for region 1 in `cc-01`, region 2 in `cc-02`, and region 3 in `cc-03`:

```
...
swift-proxy_hosts:
  cc-01:
    ip: 172.47.0.10
    container_vars:
      swift_proxy_vars:
        write_affinity: "r1"
  cc-02:
    ip: 172.47.0.10
    container_vars:
      swift_proxy_vars:
        write_affinity: "r2"
  cc-03:
```

```
        ip: 172.47.0.10
        container_vars:
          swift_proxy_vars:
            write_affinity: "r3"
```

The following `swift_hosts` section defines three Swift nodes `swn01`, `swn02`, and `swn03`. All Swift nodes will be using `sdd`, `sde`, and `sdf` disks grouped by zone id for storage availability and failure isolation purposes. The Swift nodes will be deployed within the storage network as per defined in `Chapter 3`, *OpenStack Clustering - The Cloud Controller and Common Services*, using CIDR range: `172.47.40.0/22`:

```
...
swift_hosts:
  swn01:
    ip: 172.47.44.10
    container_vars:
      swift_vars:
        zone: 0
        drives:
          - name: sdd
          - name: sde
          - name: sdf
  swn02:
    ip: 172.47.44.11
    container_vars:
      swift_vars:
        zone: 1
        drives:
          - name: sdd
          - name: sde
          - name: sdf
  swn03:
    ip: 172.47.44.12
    container_vars:
      swift_vars:
        zone: 2
        drives:
          - name: sdd
          - name: sde
          - name: sdf
```

Once the update is done, the Swift playbook can be run as follows:

```
# cd /opt/openstack-ansible/playbooks
# openstack-ansible os-swift-install.yml
```

> A complete reference to the Swift playbook and its options is available at h
> ttps://docs.openstack.org/developer/openstack-ansible/mitaka/i
> nstall-guide/configure-swift.html.

Using block storage service: Cinder

Cinder provides persistent storage management for the virtual machine's hard drives. Unlike ephemeral storage, virtual machines backed by Cinder volumes can be easily live-migrated and evacuated. In prior OpenStack releases, block storage was a part of the compute service in OpenStack **nova-volume**. Within its overwhelmed new features, block storage service has been evolved and taken a separate spot in the OpenStack ecosystem so renamed as Cinder. Under the hood, volumes expose a raw block of storage that can be attached to instances and can store data permanently. The attached volume appears as an additional hard-drive within the virtual machine. To use the attached volume within a virtual machine, it must be first partitioned and laid with a filesystem and mounted on to the filesystem hierarchy on the virtual machine.

Cinder uses iSCSI, NFS, and fiber channels to present the block device to the virtual machine. Moreover, Cinder helps you manage the quotas by limiting the tenant's usage. You can limit the quota usage by total storage utilized including snapshots, total of volumes available, or total number of snapshots taken. The following example shows the current default quota for the `packtpub_tenant` tenant by using the following command line:

```
# cinder quota-defaults packtpub_tenant
+------------+-------+
| Property   | Value |
+------------+-------+
| gigabytes  | 1000  |
| snapshots  | 50    |
| volumes    | 50    |
+------------+-------+
```

The limiting of the quotas for the `packtpub` tenant can be done in the following way:

```
# cinder quota-update --volumes 20 packtpub_tenant
# cinder quota-update --gigabytes 500 packtpub_tenant
# cinder quota-update --snapshots 20 packtpub_tenant
# cinder quota-show packtpub_tenant
+-----------+-------+
| Property  | Value |
+-----------+-------+
| gigabytes | 500   |
| snapshots | 20    |
| volumes   | 20    |
+-----------+-------+
```

The Cinder service is composed of the following components:

- Cinder API server
- Cinder scheduler
- Cinder volume server

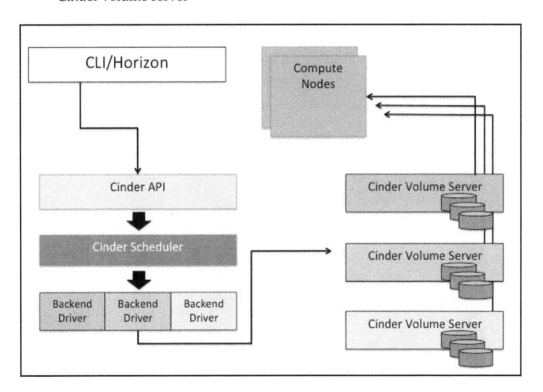

The Cinder API server interacts with the outside world using the REST interface. It receives requests for managing volumes. The Cinder volume servers are the nodes that host the volumes.

The scheduler is responsible for choosing the volume server for hosting new volume requested by the end-users.

Attaching Cinder volumes to Nova instances can be performed via command lines, but let us discover which exact storage operations could be triggered behind the scenes by going through the following steps:

1. Create a Cinder volume by specifying the volume name and its size:

    ```
    # cinder create --display_name volume1 1
    ```

    The default volume driver in Cinder is LVM over iSCSI. The volume `create` command creates a **logical volume (LV)** in the **volume group (VG)** `cinder-volumes`.

2. Next, use the `volume-attach` command to attach the Cinder volume to a Nova instance. The `volume-attach` command must be provided with the Nova instance id, the Cinder volume id, and the device name that will be presented inside the virtual machine:

    ```
    # nova volume-attach Server_ID Volume_ID Device_Name
    ```

    This command creates an **iSCSI Qualified Name (IQN)** to present the LV created in the last step to the compute node running the Nova instance.

3. The last step is to mark the volume as available to the Nova instance itself. This can be achieved by using the `libvirt` library. `Libvirt` presents the iSCSI drive as an extra block device to the virtual machine:

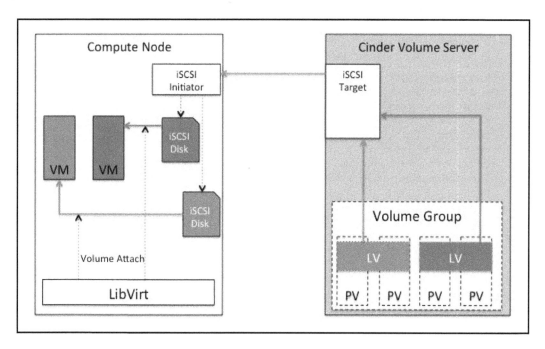

There are other use cases that are supported by Cinder, such as creating a volume from image, and booting an instance from a volume; but most of the process of volume creation and making it available to the virtual machine follows the same concept as described earlier.

Cinder backend drivers and scheduling

Like many OpenStack projects, Cinder provides a pluggable architecture by exposing different storage backend drivers. In the previous section, we discussed the process of creating a Cinder volume and attaching it to a Nova instance where we looked at the LVM-iSCSI backend driver. This is the default backend driver provided by Cinder. Additionally, Cinder can be configured with NFS, GlusterFS and various compatible storage vendors including NetApp and EMC . While we are not going to look at the configuration of various backend driver options, we will discuss about enabling multiple storage drivers and volume scheduling.

Multiple backend drivers can be enabled and used at the same time. This can be performed by enabling the `enabled_backends` flag in the `/etc/cinder/cinder.conf` configuration file. The `enabled_backends` directive should be set to the comma-separated names of the backend configuration group names as follows:

```
enabled_backends=vol-conf-grp-1, vol-conf-grp-2, vol-conf-grp-3

[vol-conf-grp-1]
volume_group=vol-grp-1
volume_driver=cinder.volume.drivers.lvm.LVMVolumeDriver
volume_backend_name=lvm-standard-bkend

[vol-conf-grp-2]
volume_group= vol-grp-2
volume_driver=cinder.volume.drivers.lvm.LVMVolumeDriver
volume_backend_name= lvm-standard-bkend

[vol-conf-grp-3]
volume_group= vol-grp-3
volume_driver=cinder.volume.drivers.lvm.LVMVolumeDriver
volume_backend_name= lvm-enhanced-bkend
```

The backend configuration groups themselves describe the backend driver. If two or more volume backends have the same names, the volume scheduler will select one of them based on capacity and weight.

The scheduler can be configured by default with the Capacity, Availability Zone and Capability Filters:

```
scheduler_default_filters=
AvailabilityZoneFilter,CapacityFilter,CapabilitiesFilter

scheduler_default_weighers= CapacityWeigher
```

By enabling the default filters and weights, the scheduler chooses the volume server with the maximum capacity within an Availability Zone matching the user requested volume size.

The Cinder scheduler can also be configured with backend driver specific filter and weight functions. This allows Cinder to place new requests on the volume server with the best backend driver match. To enable driver filters and weights add the DriverFilter and GoodnessWeigher to the scheduler_default_filters and scheduler_default_weighers list respectively. Each of the volume configuration groups should be configured with a filter and goodness function. The following example shows such a configuration:

```
[vol-conf-grp -1]
volume_group=vol-grp-1
volume_driver=cinder.volume.drivers.lvm.LVMVolumeDriver
volume_backend_name=lvm-standard-bkend
filter_function = "stats.total_capacity_gb < 500"
goodness_function = "(volume.size < 25) ? 100 : 50"
```

The Cinder scheduler refers the filter and goodness function for each backend to determine the correct backend for a volume request. Cinder also provides constructs for end user to request volumes with a specific backend driver. This is done using the Cinder volume-type definitions. The following is an example of defining volume-type and using it in volume creation:

```
# cinder type-create lvm-standard
# cinder type-key lvm-standard set volume_backend_name=lvm-standard-bkend

# cinder type-create lvm-enhanced
# cinder type-key lvm-enhanced set volume_backend_name=lvm-enhanced-bkend
```

The preceding commands create two volume-type definitions: one with the standard driver backend and another with the enhanced backend driver. To use the volume-type definition while creating a new Cinder volume, the user must enter the following command:

```
# cinder create --volume_type lvm-standard --display_name My_Std_Vol1 1
# cinder create --volume_type lvm-enhanced --display_name My_Ehn_Vol1 1
```

Deploying Cinder service

OpenStack Ansible provides playbooks to deploy Cinder services. As shown in Chapter 3, *OpenStack Cluster - The Cloud Controller and Common Services*, we will adjust the `/etc/openstack_deploy/openstack_user_config.yml` file to point to where the Cinder API service will be deployed. Based on the design model discussed in Chapter 1, *Designing OpenStack Cloud Architectural Consideration*, the Cinder API service can be deployed in the controller nodes by adding the `storage-infra_hosts` stanza as follows:

```
...
storage-infra_hosts:
  cc-01:
    ip: 172.47.0.10
  cc-02:
    ip: 172.47.0.11
  cc-03:
    ip: 172.47.0.12
```

Next, we describe the hosts that will be used for the Cinder storage nodes. The storage host can be configured with the availability zone, backend, and volume driver configuration. This can be achieved by adding the `storage_hosts` stanza with additional configuration for storage hosts with LVM and iSCSI backend as follows:

```
storage_hosts:
  lvm-storage1:
    ip: 172.47.44.5

    container_vars:
      cinder_backends:
        vol-conf-grp-1:
          volume_backend_name: lvm-standard-bkend
          volume_driver: cinder.volume.drivers.lvm.LVMVolumeDriver
          volume_group: cinder-volumes
```

 Default configuration settings using Ansible Swift playbook can be found at https://github.com/openstack/openstack-ansible-os_cinder/blo b/master/defaults/main.yml.

To run the Cinder playbook use the `openstack-ansible` command as follows:

```
# cd /opt/openstack-ansible/playbooks
```

```
# openstack-ansible os-cinder-install.yml
```

Using share storage service: Manila

The OpenStack Manila project provides file sharing as a service and has been fully integrated into the OpenStack ecosystem since Liberty release. This is yet another option for providing persistent storage to the OpenStack tenant. The most unique feature of this approach is the ability of a share to be accessed by multiple users at the same time. Taking an analogy from the physical world, the Cinder project can be compared to a SAN solution which provides a block device to the client systems, whereas the Manila project is more similar to the NAS solution which presents file share to the client system. A variety of file sharing protocol such as NFS and CIFS are supported by the Manila project. This is implemented by using multiple backend drivers for the Manila project. To understand how Manila works, we need to look at various concepts, such as the backend drivers which implement orchestration of file shares and the share network used to provide access to the file share.

Manila has a few major components, as follows:

- **The Manila API server**: This is a REST interface and is responsible for handling the client request for creating and managing new file shares
- **The Manila data service**: This is responsible for share migration and backup
- **The Manila scheduler**: This is responsible for selecting the right share server to host a newly requested files share
- **The Manila share server**: This is the one hosting the storage share requested by an OpenStack tenant

Now let's dive deeper by looking at how the shares are created and made accessible to the virtual machines. The Manila service can be configured to orchestrate just the shares on a standalone share server or deploy and manage the share servers too. The first approach is about orchestration of file shares on standalone share servers and Manila restricts its role to just managing the life cycle of the file shares.

In the second case, Manila uses Nova to launch instances, which will host the share server appliance; Cinder volumes are used to create file shares and Manila also uses Neutron to make the shares on these appliance servers accessible to the tenant virtual machines. Manila uses the network plugin to access the OpenStack network resources. Currently Nova and Neutron network plugins are supported by Manila:

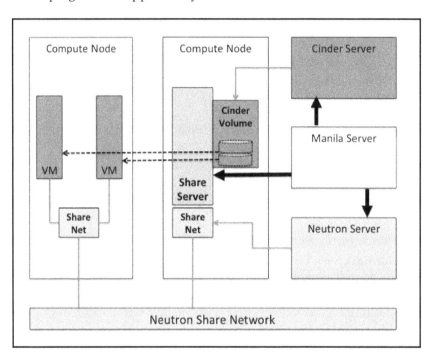

Deploying Manila and joining it to the OpenStack ecosystem can be performed as any other OpenStack service that requires the following steps in a nutshell:

1. Provide database access to the Manila service
2. Create and register the Manila user, endpoint and service registration with keystone
3. Update the Manila service configuration file at `/etc/manila/manila.conf`

 At the time of writing, no playbook has been developed for the Manila service in Ansible OpenStack project. For more information on how to deploy the Manila project, refer to the quick start guide available at `http ://docs.openstack.org/developer/manila/adminref/quick_start.ht ml`.

In case the share servers are managed by Manila, the configuration file must be updated with the Nova, Neutron, and Cinder access configuration.

The driver backend is configured with the driver details and the flag `driver_handles_share_servers` to determine whether Manila manages the share servers:

```
...
[DEFAULT]
enabled_share_backends = Backend1
enabled_share_protocols = NFS,CIFS
default_share_type = default_share_type
scheduler_driver = manila.scheduler.drivers.filter.FilterScheduler

[Backend1]
share_driver = manila.share.drivers.generic.GenericShareDriver
driver_handles_share_servers = True

service_instance_password = manila
service_instance_user = manila
service_image_name = manila-service-image

path_to_private_key = /home/stack/.ssh/id_rsa
path_to_public_key = /home/stack/.ssh/id_rsa.pub

# Custom name for share backend.
share_backend_name = Backend1
```

 The Manila service can be configured with multiple backend drivers at the same time. An example of the multi-backend-support capability for Manila can found at `https://github.com/openstack/manila/blob/mast er/doc/source/adminref/multi_backends.rst`.

Using the share service

Staring using Manila requires in the first place the creation of a default share type:

```
# manila type-create default_share_type True
```

When configured with `driver_handles_share_servers`, the `network` and `subnet-id` of the neutron network that will be attached to the share server must be provided. This can be found using the `neutron net-show` command line:

```
# manila share-network-create
  --name storage_net1
  --neutron-net-id <neutron_net_id>
  --neutron-subnet-id <neutron_subnet_id>
```

Next, create a share using the following command:

```
# manila create NFS 1 --name share1 --share-network storage_net1
```

Finally, create access rules for the share:

```
# manila access-allow share1 ip 0.0.0.0/0 --access-level rw
```

Now the file shares can be accessed from the virtual machine over NFS. To get the mount NFS source run the following command:

```
# manila share-export-location-list share1
```

Choosing the storage

While dealing with the different storage systems within OpenStack, you may wonder which option would be the best for your storage solution. Based on our previous discussions, you should be able to proceed into the next stage of discussion to question and validate the scenarios to your choice.

Why should your environment support block storage or file share and not object storage? Should you rely on the compute nodes to store your persistent storage drives? Alternatively, will the external storage nodes be more convenient, taking your budget into consideration? What about performance? Do the internal users only need reliable storage? Should they turn a blind eye to its performance capabilities? Do you need real redundant storage to meet the requirements of data-loss scenarios?

Keep in mind that there will be many possibilities. If you over engineer your storage design, you will invite complexity of deployment and maintenance.

Selecting the block storage for VMs storage backend becomes a straightforward choice due to its attractive use cases in an OpenStack environment:

- It provides persistent storage for virtual machines, which guarantees more consistency than Swift
- It offers a better read/write and input/output storage performance for the virtual machine volumes
- It resolves the trade-off between performance and availability offered by the external storage using supported storage backend.
- It has the snapshot facility to create new volumes for read/write usage

Suddenly, you might be tempted to think that we should not use Swift; the answer to this is no! There are several reasons for arguing in favor of Swift, some of which are as follows:

- Swift is a good fit if you wish to store large blobs of data, which includes a large number of images
- It is suitable for the backing up of archive storage, which brings the infrastructure-related data in to a safe zone
- It is a very cost-effective storage solution that prevents the need for an external RAID-specific controller
- With Swift, we can access specific user data from anywhere; it can serve as a Google search engine by providing metadata and indexing

As OpenStack storage facilities grow, Manila project becomes an attractive solution designed to expose and simplify the management of file shares for instances usage. Several key attributes may distinguish the use case of such a service that includes:

- Persistent data store in file shares accessible by multiple instances clients
- Ideal solution for unstructured data storage and dealing with access mount concurrency by multiple instances
- Add more granular control of share access via specific networks or access rules
- Embrace the capability of applications built on top of OpenStack to use file share as part of their infrastructure

Looking beyond the default - Ceph

If you look carefully at the comparison overview mentioned previously, you will find Ceph! It is not just a driver that has to be installed and configured as a backend for Cinder. It is standard open source distributed storage. Ceph can be used for object storage through its S3 API as well as the Swift API. If you intend to gather all the pieces from the object and network block devices, you should consider Ceph. Moreover, it can also expose the filesystem interface, which makes it possible to use it as a file share. The concept of Ceph as a scalable storage solution is almost the same as Swift that replicates data across the commodity storage nodes, but that's not all. Ceph is a good data consolidator that enables you to grab both the object, block and files share storages in a single system. You can even use it as a backend to glance for storing images.

Let's have a look at the architecture of Ceph:

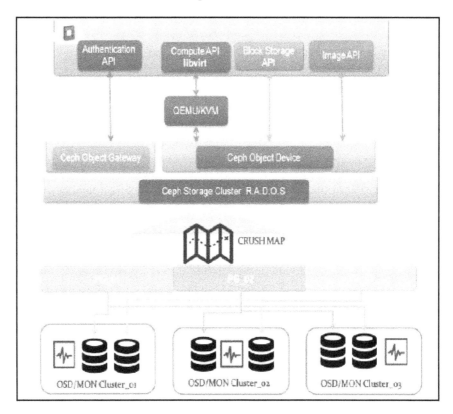

The core of Ceph is the **reliable autonomic distributed object store (RADOS)**, which is responsible for the distribution and replication of objects across the storage cluster. As illustrated in the previous figure, a block storage layer provides a **RADOS Block Device (RBD)** for the object's backend. The amazing part of this architecture is that the RBD devices are thinly provisioned within the RADOS objects and thanks to the librbd library, objects can be accessed by means of QEMU drivers, which make the link between Ceph and Nova instances. Unlike Swift, Ceph defines other basic components as follows:

- **Object Storage Devices (OSDs)**: This corresponds to the physical disks, which can be a directory residing on a regular filesystem, such as XFS or Btrfs. OSDs run the OSD daemon for the RADOS service, which will take care of the replication, coherency, and recovery of objects.

 A Linux filesystem such as XFS is required for the Ceph production environment, but Btrfs hasn't been proven to be a stable filesystem that is suitable for a production environment. Refer to the official Ceph website, h ttp://ceph.com/docs/master/rados/configuration/filesystem-reco mmendations/, for recommendation-related updates.

- **Placement groups (PGs)**: Each object stored in the Ceph cluster is mapped to a PG. The PGs are then mapped to OSDs. The reason for introducing an intermediate container is to remove tight coupling between the object stored and the OSD. The PGs create a level of abstraction and allow adding or removing OSDs without impacting the object to PG mapping. Adding or removing OSD nodes will update the PG to OSD mapping. PGs perform object replication by the pool as well. Every PG that is assigned in a pool will replicate the object into multiple OSDs within the same pool.

- **Pool**: You can compare a pool in Ceph to the concept of rings in Swift. It defines the number of PGs that are not shared. Furthermore, it provides hash maps for objects in OSDs.

- **The Controlled Replication Under Scalable Hashing (CRUSH) maps**: Based on the defined criteria, a CRUSH algorithm defines how objects are distributed over OSDs. It removes the need for a central lookup table for locating objects in the cluster. Instead, using the Ceph cluster maps and CRUSH algorithm, the Ceph client can independently calculate the object location. It also ensures that the replicated objects will not end up on the same disks, hosts, or shelves.

Besides OSD, Ceph introduces the following servers:

- **The monitor daemon server** (**MON**): This mainly focuses on checking the state of consistency of the data in each node that runs an OSD
- **The metadata server** (**MDS**): This is required for the Ceph filesystem to store their metadata if you intend to build a POSIX file on top of objects

Ceph can be integrated seamlessly with OpenStack. It has emerged as a reliable and robust storage backend for OpenStack that defines a new way of provisioning the boot-from-volume instances. This new method of provisioning is named thin provisioning. Ceph provides the **copy-on-write** cloning feature, allowing many VMs to start instantly from the templates. This shows a great improvement at the threading level along with an amazing I/O performance boost.

Thousands of VMs can be created from a single master image derived from a Glance image stored in a Ceph block device and booted by using Cinder, which requires only the space needed to store their subsequent changes:

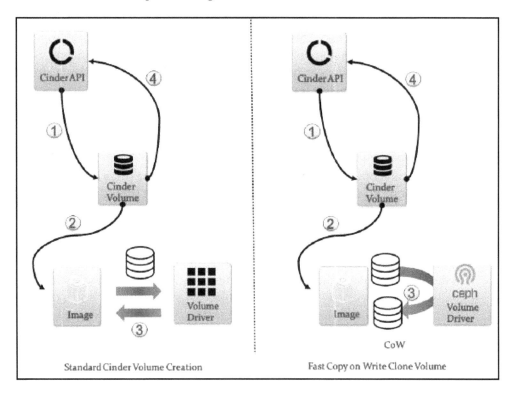

To boot the virtual machines in Ceph either from an ephemeral backend or from a volume, you must use a RAW image from Glance.

The creation of the standard Cinder volume and fast copy-on-write clone volume requires you to use the Cinder API to forward a create image request from a defined image at the Glance storage (**1**). The Cinder volume service tries to locate the image under question in the Glance image store (**2**) and forwards its volume reference back to the API (**4**). Using the standard way to boot an instance, as shown in the Standard Cinder Volume Creation section in the previous figure, an image will be pulled from Glance and streamed to the compute node, which is extremely slow (**3**). The new approach in the Fast Copy on Write Clone Volume section (**3**) gives the functionality to make a snapshot of images while they are being imported. Thus, it might be an easier and more sophisticated way to create clones from them, as well as for volume from an image.

Ceph in OpenStack

We already have an overview of OSDs, which are the workhorses for object and block storage. Moreover, partitions can be created for the OSD nodes and assigned different storage pools. Keep in mind that this setup can be an example from many others. The common point that you should stick to is the way you distribute the Ceph components across the OpenStack infrastructure. In this example, we made the `ceph-mon` daemon run in the controller node, which makes sense if you intend to centralize all the management services from a logical perspective. The `ceph-osd` nodes should run in the replica in separate storage nodes. The compute nodes need to know which Ceph node will clone the images or store the volumes that require a Ceph client to run on them.

From the network perspective, the `ceph-osd` nodes will join the private storage network while keeping the nodes that are running the Ceph daemons in the management network.

A simple integration model with OpenStack can be depicted in the following way:

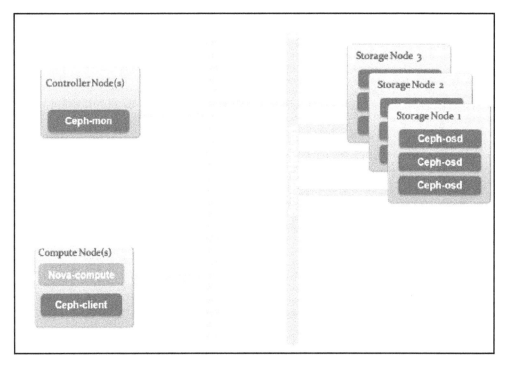

Deploying Ceph with Ansible

We will deploy Ceph using the Ceph Ansible playbook. The OpenStack Ansible project repository provides a simple playbook to install OSD and MON nodes based on `ceph-osd` and `ceph-mon` roles respectively. The OpenStack Ansible playbook for Ceph can be found at: `https://github.com/openstack/openstack-ansible/blob/master/playbooks/ceph-install.yml`.

For the current setup, we will be using a more extensive Ceph Ansible repository out of the box that can be found at: `https://github.com/ceph/ceph-ansible`. The Ceph playbook repository provides roles for deploying Ceph monitors, OSDs, MDSs, and RGWs. It allows starting with a minimal number of Ceph Nodes and adding progressively to the Ceph cluster. Start by cloning the Ceph Ansible git repository:

```
# git clone https://github.com/ceph/ceph-ansible.git
```

Next step is to review the variable definition with in the code tree. The variables are defined in the `group_vars` directory. This directory contains sample of the variable definition configuration files. We start by looking at the file `all.yml.sample`. Use the sample file as a guide:

```
# cp group_vars/all.yml.sample group_vars/all.yml
```

Next customize the variables for your setup. The variables common to the Ceph cluster are available in `group_vars/all.yml` and provide customization for source of installation packages including development branch of Ceph. You can select the filesystem type for your OSD devices. This file also defines the kernel tuning parameters like maximum number of processes and maximum number of files.

Another important parameter to configure is the cluster network used by OSDs, the public and storage network segments between the Ceph client and the Ceph cluster. You can decide on the journal location for the file system on these disks or to go with OSD directories instead of disks. This can be configured in the `group_vars/all.yml` file:

```
...
journal_size: 2048
public_network: 172.47.36.0/22
cluster_network: 172.47.44.0/22
...
```

The OSD and MON related configuration variables are available in the `group_vars/osds.yml` and `group_vars/mons.yml` respectively.

The `osds.yml` file lists the devices for use with Ceph although you can enable auto discovery of devices and Ansible will make sure that only devices without partitions are provisioned for Ceph:

```
# cp group_vars/osds.yml.sample group_vars/osds.yml
...
osd_auto_discovery: True
journal_collocation: True
...
```

The `mons.yml` file exposes more configuration directives for Ceph monitors service including Ceph file system security options :

```
# cp group_vars/mons.yml.sample group_vars/mons.yml
...
cephx: true
...
```

Next, define the inventory files with the definition of the Ceph cluster topology. Here is a sample of /etc/ansible/hosts file that includes three Ceph nodes assigned to each and OSD and MON roles as well as MDSS and RGWS:

```
[mons]
ceph-host[01:03]
[osds]
ceph-host[01:03]
mdss]
ceph-host1
[rgws]
ceph-host2
```

Once you have the inventory in place, we can start deploying the cluster by assigning roles for each server group using the site.yml file as template:

```
# cp site.yml.sample site.yml
...
- hosts: mons
  gather_facts: false
  become: True
  roles:
  - ceph-mon

- hosts: osds
  gather_facts: false
  become: True
  roles:
  - ceph-osd

- hosts: mdss
  gather_facts: false
  become: True
  roles:
  - ceph-mds

- hosts: rgws
  gather_facts: false
  become: True
  roles:
  - ceph-rgw
```

We can test the connectivity of the hosts from the Ansible deployment host before starting the deployment the Ceph cluster:

```
# ansible all -m ping
ceph-host01| success >> {
    "changed": false,
    "ping": "pong"
}

ceph-host02| success >> {
    "changed": false,
    "ping": "pong"
}

ceph-host03 | success >> {
    "changed": false,
    "ping": "pong"
}
```

Deploying the Ceph cluster can be achieved by running the `site.yml` playbook:

```
# ansible-playbook site.yml -i /etc/ansible/hosts
...
ceph-host01          : ok=13   changed=10   unreachable=0   failed=0
ceph-host02          : ok=13   changed=9    unreachable=0   failed=0
ceph-host03          : ok=13   changed=9    unreachable=0   failed=0
...
```

Storing images in Ceph

It is possible to use Ceph as a storage backend to store an operating system image for instances.

The following steps show how one can configure Glance to use Ceph as an alternative for the storage of images:

1. On the new Ceph instance, create a new Ceph pool for OpenStack Glance, as follows:

```
# ceph osd pool create images 128
```

2. On the cloud controller node, configure OpenStack Glance to use the RBD store in /etc/glance/glance-api.conf, as follows:

```
# vim /etc/glance/glance-api.conf
rbd_store_user=glance
rbd_store_pool=images
```

To enable the copy-on-write cloning feature, set the direct_url = True directive in /etc/glance/glance-api.conf.

3. Save the configuration file and restart the glance-api service, as follows:

```
#service glance-api restart
```

It is possible to reload the cloud controller configuration by commenting out the rbd_store_user and rbd_store_pool lines in the OpenStack image cookbook's attributes file.

4. On the cloud controller node, download a new image for Glance testing, as follows:

```
# wget http://cloud.centos.org/centos/7/images/CentOS-7-
x86_64-GenericCloud.qcow2.xz
```

5. Create a new Glance image from the downloaded image in the following way:

```
# glance image-create --name="CentOS-7-image" --is-public=True
--disk-format=qcow2 --container-format=ovf < CentOS-7-x86_64-
GenericCloud.qcow2.xz
```

The preceding command yields the following output:

```
+--------------------+--------------------------------------+
| Property           | Value                                |
+--------------------+--------------------------------------+
| checksum           | 346798dd32dd43449f4bd3019992b0ae     |
| container_format   | ovf                                  |
| created_at         | 2017-04-21T22:25:16Z                 |
| disk_format        | qcow2                                |
| id                 | 7fee1be4-a0bd-43dc-b695-e00b85f2c1f6 |
| min_disk           | 0                                    |
| min_ram            | 0                                    |
| name               | CentOS-7-image                       |
| owner              | 6fa47a2b492e48548c2c9596d1c2a5a2     |
| protected          | False                                |
| size               | 483780468                            |
| status             | active                               |
| tags               | □                                    |
| updated_at         | 2017-04-21T22:25:19Z                 |
| virtual_size       | None                                 |
| visibility         | private                              |
+--------------------+--------------------------------------+
```

6. You can check out the image ID in the `images` Ceph pool by issuing the following query:

```
# rados -p images ls
```

For the preceding code, we will get the following output:

```
rbd_id.7fee1be4-a0bd-43dc-b695-e00b85f2c1f6
```

The CentOS image is stored in Ceph, which refers to the CentOS image ID that is shown in the Glance image output. The object that the Glance image recently stored and imported from Ceph is identified with the help of the `rbd_id.Image_Glance_ID` format.

> It is possible to configure Cinder and Nova to use Ceph as well. You will need to create a new Ceph pool and edit the `/etc/cinder/cinder.conf` file to specify the RBD driver for Cinder. Instances in OpenStack can be booted directly into Ceph which requires defining optionally in the `/etc/nova/nova.conf` file the ephemeral backend for Nova. To read more about this specific setup, you may visit `http://ceph.com/docs/master/rbd/rbd-openstack/`.

Summary

In this chapter, we covered a vast topic pertaining to storage in OpenStack. By now, you should be more familiar with the different storage types. We delved into a variety of aspects of Swift as a former object storage solution for OpenStack.

Moreover, you should now be comfortable moving beyond the block storage component for OpenStack. You will be able to understand what fits better in your storage design against Cinder. We also discussed file share based storage and how it can be implemented with the Manila project to provide the option of share based persistent storage in OpenStack.

We discussed the different use cases for the OpenStack storage solutions and picked up an example from the many possibilities. You should now be able to take into consideration several factors such as filesystem, storage protocol, storage design, and performance.

Finally, the last section of this chapter talked about how one can mix and deploy a block, object, and filesystem storage in a system called Ceph. Thus, thanks to its APIs, you can seize the wide range of opportunities provided by OpenStack. On the other hand, making the right decision for your own storage solution is on you. Remember that any storage use case will depend on your needs or, in other words, the needs of your end users.

However, do you think that only a good storage design will be enough to make your OpenStack cloud perfect? You will have noticed that a good cloud deployment also depends on your network design and security considerations, which will be the topic of the next chapter.

6
OpenStack Networking - Choice of Connectivity Types and Networking Services

"What regresses, never progresses."
- Omar Ibn Al-Khattab

Networking is one of the core services of the cloud infrastructure. While it provides connectivity to virtual instances, it must at the same time provide the segregation of traffic from different tenants and prevent cross talk. The networking in OpenStack is designed to be self-serviced. This means the tenants can create their own network design, manage topology of multiple networks, connect networks together, access external world, and also deploy advanced networking services. As the networking services expose the cloud instances to the external world, deploying access control for the instances is imperative. The OpenStack networking project facilitates the creation of firewalls and provides the tenants with fine-grained control over network access.

Historically the Nova project provided very basic network connectivity between virtual machine instances using:

- **Flat network**: This is a single IP pool and Layer-2 domain shared by all tenants using the cloud.
- **VLAN network**: This type of network segregates traffic using VLAN tags. It requires manual VLAN configuration on the Layer-2 devices (switches).

Although these basic networking features still exist in Nova, all advanced features of networking are provided by the OpenStack networking project called **Neutron**.

In this chapter, we will discuss the following topics:

- Discovering the novelty behind Neutron networks and their implementations
- Understanding the virtual routers in OpenStack and how they work
- Learning about the virtual switches in OpenStack
- Checking out the function of various plugins and agents provided by Neutron
- Enforcing the network security in Neutron by means of security groups
- Creating self-managed firewalls using Firewall as a Service Neutron feature
- Discovering VPN as a Service capability to provide multi-site connectivity between two OpenStack environments

The architecture of Neutron

Neutron becomes a more and more effective and robust network project in the OpenStack ecosystem due to its overwhelming features and capabilities. It enables operators to build and manage a complete network topology with all the necessary elements including networks, subnets, routers, load balancers, firewalls, and ports.

The Neutron project consists of an API server, which is responsible for receiving all networking service requests. The API server is generally installed on the OpenStack controller node and multiple instances of it can be deployed to provide scalability and availability requirements:

- Neutron has been designed to follow a plugin-based architecture. Neutron plugins are responsible for adapting and providing additional network services.

- Once the API server receives a new request, it is forwarded to a specific plugin depending on how Neutron is configured. The Neutron plugins reside on the controller node and orchestrate the physical resources to instantiate the requested networking feature. A Neutron plugin can implement orchestration of resources directly by interacting with the devices or it can use agents to control the resource:

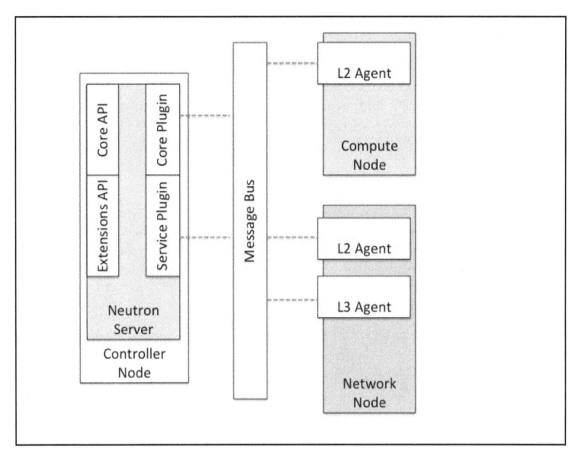

- Like other OpenStack projects, the Neutron project provides a reference implementation of plugins and agents based on open-source technologies. The agents may be deployed on the network and/or compute nodes. The network node provides resources to implement network services such as routing, firewalling, load balancing, and VPNs.
- The hardware vendors are provided with well-defined APIs to implement their own plugins and provide support for vendor networking gear. In the following section, we will discuss in detail the different plugin types and agents.

Neutron plugins

The Neutron plugins implement networking features by resource orchestration. They are broadly categorized as the core plugin and the service plugins. Core plugin

The core plugin is responsible for providing Layer-2 connectivity for the virtual machines and network elements connecting to a network. The API server calls the core plugin whenever it receives a request for creating a new virtual network or when a new port is created on the virtual network.

The core plugin implements the following Neutron resources:

- **Networks**: A Neutron network resource represents a Layer-2 domain. All virtual instances that need a network service must connect to a virtual network.
- **Ports**: A Neutron port represents a participating endpoint on the virtual network.
- **Subnet**: The Neutron subnet resource adds a Layer-3 addressing pool to a Neutron network. The subnet can have an associated DHCP server for serving IP address leases to virtual machines.

The Neutron core provides a RESTfull API interface to create and manage the mentioned resources.

Service plugin

The service plugin is called for implementing higher-level network services, such as routing between networks, implementation of firewalls, load balancers on a network, or to create VPN services.

Each of the higher layer plugins implements some virtual network constructs. For example, the L3 service plugin implements the virtual router that provides connectivity between two or more networks. It also creates Neutron resource called Floating IP that provides **network address translation** (**NAT**) functionality to expose a virtual machine to external world. In the following section we will go through each of the advance services and understand how they work.

Agents

The agents are deployed on the network and compute nodes. They interact with the Neutron server using RPC calls over the message bus. Neutron provides different types to agents to implement virtual networking services such as Layer-2 connectivity, DHCP service, and routers. The following are some of the Neutron agents:

- The Neutron L2 agent resides on all the compute and network nodes. Its main function is to connect the virtual machines and network devices like virtual routers to the Layer-2 network. It interacts with the core plugin to receive network configuration for virtual machines.
- The DHCP agent is deployed on the network node and it implements DHCP service for a given subnet.
- The Neutron L3 agent implements a routing service and provides external access to a virtual machine by implementing NAT service.
- The VPN agent implement VPN service and is installed on the network nodes.

Neutron API extensions

Extensions are provisions in the Neutron project for implementing advanced networking services. These extensions allow creating a new REST API and exposing Neutron resources. All advanced services are implemented as Neutron extensions.

Implementing virtual networks

Neutron core plugins handle the creation of virtual networks and ports. A network in Neutron is a single Layer-2 broadcast domain. Each virtual network created is associated with a separate Layer-2 domain; this helps in keeping the traffic within a virtual network isolated. The Neutron virtual networks can be created in multiple ways but broadly they can be categorized into VLAN-based and tunnel-based networks.

VLAN-based networks

The implementation of VLAN-networks, in OpenStack is based on allocating a static VLAN for each virtual network by the core plugin. This makes sure that all communication within the virtual network is confined to itself and no broadcast packet in one virtual network will impact another one.

To implement a VLAN based network the core plugin must configure the VLAN on the virtual switch on the compute and network nodes as well as orchestrate the physical network path, such as the physical switches that connect the compute and network nodes:

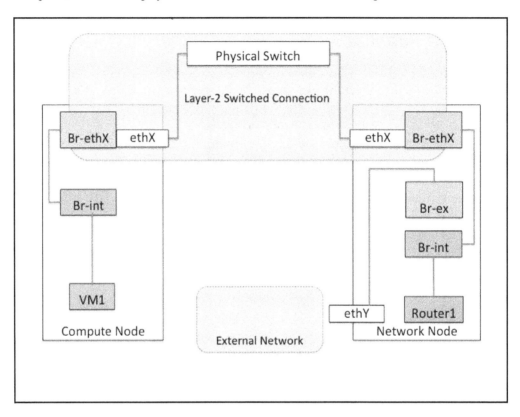

The Neutron **Modular Layer-2** (**ML2**) plugin provides a framework to implement virtual networks using various mechanisms and type drivers. In the subsequent sections, we will discuss how the ML2 plugin uses different drivers to configure the physical and virtual path.

Tunnel-based networks

The tunnel-based network creates tunnels to isolate the virtual network traffic. The tunnel-based network model functions by encapsulating packets. In such networks, the compute and network nodes are connected using IP-Fabric (a hierarchical network infrastructure that provides IP-addressing-based connectivity). An IP based network provides a single Layer-2 domain by means of **packet encapsulation** (**PE**). PE is the process of carrying the inner packet as a payload in the outer packet. The tunneled networking works by encapsulating Layer-2 packets inside IP packets. The tunnel endpoints are responsible for encapsulating and de-encapsulating the L2 packets. The IP Fabric forms the transport provider for the encapsulated network traffic. Let's take a closer look by discussing the following example:

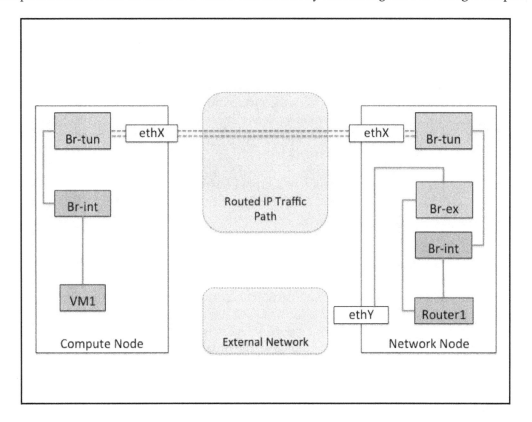

The preceding figure illustrates a VM on a compute node connected to a virtual router on the network node. As VM1 sends out a packet to another port on a virtual network, the router interface, the virtual switch on the compute node, encapsulates the L2 packet inside an IP packet and sends over the IP Fabric to the network node where the destination virtual router resides. When receiving the IP packet, the virtual switch on the destination node removes the outer IP packet to recover the L2 packet sent by the virtual machine at the origin. The packet is then delivered to the destination router port.

Thus, even though the two nodes are not part of a single Layer-2 network, the tunnels are able to emulate a Layer-2 network for the connected virtual machines.

There are certain terms that are widely used in the industry to identify the components of a tunnel based network:

- **Underlay network**: An underlay network is the IP based network connectivity (IP Fabric) between the compute and network nodes.
- **Overlay network**: An overlay network is a virtual Layer-2 domain created by encapsulating the packets from the virtual machines in to IP packets. The overlay network uses the underlay network as a means of transporting packets, while for the underlay network, the overlay packets are similar to any other data packet flowing through the IP network.

There are multiple protocols to implement a tunnel-based virtual network but the most commonly used ones are the VXLAN and GRE-based tunnels. The tunnel-based networks provide huge segmentation size; VXLAN, for instance, can create 16 million separate networks.

What would be the most suitable network segmentation mechanism? The common argument against using VLAN-based network segmentation is the limited number of segmentations that can be created. The VLAN ID is part of the Layer-2 header of the packet and its size is well defined. This puts a limit of 4048 distinct VLAN segmentations and only as many virtual networks can be created with VLANs, while the number of tunnel-based networks that can be created is much higher, in the order of millions.

Another important feature of the tunneled networks is their ability to span across multiple L2 domains in the underlay. This means it is possible to create tunneled networks with ports residing in different datacenters, thus scaling the cloud deployment to multiple locations.

However, it is worth mentioning that the VLAN-based network is much better performing compared to the tunnel-based ones, as there is no overhead of encapsulating and de-encapsulating of packets. Additionally, due to the encapsulation of packets in a tunnel-based network, each packet flowing through the overlay network carries a tunnel header and an IP header. This is an overhead on the IP Fabric and has an impact on the maximum size of packet a VM can send through the network. The encapsulation overhead can be tweaked either by adjusting the **maximum transfer unit** (**MTU**) size of the underlay network to accommodate the increased packet size, or by reducing the MTU size of the virtual network.

Virtual switches

The virtual switches are used to connect a virtual network port to the physical network. The compute and network nodes are installed with a virtual switch. The virtual machine on the compute node and network elements (virtual routers, DHCP servers) on the network node connect to the virtual switches. The virtual switches then connect to the physical switches using a Network Interface Card (NIC) of the physical node.

The Neutron server can be configured to work with the **Linux bridge** or **OpenVSwitch** (**OVS**) mechanism drivers to connect the virtual machines to the physical network. The OVS provides an extensive list of advanced switching functionalities including LACP, OpenFlow and VXLAN/GRE Tunneling. The most attractive feature of the OVS mechanism is its programmability function that leverages flow rules for packets forwarding across the network and between nodes. This makes it a very versatile switching platform. The flow rules determine how to handle packets reaching the switch. For example, it is possible to implement your own switching logic using flow rule definition. Chapter 7, *Advances Networking - A look at SDN and NFV* will examine an SDN solution that uses this feature extensively.

The Linux bridge, on the other hand, leverages the networking capabilities of the Linux kernel to provide VLAN-based isolation and tunneling. The Linux bridge has been in use for a longer period and is well tested. At the end of the day the decision for choosing one virtual switch over another is based on your features and requirements.

The ML2 plugin

In the earlier days of the OpenStack Neutron (previously known as Quantum) project, the configuration of the virtual network was handled by a single monolithic plugin. This meant it was not possible to support the creation of virtual networks with multiple vendor gears. Even in such cases where single network vendor devices were used, selecting multiple virtual switches or virtual network types was not possible. Prior to the Havana release, it was not possible to use simultaneously the Linux bridge and OpenvSwitch plugins. This feature limitation has been tackled by the creation of ML2 plugin

The ML2 plugin provides a framework of drivers to handle different flavors of virtual switches; both OVS and Linux bridge-based configurations are supported. It also supports different types of network segmentation based on VLANs, VXLAN, and GRE tunnels. It provides APIs for writing drivers for different vendor devices that can coexist and for implementing new network types. The ML2 drivers are classified as type drivers and mechanism drivers. The type drivers implement a network isolation type such as VLAN, VXLAN, and GRE. The mechanism drivers, on the other hand, implement an orchestration mechanism for physical or virtual switches:

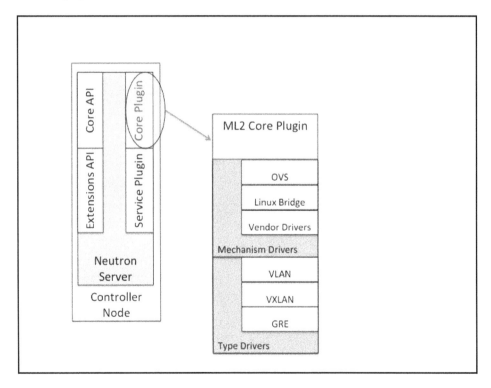

Network types

The addition of the concept of plugins in Neutron implies the support of different network types that vary regarding their usage in an OpenStack setup.

It should be noted that the network types are not related to how they are implemented in reality (Flat, VLAN, VXLAN, or GRE) but distinguished by their usage. The following network types are often used while describing the virtual network topology:

- **Tenant networks**: This are virtual networks created by tenants.
- **Provider networks**: These are created by the OpenStack operators and associated with an existing network in the data center. Provider networks can be tagged (VLAN) or untagged (flat) allowing tenants to access existing networks that can be shared or dedicated to a specific tenant.
- **External networks**: These allow access to the external world, typically the Internet. External networks should provide default gateway(s) for routing to the Internet into the OpenStack environment. Instances can be assigned with floating IPs to make them publicly accessible.

Neutron subnets

The subnets define a pool of IP addresses associated to a network. The definition of subnets in Neutron contains the IP pool in the form of **Classless Inter-Domain Routing (CIDR)**. Optionally, the gateway of the subnet can be adjusted by default as the first IP address in the pool.

It should be noted that Neutron allows the association of multiple subnets to a single network.

Creating virtual networks and subnets

Now that we have a clear understanding of the virtual networks, we can start creating virtual networks. Creating virtual networks can be performed using the following Neutron command line:

```
# neutron net-create network1
```

To create a subnet associated with this virtual network, use the `subnet-create` argument in the Neutron command line. To specify the gateway address, use the `--gateway` option. Use the `--disable-dhcp` option to disable the DHCP service for the subnet. It is also possible to set the name servers for the subnet up to five per subnet using the `--dns-nameserver` option:

```
# neutron subnet-create --disable-dhcp --gateway 192.168.20.100
--dns-nameserver 192.168.20.100 network1 192.168.20.0/24
```

Understanding network port connectivity

In this section, we will walk through the mechanism of connecting a virtual port to the network. We will be examining the virtual switches on the compute and network nodes. Neutron server uses Layer-2 agents running on the nodes to orchestrate the virtual switch.

Understanding Linux bridge-based connectivity

Let's start by understanding how a node installed with Linux bridge connects a virtual machine to the physical network. We will take the example of VLAN-based networks and then apply the same mechanism to understand tunneled networks. As mentioned earlier, Linux bridge provides basic switching functions, it does not support VLAN tagging or tunneling. Then how does Neutron use Linux bridge to provide VLAN and tunnel-based isolation? The answer to this question can be found in the Linux kernel. The kernel exposes features allowing the creation of sub-interfaces that can perform VLAN tagging or tunneling.

The following figure shows how the tagged sub-interfaces are created from a parent physical NIC and how they are then plugged into the bridges:

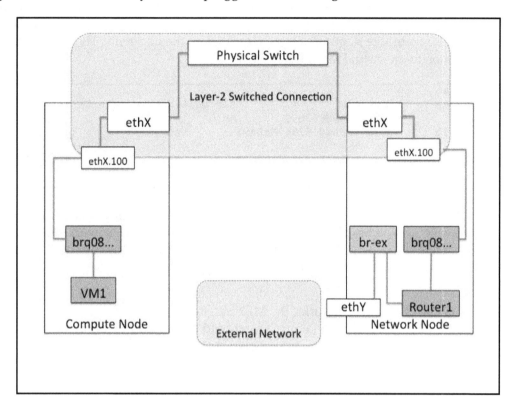

The Neutron L2 agent creates a separate sub-interface and Linux bridge per VLAN segment and then plugs them together. When a virtual machine tries to connect to a network, the ports of the virtual machines are then connected to the correct bridge corresponding to the virtual network. The following output shows the VLAN sub-interface `eth1.111` and the corresponding Linux bridge `brq08c3182b-c3` created by the L2 agents. The tap interfaces are the connection to the virtual instances:

```
$ brctl show
bridge name       bridge id              STP enabled      interfaces
br-ex            8000.000000000000           no
brq08c3182b-c3            8000.525400c8d9da            no                    eth1.111
                                                                    tape9caa6d2-9d
brq85ceb988-63            8000.525400c8d9da            no                    eth1.165
                                                                    tap3390b56b-ab
```

In this layout, the Linux kernel is responsible for tagging and untagging packets. The bridge just provides Layer-2 switching between the interfaces. The tunneled networks are also implemented using the same mechanism, the only difference is that the sub-interfaces are created by the L2 agent of tunnel sub-interfaces, which encapsulate packet instead of tagging them.

To enable Linux bridge-based networks, the **ML2** plugin configuration file `/etc/neutron/plugins/ml2/ml2_conf.ini` should be updated as follows:

```
[ml2]
tenant_network_types = vlan
type_drivers =..,vlan,..
mechanism_drivers = linuxbridge

[ml2_type_vlan]
network_vlan_ranges = default:100:300

[linux_bridge]
physical_interface_mappings = default:eth1
```

Understanding OpenVSwitch-based connectivity

The OVS plugin provides more advanced networking features and implements VLAN and tunneling. Let's parse briefly how a compute and network node deployed with OVS implements virtual networks.

The OVS uses multiple interconnected switches to perform Layer-2 isolation. The OVS uses three bridges to connect the virtual machines to the physical network. We will start our discussion by first looking at VXLAN-based networks.

To configure the ML2 plugin to use VXLAN-based networks, update the ML2 configuration file `/etc/neutron/plugins/ml2/ml2_conf.ini` as follows:

```
[ml2]
tenant_network_types = vxlan
type_drivers = ..,vxlan
mechanism_drivers = openvswitch

[ml2_type_vxlan]
vni_ranges = 1001:2000

[agent]
tunnel_types = vxlan

[ovs]
datapath_type = system
tunnel_bridge = br-tun
local_ip = <tunnel endpoint ip>
```

One major difference between OVS and Linux bridge implementations is the number of virtual devices and interfaces presented for each mechanism. OVS introduces additional virtual interfaces inside the host identified as bridges and classified as follows:

- `br-int`: The `br-int` is the integration bridge. All virtual instances that use the networking service connect to this bridge. This includes virtual machines, routers, and DHCP server.
- `br-tun`: In the case of tunnel-based networks, the `br-ethX` (provider bridge) is replaced with a tunnel bridge called `br-tun`. The `br-tun` bridge is configured to handle encapsulation and de-encapsulation of packets.
- `br-ex`: This bridge is connected to a physical interface that provides connectivity to the external world.

The virtual machines connect to the integration bridge using VLAN segmentation. The VLAN IDs used to connect the virtual machines to the integration bridge are local to the compute node (a similar approach is used on the network node to connect router interfaces). It should be noted that the local VLANs are also used in the case of VLAN-based networks. The local VLANs are never exposed outside of the compute or network nodes.

The following illustration shows the OVS configuration on a network node. The `ovs-vsctl show` command shows the OVS configuration. Notice that the interfaces connected to the `br-int` bridge are tagged with VLAN 1:

```
# ovs-vsctl show
```

```
    Bridge br-int
        fail_mode: secure
        Port patch-tun
            Interface patch-tun
                type: patch
                options: {peer=patch-int}
        Port "tap91e5d7cc-0a"
            tag: 1
            Interface "tap91e5d7cc-0a"
                type: internal
        Port br-int
            Interface br-int
                type: internal
        Port "qr-82c29b26-db"
            tag: 1
            Interface "qr-82c29b26-db"
                type: internal
        Port "qr-893f0eb2-31"
            tag: 1
            Interface "qr-893f0eb2-31"
                type: internal
    Bridge br-tun
        fail_mode: secure
        Port "vxlan-c0a87aa3"
            Interface "vxlan-c0a87aa3"
                type: vxlan
                options: {df_default="true", in_key=flow,
local_ip="192.168.122.142", out_key=flow, remote_ip="192.168.122.163"}
        Port patch-int
            Interface patch-int
                type: patch
                options: {peer=patch-tun}
        Port br-tun
            Interface br-tun
```

If the destination virtual machine is on the same compute node, the integration bridge switches the packet locally and delivers it to the destination virtual machine port.

If the destination port is on a different node, the packet is transferred to the `br-tun` bridge over the patch port. The `br-tun` bridge encapsulates then the L2 packet inside a VXLAN packet and swaps the local VLAN with the VXLAN tunnel ID that is allocated by the ML2 VXLAN driver for the virtual network. Use the `ovs-ofctl dump-flows` command to see the flow rules on the `br-tun` bridge. In the following illustration VXLAN ID 0x426 or 1062 is used to replace the local VLAN ID 1:

```
$ sudo ovs-ofctl dump-flows br-tun
NXST_FLOW reply (xid=0x4):
 cookie=0x973705127896e35e, duration=3326.399s, table=0, n_packets=548,
n_bytes=63588, idle_age=5, priority=1,in_port=1 actions=resubmit(,2)
 cookie=0x973705127896e35e, duration=3255.875s, table=0, n_packets=706,
n_bytes=30412, idle_age=833, priority=1,in_port=2 actions=resubmit(,4)
 cookie=0x973705127896e35e, duration=3326.399s, table=0, n_packets=2, n_bytes=180,
idle_age=3286, priority=0 actions=drop
 cookie=0x973705127896e35e, duration=3303.882s, table=4, n_packets=0, n_bytes=0,
idle_age=3303, priority=1,tun_id=0x426 actions=mod_vlan_vid:1,resubmit(,10)
 cookie=0x973705127896e35e, duration=3326.397s, table=4, n_packets=706,
n_bytes=30412, idle_age=833, priority=0 actions=drop
 cookie=0x973705127896e35e, duration=3326.397s, table=6, n_packets=0, n_bytes=0,
idle_age=3326, priority=0 actions=drop
 cookie=0x973705127896e35e, duration=3326.396s, table=10, n_packets=0, n_bytes=0,
idle_age=3326, priority=1 actions=learn
(table=20,hard_timeout=300,priority=1,cookie=0x973705127896e35e,NXM_OF_VLAN_TCI
[0..11],NXM_OF_ETH_DST[]=NXM_OF_ETH_SRC[],load:0->NXM_OF_VLAN_TCI
[],load:NXM_NX_TUN_ID[]->NXM_NX_TUN_ID[],output:NXM_OF_IN_PORT[]),output:1
 cookie=0x973705127896e35e, duration=3326.396s, table=20, n_packets=0, n_bytes=0,
idle_age=3326, priority=0 actions=resubmit(,22)
 cookie=0x973705127896e35e, duration=3255.868s, table=22, n_packets=508,
n_bytes=59944, idle_age=5, dl_vlan=1 actions=strip_vlan,set_tunnel:0x426,output:2
 cookie=0x973705127896e35e, duration=3326.379s, table=22, n_packets=40,
n_bytes=3644, idle_age=3257, priority=0 actions=drop
```

The OVS flow configuration then outputs the packet on port 2, which is the VXLAN port, as can be seen in the output of `ovs-ofctl show br-tun`:

```
$ sudo ovs-ofctl show br-tun
OFPT_FEATURES_REPLY (xid=0x2): dpid:00000a32ebaa1547
n_tables:254, n_buffers:256
capabilities: FLOW_STATS TABLE_STATS PORT_STATS QUEUE_STATS ARP_MATCH_IP
actions: OUTPUT SET_VLAN_VID SET_VLAN_PCP STRIP_VLAN SET_DL_SRC SET_DL_DST SET_NW_SRC
 1(patch-int): addr:ba:2b:3e:1e:ff:e5
     config:    0
     state:     0
     speed: 0 Mbps now, 0 Mbps max
 2(vxlan-c0a87aa3): addr:16:32:1f:e3:fa:a7
     config:    0
     state:     0
     speed: 0 Mbps now, 0 Mbps max
 LOCAL(br-tun): addr:0a:32:eb:aa:15:47
     config:    0
     state:     0
     speed: 0 Mbps now, 0 Mbps max
OFPT_GET_CONFIG_REPLY (xid=0x4): frags=normal miss_send_len=0
```

This packet is then sent over the IP Fabric to the tunnel endpoint on the destination node.

On reaching the destination node, the `br-tun` on the destination node de-encapsulates the IP header, swaps the VXLAN ID to a local VLAN ID and passes it to the `br-int` bridge that finally delivers the packet to the destination port.

In the case of VLAN-based networks, the `br-tun` is replaced with `br-ethX`. This bridge connects to the physical interface `ethX`. The convention is to name the bridge after the physical interface: for example, the bridge connecting to `eth1` is called `br-eth1`. The `ethX` is the NIC on the compute or network server that connects to the physical switch providing the tenant network. In the case of VLAN-based networks, the `br-ethX` is responsible for swapping the local VLAN with the static VLAN allocated by the core plugin.

Connecting virtual networks with routers

The virtual network can connect together multiple virtual machines and provide a communication path between them, but what if you wanted to cross the Layer-2 network boundary and communicate across the networks. This is where the virtual router comes into the picture. With virtual routers you can connect multiple networks to each other. The way this works is, the tenant adds the subnet associated virtual network to the router. This creates a port on the virtual network and the port is assigned the IP address of the gateway for the subnet. When the virtual machines are offered IP addresses by the DHCP server on the network, the offer contains the IP address for the network gateway. The virtual router forwards the IP packets between the connected networks.

The default L3 plugin for Neutron implements these virtual routers using Linux network namespaces. A network namespace can be thought of as completely isolated networking stack. It has its own network configuration, routing table, IPtables rules, packet forwarding configuration, and so on.

Configuring the routing service

To provide the routing service, Neutron server must be configured with the router service plugin. To do this, update the service plugin list in Neutron configuration file /etc/neutron/neutron.conf:

```
[DEFAULT]
service_plugins = router
```

The router plugin implements virtual router instances using Linux namespaces. This is done using the L3 agent deployed on the network node. The router plugin and L3 agent communicate over the message bus. The L3 agent configuration file is present at `/etc/neutron/l3_agent.ini`:

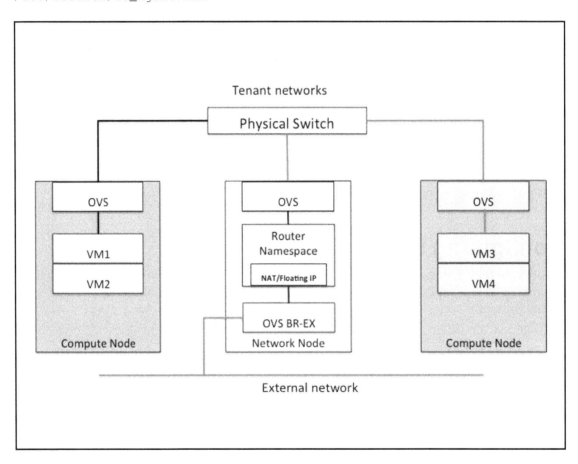

The router plugin also provides external access using NAT and floating IP configuration. NAT and floating IP requires a configured network node with the external network bridge. Assuming the third NIC on the network node is used for providing external access, use the following OVS commands to create the external access bridge:

```
# ovs-vsctl add-br br-ex
# ovs-vsctl add-port br-ex eth3
```

Connecting networks using a virtual router

To create a virtual router use the `router-create` command as follows:

```
$ neutron router-create router1
```

Next add the subnets to the router using the `router-interface-add` command:

```
$ neutron router-interface-add subnet1
```

Once the router interfaces are added, you can check the namespace created by the L3 agent on the network node. To do this, use the `ip netns` commands as follows:

```
$ ip netns list
qdhcp-26adf398-409d-4f6e-9c44-918779d8f57f
qrouter-65ef2787-541c-4ff2-8b69-24ae48094d68
```

`65ef2787-541c-4ff2-8b69-24ae48094d68` is the router id. Next you can check the routing table in the virtual router, as follows, by selecting the router namespace:

```
$ sudo ip netns exec qrouter-65ef2787-541c-4ff2-8b69-24ae48094d68 route -n
```

```
Kernel IP routing table
Destination     Gateway         Genmask         Flags Metric Ref    Use Iface
0.0.0.0         10.0.2.2        0.0.0.0         UG    0      0        0 qg-d8e8a74b-6c
10.0.2.0        0.0.0.0         255.255.255.0   U     0      0        0 qg-d8e8a74b-6c
10.15.15.0      0.0.0.0         255.255.255.0   U     0      0        0 qr-c2902c14-3b
```

Connecting to the external world

How do we provide access to the Internet to our virtual machines? This can be done in a couple of ways:

- The easiest approach is to connect the virtual machine directly to a network that has access to the Internet. For example, connecting the virtual machines directly to the management network can give the virtual machines access to the Internet. To do this, the admin can create a provider network and make the management network accessible to the OpenStack users.

- The second option is to use a router to access the Internet. In the previous discussions, we learned how two or more networks can be connected to each other. Now that the virtual machines are able to communicate across the network boundary, the next question is, can we access the Internet using the virtual router? Theoretically if the virtual router is interfaced with the external world, we could of course send packets to the outside world. On the other hand, the used IP address while creating the subnets are not routable from the Internet. So even if we could send a packet out the response will never be able to get back to us. This problem can be solved in two ways:
    - The first option is to use routable addresses in the virtual networks. This may not be always possible as getting a lot of routable IP address space is a costly affair.
    - The second option is to use NAT. The way this works is by connecting the router to an external network. Then use the external IP address on the router to implement SNAT. The SNAT process translates the source address of the packets going from the internal networks to the external IP Address. As the external IP address is routable, the responses packet from the Internet will be received on the router. The router then reverses the translation and changes the destination to the internal IP and forwards the packet to the virtual machine on the internal network.

Providing connectivity from the external world

In the previous discussion, we covered different approaches of providing Internet access to the virtual machines. In the NAT-based approach, the virtual machines can access the external world but this approach does not allow access to the virtual machine from the Internet.

To expose a virtual machine to the Internet, OpenStack provides the concept of floating IPs. The floating IP is an external IP address that is associated with a virtual machine. Behind the scene, the floating IP is implemented using DNAT. This allows the virtual machine to be addressable to the external network using the associated floating IP. The floating IP is configured in the external interface of the router; when a packet is sent to the floating IP address, the DNAT rule configured in the router forwards the packet to the virtual machine. The response from the virtual machine is sent to the Internet with the source address translated to the floating IP.

Associating a floating IP to a virtual machine

A floating IP is an address on an external network. Creating an external network is a pre-requisite for floating IPs. Let's first create an external network:

```
$ neutron net-create external1 -shared --router:external True
$ neutron subnet-create external1 --name external-subnet1
--gateway 10.56.11.1 10.56.11.0/24
```

Next, use this network to set the gateway for your virtual router:

```
$ neturon router-gateway-set router1 external1
```

This will add a port on the external network to the router and sets the gateway of the external network as default one of the router. For example, in the previous example, the router `router1` will have its default gateway set to `10.56.11.1`. The virtual machines connected to this router can access the Internet using SNAT.

Finally, create and associate the floating IP. This will make the virtual machine accessible to the Internet by associating external IP to it and implementing DNAT. To do this use the following command:

```
$ neutron floatingip-create external1
$ neutron floatingip-associate floating_ip_id instance_port_id
```

At this point the floating IP is set and DNAT rules are added to the router namespace to forward any traffic to the floating IP address to the IP address of the specified port instance.

Implementing network security in OpenStack

OpenStack provides network security to control access to the virtual networks. Like other network services, the security policy applied to the virtual networks are offered as a self-service feature. The security services are provided either at a network port level using security groups or at the network boundary using the firewall service. In this section, we will discuss the security services provided by the Neutron project.

The security rules that are applied to the incoming and outgoing traffic are based on match condition, which includes the following:

- The source and destination addresses to which the security policy must be applied
- The source and destination ports for the network flow
- The directionality of traffic, Egress/Ingress traffic

The Neutron security services use Linux IPtables to implement security policies.

 For more information on how IPtables works on Linux, `https://www.cen tos.org/docs/5/html/Deployment_Guide-en-US/ch-iptables.html` is a very useful reference.
A complete list of possible target values in IPtables can be found here: `http://www.iptables.info/en/iptables-targets-and-jumps.html`.

Security groups

The security groups are Neutron extensions that allow configuration of network access rules at a port level. With security groups, the tenant can create an access policy to control access to resources within the virtual network. IPtables are configured by means of security groups to perform traffic filtering.

Creating security group policies

The security group rules can be created either using the Neutron CLI or through the OpenStack dashboard. To create the security group using the Neutron CLI, use the `security-group-create` command:

```
$ neutron security-group-create SG1

Created a new security_group:
+----------------------+----------------------------------------------------------------------------------------------------------+
| Field                | Value                                                                                                    |
+----------------------+----------------------------------------------------------------------------------------------------------+
| description          |                                                                                                          |
| id                   | 81ab3baf-a527-4de3-a81e-ea5c9c1cc3aa                                                                     |
| name                 | SG1                                                                                                      |
| security_group_rules | {"remote_group_id": null, "direction": "egress", "protocol": null, "description": "", "ethertype": "IPv4", "remote_ip_prefix": |
|                      | null, "port_range_max": null, "security_group_id": "81ab3baf-a527-4de3-a81e-ea5c9c1cc3aa", "port_range_min": null, "tenant_id": |
|                      | "f8255416667a46168754fc6d8cc5e81b", "id": "3ad1329a-02d7-42b9-9d1d-2e5e3ea93ac6"}                        |
|                      | {"remote_group_id": null, "direction": "egress", "protocol": null, "description": "", "ethertype": "IPv6", "remote_ip_prefix": |
|                      | null, "port_range_max": null, "security_group_id": "81ab3baf-a527-4de3-a81e-ea5c9c1cc3aa", "port_range_min": null, "tenant_id": |
|                      | "f8255416667a46168754fc6d8cc5e81b", "id": "dafcc823-0310-474c-a1bc-247db250d7e1"}                        |
| tenant_id            | f8255416667a46168754fc6d8cc5e81b                                                                         |
+----------------------+----------------------------------------------------------------------------------------------------------+
```

Then to add new rules to the security group, use the Neutron `security-group-rule-create` command. To create the rule, you need to provide the remote address, the protocol that can be TCP, UDP, or ICMP, the protocol port, for example, `80` for HTTP traffic, and the direction of traffic, for example egress for traffic going out or ingress for traffic coming in:

```
$ neutron security-group-rule-create --description "Allow HTTP traffic from anywhere" \
--direction ingress --ethertype IPv4 \
--protocol tcp --port-range-min 80 --port-range-max 80 \
--remote-ip-prefix 0.0.0.0/0 SG1 \

Created a new security_group_rule:
+--------------------+--------------------------------------+
| Field              | Value                                |
+--------------------+--------------------------------------+
| description        |                                      |
| direction          | ingress                              |
| ethertype          | IPv4                                 |
| id                 | f1f2acba-b332-483e-8666-4e669df5ab07 |
| port_range_max     | 80                                   |
| port_range_min     | 80                                   |
| protocol           | tcp                                  |
| remote_group_id    |                                      |
| remote_ip_prefix   | 0.0.0.0/0                            |
| security_group_id  | 81ab3baf-a527-4de3-a81e-ea5c9c1cc3aa |
| tenant_id          | f8255416667a46168754fc6d8cc5e81b     |
+--------------------+--------------------------------------+
```

The same operation can also be performed using the OpenStack dashboard. To manage security groups, navigate to **Compute | Access & Security | Security Group**. Use the **+Create Security Group** button to create a new security group. Use the **Manage Rule** drop down menu to add **Rules** to the security group:

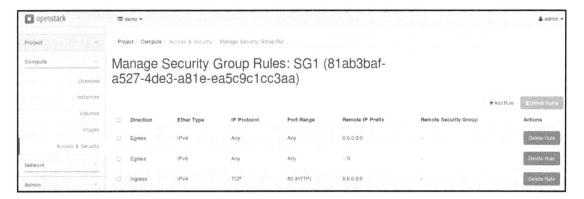

Firewall as a service

The firewall service allows controlling traffic that crosses the network boundary. Firewall policies are applied at the routers, which connect multiple networks. The default firewall driver in Neutron uses IPtables to configure access rules within the router. Unlike the security groups approach which is based on a default deny policy and only creates rules to allow specific traffic, the firewall service allows creation of both allow and deny rules.

Configuring the firewall service

To configure the firewall service, the Neutron configuration file should be updated with the firewall service plugin. The following example shows the settings in `/etc/neutron/neutron.conf` required for the firewall service:

```
[DEFAULT]
service_plugins = router,firewall
```

Next, update the L3 agent configuration file with the firewall driver. The firewall service uses the Neutron L3 agent to configure the IPtables rules:

```
[fwaas]
driver = netron_fwaas.services.firewall.drivers.linux.
iptables_fwaas.IptablesFwaasDriver
enabled = True
```

Next, we will enable the `FWaaS` dashboard in Horizon by updating the OpenStack dashboard configuration file `/usr/share/openstack-dashboard/openstack_dashboard/local/local_settings.py` as follows:

```
...
'enable_FWaaS': True,
```

Finally, restart the Neutron server to load the service plugin and the web server to restart Horizon with the firewall dashboard:

```
$ sudo service httpd restart
$ sudo service neutron-server restart
```

Creating firewall policies and rules

The OpenStack tenant can define network access policies using the Neutron firewall service. The firewall policies are applied at the Layer-3 and control traffic entering or leaving a network. Firewall definition is composed of policies, the firewall policies themselves are composed of individual rules. The rules are defined based on match condition to identify flows of traffic. A firewall rule can explicitly allow or reject traffic flows.

To create a firewall, use the `firewall-policy-create` command to create an empty firewall policy:

```
$ neutron firewall-policy-create  fw-pol1
Created a new firewall_policy:
+------------------+------------------------------------------+
| Field            | Value                                    |
+------------------+------------------------------------------+
| audited          | False                                    |
| description      |                                          |
| firewall_rules   |                                          |
| id               | 39fd89c4-b3ba-4046-89fe-d59ccf60ddc0     |
| name             | fw-pol1                                  |
| shared           | False                                    |
| tenant_id        | f8255416667a46168754fc6d8cc5e81b         |
+------------------+------------------------------------------+
```

Then create a firewall by associating the policy created in the previous step and a router using the `firewall-create` command:

```
$ neutron firewall-create fw-pol1 --router router1
Created a new firewall:
+--------------------+------------------------------------------+
| Field              | Value                                    |
+--------------------+------------------------------------------+
| admin_state_up     | True                                     |
| description        |                                          |
| firewall_policy_id | 39fd89c4-b3ba-4046-89fe-d59ccf60ddc0     |
| id                 | 0546c469-b2c6-47d2-86fa-fe609fa0ef21     |
| name               |                                          |
| router_ids         | ba10e7eb-1f10-4dcf-9b28-ed05eacc9385     |
| status             | PENDING_CREATE                           |
| tenant_id          | f8255416667a46168754fc6d8cc5e81b         |
+--------------------+------------------------------------------+
```

Access rules can be added to the firewall policy using the `firewall-rule-create` command:

```
$ neutron firewall-rule-create --source-ip-address 0.0.0.0/0 \
--destination-ip-address 192.168.0.20 --destination-port 80 \
--protocol tcp --action allow

Created a new firewall_rule:
+------------------------+--------------------------------------+
| Field                  | Value                                |
+------------------------+--------------------------------------+
| action                 | allow                                |
| description            |                                      |
| destination_ip_address | 192.168.0.20                         |
| destination_port       | 80                                   |
| enabled                | True                                 |
| firewall_policy_id     |                                      |
| id                     | a1c8d52a-8207-4e4f-aef2-6422b0c6f065 |
| ip_version             | 4                                    |
| name                   |                                      |
| position               |                                      |
| protocol               | tcp                                  |
| shared                 | False                                |
| source_ip_address      | 0.0.0.0/0                            |
| source_port            |                                      |
| tenant_id              | f8255416667a46168754fc6d8cc5e81b     |
+------------------------+--------------------------------------+
```

Then use the `firewall-policy-update` or `firewall-policy-insert-rule` command to update the firewall policy. The order of rules added to the firewall policy determines how packets traversing the firewall will be evaluated. This point must be kept in mind while providing the rule list during the firewall policy update. The `firewall-policy-insert-rule` command can be used to insert a single rule in the firewall policy. To identify the position of the rule in the firewall policy, use the `--insert-before` or `--insert-after` option.

```
$ neutron firewall-policy-update --firewall-rules a1c8d52a-8207-4e4f-aef2-6422b0c6f065 fw-pol1
Updated firewall_policy: fw-pol1


$ neutron firewall-policy-show fw-pol1
+-----------------+-------------------------------------------+
| Field           | Value                                     |
+-----------------+-------------------------------------------+
| audited         | False                                     |
| description     |                                           |
| firewall_rules  | a1c8d52a-8207-4e4f-aef2-6422b0c6f065      |
| id              | 39fd89c4-b3ba-4046-89fe-d59ccf60ddc0      |
| name            | fw-pol1                                   |
| shared          | False                                     |
| tenant_id       | f8255416667a46168754fc6d8cc5e81b          |
+-----------------+-------------------------------------------+
```

To verify the applied firewall policy, check the IPtables configuration in the router
namespace:

```
$ sudo ip netns exec qrouter-ba10e7eb-1f10-4dcf-9b28-ed05eacc9385 iptables -L -n|grep 80
ACCEPT     tcp  --  0.0.0.0/0              192.168.0.20           tcp dpt:80
ACCEPT     tcp  --  0.0.0.0/0              192.168.0.20           tcp dpt:80
```

Inter-site connectivity with VPN service

As business grows, it might be necessary to expand the cloud environment to multiple data
centers. Of course, the implementation of a VPN setup whether it is a simple SSL one or an
IPSEC solution will provide a secure communication path for the tenant traffic across the
Internet. OpenStack provides isolated networks and network access control to avoid traffic
congestion and improve the security of the internal network of the OpenStack environment.
The **VPN as a Service** (**VPNaaS**) function protects the integrity of data by using the
tunneling and encryption to provide a secure connection between machines that are
geographically located in different data centers.

The next figure depicts two different OpenStack data centers, and we intend to link their associated tenants. You may remember that a project in horizon presents a tenant description that includes its private networks, routers, and subnets:

 Add an admin user to each project in the admin role. This will allow you to fully perform administrative tasks in horizon. Additionally, you can create different users per project and assign a service type to it using an admin account.

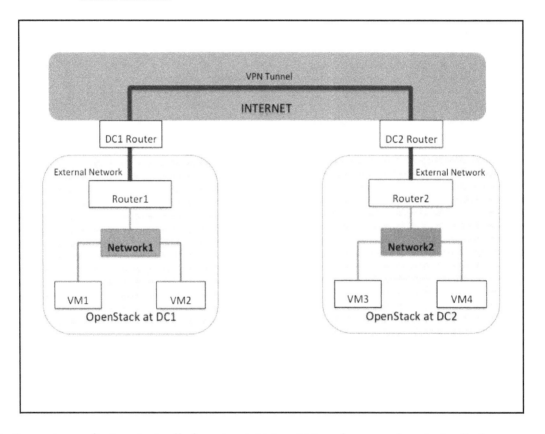

Let's create our first project called `PackPub01` in `DC01` and a second project called `PacktPub02` in `DC02`.

Based on the previous illustration, we intend to let the machines in both the OpenStack subnets talk to each other. Note that each subnet sits behind a gateway router. Each project's network has a defined subnet that serves local IP addresses, whereas a router connects to the external public interface of each network. The connection between both the public IP addresses will be encrypted and sent over a tunnel by means of VPN service.

The following table shows the topology at DC1 and DC2 and the network addressing:

Data center	Network	Subnet	Router	Router external net IP
DC1	Network1	192.168.47.0/24	Router1	172.24.4.X
DC2	Network2	192.168.48.0/24	Router2	172.24.4.Y

The router gateway IP can be found by navigating to **Network│Router** then selecting the router and navigating to the**Overview tab**. The **External Fixed IPs** shows the router external net IP.

 Subnets in different datacenters must have non-overlapping IP address ranges.

Configuring the VPN service plugin

Let's bring up the VPN service by using the following steps:

1. To create a full site-to-site IPsec VPN, we will use Openswan IPsec implementation for Linux. Neutron supports Openswan by providing a driver, which needs to be configured and started. Additionally, we will need the neutron-plugin-vpn-agent package to be installed on the network nodes in each site as follows:

   ```
   $ sudo yum install neutron-vpn-agent openswan
   $ sudo service ipsec start
   ```

2. Update the VPN service agent file /etc/neutron/vpn_agent.ini to use the Openswan driver as follows:

   ```
   ...
   [vpnagent]
   vpn_device_driver=neutron.services.vpn.
   device_drivers.ipsec.OpenSwanDriver
   ```

3. Enable VPN service in Neutron by adding `vpnaas` to the list of service plugins in `/etc/neutron/neutron.conf` as follows:

```
[DEFAULT]
service_plugins =.. ,vpnaas
```

4. In the same file, enable the VPN service provider to use the `openswan` driver in the `service_provider` section as follows:

```
...
[service_providers]
service_provider= VPN:openswan:neutron.services.vpn.
service_drivers.ipsec.IPsecVPNDriver:default
```

5. Next, we will enable the `VPNaaS` dashboard in horizon by updating `/usr/share/openstack-dashboard/openstack_dashboard/local/local_settings.py` as follows:

```
'enable_VPNaaS': True,
```

6. Finally, restart `neutron-server` and `neutron-vpn-agent` services, and the web server, as follows:

```
$ sudo service httpd restart
$ sudo service neutron-server restart
$ sudo service neutron-vpn-agent restart
```

To read more about Openswan, check the official website: `https://www.openswan.org/`.

Creating the VPN service

Let's create the VPN connection to connect the two networks in DC1 and DC2. We will start by configuring VPN on DC1.

Creating the Internet Key Exchange policy

In Horizon, we can create the **Internet Key Exchange (IKE)** policy in the first VPN phase. The following screenshot shows a simple IKE setup of an OpenStack environment that is in the DC01 site:

An IKE policy can also be created by using the `neutron` command line, as follows:

$ neutron vpn-ikepolicy-create --auth-algorithm sha1 --encryption-algorithm aes-256 --ike-version v2 --lifetime units=seconds,value=3600 --pfs group5 --phase1-negotiation-mode main --name PP-IKE-Policy

Creating an IPSec policy

The creation of an IPSec policy in the OpenStack environment that is in the `DC01` site in horizon can be done in the following way:

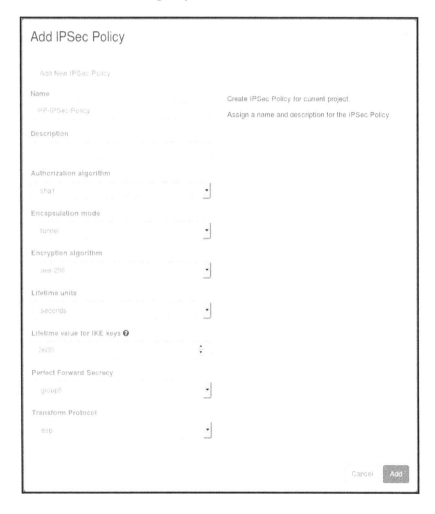

An IPSec policy can also be created by using the `neutron` command line, as follows:

$ neutron vpn-ipsecpolicy-create --auth-algorithm sha1 --encapsulation-mode tunnel --encryption-algorithm aes-256 --lifetime units=seconds,value=36000 --pfs group5 --transform-protocol esp -name PP_IPSEC_Policy

Standard VPN settings, such as **Encapsulation mode**, **Encryption algorithm**, **Perfect Forward Secrecy**, and **Transform Protocol,** should remain the same in both the sites for phase 1.

If you face a VPN connectivity problem, a best practice of troubleshooting before filtering or debugging the traffic is to begin checking the existence of any mismatch of the phase 1 and phase 2 settings in both sites.

Creating a VPN service

To create a VPN service, we will need to specify the router facing the external interface and attach the web server instance to the private network in the `DC01` site. The router will act as a VPN gateway. We can add a new VPN service from Horizon in the following way:

A VPN service can also be created by using the neutron command line, as follows:

$ neutron vpn-service-create --tenant-id c4ea3292ca234ddea5d50260e7e58193 --name PP_VPN_Service Router-VPN public_subnet

Keep in mind that a VPN service is needed to select the router that will perform your VPN gateway. Note that here, we have exposed our local subnet 192.168.47.0/24.

Creating an IPSec site connection

The last step needs some information. Usually, we need to set up an external IP address of the other peer for a VPN site. In OpenStack, you can check it by logging on as an admin and from the PacktPub02 tenant, clicking on the**Router** section. Here, you get the necessary details , which present information regarding the external gateway interface, 172.24.4.227. The **Remote peer subnet(s)** value is the CIDR notation 192.168.48.0/24. We will finish our first project, the DC01 VPNaaS connection, by setting the secret preshared key to AwEsOmEVPn. The key will be the same for both the sides. The process of setting the key is depicted in the following screenshot:

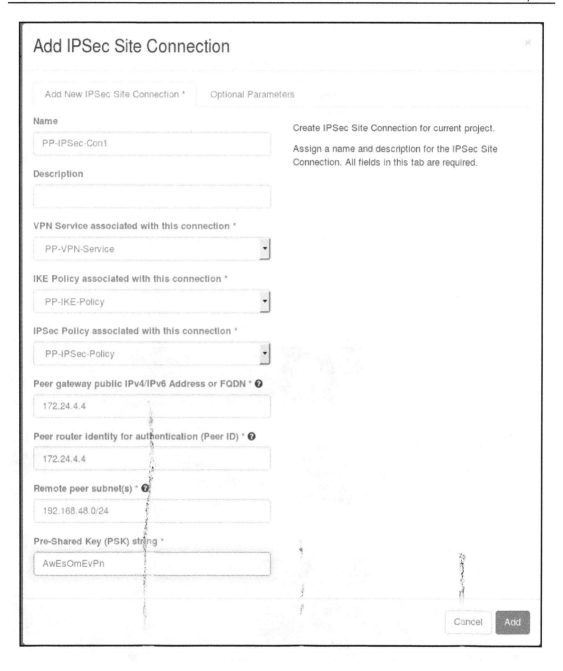

Add IPSec Site Connection

| Add New IPSec Site Connection * | Optional Parameters |

Name

PP-IPSec-Con1

Description

VPN Service associated with this connection *

PP-VPN-Service

IKE Policy associated with this connection *

PP-IKE-Policy

IPSec Policy associated with this connection *

PP-IPSec-Policy

Peer gateway public IPv4/IPv6 Address or FQDN * ❷

172.24.4.4

Peer router identity for authentication (Peer ID) * ❷

172.24.4.4

Remote peer subnet(s) * ❷

192.168.48.0/24

Pre-Shared Key (PSK) string *

AwEsOmEvPn

Create IPSec Site Connection for current project.

Assign a name and description for the IPSec Site Connection. All fields in this tab are required.

Cancel   Add

A VPN service can also be created by using the `neutron` command line, as follows:

**# neutron ipsec-site-connection-create --name PP_IPSEC
---vpnservice-id PP_VPN_Service --ikepolicy-id
PP-IKE-Policy --ipsecpolicy-id PP_IPSEC_Policy
--peer-address 192.168.48.0/24 --peer-id 172.24.4.232
--psk AwEsOmEvPn**

The peer gateway public IPv4 address can be obtained from the router details of `DC02`. We will need to hit the external interface, as shown in the following screenshot:

To finish the VPN setup, you will need to follow the latter steps, but changing the IP gateway addresses of `DC01` and the remote subnet to `192.168.47.0/24`. Note that the VPN settings, encryption algorithms and protocols, and the shared password must be the same on both the sides.

A small smoke test can evaluate our setup.

From an instance in `DC01`, we can ping the `DC02` site via `192.168.48.12`, as follows:

```
$ ip addr list
1: lo: <LOOPBACK,UP,LOWER_UP> mtu 16436 qdisc noqueue
    link/loopback 00:00:00:00:00:00 brd 00:00:00:00:00:00
    inet 127.0.0.1/8 scope host lo
    inet6 ::1/128 scope host
       valid_lft forever preferred_lft forever
2: eth0: <BROADCAST,MULTICAST,UP,LOWER_UP> mtu 1450 qdisc pfifo_fast qlen 1000
    link/ether fa:16:3e:ca:1c:5c brd ff:ff:ff:ff:ff:ff
    inet 192.168.47.4/24 brd 192.168.47.255 scope global eth0
    inet6 fe80::f816:3eff:feca:1c5c/64 scope link
       valid_lft forever preferred_lft forever
$ ping 192.168.48.1
PING 192.168.48.1 (192.168.48.1): 56 data bytes
64 bytes from 192.168.48.1: seq=0 ttl=63 time=2.575 ms
64 bytes from 192.168.48.1: seq=1 ttl=63 time=1.370 ms
64 bytes from 192.168.48.1: seq=2 ttl=63 time=8.423 ms

--- 192.168.48.1 ping statistics ---
3 packets transmitted, 3 packets received, 0% packet loss
round-trip min/avg/max = 1.370/4.122/8.423 ms
$
```

Make sure that you have enabled ICMP on the DC02 router to allow ping traffic.

Summary

In this chapter, we delved into the various aspects of networking services in OpenStack. At this point, you should be comfortable with networking services. You should also be aware of the benefits of the Neutron API and the support of several plugins that allow you to diversify the networking hardware setup within OpenStack.

We started with Layer-2 networking choices and discussed about the routing service. Next, we discussed security functions such as FWaaS and security groups. At this stage, you should be able to understand the difference between FWaaS and the security groups and how to configure them at the network and port level.

Finally, a straightforward step-by-step guide showed another awesome point of Neutron by leveraging the networking security using VPNaaS-Neutron is very extensible and powerful. As it is a critical aspect of your OpenStack infrastructure that is responsible for network management, you should consider that Neutron can be a single point of failure as well as any other OpenStack node in your environment.

In the next chapter, we will look at more advanced networking topic such as SDN and NFV and understand how they fit in to the OpenStack environment.

7

Advanced Networking - A Look at SDN and NFV

"Without education, you are not going anywhere in this world."
- Malcolm X

Networking is one of the most complex services in the cloud-computing stack. The advent of cloud computing has put extraordinary demands on the networking service. The modern network service, on the one hand, must be able to deal with the use cases of extreme flexibility for connecting arbitrary endpoints. On the other hand, the networking infrastructure must provide high performance communication channels and allow for quick provisioning of new services.

The service providers are looking for a minimal ordering lead time to provision new infrastructure for ever-increasing demand for network services, while at the same time they demand an infrastructure that can scale up to customer demand and scale down during the full period to save power, infrastructure, and real estate cost.

OpenStack has embraced new projects to enable these new use cases. In this chapter, we will look at new networking services, which are quickly evolving to cater to the demands the cloud has put on the network:

- We will look at **Open Virtual Network (OVN)** as an SDN implementation
- We will look at Tacker, which provides an NFV platform using OpenStack
- Finally we will look at the LBaaS v2 implementation with Octavia, which uses virtual appliances to provide a load balancer service

Let's start our journey by exploring the SDN-based networks.

Understanding SDN-based networks

One of the emerging approaches to networking is **software-defined networking** (**SDN**). The SDN philosophy proposes a programmable network that provides the flexibility of defining how packets will be forwarded in the network. The forwarding rules can be programmed using a controller. In a cloud infrastructure where the knowledge of topology and location of network endpoints are centrally available to the cloud, the cloud controller, SDN provides the APIs for programming how the networking infrastructure will transfer packets between the various consumers of the networking service.

SDN brings in the concept of programmable networks, where the flow of packets in the network can be controlled and defined using software-based control. One of the implementations of this approach uses a centralized controller to program switches with packet flow entries. The packet flow entries are a combination of a match condition and corresponding action, which must be performed on a packet. A simple example of this may be a packet drop rule for a certain destination.

To enable this kind of control over the packet forwarding path, the networking device must expose an interface to the low-level flow control.

The OpenFlow specification describes a standard to expose this low level control using flow entry programming. It provides the programming semantics for the flow definition. An OpenFlow enabled switch is managed by a controller, which can install flow entries on the managed switch over a secure connection. The OpenFlow specification describes how these rules should be arranged to match tables. When a packet arrives on the switch, it passes through a series of flow rules, which try to match the packet and take an appropriate forwarding decision, or forward the table to the next table. If the packet does not match any rule, it is forwarded to the controller which analyzes the packet and generates flow rules to handle the packet and installs them on the switch. This type of rule install is called reactive flow programming. As the controller is a centralized entity, which can interface with other network and compute management software, it can gain complete knowledge of the network topology. Using this knowledge, it can pre-populate rules on the switch using proactive programming. An example of proactive flow programming would be to install flow rules for a virtual machine which is yet to be provisioned.

With an SDN-based approach, the control function of the network devices is decoupled from the forwarding function. A central SDN controller handles the control of the network flows while the switch handles the high throughput forwarding function.

The SDN architecture challenges the basic constructs of current networking implementation where the forwarding functions are statically defined; for example, the layer 2 learning in a switch is a well-defined process and is mostly a static one.

SDN proposes a more flexible and software controllable packet forwarding architecture.

OVS architecture

We have already discussed about OpenVSwitch in `Chapter 6`, *OpenStack Networking - Choice of Connectivity Types and Networking Services*. OVS is a virtual switch implementation; it uses flow programming semantics of the OpenFlow specification. It exposes interfaces for switch management using the OVSDB protocol and flow programming using the OpenFlow specification. An OVS instance can be either locally configured with flow rules or it can connect to an SDN controller which pushes the flow entries.

On an OpenStack node installed with an OVS switch, you can see the flow specification using the `ovs-ofctl dump-flows br-int` command.

The following diagram shows OVS instances managed by an SDN controller:

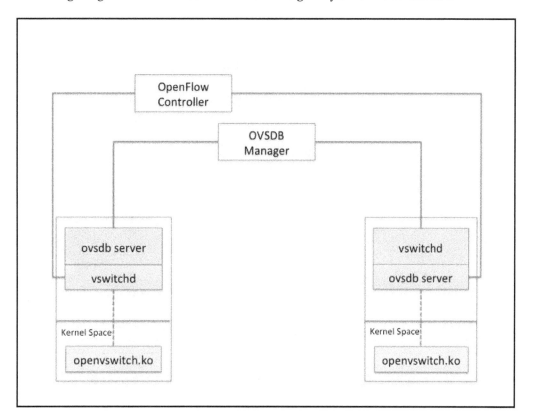

The OVS switch consists of a user-space database called ovsdb that can connect to an ovsdb manager and receives switch configuration data. The vswitchd daemon, on the other hand, connects to the SDN controller and receives flow programming data.

Architecture of OVN

The OVN is an implementation based on SDN architecture. As the SDN architecture evolved, it became apparent that the centralized controller could be a bottleneck when deployed in large networks with hundreds of switches. The architecture of OVN removes this drawback by using multiple OVS databases and controllers to provide a programmable virtual networking solution:

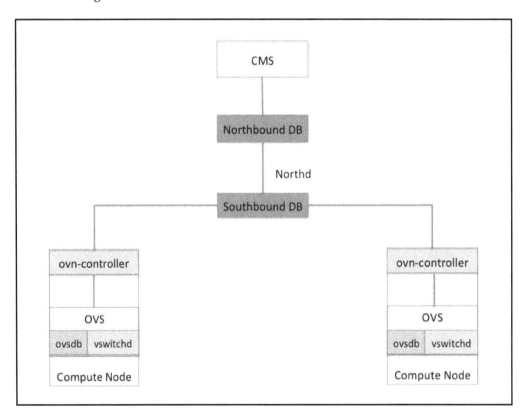

In this section, we will learn about the OVN components and their integration with OpenStack.

Components of OVN

The core of the OVN solution is the OpenVSwitch that implements programmable flow rules using OpenFlow. Unlike other SDN solutions that are based on a centralized controller and the virtual switches connecting to it, the OVN project uses multiple levels of controllers. These controllers manage abstractions that are stored in different ovsdb databases.

The OVN project is composed of the following components:

- **Northbound database**: The northbound database is an instance of ovsdb used by OVN to store high-level abstraction of the virtual networks. The Northbound database stores the virtual network abstractions that match the concepts of the **cloud management system** (**CMS**) such as OpenStack. Some examples of the tables in this database are, `Logical_Switch`, `ACL`, `Logical_Router`, and `Logical_Switch_Port`. As can be seen from the table names, there is a close relationship of the information in this database with the OpenStack networking abstractions.

- **Southbound database**: The southbound database, on the other hand, is closer to the implementation details. The Southbound database stores the physical and logical network data. It also contains the data binding between the logical and physical networks, logical flows. Some of the examples of the tables in this database are `Port_Binding`, `Mac_Binding`, and `Logicla_Flow`.

- **OVN-controller**: The OVN-controller acts like a conventional L2 agent. It is installed on the compute nodes. It connects to the OVN southbound database over the TCP connection and receives updates. The controller then programs the OpenFlow rules on the OVS switch. It uses a Unix domain socket to connect to the local ovsdb database.

- **OVS**: The OVS switch provides the data path for packet forwarding. It gets its forwarding rules updated by the OVN-controller.

- **OVN-northd daemon**: The job of the OVN-northd daemon is to connect the northbound database to the southbound database. It provides translation of high level abstraction stored in the northbound database to a format more suitable for use by the OVN-controller.

Integrating OVN with OpenStack

The OVN project provides switching and routing services between the virtual instances. It also provides a gateway service to connect virtual networks to physical networks. OVN can integrate with CMS such as OpenStack using an ML2 mechanism driver and L3 service plugin. It also provides an implementation of the security group APIs.

OVN can be installed using the following packages: the `openvswitch-ovn` package on RedHat-based distributions, and `ovn-central`, `ovn-host`, `ovn-docker`, and `ovn-common` for Ubuntu systems. This should install the required OVS packages. The OVN drivers for neutron can be installed using the `python-networking-ovn` package.

The controller node runs the ovsdb northbound and southbound servers. It also runs the OVN northd daemon, while the compute nodes run the OVN controller.

To configure the OVN ML2 driver, use the following configuration in `/etc/neutron/plugins/ml2/ml2_conf.ini` on the controller node:

```
[ml2]
tenant_network_types = geneve
extension_drivers = port_security
type_drivers = local,flat,vlan,geneve
mechanism_drivers = ovn,logger
[ml2_type_geneve]
max_header_size = 58
vni_ranges = 1:65536
```

OVN uses `geneve` as the tunneling protocol to create virtual overlay networks. The advantage of using `geneve` encapsulation is its ability to encode networking metadata in the encapsulation header. An encapsulation format such as VXLAN is still supported for gateway devices such as physical switches that connect a tunneled network to a physical network. However, the VXLAN encapsulation can only encode the **virtual network identifier** (**VNI**) in the encapsulation header, while `geneve` uses extensible TLVs to encapsulate variable length metadata in the header that can be used to carry information such as packet ingress and egress ports. Another advantage of using `geneve` is the use of a randomized source port for creating the tunnels. This is a big gain when used with ECMP, which uses the source port as one of the parameters to determine the tunnel path.

The OVN controller manages the local OVS instance on the compute node and receives its configuration by connecting to the OVN Southbound database on the controller node.

On the compute nodes, the OVN controller must be told about the location of the northbound and southbound databases. This can be done using the following settings in the `ml2_config.ini`:

```
[ovn]
ovn_l3_mode = True
ovn_sb_connection = tcp:192.168.122.126:6642
ovn_nb_connection = tcp:192.168.122.126:6641
```

The OVN project also provides an L3 service plugin. To use the L3 plugin, use the following configuration in the `/etc/neutron/neutron.conf` file:

```
service_plugins = L3_SERVICE
```

Implementing virtual networks with OVN

Once the OVN plugins are configured, OVN handles the creation of virtual networks and routers. In this section, we will explore the mapping between OpenStack abstractions such as virtual networks, ports, and the corresponding entries in the OVN northbound and southbound databases.

Let's start by examining the L2 networks and ports and how they are mapped to the OVN northbound abstractions. List the virtual networks using the `neutron net-list` commands:

```
$ neutron net-list
+--------------------------------------+---------+--------------------------------------------------------------------+
| id                                   | name    | subnets                                                            |
+--------------------------------------+---------+--------------------------------------------------------------------+
| 4ae49ded-5b49-4cf5-92b4-a31690894461 | public  | 228c523c-fbd3-4603-aa71-1a49401d7ebb                               |
|                                      |         | 92f8f390-a70a-4dad-ac7e-fbf9551023a3                               |
| 9047a3be-a2a6-42cb-9c44-8752da25abcd | private | 5382d80c-ee3f-4cc6-9923-77397856111b 10.0.0.0/24                   |
|                                      |         | 2272a2ac-26f1-410f-9d8f-a608645fc463 fd5e:cb35:8d04::/64           |
+--------------------------------------+---------+--------------------------------------------------------------------+
```

OVN maps the virtual networks to **logical switches (ls)** and the virtual ports to **logical switch ports (lsp)**. To view the corresponding entries in the northbound database, use the `ovn-nbctl ls-list` command:

```
$ sudo ovn-nbctl ls-list
f548a9b1-d868-47da-b180-1616337c35f0 (neutron-4ae49ded-5b49-4cf5-92b4-a31690894461)
23ac2ea6-a6e5-4ca2-ae08-e09326db506f (neutron-9047a3be-a2a6-42cb-9c44-8752da25abcd)
```

You can also examine the logical switch and the ports attached to the logical switch using the `ovn-nbctl lsp-list` and `show` commands:

```
$ sudo ovn-nbctl show f548a9b1-d868-47da-b180-1616337c35f0
    switch f548a9b1-d868-47da-b180-1616337c35f0 (neutron-4ae49ded-5b49-4cf5-92b4-a31690894461)
        port 6596f75e-ac45-4ff1-9989-91a6f31eadfa
            addresses: ["fa:16:3e:59:96:e3 172.24.4.4 2001:db8::a"]

$ sudo ovn-nbctl lsp-list f548a9b1-d868-47da-b180-1616337c35f0
0013af45-15e1-4a5d-bd5c-028142b3531c (6596f75e-ac45-4ff1-9989-91a6f31eadfa)
```

OVN refers to the virtual router and router ports and the **logical router** (**lr**) and **logical router ports** (**lrp**). To check the L3 router and router ports use the `ovn-nbctl lr-list` command:

```
$ neutron router-list
+--------------------------------------+---------+-----------------------------------------------------------------------------------------------+
| id                                   | name    | external_gateway_info                                                                         |
+--------------------------------------+---------+-----------------------------------------------------------------------------------------------+
| e1c54e0c-2f2f-46f5-ae9a-d8b5bd0e2340 | router1 | {"network_id": "4ae49ded-5b49-4cf5-92b4-a31690894461", "external_fixed_ips": [{"subnet_id": "92f8f390 |
|                                      |         | -a70a-4dad-ac7e-fbf9551023a3", "ip_address": "172.24.4.4"}, {"subnet_id": "228c523c-           |
|                                      |         | fbd3-4603-aa71-1a49401d7ebb", "ip_address": "2001:db8::a"}]}                                   |
+--------------------------------------+---------+-----------------------------------------------------------------------------------------------+

$ sudo ovn-nbctl lr-list
067821ab-308b-493d-8618-d3e2b2624d40 (neutron-e1c54e0c-2f2f-46f5-ae9a-d8b5bd0e2340)

$ sudo ovn-nbctl show 067821ab-308b-493d-8618-d3e2b2624d40
    router 067821ab-308b-493d-8618-d3e2b2624d40 (neutron-e1c54e0c-2f2f-46f5-ae9a-d8b5bd0e2340)
        port lrp-a314242e-7dab-4c7c-b6b6-7f8d1453594e
            mac: "fa:16:3e:55:66:fd"
        port lrp-530cca5c-5338-4273-86dd-644832b5ba72
            mac: "fa:16:3e:48:48:3a"
```

The high-level entities stored in the northbound database are then converted to logical flow entries by the `ovn-northd` daemon and stored in the southbound database. You can view these flow entries using the `ovn-sbctl lflow-list` command:

```
$ sudo ovn-sbctl lflow-list
Datapath: 01fbe7e4-a2c6-45bb-bacd-f64fb6f09f8a  Pipeline: ingress
  table=0(ls_in_port_sec_l2), priority= 100, match=(eth.src[40]), action=(drop;)
  table=0(ls_in_port_sec_l2), priority= 100, match=(vlan.present), action=(drop;)
  table=0(ls_in_port_sec_l2), priority=  50, match=(inport == "530cca5c-5338-4273-86dd-644832b5ba72"), action=(next;)
  table=0(ls_in_port_sec_l2), priority=  50, match=(inport == "a314242e-7dab-4c7c-b6b6-7f8d1453594e"), action=(next;)
  table=0(ls_in_port_sec_l2), priority=  50, match=(inport == "e1077206-4cad-4631-b1ea-257304db7d26"), action=(next;)
  table=1(ls_in_port_sec_ip), priority=   0, match=(1), action=(next;)
  table=2(ls_in_port_sec_nd), priority=   0, match=(1), action=(next;)
  table=3(   ls_in_pre_acl), priority=   0, match=(1), action=(next;)
  table=4(    ls_in_pre_lb), priority=   0, match=(1), action=(next;)
  table=5(ls_in_pre_stateful), priority= 100, match=(reg0[0] == 1), action=(ct_next;)
  table=5(ls_in_pre_stateful), priority=   0, match=(1), action=(next;)
  table=6(      ls_in_acl), priority=   0, match=(1), action=(next;)
  table=7(       ls_in_lb), priority=   0, match=(1), action=(next;)
  table=8(  ls_in_stateful), priority= 100, match=(reg0[1] == 1), action=(ct_commit; next;)
  table=8(  ls_in_stateful), priority= 100, match=(reg0[2] == 1), action=(ct_lb;)
  table=8(  ls_in_stateful), priority=   0, match=(1), action=(next;)
```

Finally, the ovn-controller on the compute nodes connects to the OVN southbound database to receive the logical flow entries and configure the local OVS switch. We have already discussed how to view the OVS switch configuration and flow entries in Chapter 6, *OpenStack Networking - Choice of Connectivity Types and Networking Services*, using the ovs-vsctl show and ovs-ofctl dump-flows commands.

Understanding network function virtualization

While SDN is all about flexibility and programmability of how the packets flow in the network, the next topic of discussion focuses on how the network services are provisioned. In the legacy approach to accommodate new networking services, the service providers must acquire new equipment, allocate power and data center real estate for the device, and then start the provisioning of services. This approach is both costly and inflexible in terms of resource allocation. NFV advocates the virtualization of network infrastructures such as routers, firewalls, and load balancers. In our discussion of NFV, we will understand how NFV brings in elasticity of network resources and look at the OpenStack-based NFV solution.

With the growth of virtual data centers and on-demand networks, there is an increasing need for an elastic networking infrastructure that can be brought to life to handle increased connectivity demands and can be decommissioned when the requirements go down. This is a challenge that the network service providers have been facing. In the conventional approach, to provision a new service meant procuring new physical devices allocating power and space in the data center, connecting the device to the network. The disadvantage of this approach is the long wait time in ordering devices and increasing real estate, connectivity, and power cost, but the most important one is the non-existence of a scale down option.

NFV is the proposed solution to the current situation; it aims to virtualize the networking function within the data center. This requires conversion of physical network devices such as routers, firewalls, and load-balancers to be converted to virtual form factors known as the **virtual network function** (**VNF**). The network service provider can then scale up the network infrastructure by spawning new instances of the VNF devices and scale down infrastructure by shutting off unused NFV instances. This provides the service providers with the required flexibility for dealing with changing connectivity demands.

The Management and Orchestration (MANO) specifications

With the realization of converting a network function in to a virtualized form comes the next set of challenges: the management of these VNFs in the data center. Although the concept of NFV shows the path to a scalable network infrastructure, it does not specify how to manage the life cycle of these virtual functions. The MANO specification describes the management of the NFV platform. It describes the following concepts:

- **Virtual Infrastructure Manager** (**VIM**): The VIM manages the compute, network, and storage resources required to host a virtualized network function such as a virtual router.
- **NFV Manager** (**NFVM**): A NFVM is responsible for on-boarding new virtualized network function appliances. It maintains a catalog of available virtualized network functions. The user can then launch these virtual appliances in the VIM.
- **NFV Orchestrator** (**NFVO**): The function of the NFVO is to manage the life cycle of the VNF instance.

Topology and Orchestration Specification for Cloud Applications (TOSCA) templates

Now that we understand the need for NFV and its related management concepts, let's talk about the VNF itself. The VNF is a virtual form of a conventional networking device. The virtual instance must be described in terms of its storage, compute, and connectivity requirements. This is where the TOSCA templates come into the picture. In reality, the TOSCA templates can describe much more than a simple VNF. It can describe network resources such as subnets, images to deploy, and the memory and CPU allocation for the VNF.

Looking at the Tacker project

So where does OpenStack fit in to this NFV ecosystem? NFV deployment requires a VIM. We discussed earlier that the VIM manages the compute, storage, and network resources needed to instantiate a VNF. This job can be easily done by a cloud system such as OpenStack. The Tacker project augments the services of OpenStack by providing the NFV manager and NFV Orchestrator components. Let's look at the process of creatiing a VNF instance on an OpenStack deployment.

We start by registering the OpenStack infrastructure as the VIM for deploying VNFs. To do this, navigate to the **NFV** | **NFV Orchestration** | **VIM Management** panel:

Register your OpenStack installation; the local installation is already registered but you can add another one if needed:

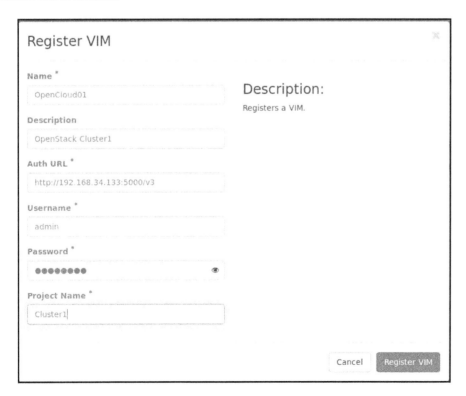

Once the VIM is ready, the next step is to add a VNF template. This process is called VNF onboarding. To do this, navigate to the **VNF Management** | **VNF catalog** and click **OnBoard VNF**. To onboard a new VNF, you must provide a TOSCA template that describes the VNF:

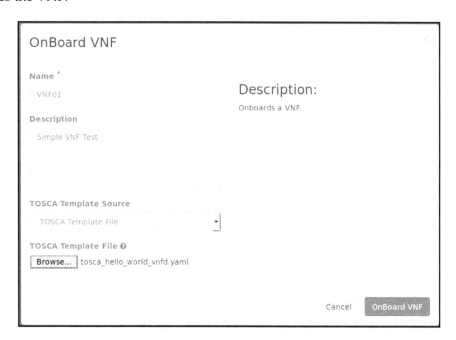

The next step is to deploy instances of a VNF. To do this, navigate to **NFV** | **VNF Management** | **VNF Manager** and click on **Deploy VNF**:

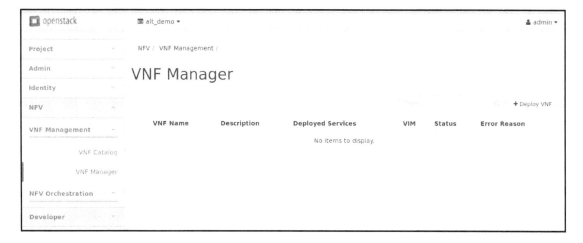

To create a new VNF, you have to select the VNF template from the catalog. You can also pass parameters to customize your VNF instance:

Once you have launched the VNF instance, you can view the same at **Admin** | **System** | **Instance**:

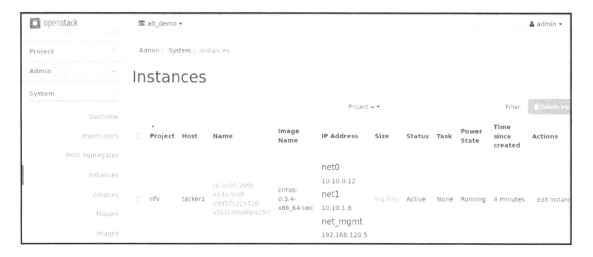

Deploying LBaaS service with Octavia

The load balancer service in neutron has evolved to v2 APIs. The new LBaaS APIs allow for creating multiple listeners on a single load balancer IP. Octavia is an implementation of LBaaS v2 APIs. Octavia uses a virtual appliance-based approach for providing the load balancer service.

Configuring Octavia

To configure Octavia, update the service plugin in neutron.conf to include the following:

```
service_plugins =
neutron_lbaas.services.loadbalancer.plugin.LoadBalancerPluginv2
service_provider =
LOADBALANCERV2:Octavia:neutron_lbaas.drivers.octavia.driver.OctaviaDriver:d
efault
```

Creating a load balancer

To create a `loadbalancer`, we start by creating two server instances that will run the actual service. You should note the IP address assigned to this server:

```
$ nova list
+--------------------------------------+-------+--------+------------+-------------+------------------------------------------------------------+
| ID                                   | Name  | Status | Task State | Power State | Networks                                                   |
+--------------------------------------+-------+--------+------------+-------------+------------------------------------------------------------+
| d4bba922-bc85-4025-8206-b8240db7a4a3 | node1 | ACTIVE | -          | Running     | private=fd96:a0e7:78f4:0:f816:3eff:fe53:b46e, 10.0.0.10    |
| 1b2966d7-abe4-4c40-993b-79e4f9799217 | node2 | ACTIVE | -          | Running     | private=fd96:a0e7:78f4:0:f816:3eff:fe75:c1c4, 10.0.0.8     |
+--------------------------------------+-------+--------+------------+-------------+------------------------------------------------------------+
```

Next we create the `loadbalancer` instance. This step will launch a virtual appliance that provides the `lbaaS` service:

```
$ neutron lbaas-loadbalancer-create --name lb1 private-subnet
Created a new loadbalancer:
+---------------------+--------------------------------------+
| Field               | Value                                |
+---------------------+--------------------------------------+
| admin_state_up      | True                                 |
| description         |                                      |
| id                  | 08583f1a-316f-4db5-bcfa-95f7d319543c |
| listeners           |                                      |
| name                | lb1                                  |
| operating_status    | OFFLINE                              |
| pools               |                                      |
| provider            | octavia                              |
| provisioning_status | PENDING_CREATE                       |
| tenant_id           | 96a927af6870461fa427732d8b73da1b     |
| vip_address         | 10.0.0.7                             |
| vip_port_id         | 318beb73-6f2d-44ac-bec3-e7c405e3258d |
| vip_subnet_id       | 5330af21-0640-465e-8be0-d6a4bd0961cd |
+---------------------+--------------------------------------+
```

It takes a little time for the virtual machine to come up and be active:

```
$ neutron lbaas-loadbalancer-show lb1
+---------------------+------------------------------------------+
| Field               | Value                                    |
+---------------------+------------------------------------------+
| admin_state_up      | True                                     |
| description         |                                          |
| id                  | 08583f1a-316f-4db5-bcfa-95f7d319543c     |
| listeners           |                                          |
| name                | lb1                                      |
| operating_status    | ONLINE                                   |
| pools               |                                          |
| provider            | octavia                                  |
| provisioning_status | ACTIVE                                   |
| tenant_id           | 96a927af6870461fa427732d8b73da1b         |
| vip_address         | 10.0.0.7                                 |
| vip_port_id         | 318beb73-6f2d-44ac-bec3-e7c405e3258d     |
| vip_subnet_id       | 5330af21-0640-465e-8be0-d6a4bd0961cd     |
+---------------------+------------------------------------------+
```

Once the `loadbalancer` service becomes active, create a `listener` for the `loadbalancer`. A `listener` is associated with a `port` on the `loadbalancer` IP. Note that multiple listeners using different ports can be associated with the `loadbalancer`:

```
$ neutron lbaas-listener-create --loadbalancer lb1 --protocol HTTP --protocol-port 80 --name listener1
Created a new listener:
+--------------------------+------------------------------------------------+
| Field                    | Value                                          |
+--------------------------+------------------------------------------------+
| admin_state_up           | True                                           |
| connection_limit         | -1                                             |
| default_pool_id          |                                                |
| default_tls_container_ref |                                               |
| description              |                                                |
| id                       | c0b38610-6b2d-4025-9554-c7e216c4f04b           |
| loadbalancers            | {"id": "08583f1a-316f-4db5-bcfa-95f7d319543c"} |
| name                     | listener1                                      |
| protocol                 | HTTP                                           |
| protocol_port            | 80                                             |
| sni_container_refs       |                                                |
| tenant_id                | 96a927af6870461fa427732d8b73da1b               |
+--------------------------+------------------------------------------------+
```

Next create a `pool` and associate it with the `listener`. While creating the `pool`, you must also mention the load balancing strategy. In the following example, we have used `ROUND_ROBIN` as the `lb-algorithm`:

```
$ neutron lbaas-pool-create --lb-algorithm ROUND_ROBIN --listener listener1 --protocol HTTP --name pool1
Created a new pool:
+---------------------+------------------------------------------------+
| Field               | Value                                          |
+---------------------+------------------------------------------------+
| admin_state_up      | True                                           |
| description         |                                                |
| healthmonitor_id    |                                                |
| id                  | b4248e89-9055-4716-9378-b4bb975fdc11           |
| lb_algorithm        | ROUND_ROBIN                                    |
| listeners           | {"id": "c0b38610-6b2d-4025-9554-c7e216c4f04b"} |
| loadbalancers       | {"id": "08583f1a-316f-4db5-bcfa-95f7d319543c"} |
| members             |                                                |
| name                | pool1                                          |
| protocol            | HTTP                                           |
| session_persistence |                                                |
| tenant_id           | 96a927af6870461fa427732d8b73da1b               |
+---------------------+------------------------------------------------+
```

Now add the servers to the `pool` that will be running the actual service:

```
$ neutron lbaas-member-create  --subnet private-subnet --address 10.0.0.8 --protocol-port 80 pool1
Created a new member:
+----------------+--------------------------------------+
| Field          | Value                                |
+----------------+--------------------------------------+
| address        | 10.0.0.8                             |
| admin_state_up | True                                 |
| id             | 6cee56ad-d6ad-4274-afc8-a459a6bd9263 |
| name           |                                      |
| protocol_port  | 80                                   |
| subnet_id      | 5330af21-0640-465e-8be0-d6a4bd0961cd |
| tenant_id      | 96a927af6870461fa427732d8b73da1b     |
| weight         | 1                                    |
+----------------+--------------------------------------+
```

Next start the service on the `nova` instances. For a quick test, we will mimic an HTTP server as follows. This must be done on all the servers in the `pool`:

```
# ssh cirros@10.0.0.10
The authenticity of host '10.0.0.10 (10.0.0.10)' can't be established.
RSA key fingerprint is 96:73:2a:b5:01:b5:e5:ec:24:20:ec:a5:1d:f3:2b:f0.
Are you sure you want to continue connecting (yes/no)? yes
Warning: Permanently added '10.0.0.10' (RSA) to the list of known hosts.
cirros@10.0.0.10's password:
$ MYIP=$(ifconfig eth0|grep 'inet addr'|awk -F: '{print $2}'| awk '{print $1}')
$ while true; do echo -e "HTTP/1.0 200 OK\r\n\r\nWelcome to $MYIP" | sudo nc -l -p 80 ; done&
$ Connection to 10.0.0.10 closed.
```

Finally we can test your `loadbalancer` by connecting to `port 80` on the `loadbalancer` IP. As the load-balancing algorithm is `ROUND_ROBIN`, a consecutive client request will be served by different servers:

```
# curl 10.0.0.7
Welcome to 10.0.0.8
# curl 10.0.0.7
Welcome to 10.0.0.10
```

Next associate a `healthmonitor` to the `loadbalancer`:

```
$ neutron lbaas-healthmonitor-create --delay 5 --max-retries 2 \
   --timeout 10 --type HTTP --pool pool1
```

Summary

In this chapter, we looked at the advanced network services. Most of these projects are still in active development and are constantly changing. At the same time, they are responding to the changing customer demands of flexibility and scale.

We looked at the OVN project which implements an SDN-like architecture and uses OpenFlow to program the switches. It uses multiple controllers and multiple databases to tackle the challenge of scale.

We then looked at the NFV solution called Tacker, which uses OpenStack as a virtual infrastructure manager. The Tacker project also enables life cycle management of the VNF calatog and instances.

Finally, we looked at the LBaaS project and Octavia, which is an implementation of the new LBaaS APIs. The Octavia project uses a virtual machine to start the load balancer service.

8
Operating the OpenStack Infrastructure - The User Perspective

The previous chapters described the designing elements involved in the OpenStack infrastructure configuration and deployment. Now it is time to let the users and administrators enjoy the rest of the journey and operate the OpenStack platform.

This chapter will expose a test-driven OpenStack experience through the usage of its **Application Programming Interface** (**API**) and **Command Line Interface** (**CLI**). Ultimately, the chapter will gather the discussed pieces from the previous chapters together and show how OpenStack services can be consumed from an end-user perspective as a real-life experience.

One of the key successes of a reliable infrastructure is being consistent and repeatable. This is where the usage of the server **Template** concept comes into play. As OpenStack itself was built based on the principles of **Infrastructure as Code** (**IaC**), it also provides an orchestration service where its resources are described in code and assembled in templates. This chapter will cover the following topics:

- Managing users, projects, and quotas
- Exploring the OpenStack orchestration service named Heat
- Making your development and testing teams more agile by delivering an environment in no time
- Learning how to use Heat templates and how to extend them
- Operating the OpenStack infrastructure from code efficiently using Terraform

Operating the OpenStack tenancy

OpenStack supports a multi-tenancy model. The latter naming convention of **Tenant** in OpenStack is transformed to **Project**. As discussed in Chapter 3, *OpenStack Cluster - The Cloud Controller and Common Services*, Keystone is the OpenStack component that manages access to resources by grouping and isolating them by a defined project or tenant. This means that any user or newly created user group can have access to a given project. To permit a user access to a certain number of predefined sets of resources is ensured by assigning roles. The role concept in OpenStack denotes which service or group of services a user is authorized to have access to.

In a real production OpenStack environment, several users would need to access several types of services and have a certain liberty to exploit their underlying resources. As an OpenStack administrator, you should be able to denote the hierarchy of the organization and thus identify the needs of each project in terms of resource management and consumption.

Let's open the curtains of the deployed OpenStack environment to the end users by creating our first project, a user, and assigning a specific role in OpenStack.

Managing projects and users

Development and QA teams in the organization are willing to extend their test and staging environments. For this purpose, different team members will need access to separate environments in OpenStack and launch instances. Now, recall what was mentioned in the previous section. We can create two different projects and add the users classified by project: test and staging. A user pp_test_user can be added to a project Testing_PP. Using the Keystone CLI, create a new project as follows:

```
# keystone tenant-create --name Testing_PP --description "Test
Environment Project"
+-------------+----------------------------------+
|  Property   |              Value               |
+-------------+----------------------------------+
| description |     Test Environment Project     |
|   enabled   |               True               |
|     id      | 832bd4c20caa44778f4acf5481d4a4a9 |
|    name     |            Testing_PP            |
+-------------+----------------------------------+
```

Create a new user named `pp_test_user` as follows:

```
# keystone user-create --name pp_test_user --pass password --email
pptest@testos.com
+----------+-----------------------------------+
| Property |              Value                |
+----------+-----------------------------------+
|  email   |         pptest@testos.com         |
| enabled  |               True                |
|   id     | 4117dc3cc0054db4b8860cc89ac21278  |
|   name   |          pp_test_user             |
| username |          pp_test_user             |
+----------+-----------------------------------+
```

The new user can be assigned to the newly created tenant as a `member` role as follows:

```
# keystone user-role-add --user pp_test_user --tenant Testing_PP --role
_member_
```

To list all the roles assigned to a given user, use the OpenStack CLI that gives more flexibility to query roles by users and projects as follows:

```
# openstack role list -user pp_test_user -project Testing_PP
+------------------------------+--------+-----------+-----------+
| ID                           | Name   |Project    | User      |
+------------------------------+--------+-----------+-----------+
9fe2ff9ee4384b1894a90878d3e92bab|_member_|Testing_PP |pp_test_user
+------------------------------+--------+-----------+-----------+
```

Managing user capabilities

So far, we have a first project created in OpenStack and assigned its first member user. The new user can log in to the Horizon dashboard and start creating and managing his/her own resources in a completely separated logical environment. On the other hand, existing default roles in OpenStack might not satisfy a custom authorization setup for a given user or group of users. In some cases, some users would need less restricted access to some resources. Our new user is assigned to a `_member_` role that could prevent performing some operations. As an OpenStack administrator, you can get as much flexibility as you want by defining custom roles that map certain rights and user capabilities.

Every service in OpenStack exposes a `policy.json` file that is parsed by a service policy engine.

 The policy files are generally located at: `/etc/OPENSTACK_SERVICE/policy.json` `OPENSTACK_SERVICE` includes the name of any OpenStack service that is installed, up and running.

The policy file is composed of a set of rules and classified as follows:

- **Generic rules**: These evaluate a comparison between one or many users' security credential attributes against one or many resource attributes
- **Role-based rules**: If the user assigned the matched role is mentioned in the rule then it returns a success and resources are granted
- **Field-based rules**: If the resource supports one or many fields that match very specific value(s) then it returns a success and resources are granted

So far, the new user will not be able to accomplish all his/her operational tasks. For example, the `_member_` role will not allow the newly created user to create routers. Depending on the administrative rules, it is not a good idea to assign, for example, an `admin` role for less restricted users. As a `pp_test_user` user, the following output shows that only `admin` is able to create routers:

```
~(keystone_pp_test_user)]# neutron router-create test-router-1
You are not authorized to perform the requested action: admin_required
(HTTP 403) (Request-ID: req-746f8266-4e2e-4e4c-b01d-e8fc10069bfd)
```

To overcome such authorization user restriction, it is possible to create a new role that gives power to any associated role user to create routers. The following command line will create a new role called `router_owner`:

```
# keystone role-create --name router_owner
+----------+----------------------------------+
| Property |               Value              |
+----------+----------------------------------+
|    id    | e4410d9ae5ad44e4a1e1256903887131 |
|   name   |           router_owner           |
+----------+----------------------------------+
```

Then add the newly created role to the user `pp_test_user`:

```
# keystone user-role-add --user pp_test_user --tenant Testing_PP --role
router_owner
```

Once assigned, the last step is to edit the default `/etc/neutron/policy.json` file by looking for the desired rule line. You may notice that the `create_router` rule is configured by default as a role-based rule. Appending that line will enable our new user to create routers, as shown in the following extract:

```
# vim /etc/neutron/policy.json
...
"create_router": "rule:admin_only or role:router_owner"
...
```

Logged as `pp_test_user`, creating a new router will end up with a successful authorization call as follows:

```
~(keystone_pp_test_user)]# neutron router-create test-router-1
Created a new router:
+----------------------+--------------------------------------+
| Field                | Value                                |
+----------------------+--------------------------------------+
| admin_state_up       | True                                 |
| external_gateway_info|                                      |
| id                   | 7151c4ca-336f-43ef-99bc-396a3329ac2f |
| name                 | test-router-1                        |
| routes               |                                      |
| status               | ACTIVE                               |
| tenant_id            | 832bd4c20caa44778f4acf5481d4a4a9     |
+----------------------+--------------------------------------+
```

At the time of writing of this book, the user interface is supposed to not expose the router creation and management dashboard (for example, when rules are set to deny). Additionally, updating rules by service policy does not require a restart of the associated service.

Managing quotas

Before letting tester and developer users take advantage of the OpenStack capabilities, we should proceed first by defining a preventive policy to limit the usage of the OpenStack resources by a project or tenant. This can be controlled by means of a quota. As we have created a project in the previous section, a default quota is applied. Quotas can be managed easily for the OpenStack services, including compute, network, block storage, and orchestration services.

Compute service quotas

The following command line displays, for example, the quota information for our new created tenant for the compute service, **nova**:

```
# nova quota-show --tenant 832bd4c20caa44778f4acf5481d4a4a9
+----------------------------+-------+
| Quota                      | Limit |
+----------------------------+-------+
| instances                  | 10    |
| cores                      | 20    |
| ram                        | 51200 |
| floating_ips               | 10    |
| fixed_ips                  | -1    |
| metadata_items             | 128   |
| injected_files             | 5     |
| injected_file_content_bytes| 10240 |
| injected_file_path_bytes   | 255   |
| key_pairs                  | 100   |
| security_groups            | 100   |
| security_group_rules       | 200   |
| server_groups              | 10    |
| server_group_members       | 10    |
+----------------------------+-------+
```

To list the compute service quota set per tenant or project, use the following command line:
```
# nova quota-show --tenant TENANT_ID
```
Where:
TENANT_ID: This is the tenant ID input that can be listed by checking the keystone tenant-list command line.

Updating the compute quotas, for example, is very straightforward. The following command line shows how to increase, for example, the default quota set for the `Testing_PP` tenant from 10 up to a 20 instances limit and decrease the RAM quota limit down to 25000 MB:

```
# nova quota-update --instances 20 ram 25000
832bd4c20caa44778f4acf5481d4a4a9
```

To update the compute service quota set per tenant or project, use the following command line:

```
# nova quota-update QUOTA_KEY QUOTA_VALUE TENANT_ID
```

Here:

QUOTA_KEY: This is the quota item displayed from the `nova quota-show` command line

QUOTA_VALUE: This is the desired new quota value to assign to the specified quota key

TENANT_ID: This is the tenant ID input that can be listed by checking the `keystone tenant-list` command line

Any user added to the project will have the same quota as the project or tenant quota. As an OpenStack administrator, you will need in some cases to set different quotas per tenant and even in a more granular way, by user. For example, 10 users sharing a new project will perform different tests classified by application, database, and network levels. You should understand that increasing the quota limits per project will apply for all underlying users. The latest tenant quota updates can be checked by the user quota as follows:

```
# nova quota-show --user 411dabfe17304da99ac8e62ac3413cc5 --tenant
832bd4c20caa44778f4acf5481d4a4a9
+----------------------------+-------+
| Quota                      | Limit |
+----------------------------+-------+
| instances                  | 20    |
| cores                      | 20    |
| ram                        | 25000 |
```

To list the compute service quota set per tenant user or project user, use the following command line:

```
# nova quota-show --user USER_ID --tenant TENANT_ID
```

Where:

USER_ID: This is the user ID displayed from the `keystoneuser-list` command line

TENANT_ID: This is the tenant ID that can be listed by checking the `keystone tenant-list` command line

Suppose that `pp_test_user` will need just to perform a few tests for auto scaling the group for a new application fronted by a fleet of web servers, the application test benchmarks would require using a maximum of three web servers for the auto-scaling group and a minimum of one. In this case, it will be more useful to limit resources usage per `pp_test_user` user instead of per tenant. This can be performed as follows:

```
# nova quota-update --user 411dabfe17304da99ac8e62ac3413cc5 --instances 3
```

> To update the compute service quota set per tenant user or project user, use the following command line:
> ```
> # nova quota-update --user USER_ID QUOTA_KEY QUOTA_VALUE
> ```
> Where:
> **USER_ID**: This is the user ID displayed from the `keystone user-list` command line
> **QUOTA_KEY**: This is the quota item displayed from the `nova quota-show` command line
> **QUOTA_VALUE**: This is the desired new quota value to assign to the specified quota key.

Block storage service quotas

Like Nova, Cinder offers quota settings to limit the usage of the amount of block storage space, and the number of volumes and snapshots per tenant. The quotas of a given tenant can be checked using the Cinder CLI as follows:

```
#cinder quota-show Testing_PP
+-----------+-------+
| Property  | Value |
+-----------+-------+
| gigabytes |  500  |
| snapshots |   10  |
| volumes   |   10  |
+-----------+-------+
```

Cinder quotas can be updated simply by specifying the needed quota property and tenant ID. For example, increasing the number of snapshots to 50 for our `Testing_PP` tenant can be performed by running the following command line:

```
# cinder quota-update -snapshots 50  832bd4c20caa44778f4acf5481d4a4a9
```

To update the block storage service quota set per tenant, use the following command line:

```
# cinder quota-update --QUOTA_NAME QUOTA_VALUE TENANT_ID
```

Where:

QUOTA_NAME: This is the quota item displayed from the `cinder quota-show` command line. Available Cinder resources are gigabytes, snapshots, and volumes.

QUOTA_VALUE: This is the desired new quota value to assign to the specified quota key.

TENANT_ID: This is the tenant ID displayed from the `keystone tenant-list` command line.

The latest update can be checked as follows:

```
# cinder quota-show Testing_PP
+-----------+-------+
|  Property | Value |
+-----------+-------+
| gigabytes |  500  |
| snapshots |   50  |
|  volumes  |   10  |
+-----------+-------+
```

More default quota settings can be found in the main Cinder configuration file at `/etc/cinder/cinder.conf`. This includes additional options such as number of volume **backups** per tenant and total amount of storage for overall **backups** per **tenant**.

Network service quotas

Quotas per tenant for the Neutron service can be managed bit more differently than Nova and Cinder. By default, the quota limit per tenant is disabled so all tenants will have the same number of network resources. To set a quota limit per tenant, uncomment the *quota_driver* directive in the `/etc/neutron/neutron.conf` file as follows:

```
...
quota_driver = neutron.db.quota_db_DbQuotaDriver
...
```

Once enabled, it becomes possible to check the quotas per tenant. The Neutron CLI supports the quota option to query the list of tenants within "per-tenant" quota enabled:

```
# neutron quota-list
```

```
+------------+---------+------+--------+--------+----------------------------------+
| floatingip | network | port | router | subnet | tenant_id                        |
+------------+---------+------+--------+--------+----------------------------------+
|         25 |      10 |   30 |     15 |     10 | 832bd4c20caa44778f4acf5481d4a4a9 |
+------------+---------+------+--------+--------+----------------------------------+
```

Updating the quota of a tenant is very straightforward using the **quota-update** Neutron subcommand. The following command line updates the limits of the Neutron subnet and floating IP resources for the `Testing_PP` tenant:

```
# neutron quota-update --tenant_id  832bd4c20caa44778f4acf5481d4a4a9
--subnet 15 --floatingip 30
```

> To update the network service quota set per tenant, use the following command line:
> ```
> # neutron quota-update --TENANT_ID --QUOTA_NAME
> QUOTA_VALUE
> ```
> Where:
> **TENANT_ID**: This is the tenant ID displayed from the `keystone` `tenant-list` command line.
> **QUOTA_NAME**: This is the quota item displayed from the `neutron` `quota-show` command line. Available Neutron resources are floatingip, network, port, router, and subnet.
> **QUOTA_VALUE**: This is the desired new quota value to assign to the specified quota key.

The latest update can be checked as follows:

```
# neutron quota-show --tenant_id 832bd4c20caa44778f4acf5481d4a4a9
+------------+-------+
| Field      | Value |
+------------+-------+
| floatingip | 30    |
| network    | 10    |
| port       | 30    |
| router     | 15    |
| subnet     | 15    |
```

Neutron configuration gives more flexibility in the way of controlling quotas for a specific number of networking resources. This can be achieved by configuring the `/etc/neutron/neutron.conf` file to enable or disable a given Neutron resource in the quotas section. The following excerpt enables the quota only for the network and port defined in the `quota_items` directive:

```
...
[quotas]
quota_items = network, port
```

Since the Mitaka release, Neutron supports the definition of quotas for security groups and the number of security rules per group. Security group quotas can be set by adding the following lines in the neutron.conf file within the same quota section:

```
...
[quotas]
...
quota_secuirty_gourp = 20
quota_security_group_rule = 100
...
```

Orchestration service quotas

Stacks in OpenStack are managed by Heat. As we will see in the next section, the orchestration component in OpenStack enables assembling different resources to run a complete stack from code. This is an ideal use case for DevOps to provision resources in no time and leverage testing code and application functionality from one template file. On the other hand, controlling stacks for users can be more challenging as resources can be more demanded and rapidly exhausted. Heat also exposes quotas to control the number for stacks per tenant and resources per stack. Individual management of resources per stack in Heat is not straightforward. Increasing the limits, for example, of given resource quotas should be performed firstly by adjusting them individually from the CLI as shown in the previous sections. The Heat main configuration file allows you to set the following quota directives per tenant and per stack resource:

- `max_stacks_per_tenant = 200`: Sets a maximum of 200 stacks by default per tenant
- `max_resources_per_stack = 2000`: Sets a maximum of 2,000 resources by default per stack
- `max_template_size = 1000000`: Sets a maximum of 1,000,000 raw byte size by default per template

- `max_nested_stack_depth = 10`: Sets a maximum of 10 for the degree of depth when using nested templates
- `max_events_per_stack = 2000`: Sets a maximum of 2000 events by default per stack

Orchestration in OpenStack

As the title promises, here's building stacks in OpenStack! As you may have guessed from the stack terminology, this includes any group of connected OpenStack resources, including instances, volumes, virtual routers, firewalls, load balancers, and so on, that form a stack. However, how can stacks be created and managed? Starting from the Grizzly release, a new orchestration service named Heat has been added. Using YAML-based template languages called the **Heat Orchestration Template** (**HOT**), you will be able to spin up multiple instances, logical networks, and many other cloud services in an automated fashion. Now, you can guess the rest: you can create stacks from templates.

 If you are familiar with the AWS cloud formation service, Heat is fully compatible with AWS templates and provides an API to align the AWS specification using CFN-formatted templates expressed in JSON.

Demystifying the power of Heat

OpenStack is considered as a dynamic infrastructure platform where computing, storage, and networking resources are exposed to end users to be consumed in a programmatic fashion. As a project or tenant starts growing rapidly, more OpenStack resources will be consumed and OpenStack operators will need more sophisticated ways to manage their large allocated OpenStack resources running applications. Users can achieve this by defining an infrastructure pattern based on the Infrastructure as Code approach. The challenge comes next by defining how users or operators would react against their application changes from infrastructure and resource perspectives. In one respect, this can be resolved by designing the application to accept frequent changes when the infrastructure grows and shrinks in terms of resources.

Giving a succinct overview of the Heat architecture components might be helpful, not only for an OpenStack administrator but also for operators and users when it comes to dealing with certain setups. Essentially, Heat has a few major components, as follows:

- **heat-api**: This is a native OpenStack HTTPd RESTful API. It mainly processes API calls by sending them to the Heat engine via an advanced message queuing protocol.
- **heat-api-cfn**: This is a Cloud Formation API service that's compatible with Heat. It forwards API requests to the Heat engine via an advanced messaging queuing protocol.
- **Heat engine**: This is the main part of the orchestration service where templates are processed and launched.

> Note that the Heat engine can provide auto-scaling and high availability functionalities implemented in its core.

- **Heat CLI tools**: The Heat tool client CLI communicates with heat-api.
- **heat-api-cloudwatch**: This is an additional API that is essentially responsible for monitoring stacks and orchestration services when the AWS Cloud Formation service is used.

It is time to unleash the power of Heat in OpenStack by drilling down into the terminology of **stack**.

Stacking in OpenStack

OpenStack allows cloud operators and end users to create resources individually or by a set of collected infrastructure elements defined as one single unit. The orchestration project, Heat, aims to leverage the power of automating the resources usage in OpenStack. By adopting the concept of **Stack**, end users will explicitly structure their applications in a very simple way rather than going through a painful journey of routines and firefighting.

Whichever stacks are being used and applied; the end user will focus on how the application will be deployed and see it as a single unit. Heat uses the **Heat Orchestration Template** (**HOT**), written in YAML; it enables users to automate the resource allocation in OpenStack from code. The textual description in a HOT file will act as the *eye of contact* between users and their application environments. Stacking in OpenStack is just the act of provisioning a whole application environment stack from HOT file(s). A typical HOT structure would look like the following code skeleton:

```
heat_template_version:
description:
parameters:
  param1
    type:
    label:
    description:
    default:
  param2:
      ….
resources:
  resource_name:
    type: OS::*::*
    properties:
      prop1: { get_param: param1}
      prop2: { get_param: param2}
      .......
outputs:
  output1:
   description:
   value: { get_attr: resource_name,attr] }
          ......
```

Let's check out the overall sections of the previous template:

- `heat_template_version`: This specifies the version of the template syntax that is used. Standard versions are 2013-05-23, while new ones, labeled 2014-10-16, are introduced with the Juno release and contain a few additions.
- `description`: This includes the description of the template.
- `parameters`: These declare a list of inputs. Each parameter is given a name, type, and description; the default value is optional. Parameters can include any information, such as a specific image or a network ID specified by the user.
- `resources`: These can be referred to as objects that Heat will create or modify as part of its operation. The resources section is where the different components are defined. For example, `resource_name` can be `virtual_web` with the `OS::Nova::Server` type, which indicates the type of Nova compute instance. It can be forwarded by a list of sub-properties that identify which image, flavor, and private network can be used for the `virtual_web` instance resource.
- `outputs`: It is possible to export the attributes of a stack after its deployment back to the Heat engine.

> Recent updated resource descriptions can be found at
> `http://docs.openstack.org/developer/heat/template_guide/openstack.html`

Organizing the stacks

Deploying applications using Heat can be seen very simple at the beginning, when users define simple stacks. As the application infrastructure grows, more resource sections will be added in the stack template, resulting in a long one. Continuing to use a monolithic defined template might raise several issues to maintain a sprawling infrastructure and become hard to inject any needed stack change and update.

A very promising way to overcome the monolithic stack approach is to divide the application environment into multiple stacks. Heat is designed to make stacks reusable in different locations for a given application. The following schema illustrates a multi-tiered application environment divided into several stacks where each is built and modified separately: **Networking**, **Web Server**, **Application**, and **Database**:

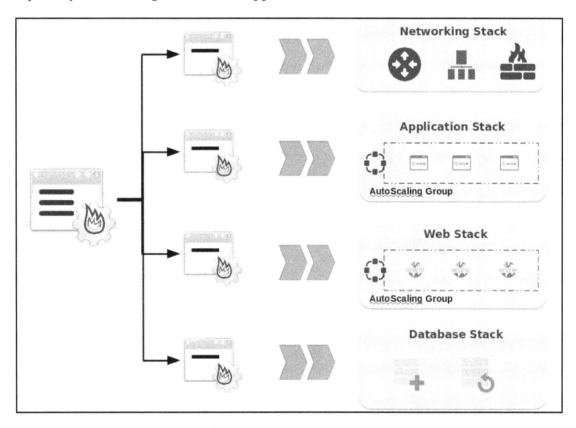

As shown in the preceding illustration, a user can define the application layout from a parent template as an entry point to the rest of the stack resources. Any other resource group definition will be described in a child stack template. Configuration parameters between stacks can be managed by the parent stack, which uses the outputs of each created stack as input parameters of another child stack, if mentioned.

Modularizing the stacks

Users can speed up their development tenfold by organizing the infrastructure code using nested templates. The following example will combine several reusable templates to deploy a multi-tier application in Heat, including:

- A load balancer
- A fleet of two load-balanced web server instances running **HTTPD**
- A database running the **MariaDB** database instance

We can start by defining our Heat templates for each stack created with the following structure:

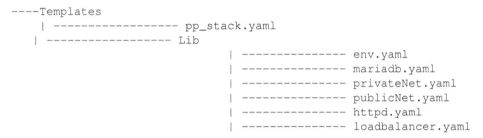

```
----Templates
    | ----------------- pp_stack.yaml
    | ----------------- Lib
                            | -------------- env.yaml
                            | -------------- mariadb.yaml
                            | -------------- privateNet.yaml
                            | -------------- publicNet.yaml
                            | -------------- httpd.yaml
                            | -------------- loadbalancer.yaml
```

We will consider `pp_stack.yaml` as our parent stack template. We will need to prepare the children ones which will be stored as library templates for re-usability purposes with the following:

- `env.yaml`: This contains a customization of the defined Heat templates. It is mainly used to map names to templates. The environment file can include three sections:
  - `Resource_registry`: This defines custom name definitions of resources to the parent stack template
  - `Parameters`: This defines specific parameters only for the parent template and not to the resources in the children templates
  - `Parameter_defaults`: This defines a global value by default for all parameters in both parent and nested templates

In our case, we will define the `resource_registry` section as the following:

- The naming convention in our environment file is prefixed by `Lib` and is followed by `PacktPub` as a customized namespace for every template deployment, and it then gives the names for each template within its path:

```
resource_registry:
 Lib::PacktPub::MariaDB: mariadb.yaml
 Lib::PacktPub::PrivNet:privateNet.yaml
 Lib::PacktPub::PubNet:publicNet.yaml
 Lib::PacktPub::Httpd:httpd.yaml
 Lib::PacktPub::LoadBalancer:loadbalancer.yaml
```

- `mariadb.yaml`: This defines a nested database template to install mariadb and mariadb-server. This also includes setting a secured **DMZ** by means of security groups. Basically, the database will not be attached to any external network. This can be extended by setting a **NAT** instance to enable Egress traffic from the mariadb server to download packages. For example:

```
heat_template_version: 2013-05-23

description: installs a maridb server with a database.

parameters:
  image:
    type: string
    default: centos7
  flavor:
    type: string
    default: m1.medium
  key:
    type: string
    default: my_key
  private_network:
    type: string
    default: Private_Network
  database_name:
    type: string
  database_user:
    type: string


resources:
 database_root_password:
   type: OS::Heat::RandomString
 database_password:
   type: OS::Heat::RandomString
```

```
database_root_password:
  type: OS::Heat::RandomString

security_group:
  type: OS::Neutron::SecurityGroup
  properties:
    name: db_server_security_group
    rules:
      - protocol: tcp
        port_range_min: 3306
        port_range_max: 3306
port:
  type: OS::Neutron::Port
  properties:
    network: { get_param: private_network }
    security_groups:
      - { get_resource: security_group }

mariadb_instance:
  type: OS::Nova::Server
  properties:
    image: { get_param: image }
    flavor: { get_param: flavor }
    key_name: { get_param: key }
    networks:
      - port: { get_resource: port }
    user_data_format: RAW
    user_data:
      str_replace:
        params:
          __database_root_password__: { get_attr:
[database_root_password, value] }
          __database_name__: { get_param: database_name }
          __database_user__: { get_param: database_user }
          __database_password__: { get_attr:
[database_password, value] }
        template: |
          #!/bin/bash -v
          yum -y install mariadb mariadb-server
          systemctl enable mariadb.service
          systemctl start mariadb.service
          mysqladmin -u root password $db_rootpassword
          cat << EOF | mysql -u root --
password=$db_rootpassword
          CREATE DATABASE $db_name;
          GRANT ALL PRIVILEGES ON $db_name.* TO "$db_user"@"%"
          IDENTIFIED BY "$db_password";
          FLUSH PRIVILEGES;
```

```
                    EXIT
                    EOF

        outputs:
         name:
            description: Database Name.
            value: { get_attr: [mariadb_instance, name] }
         ip:
            description: Database IP address.
            value: { get_attr: [mariadb_instance, first_address] }
         port:
            description: Database port number.
            value: { get_resource: port }
        database_password:
            description: Database password.
            value: { get_attr: [database_password, value] }
```

- privateNet.yaml: This defines the creation of a private network dedicated to the instances mentioned in the parent template. This way it will enable you to add whole stacks as much as you want, without digging into different files to specify the network range that all instances will be assigned. Additionally, the template will create a router and attach its interface to the private network to connect to the external network:

```
        heat_template_version: 2013-05-23

        description: Template that creates a private network

        parameters:
         public_network:
            type: string
            default: Public_Network
         cidr:
            type: string
            default: '10.10.10.0/24'
         dns:
            default: '8.8.8.8'


        resources:
         private_network:
            type: OS::Neutron::Net


         private_subnet:
            type: OS::Neutron::Subnet
            properties:
```

```
          network_id: { get_resource: private_network }
          cidr: 10.10.10.0/24
          dns_nameservers: { get_param: dns }


      router:
        type: OS::Neutron::Router
        properties:
          external_gateway_info:
            network: { get_param: public_network }


      router-interface:
        type: OS::Neutron::RouterInterface
        properties:
          router_id: { get_resource: router }
          subnet: { get_resource: private_subnet }


  outputs:
   name:
      description: Private Network.
      value: { get_attr: [private_network, name] }
```

- `publicNet.yaml`: This defines how instances should connect to the external network. This can be performed by allocating floating IPs to the web servers as follows:

```
        heat_template_version: 2013-05-23
        description: Associate floating IP to servers to access
public network.

  parameters:
   port:
      type: string

   public_network:
      type: string.
      default: Public_Network

  resources:
   floating_ip:
      type: OS::Neutron::FloatingIP
      properties:
        floating_network: { get_param: public_network }


   floating_ip_assoc:
```

```
          type: OS::Neutron::FloatingIPAssociation
          properties:
            floatingip_id: { get_resource: floating_ip }
            port_id: { get_param: port }

      outputs:
       ip:
          description: The floating IP address assigned to the server.
          value: { get_attr: [floating_ip, floating_ip_address] }
```

- `httpd.yaml`: This creates a simple web server running HTTPD. The web server template will create a new security group, allowing only **HTTP** and **HTTPS** traffic:

```
      heat_template_version: 2013-05-23
      description: Installs a web server running httpd.

      parameters:
       image:
          type: string
          default: centos7
       flavor:
          type: string
          default: m1.small
       key:
          type: string
          default: my_key
       private_network:
          type: string
          default: Private_Network


      resources:
       security_group:
          type: OS::Neutron::SecurityGroup
          properties:
            name: web_server_sg
            rules:
              - remote_ip_prefix: 0.0.0.0/0
                protocol: tcp
                port_range_min: 80
                port_range_max: 80


              - remote_ip_prefix: 0.0.0.0/0
                protocol: tcp
                port_range_min: 443
                port_range_max: 443
```

```
      port:
        type: OS::Neutron::Port
        properties:
          network: { get_param: private_network }
          security_groups:
            - { get_resource: security_group }


    ws_instance:
      type: OS::Nova::Server
      properties:
        image: { get_param: image }
        flavor: { get_param: flavor }
        key_name: { get_param: key }
        networks:
          - port: { get_resource: port }
        user_data_format: RAW
        user_data:
          str_replace:
           template: |
            #!/bin/bash -ex
            yum -y install httpd
            systemctl enable httpd.service
            systemctl start httpd.service
            setsebool -P httpd_can_network_connect_db=1

outputs:
 name:
    description: Web Server instance.
    value: { get_attr: [ws_instance, name] }
 ip:
    description: Web Server IP address.
    value: { get_attr: [ws_instance, first_address] }
 port:
    description: Web Server Port number.
    value: { get_resource: port }
```

- `loadbalancer.yaml`: This creates a simple `load-balancer`. All initiated requests will be accepted and internally dispatched to the servers running behind the `load-balancer`:

```
heat_template_version: 2013-05-23
description: A load-balancer server
parameters:
 image:
    type: string
 key_name:
    type: string
```

```
            flavor:
              type: string
            pool_id:
              type: string
            user_data:
              type: string
            metadata:
              type: json
            network:
              type: string


            resources:
              server:
                type: OS::Nova::Server
                properties:
                  flavor: {get_param: flavor}
                  image: {get_param: image}
                  key_name: {get_param: key_name}
                  metadata: {get_param: metadata}
                  user_data: {get_param: user_data}
                  user_data_format: RAW
                  networks: [{network: {get_param: network} }]
              member:
                type: OS::Neutron::PoolMember
                properties:
                  pool_id: {get_param: pool_id}
                  address: {get_attr: [server, first_address]}
                  protocol_port: 80


            outputs:
              server_ip:
                description: Load Balancer IP Address
                value: { get_attr: [server, first_address] }
              lb_member:
                description: LB member details.
                value: { get_attr: [member, show] }
```

- `pp_stack.yaml`: This defines the master template where nested templates created previously will be used. Resources in the master template will be declared simply by calling the namespace of each invoked nested template:

```
            heat_template_version: 2013-05-23
            description: Create Multi-Tier Application Stack
            parameters:
             image:
               type: string
```

```
      default: centos7
 flavor:
   type: string
   default: m1.medium
 key:
   type: string
   default: my_key
 public_network:
   type: string
   default: Public_Network
resources:
 network:
   type: Lib::PacktPub::PrivNet
   properties:
     public_network: { get_param: public_network }

 mariadb:
   type: Lib::PacktPub::MariaDB
   properties:
     image: { get_param: image }
     flavor: { get_param: flavor }
     key: { get_param: key }
     private_network: { get_attr: [network, name] }
     database_name: website
     database_user: website_user
 server:
   type: Lib::PacktPub::Httpd
   properties:
     image: { get_param: image }
     flavor: { get_param: flavor }
     key: { get_param: key }
     private_network: { get_attr: [network, name] }
     mariadb: { get_attr: [mariadb, ip] }
     database_name: website
     database_user: website_user
     database_password: { get_attr: [mariadb,
database_password] }

 public_ip:
   type: Lib::PacktPub::PubNet
   properties:
     port: { get_attr: [server, port] }
     public_network: { get_param: public_network }

outputs:
 ip:
   description: Web Server Public IP
   value: { get_attr: [public_ip, ip] }
```

Before creating any stack, it is very useful to validate each template using the following command line:

```
# heat template-validate --template-file hot_template_file.yaml
```

To deploy the multi-tier application stack, make sure to point to the environment file which references to the nested templates and uploads all of them to Heat automatically:

```
# heat stack-create multi_tier_app -f pp_stack.yaml -e Lib/env.yaml
```

Embracing OpenStack orchestration - Terraform

As demonstrated previously, Heat is very capable of provisioning almost any resource in OpenStack. Although it has great nesting and template reusability functions, it might become quite complicated to keep a simple and easy way to read infrastructure code when the underlying stack's resources are growing. Additionally, Heat templates are YAML document code based, and are verbose when running different environments for the same underlying infrastructure. You will need at some point to modularize the code per template, which is not obvious in Heat.

In this respect, we will discover a new kind of infrastructure management tool called **Terraform**. Like Heat, the Terraform tool allows users to orchestrate the provisioning of infrastructure resources of one or many cloud providers by defining configuration files. On the other hand, unlike Heat, Terraform is considered easier to manage and safer to update the underlying infrastructure managed by OpenStack.

Terraform is a Hashicorp tool developed as a provider-agnostic supporting AWS, OpenStack, VMware vCloud, DigitalOcean, and many other cloud providers. Note that not all the resources are supported by Terraform, and supported resources will vary from one provider to another. More documentation regarding OpenStack support by Terraform can be found at: https://www.terraform.io/docs/providers/openstack/

Terraform supports several modules for OpenStack, including compute, block storage, object storage, network, load balancer, and firewall resources. At the time of writing, the supported resource list is extending to include more OpenStack modules in Terraform.

Terraform in action

Giving succinct hints on Terraform compared to Heat might be helpful in distinguishing the main differences between both orchestration tools and checking the best outfit for a particular infrastructure setup, as follows:

- **Resources abstraction**: All resources in Terraform are described in a DSL-friendly language and parsed internally by the **GO** programming language. Users will need to focus only on writing code that describes the resources. Additionally, Terraform is designed to reuse environments by the means of modules instead of duplicating each environment code file.

 GO, also known as **Golang**, is a simple programming language created by Google providing many features and an excellent standard library. The official website of Golang is `https://golang.org/`.

- **Change visibility**: Using Terraform, any change can be traceable by splitting it into two phases: plan and execution. During the plan phase, Terraform draws an action plan about the exact OpenStack resources that will be added, modified, or destroyed. The user can review the plan action list of each resource and decide to apply them or not. The next phase includes applying changes of the code infrastructure managed by OpenStack.
- **Infrastructure state management**: Terraform enables holding the last-known state of the infrastructure. Additionally, within every infrastructure update, a new state file will be created locally and can be stored for backup-versioning purposes.
- **Failure handling**: Another great feature provided by Terraform is the ability to handle failure when provisioning resources. Unlike Heat in OpenStack, Terraform marks the failed provisioned resource as **tainted**. That will be replaced in the next execution by re-provisioning only the tainted resource without redeploying the whole infrastructure resources from scratch.

Terraform in OpenStack

Before provisioning our second infrastructure into OpenStack, we will need to install Terraform. This can be done from your local machine as follows:

1. Get the latest Terraform release from the official Hashicorp repository. At the time of writing this chapter, Terraform 0.7.7 will be used:

    ```
    # wget https://releases.hashicorp.com/terraform/0.7.7/
      terraform_0.7.7_linux_amd64.zip
    ```

2. Unzip the Terraform package and set your `local PATH` environment to the extracted `terraform` directory:

    ```
    # unzip terraform_0.7.7_linux_amd64.zip
    # vim ~/.bash_profile
    PATH=$PATH:<filepath>
    ```

    Where `<filepath>` is the path of the extracted Terraform file.

3. Populate the new `PATH` at your local environment:

    ```
    # source ~/.bash_profile
    ```

4. Check the `terraform` installation:

    ```
    # terraform --version
    Terraform v0.7.7
    ```

The next part will guide you through a few steps to provision a web server accessible from a public network and attach it to an existing private network. Terraform uses files within the `.TF` extension, which will be presented as follows:

*   `variables.tf`: This contains different variables to be assigned to resource attributes
*   `provider.tf`: This is a separate file, which incorporates the OpenStack tenant and user credentials
*   `infra.tf`: This incorporates all resource descriptions, including compute and network resources
*   `postscript.sh`: This is the user data postscript file, which installs the required packages for the web server

We can start by defining our `variable.tf` file, which will specify an environment for a specific configuration in OpenStack, including credentials, image, flavor, and network variables as follows:

```
variable "OS_USERNAME" {
    description = "The username for the Tenant."
    default  = "pp_user"
}

variable "OS_TENANT" {
    description = "The name of the Tenant."
    default  = "pp_tenant"
}

variable "OS_PASSWORD" {
    description = "The password for the Tenant."
    default  = "367811794c1d45b4"
}

variable "OS_AUTH_URL" {
    description = "The endpoint url to connect to the Cloud Controller
OpenStack."
    default  = "http://10.0.10.10:5000/v2.0"
}


variable "OS_REGION_NAME" {
    description = "The region to be used."
    default  = "RegionOne"
}
```

In the same file, we define the uploaded Glance image, the public key, the default SSH user, and the flavor that will be used for our web server:

```
variable "image" {
 description = "Default image for web server"
 default = "centos"
}

variable "flavor" {
  description = "Default flavor for web server instance"
  default = "m1.small"
}

variable "ssh_key_file" {
  description = "Public SSH key for passwordless access the server."
  default = "~/.ssh/pubkey"
}
```

```
variable "ssh_user_name" {
 description = "Default SSH user configured in the centos image uploaded by
glance."
 default = "centos"
}
```

Other network variables will be added as well to assign which network the web server will
be attached to as follows:

```
variable "private_network" {
 description = "Default private network created in OpenStack"
 default = "Private_Network"
}

variable "private_subnet" {
 description = "Default private subnet network which the web server will be
attached to"
 default = "Private_Subnet"
}

variable "router" {
description = "Default Neutron Router created in OpenStack"
default = "pp_router"
}

variable "external_gateway" {
description = "Default External Router Interface ID"
default =  "ac708df9-23b1-42dd-8bf1-458189db71c8"
}

variable "public_pool" {
 description = "Default public network to assign floating IP for external
access"
 default = "Public_Network"
}
```

The `postscript.sh` will install the required web server packages and start the `httpd` as
follows:

```
#!/bin/bash
yum -y install httpd
systemctl enable httpd.service
systemctl start httpd.service
chkconfig --level 2345 httpd on
```

Next, we can start elaborating the rest of the Terraform files by defining the set of defined variables. The `provider.tf` will be used to populate proper credentials for the OpenStack provider as follows:

```
provider "openstack" {
  user_name = "${var.OS_USERNAME}"
  tenant_name = "${var.OS_TENANT}"
  password   = "${var.OS_PASSWORD}"
  auth_url   = "${var.OS_AUTH_URL}"
}
```

The next `infra.tf` file will contain all the building blocks of our web server by assigning to each resource its predefined variable. The first configuration section defines the key pair as follows:

```
resource "openstack_compute_keypair_v2" "mykey" {
  name       = "mykey"
  public_key = "${file("${var.ssh_key_file}.pub")}"
}
```

The following section will create a new security group for the web server by allowing only HTTP and HTTPS traffic from the Internet and SSH access from the internal network:

```
resource "openstack_compute_secgroup_v2" "ws_sg" {
  name        = "ws_sg"
  description = "Security group for the Web Server instances"

  rule {
    from_port   = 22
    to_port     = 22
    ip_protocol = "tcp"
    cidr        = "192.168.0.0/16"
  }

  rule {
    from_port   = 80
    to_port     = 80
    ip_protocol = "tcp"
    cidr        = "0.0.0.0/0"
  }
```

```
rule {
   from_port   = 443
   to_port     = 443
   ip_protocol = "tcp"
   cidr        = "0.0.0.0/0"
  }
}
```

To enable external access for the web server, we will need to assign a floating IP from the existing public pool by defining the following OpenStack resource in the Terraform file:

```
resource "openstack_compute_floatingip_v2" "fip" {
 pool        = "${var.public_pool}"
 }
```

After defining the needed variables, we can describe the web server resource attributes, including the network that they will be attached to, as shown here:

```
resource "openstack_compute_instance_v2" "web_server" {
 name             = "web_server"
 image_name       = "${var.image}"
 flavor_name      = "${var.flavor}"
 key_pair         = "${openstack_compute_keypair_v2.mykey.name}"
 security_groups  = ["${openstack_compute_secgroup_v2.ws_sg.name}"]
 floating_ip      = "${openstack_compute_floatingip_v2.fip.address}"

 network {
   uuid = "${var.Private_Network}"
 }
```

Next, we define how the resources will be accessed for provisioning. This can be achieved by configuring the provisioner as `remote-exec` that will establish an SSH connection to the remote resource and applies the `postscript.sh` script defined in the `user_data`, section as follows:

```
 provisioner "remote-exec" {
  connection {
    user      = "${var.ssh_user_name}"
    secret_key_ = "/root/.ssh/id_rsa"
    timeout = "20m"
  }

  user_data = "${file("postscript.sh")}"


 }
}
```

Alternatively, it is possible to use an **inline** directive in the provisioner section supported by Terraform, instead of pointing to an external postscript file. The `user_data` directive can be replaced by the following section:

```
inline = [
        "yum -y install httpd",
        "systemctl enable httpd.service"
        "systemctl start httpd.service",
        "chkconfig --level 2345 httpd on"
    ]
```

Before deploying the new resources, we can take advantage of the planning feature provided by Terraform prior to applying any change, so we can review our infrastructure changes as follows:

```
# terraform plan
```

```
    stop_before_destroy:            "false"

+ openstack_compute_keypair_v2.terraform
    name:          "mykey"
    public_key: "ssh-rsa AAAAB3NzaC1yc2EAAAADAQABAAA
PCs0Z4tgtq0v0o20a5aahLve6WpKYM+D6ieMDY2iH056jg9d9S9b
oz+eh1/S4Q8y0QA6Pn93sytFe8dezoh7UlFlBy0530WN6HSxP5Tc
    region:        "RegionOne"

+ openstack_compute_secgroup_v2.terraform
    description:                    "Security group f
    name:                           "ws_sg"
    region:                         "RegionOne"
    rule.#:                         "3"
    rule.2180185248.cidr:           "0.0.0.0/0"
    rule.2180185248.from_group_id:  ""
    rule.2180185248.from_port:      "-1"
    rule.2180185248.id:             "<computed>"
    rule.2180185248.ip_protocol:    "icmp"
    rule.2180185248.self:           "false"
    rule.2180185248.to_port:        "-1"
    rule.3719211069.cidr:           "0.0.0.0/0"
    rule.3719211069.from_group_id:  ""
    rule.3719211069.from_port:      "80"
    rule.3719211069.id:             "<computed>"
    rule.3719211069.ip_protocol:    "tcp"
    rule.3719211069.self:           "false"
    rule.3719211069.to_port:        "80"
    rule.836640770.cidr:            "0.0.0.0/0"
    rule.836640770.from_group_id:   ""
    rule.836640770.from_port:       "22"
    rule.836640770.id:              "<computed>"
    rule.836640770.ip_protocol:     "tcp"
    rule.836640770.self:            "false"
    rule.836640770.to_port:         "22"

Plan: 4 to add, 0 to change, 0 to destroy.
```

The plan command line gives details on how many instances will be added, changed, or destroyed during the Terraform dry run. We can agree about our expected provisioned state and execute the plan based on the previous outcome as follows:

```
# terraform apply
```

```
openstack_compute_secgroup_v2.terraform: Refreshing state... (ID: 95002a0d-3fb6-4d26-83b5-8a5b7d4ce25a)
openstack_compute_keypair_v2.terraform: Refreshing state... (ID: mykey)
openstack_compute_floatingip_v2.terraform: Creating...
  address:        "" => "<computed>"
  fixed_ip:       "" => "<computed>"
  instance_id:    "" => "<computed>"
  pool:           "" => "public_network"
  region:         "" => "RegionOne"
openstack_compute_floatingip_v2.terraform: Creation complete
openstack_compute_instance_v2.terraform: Creating...
  access_ip_v4:              "" => "<computed>"
  access_ip_v6:              "" => "<computed>"
  flavor_id:                 "" => "<computed>"
  flavor_name:               "" => "m1.small"
  floating_ip:               "" => "10.0.2.96"
  image_id:                  "" => "<computed>"
  image_name:                "" => "centos"
  key_pair:                  "" => "mykey"
  name:                      "" => "web_server"
  network.#:                 "" => "1"
  network.0.access_network:  "" => "false"
  network.0.fixed_ip_v4:     "" => "<computed>"
  network.0.fixed_ip_v6:     "" => "<computed>"
  network.0.floating_ip:     "" => "<computed>"
  network.0.mac:             "" => "<computed>"
  network.0.name:            "" => "<computed>"
  network.0.port:            "" => "<computed>"
  network.0.uuid:            "" => "26adf398-409d-4f6e-9c44-918779d8f57f"
  region:                    "" => "RegionOne"
  security_groups.#:         "" => "1"
  security_groups.1149137907: "" => "ws_sg"
  stop_before_destroy:       "" => "false"
openstack_compute_instance_v2.terraform: Still creating... (10s elapsed)
```

The deployment might take a while, depending on how many resources need to be created. In our example, a new web server will be deployed within a floating IP. This can be checked as follows:

```
# nova list
```

```
| web_server          | ACTIVE | -          | Running  | private_network=10.15.15.110, 10.0.2.96
+---------------------+--------+------------+----------+----------------------------------------
```

The default page of the instance can be requested to check the availability of the web server from the external network by using the floating IP assigned to it as follows:

```
# curl http://10.0.2.96
```

```
<!DOCTYPE html PUBLIC "-//W3C//DTD XHTML 1.1//EN" "http://www.w3.org/TR/xhtml11/DTD/xhtml11.dtd"><html><head>
<meta http-equiv="content-type" content="text/html; charset=UTF-8">
        <title>Apache HTTP Server Test Page powered by CentOS</title>
        <meta http-equiv="Content-Type" content="text/html; charset=UTF-8">
```

Another amazing feature that Terraform provides is a safe cleanup of the running infrastructure we have just deployed using the Terraform destroy command line:

```
public  -var  pool=public_network
Do you really want to destroy?
    Terraform will delete all your managed infrastructure.
    There is no undo. Only 'yes' will be accepted to confirm.

    Enter a value: yes
```

Deleting resources using Terraform can be also planned by using the following command line:

```
# terraform plan -destroy
```

```
openstack_compute_keypair_v2.terraform: Refreshing state... (ID: mykey)
openstack_compute_secgroup_v2.terraform: Refreshing state... (ID: 95002a0d-3
openstack_compute_floatingip_v2.terraform: Refreshing state... (ID: c599a799
openstack_compute_instance_v2.terraform: Refreshing state... (ID: 91854f04-4
openstack_compute_instance_v2.terraform: Destroying...
openstack_compute_instance_v2.terraform: Still destroying... (10s elapsed)
openstack_compute_instance_v2.terraform: Destruction complete
openstack_compute_keypair_v2.terraform: Destroying...
openstack_compute_floatingip_v2.terraform: Destroying...
openstack_compute_secgroup_v2.terraform: Destroying...
openstack_compute_keypair_v2.terraform: Destruction complete
openstack_compute_floatingip_v2.terraform: Destruction complete
openstack_compute_secgroup_v2.terraform: Still destroying... (10s elapsed)
openstack_compute_secgroup_v2.terraform: Destruction complete

Destroy complete! Resources: 4 destroyed.
```

Summary

This chapter covers several topics on using OpenStack services from the user perspective. The beginning of the chapter provides a general background on how users can be assigned to projects. From an administrative perspective, it is essential to understand how quotas should be spread among a list of users by setting limits for the OpenStack resource consumption. The next part of this chapter unleashed the power of the orchestration service, Heat, in OpenStack. Discovering the greatness of such OpenStack project will allow users to treat their intended application infrastructure as code. You should be able to understand how Heat provisions resources in OpenStack using templates and without going through a manual and error-prone setup, either from Horizon or via the CLI. Additionally, a third-party and amazing tool comparable to Heat is explored: Terraform. We have seen how flexible and easy it is to manage an application stack lifecycle when using the Terraform tool. Although it does not cover as many resources as Heat, it is continuously growing its OpenStack modules support.

Orchestrating resource provisioning in OpenStack by end users might massively increase the workload in the underlying infrastructure and operators should be prepared to face such sudden peaks. As discussed in previous chapters, OpenStack is designed to scale. Additionally, we will need to make sure that every OpenStack service is fault tolerant. Our next topic will investigate architecting a highly available OpenStack environment to overcome failure at every layer of the cloud infrastructure.

9

OpenStack HA and Failover

"Once we accept our limits, we go beyond them."
- Albert Einstein

So far, you have gained a good knowledge of all the components needed to provide a functional OpenStack infrastructure. In Chapter 1, *Designing OpenStack Cloud Architectural Consideration*, we saw one of the many ways to design a complete OpenStack environment. Chapter 3, *OpenStack Cluster - The Cloud Controllers and Common Services* and Chapter 4, *OpenStack Compute - Choice of Hypervisor and Node Segregation*, looked at one of the most important logical and physical designs of OpenStack clustering in depth, by iterating through cloud controller and compute nodes. Distributing services through the mentioned nodes after considering the standalone storage cluster, as seen in Chapter 5, *OpenStack Storage - Block, Object, and File Share*, aims to reduce the downtime for a given service. Many design approaches can fulfill such high availability goals in OpenStack. On the other hand, achieving **High Availability** (**HA**) in the production environment may not be as simple as the name suggests: it's the effort to eliminate any **Single Point of Failure** (**SPOF**) on every layer in your architecture. OpenStack components can be brought and distributed in different nodes while maintaining a sense of teamwork, which OpenStack is good at - again, thanks to our messaging service. In this chapter, we will cover the following topics:

- Understanding how HA and failover mechanisms can guarantee OpenStack business continuity
- Looking for a workaround on how to make different OpenStack components configured in HA
- Checking out different ways to validate a complete HA setup for database and messaging queue services
- Implementing an HA setup for native OpenStack API services
- Empowering the high availability of network services in OpenStack

HA under the scope

OpenStack is designed to provide more flexibility when setting up your building block architecture. A real robust OpenStack cloud platform includes fault tolerance at every level of the architecture. This can be marked as successful if it is planned ahead. Starting with a small cluster is easy and achievable, but growing it is a challenge. The hallmark of the OpenStack basic component itself is that it can run in commodity hardware. OpenStack is designed to scale massively and provide HA by leveraging more advanced HA techniques in each level of the infrastructure. This can include automatic failover and geo-redundancy.

Whatever the reason for a node failure, end users should keep running their applications and spawning instances with minimum disturbance or data loss.

For this reason, an OpenStack operator would be able to measure its cloud platform availability. A general formula to check the total uptime of a system is as follows:

Availability = MTTF/ (MTTF + MTTR)

Here:

- **MTTF** (**Mean Time to Failures**): This is an estimate of the average time that a system is functional before its failure
- **MTTR** (**Mean Time to Repair**): This is an estimate of the average time to repair a part or component of a system

 There may be different definitions of how to estimate the availability of a system. This can be also computed using a different metric:
Availabilty = MTBF/(MTTR+MTBF)
Here, **MTBF** (Mean Time between Failures) is the estimated time between recurrent failures of a part or component of a system.

Finding the right value of high availability cannot be directly obvious without designing and testing continuously. During such an exercise, a few critical performance metrics will be taken into consideration, including:

- Response time
- System uptime percentage
- System downtime percentage
- System throughput

When architecting for an HA OpenStack is setup, failures should be planned for at every single layer of the cloud architecture. Due to advanced HA models and techniques, this can be achieved. Moreover, OpenStack exposes more features and scenarios that embrace the availability not only for its components but also for user applications. For example, traditional applications suffer from misleading infrastructures. If a host fails, the application running on it will not be accessible anymore. By adopting the OpenStack capabilities, the guest instance, for example, can be relocated to a new, healthy host. For an extended OpenStack setup, the cloud environment could scale even more to domain failures by recalling Availability Zones.

Some high availability design patterns can be summarized in the following points:

- Eliminate any SPOF
- Adopt a Geo-Replication design
- Automate monitoring
- Plan for disaster and fast recovery
- Decouple and isolate OpenStack components as much as possible

Do not mix them

We still remember that one of the several purposes of OpenStack clustering is to make sure that services remain running in the case of a node failure. The HA functionality aims to make sure that the different nodes participating in a given cluster work in tandem to satisfy certain downtime. HA, in fact, is a golden goal for any organization where some useful concepts can be used to reach it with minimum downtime, such as the following:

- **Failover**: Migrates a service running on the failed node to a working one (switches between primary and secondary)
- **Fallback**: Once a primary is back after a failed event, the service can be migrated back from the secondary
- **Switchover**: Manually switches between nodes to run the required service

There is also a different terminology, which you may have most likely already experienced, and that is **load balancing**. In a heavily loaded environment, load balancers are introduced to redistribute a bunch of requests to less loaded servers. This can be similar to the **high performance clustering** concept, but you should note that this cluster logic takes care of working on the same request, whereas a load balancer aims to relatively distribute the load based on its task handler in an optimal way.

HA levels in OpenStack

It might be important to understand the context of HA deployments in OpenStack. This makes it imperative to distinguish the different levels of HA in order to consider the following in the cloud environment:

- **L1**: This includes physical hosts, network and storage devices, and hypervisors
- **L2**: This includes OpenStack services, including compute, network, and storage controllers, as well as databases and message queuing systems
- **L3**: This includes the virtual machines running on hosts that are managed by OpenStack services
- **L4**: This includes applications running in the virtual machines themselves

The main focus of supporting HA in OpenStack has been on L1 and L2, which are covered in this chapter. Additionally, L3 HA has been improved and supported by the OpenStack community. By virtue of its multi-storage backend support, OpenStack is able to bring instances online in the case of host failure by means of **live migration**.

Nova also supports the **Nova evacuate** implementation, which fires up API calls for VM evacuation to a different host due to a compute node failure.

 Live migration is the ability to move running instances from one host to another with, ideally, no service downtime. By default, live migration in OpenStack requires a shared filesystem, such as a Network File System (NFS). It also supports block live migration when virtual disks can be copied over TCP without the need for a shared filesystem. Read more on VM migration support within the last OpenStack release at `http://docs.openstack.org/admin-guide/compute-configuring-migrations.html#section-configuring-compute-migrations`.

A strict service-level agreement

Normally, if you plan to invest time and money in OpenStack clustering, you should refer to the HA architectural approaches in the first place. They guarantee business continuity and service reliability. At this point, meeting these challenges will drive you to acquire skills you never thought you could master. Moreover, exposing an infrastructure that accepts failures might distinguish your environment as a blockbuster private cloud. Remember that this topic is very important in that all you have built within OpenStack components must be available to your end user.

Availability means that not only is a service running, but it is also exposed and able to be consumed. Let's see a small overview regarding the maximum downtime by looking at the availability percentage or HA as X-nines:

Availability Level	Availability %	Downtime/year	Downtime/Day
1 Nine	90	~ 36.5 days	~ 2.4 hours
2 Nines	99	~ 3.65 days	~ 14 minutes
3 Nines	99.9	~ 8.76 hours	~ 86 seconds
4 Nines	99.99	~ 52.6 minutes	~ 8.6 seconds
5 Nines	99.999	~ 5.25 minutes	~ 0.86 seconds
6 Nines	99.9999	~ 31.5 seconds	~ 0.0086 seconds

Basically, availability management is a part of IT best practice when it comes to making sure that IT services are *running* when needed, which reflects your **service-level agreement** (**SLA**):

- Minimized downtime and data loss
- User satisfaction
- No repeat incidents
- Services must be consistently accessible

A paradox may appear between the lines when we consider that eliminating the SPOF in a given OpenStack environment will include the addition of more hardware to join the cluster. At this point, you might be exposed to creating more SPOF and, even worse, complicated infrastructure where maintenance turns into a difficult task.

Measuring HA

The following is a simple tip: if you do not measure something, you cannot manage it. But what kind of metrics can be measured in a highly available OpenStack infrastructure?

Agreed, HA techniques come across as increasing the availability of resources, but still, there are always occasions where you may face an interruption at some point! You may notice that the previous table did not mention any value equal to 100 percent uptime.

First, you may appreciate the non-vendor lock-in hallmark that OpenStack offers on this topic. Basically, you should mark the differences between HA functionalities that exist in a virtual infrastructure. Several HA solutions provide protection to virtual machines when there is a sudden failure in the host machine. Then, it will perform a restore situation for the instance on a different host. What about the virtual machine itself? Does it hang? So far, we have seen different levels of HA. In OpenStack, we have already seen cloud controllers run manageable services and compute hosts, which can be any hypervisor engine and third-rank of the instance itself!

The last level might not be a cloud administrator task that maximizes its internal services' availability as it belongs to the end user. However, what should be taken into consideration is what really affects the instance externally, such as the following:

- Storage attachment
- Bonded network devices

A good practice is to design the architecture with an approach that is as simple as possible by keeping an efficient track of every HA level in our OpenStack cluster.

 Eliminating any SPOF while designing the OpenStack infrastructure will help in reaching a scalable environment.

A good strategy to follow is to design an **untrustworthy SPOF** principle by ruling. This keyword can be found anywhere in any system. In Chapter 1, *Designing OpenStack Cloud Architectural Consideration*, within our first design, we highlighted a simple architecture that brings in many instances to maximize availability.

Nowadays, large IT infrastructures are likely to suffer from database scalability across multiple nodes. Without exception, the database in the OpenStack environment will need to scale as well. We will cover how to implement a database HA solution in more detail later in this chapter.

 High availability in OpenStack does not necessarily mean that it is designed to achieve maximum performance. On the other hand, you should consider the limitations of the overhead result on updating different nodes running the same service.

The HA dictionary

To make it easier to understand the following sections of this chapter, it might be necessary to remember a few terminologies to justify high availability and failover decisions later:

- **Stateless service**: This is the service that does not require any record of the previous request. Basically, each interaction request will be handled based on the information that comes with it. In other words, there is no dependency between requests where data, for example, does not need any replication. If a request fails, it can be performed on a different server.

- **Stateful service**: This is the service where request dependencies come into play. Any request will depend on the results of the previous and the subsequent ones. Stateful services are difficult to manage, and they need to be synchronized in order to preserve consistency.

Let's apply our former definition to our OpenStack services:

Stateful services	Stateless services
MySQL, RabbitMQ	nova-api, nova-conductor, glance-api, keystone-api, neutron-api, nova-scheduler, webserver [Apache/Nginx]

Any HA architecture introduces an *active/active* or *active/passive* deployment, as covered in `Chapter 1`, *Designing OpenStack Cloud Architectural Consideration*. This is where your OpenStack environment will highlight its scalability level.

First, let's see the difference between both concepts in a nutshell to justify your decision:

- **Active/active**: Basically, all OpenStack nodes running the same stateful service will have an identical state. For example, deploying a MySQL cluster in the active/active mode will bring in a multi-master MySQL node design, which involves any update to one instance that may be propagated to all other nodes. Regarding the stateless services, redundancy will invoke instances to be load-balanced.

- **Active/passive**: In the case of stateful services, a failure event in one node will bring its associated redundant instance online. For example, within database clustering, only one master node comes into play, where the secondary node will act as a listener when failover occurs. It keeps load balancing handling requests within stateless services.

Hands-on HA

Chapter 1, *Designing OpenStack Cloud Architectural Consideration*, provided a few hints on how to prepare for the first design steps; do not lock the keys inside your car. At this point, we can go further due to the emerging different topologies, and it is up to you to decide what will fit best. This is the first question that may come into your mind: OpenStack does not include native HA components; how you can include them? There are widely used solutions for each component that we cited in the previous chapter in a nutshell.

Understanding HAProxy

HAProxy stands for **High Availability Proxy**. It is a free load balancing software tool that aims to proxy and direct requests to the most available nodes based on **TCP/HTTP** traffic. This includes a load balancer feature that can be a frontend server. At this point, we find two different servers within an HAProxy setup:

- A frontend server listens for requests coming on a specific IP and port, and determines where the connection or request should be forwarded
- A backend server defines a different set of servers in the cluster receiving the forwarded requests

Basically, HAProxy defines two different load balancing modes:

- **Load balancing layer** 4: Load balancing is performed in the transport layer in the OSI model. All the user traffic will be forwarded based on a specific IP address and port to the backend servers. For example, a load balancer might forward the internal OpenStack system's request to the Horizon web backend group of backend servers. To do this, whichever backend Horizon is selected should respond to the request under scope. This is true in the case of all the servers in the web backend serving identical content. The previous example illustrates the connection of the set servers to a single database. In our case, all services will reach the same database cluster.
- **Load balancing layer** 7: The application layer will be used for load balancing. This is a good way to load balance network traffic. Simply put, this mode allows you to forward requests to different backend servers based on the content of the request itself.

Many load balancing algorithms are introduced within the HAProxy setup. This is the job of the algorithm, which determines the server in the backend that should be selected to acquire the load. Some of them are as follows:

- **Round robin**: Here, each server is exploited in turn. As a simple HAProxy setup, round robin is a dynamic algorithm that defines the server's weight and adjusts it on the fly when the called instance hangs or starts slowly.
- **Leastconn**: The selection of the server is based on the lucky node that has the lowest number of connections.

> It is highly recommended that you use the *leastconn* algorithm in the case of long HTTP sessions.

- **Source**: This algorithm ensures that the request will be forwarded to the same server based on a hash of the source IP as long as the server is still up.

> Contrary to RR and leastconn, the source algorithm is considered a static algorithm, which presumes that any change to the server's weight on the fly does not have any effect on processing the load.

- **URI**: This ensures that the request will be forwarded to the same server based on its URI. It is ideal to increase the cache-hit rate in the case of proxy caches' implementations.

> Like the source, the URI algorithm is static in that updating the server's weight on the fly will not have any effect on processing the load.

You may wonder how the previous algorithms determine which servers in OpenStack should be selected. Eventually, the hallmark of HAProxy is a healthy check of the server's availability. HAProxy uses a health check by automatically disabling any backend server that is not listening on a particular IP address and port.

But how does HAProxy handle connections? To answer this question, you should refer to the first logical design in Chapter 1, *Designing OpenStack Cloud Architectural Consideration*, which is created with a **virtual IP** (**VIP**). Let's refresh our memory about the things that we can see there by treating a few use cases within a **VIP**.

Services should not fail

A VIP can be assigned to the active servers running all the OpenStack services that need to be configured to use the address of the server. For example, in the case of a failover of the nova-api service in controller node 1, the IP address will follow the nova-api in controller node 2, and all clients' requests, which are the internal system requests in our case, will continue to work:

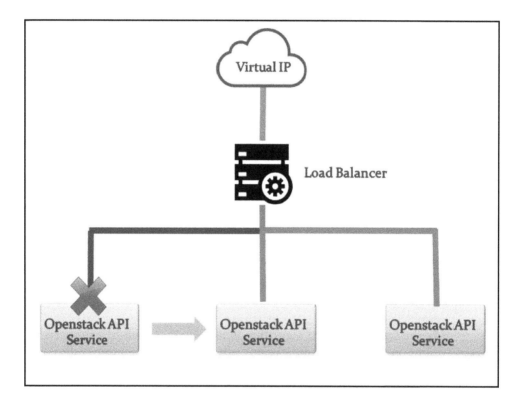

Load balancer should not fail

The previous use case assumes that the load balancer never fails! But in reality, this is a SPOF that we have to arm by adding a VIP on top of the load balancer's set. Usually, we need a stateless load balancer in OpenStack services. Thus, we can undertake such challenges using software similar to **Keepalived**:

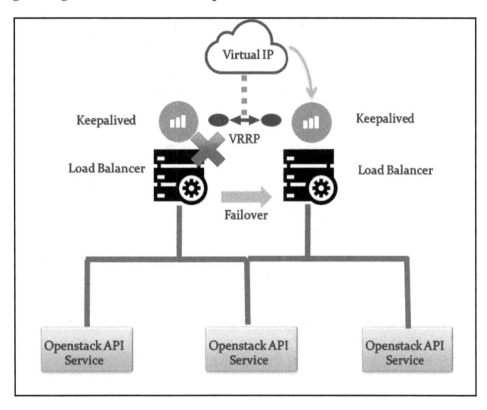

Keepalived is a free software tool that provides high availability and load balancing facilities based on its framework, to check a **Linux Virtual Server** (**LVS**) pool state.

LVS is a highly available server built on a cluster of real servers, by running a load balancer on the Linux operating system. It is mostly used to build scalable web, mail, and FTP services.

As shown in the previous illustration, nothing is magic! Keepalived uses the Virtual **Router Redundancy Protocol** (**VRRP**) protocol to eliminate SPOF by making IPs highly available. The VRRP implements virtual routing between two or more servers in a static, default routed environment. Considering a master router failure event, the backup node takes the master state after a period of time.

 In a standard VRRP setup, the backup node keeps listening for multicast packets from the master node with a given priority. If the backup node fails to receive any VRRP advertisement packets for a certain period, it will take over the master state by assigning the routed IP to itself. In a multi-backup setup, the backup node with the same priority will be selected within its highest IP value to be the master one.

OpenStack HA under the hood

Deep down in the murky depths of HA, the setup of our magnificent OpenStack environment is much diversified! It may come across as a bit biased to favor a given HA setup, but remember that, depending on which software clustering solution you feel more comfortable with, you can implement your HA OpenStack setup.

Let's shine the spotlight brightly on our first OpenStack design in `Chapter 1`, *Designing OpenStack Cloud Architectural Consideration*, and take a closer look at the pieces in the HA mode.

Next, we will move on to specific OpenStack core components and end up with exposing different possible topologies.

HA in the database

There's no doubt that behind any cluster lies a story! Creating your database in the HA mode in an OpenStack environment is not negotiable. We have set up MySQL in cloud controller nodes that can also be installed on separate ones. Most importantly, keep it safe not only from water, but also from fire. Many clustering techniques have been proposed to make MySQL highly available. Some of the MySQL architectures can be listed as follows:

- **Master/slave replication**: As exemplified in the following figure, a VIP that can be optionally moved has been used. A drawback of such a setup is the probability of data inconsistency due to delay in the VIP failing over (data loss):

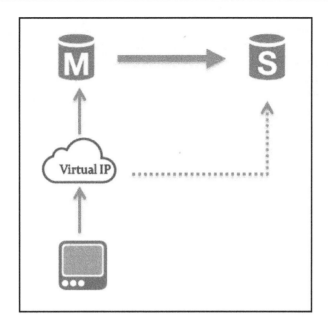

- **MMM replication**: By setting two servers, both of them become masters by keeping only one acceptable write query at a given time. This is still not a very reliable solution for OpenStack database HA, as in the event of failure of the master, it might lose a certain number of transactions:

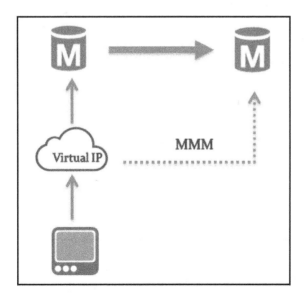

- **MySQL shared storage**: Both servers will depend on a redundant shared storage. As shown in the following figure, a separation between servers processing the data and the storage devices is required. Note that an active node may exist at any point in time. If it fails, the other node will take over the VIP after checking the inactivity of the failed node, and turn it off. The service will be resumed in a different node by mounting the shared storage within the taken VIP:

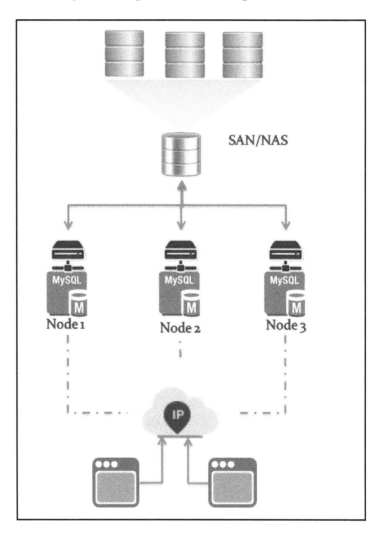

- Such a solution is excellent in terms of uptime but may require a powerful storage/hardware system that can be extremely expensive.
- **Block-level replication**: One of the most adopted HA implementations is the **Distributed Replicated Block Device** (**DRBD**) replication. Simply put, it replicates data in the block device, which is the physical hard drive between OpenStack MySQL nodes:

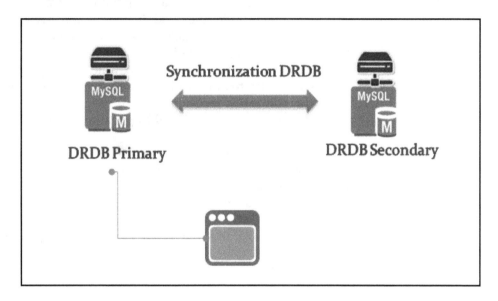

What you need are just Linux boxes. The DRBD works on their kernel layer exactly at the bottom of the system I/O stack.

With shared storage devices, writing to multiple nodes simultaneously requires a cluster-aware filesystem, such as the Linux **Global File System** (**GFS**).

DRBD can be a costless solution, but performance-wise, it cannot be a deal when you rely on hundreds of nodes. This can also affect the scalability of the replicated cluster.

- **MySQL Galera multi-master replication**: Based on multi-master replication, the Galera solution has a few performance challenges within an MMM architecture for the MySQL/innoDB database cluster. Essentially, it uses synchronous replication, where data is replicated across the whole cluster. As was stated in our first logical design in `Chapter 1`, *Designing OpenStack Cloud Architectural Consideration*, a requirement of the Galera setup is the need for at least three nodes, to run it properly. Let's dive into the Galera setup within our OpenStack environment and see what happens under the hood. In general, any MySQL replication setup can be simple to set up and make HA-capable, but data can be lost during the failing over. Galera is tightly designed to resolve such a conflict in the multi-master database environment. An issue you may face in a typical multi-master setup is that all the nodes try to update the same database with different data, especially when a synchronization problem occurs during the master failure. This is why Galera uses **Certification Based Replication** (**CBR**).

Keep things simple: the main idea of CBR is to assume that the database can roll back uncommitted changes, and it is **transactional** in addition to applying replicated events in the same order across all the instances. Replication is truly parallel; each one has an ID check. What Galera can bring as an added value to our OpenStack MySQL HA is the ease of scalability; there are a few more things to it, such as joining a node to Galera while it is automated in production. The end design brings an active/active multi-master topology with less latency and transaction loss:

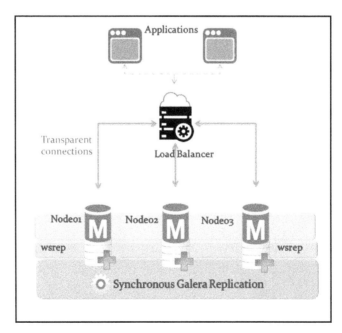

A very interesting point in the preceding diagram is that every MySQL node in the OpenStack cluster should be patched within a **Write-Set Replication (wsrep)** API. If you already have a MySQL master-master actively working, you will need to install **wsrep** and configure your cluster.

 Wsrep is a project that aims to develop a generic replication plugin interface for databases. Galera is one of the projects that use wsrep APIs by working on its wsrep replication library calls.

You can download and install Galera from `https://github.com/codership/galera`. Every node will need a certain number of steps to configure a complete MySQL cluster setup.

HA in the queue

RabbitMQ is mainly responsible for communication between different OpenStack services. The issue is fairly simple: no queue, no OpenStack service intercommunication. Now that you get the point, another critical service needs to be available and survive the failures. RabbitMQ is mature enough to support its own cluster setup without the need to go for Pacemaker or another clustering software solution.

The amazing part about using RabbitMQ is the different ways by which such a messaging system can reach scalability using an active/active design with the following:

- **RabbitMQ clustering**: Any data or state needed for the RabbitMQ broker to be operational is replicated across all nodes.
- **RabbitMQ mirrored queues**: As the message queue cannot survive in nodes in which it resides, RabbitMQ can act in active/active HA message queues. Simply put, queues will be mirrored on other nodes within the same RabbitMQ cluster. Thus, any node failure will automatically switch to using one of the queue mirrors.

 Exchanges and bindings can survive failure, as they exist in all nodes. Setting up queue mirroring does not enhance any load distribution across the cluster and only guarantees availability. A good reference on the HA of queues within RabbitMQ can be found at `https://www.rabbitmq.com/ha.html`.

Like any standard cluster setup, the original node handling the queue can be thought of as a master, while the mirrored queues in different nodes are purely slave copies. The failure of the master will result in the selection of the oldest slave to be the new master.

Keep calm and implement HA

So far, we have introduced most of the possibilities that can make our OpenStack environment highly available. OpenStack cloud controller nodes, database clusters, and network nodes can be deployed in redundancy in the following ways:

- MySQL high availability through Galera active/active multi-master deployment and Keepalived
- RabbitMQ active/active high availability using mirrored queues and HAProxy for load balancing
- The OpenStack API services' inclusion of the nova-scheduler and glance-registry in cloud controllers nodes in the active-passive model using Pacemaker and Corosync
- Neutron Layer 3 agents by internal routing redundancy

Implementing HA on MySQL

In this implementation, we will need three separate MySQL nodes and two HAProxy servers so that we guarantee our load balancer can fail over in case one of them fails. Keepalived will be installed in each HAProxy to control the Virtual IP. Different nodes in this setup will be assigned as the following:

- Virtual IP: 192.168.47.47
- HAProxy01: 192.168.47.120
- HAProxy02: 192.168.47.121
- MySQL01: 192.168.47.125
- MySQL02: 192.168.47.126
- MySQL03: 192.168.47.127

In order to implement HA on MySQL, go through the following steps:

1. Let's start first by installing and configuring our HAProxy servers:

    ```
    packtpub@haproxy1$ yum update
    packtpub@haproxy1$ yum install haproxy keepalived
    ```

2. We check whether the HAProxy is properly installed:

    ```
    packtpub@haproxy1$ haproxy -v
    HA-Proxy version 1.5.2 2014/07/12
    ```

3. Let's configure our first HAProxy node. We start by backing up the default configuration file:

```
packtpub@haproxy1$ cp /etc/haproxy/haproxy.cfg
/etc/haproxy/haproxy.cfg.bak
packtpub@haproxy1$ nano /etc/haproxy/haproxy.cfg
  global
  log        127.0.0.1 local2
  chroot     /var/lib/haproxy
  pidfile    /var/run/haproxy.pid
  maxconn    1020 # See also: ulimit -n
  user haproxy
  group haproxy
  daemon
  stats socket /var/lib/haproxy/stats.sock mode 600 level admin
  stats timeout 2m
  defaults
  mode     tcp
  log      global
  option   dontlognull
  option   redispatch
  retries          3
  timeout queue    45s
  timeout connect  5s
  timeout client   1m
  timeout server   1m
  timeout check    10s
  maxconn          1020
  listen haproxy-monitoring *:80
  mode     tcp
  stats    enable
  stats    show-legends
  stats    refresh    5s
  stats    uri        /
  stats    realm      Haproxy Statistics
  stats    auth       monitor:packadmin
  stats    admin      if TRUE
  frontend haproxy1 # change on 2nd HAProxy
  bind *:3306
  default_backend      mysql-os-cluster
  backend mysql-os-cluster
  balance roundrobin
  server mysql01      192.168.47.125:3306 maxconn 151 check
  server mysql02      192.168.47.126:3306 maxconn 151 check
  server mysql03      192.168.47.127:3306 maxconn 151 check
```

4. Start the `haproxy` service:

```
packtpub@haproxy1$ sudo service haproxy start
```

5. Repeat steps 1-4, replacing `haproxy1` with `haproxy2` in the frontend section.

6. Now we arm our HAProxy servers by adding the VRRP `/etc/keepalived/keepalived.conf` file. But first we back up the original configuration file:

```
packtpub@haproxy1$ sudo cp /etc/keepalived/keepalived.conf
/etc/keepalived/keepalived.conf.bak
packtpub@haproxy1$ sudo nano /etc/keepalived/keepalived.conf
```

To bind a virtual address that does not exist physically on the server, you can add to sysctl.conf in your CentOS box the following option:

```
net.ipv4.ip_nonlocal_bind=1
```

Do not forget to activate the change using the following:

```
packtpub@haproxy1$ sudo sysctl -p
packtpub@haproxy1$ sudo nano /etc/keepalived/keepalived.conf
vrrp_script chk_haproxy {
  script "killall -0 haproxy"
  interval 2
  weight 2
}
vrrp_instance MYSQL_VIP {
  interface eth0
  virtual_router_id 120
  priority 111 # Second HAProxy is 110
  advert_int 1
virtual_ipaddress {
    192.168.47.47/32 dev eth0
  }
  track_script {
    chk_haproxy
  }
}
```

7. Repeat step 6 by setting the priority configuration directive to 110 in the `vrrp_instance MYSQL_VIP` stanza for node HAProxy2.

8. Check whether the Virtual IP was assigned to eth0 in both nodes:

    ```
    packtpub@haproxy1$ ip addr show eth0
    packtpub@haproxy2$ ip addr show eth0
    ```

11. Now you have HAProxy and Keepalived configured, we need only to set up the Galera plugin through all MySQL nodes in the cluster:

    ```
    packtpub@db01$ wget
    https://launchpad.net/codership-mysql/5.6/5.6.16-25.5/+download/MyS
    QL-server-5.6.16_wsrep_25.5-1.rhel6.x86_64.rpm
    packtpub@db01$ wget https://launchpad.net/galera/0.8/0.8.0/
    +download/galera-0.8.0-x86_64.rpm
    ```

10. We need to install the previously downloaded RPM files using the following command lines:

    ```
    packtpub@db01$ rpm -Uhv galera-0.8.0-x86_64.rpm
    packtpub@db01$ rpm -Uhv MySQL-server-5.6.16_wsrep_25.5
    1.rhel6.x86_64.rpm
    ```

> If you did not install MySQL within Galera from scratch, you should stop the MySQL service first before proceeding with the Galera plugin installation. The example assumes that MySQL is installed and stopped.

11. Once the Galera plugin is installed, log in to your MySQL nodes and create a new user galera with the password galerapass and, optionally, the haproxy username for HAProxy monitoring, without a password for the sake of simplicity. Note that for MySQL clustering, a new user sst must exist. We will set up a new password sstpassword for node authentication:

    ```
    mysql> GRANT USAGE ON *.* to sst@'%' IDENTIFIED BY 'sstpassword';
    mysql> GRANT ALL PRIVILEGES on *.* to sst@'%';
    mysql> GRANT USAGE on *.* to galera@'%' IDENTIFIED BY 'galerapass';
    mysql> INSERT INTO mysql.user (host,user) values ('%','haproxy');
    mysql> FLUSH PRIVILEGES;mysql> quit
    ```

12. Configure the MySQL wsrep Galera library in each MySQL node in /etc/mysql/conf.d/wsrep.cnf as follows, For db01.packtpub.com:

    ```
    wsrep_provider=/usr/lib64/galera/libgalera_smm.so
    wsrep_cluster_address="gcomm://"
    wsrep_sst_method=rsync
    wsrep_sst_auth=sst:sstpass
    ```

Restart the MySQL server:

```
packtpub@db01$ sudo /etc/init.d/mysql restart
```

For db02.packtpub.com:

```
wsrep_provider=/usr/lib64/galera/libgalera_smm.so
wsrep_cluster_address="gcomm://192.168.47.125"
wsrep_sst_method=rsync
wsrep_sst_auth=sst:sstpass
```

Restart the MySQL server:

```
packtpub@db01$ sudo /etc/init.d/mysql restart
```

For db03.packtpub.com:

```
wsrep_provider=/usr/lib64/galera/libgalera_smm.so
wsrep_cluster_address="gcomm://192.168.47.126"
wsrep_sst_method=rsync
wsrep_sst_auth=sst:sstpass
```

Restart the MySQL server:

```
packtpub@db01$ sudo /etc/init.d/mysql restart
```

Note that the db01.packtpub.com gcomm:// address is left empty to create the new cluster. The last step will connect to the db03.packtpub.com node.

To reconfigure it, we will need to modify our /etc/mysql/conf.d/wsrep.cnf file and point to 192.168.47.127:

```
wresp_cluster_address ="gcomm://192.168.47.127"
```

From the mysql command line, set your global MySQL settings as the following:

```
mysql> set global
wsrep_cluster_address='gcomm://192.168.1.140:4567';
```

13. Check whether the Galera replication is running as it should be:

```
packtpub@db01$ mysql -e "show status like 'wsrep%' "
```

14. If your cluster is fine, you should see something like the following:

```
wsrep_ready = ON
```

15. An additional check can be verified from the MySQL command line. In db01.packtpub.com, you can run the following:

```
Mysql> show status like 'wsrep%';
|wsrep_cluster_size   | 3       |
|wsrep_cluster_status | Primary |
| wsrep_connected     | ON      |
```

> wsrep_cluster_size is showing value 3, which means our cluster is aware of three nodes connected while the current node is designated as a primary node, wsrep_cluster_status.status.

16. Starting from step 9, you can add new a MySQL node and join the cluster.

 We have separated our MySQL cluster from the cloud controller, which means that OpenStack services running in the former node, including Keystone, Glance, Nova, Cinder, and Neutron nodes, need to point to the right MySQL server. Remember that we are using HAProxy, while VIP is managed by Keepalived for MySQL high availability.

We will need to reconfigure the Virtual IP as the following in each service:

```
Nova: /etc/nova/nova.conf
sql_connection=mysql://nova:openstack@192.168.47.47/nova
Keystone: /etc/keystone/keystone.conf
sql_connection=mysql://keystone:openstack@192.168.47.47/keystone
Glance: /etc/glance/glance-registry.conf
sql_connection=mysql://glance:openstack@192.168.47.47/glance
Neutron: /etc/neutron/plugins/openvswitch/ovs_neutron_plugin.ini
sql_connection=mysql://neutron:openstack@192.168.47.47/neutron
Cinder: /etc/cinder/cinder.conf
sql_connection=mysql://cinder:openstack@192.168.47.47/cinder
```

Remember that editing your OpenStack configuration files means you will need to restart the corresponding services. Be sure that after each restart, the service is up and running and does not show any error in the log files.

If you are familiar with the `sed` and `awk` command lines, it might be easier to reconfigure files using them. You can have a look at another useful shell tool for manipulating `ini` and `conf` files, crudini, which can be found at: `http://www.pixelbeat.org/programs/crudini/`. To update an existing configuration file, the command line is fairly simple:

```
# crudini --set <Config_File_Path> <Section_Name> <Parameter> <Value>
```

For example, to update the `/etc/nova/nova.conf` file shown previously, you can enter the following command line:

```
# crudini --set /etc/nova/nova.conf database connection
mysql://nova:openstack@192.168.47.47/nova
```

Implementing HA on RabbitMQ

In this setup, we will need to introduce minor changes in our RabbitMQ instances running in cloud controller nodes. We will enable mirrored options in our RabbitMQ brokers. In this example, we assume that the RabbitMQ service is running on three OpenStack cloud controller nodes as follows:

- Virtual IP: 192.168.47.47
- HAProxy01: 192.168.47.120
- HAProxy02: 192.168.47.121
- Cloud Controller 01: 192.168.47.100
- Cloud Controller 02: 192.168.47.101
- Cloud Controller 03: 192.168.47.102

In order to implement HA on RabbitMQ, go through the following steps:

1. Stop RabbitMQ services on the second and third cloud controller. Copy the erlang cookie from the first cloud controller to the additional nodes:

   ```
   packtpub@cc01$ scp /var/lib/rabbitmq/.erlang.cookie root
   @cc02:/var/lib/rabbitmq/.erlang.cookie
   packtpub@cc01$ scp /var/lib/rabbitmq/.erlang.cookie root
   @cc03:/var/lib/rabbitmq/.erlang.cookie
   ```

2. Set the RabbitMQ group and user with *400* file permissions in both additional nodes:

```
packtpub@cc02$ sudo chown rabbitmq:rabbitmq
/var/lib/rabbitmq/.erlang.cookie
packtpub@cc02$ sudo chmod 400 /var/lib/rabbitmq/.erlang.cookie
packtpub@cc03$ sudo chown rabbitmq:rabbitmq
/var/lib/rabbitmq/.erlang.cookie
packtpub@cc03$ sudo chmod 400 /var/lib/rabbitmq/.erlang.cookie
```

3. Start the RabbitMQ service in cc02 and cc03:

```
packtpub@cc02$ service rabbitmq-server start
packtpub@cc02$chkconfig rabbitmq-server on
packtpub@cc03$ service rabbitmq-server start
packtpub@cc03$chkconfig rabbitmq-server on
```

Now it is time to build the cluster and enable the mirrored queues option. Currently, all the three RabbitMQ brokers are independent and they are not aware of each other. Let's instruct them to join one cluster unit. First, stop the rabbimqctl daemon.

On node cc02:

```
# rabbitmqctl stop_app
Stopping node 'rabbit@cc02' ...
...done.
# rabbitmqctl join-cluster rabbit@cc01
Clustering node 'rabbit@cc02' with 'rabbit@cc01' ...
...done.
# rabbitmqctl start_app
Starting node 'rabbit@cc02' ...
... done
```

On node cc03:

```
# rabbitmqctl stop_app
Stopping node 'rabbit@cc03' ...
...done.
# rabbitmqctl join-cluster rabbit@cc01
Clustering node 'rabbit@cc03' with 'rabbit@cc01' ...
...done.
# rabbitmqctl start_app
Starting node 'rabbit@cc03' ...
... done
```

Check the nodes in the cluster by running from any RabbitMQ node:

```
# rabbitmqctl cluster_status
Cluster status of node 'rabbit@cc03' ...
[{nodes,[{disc,['rabbit@cc01','rabbit@cc02',
'rabbit@cc03']}]},
{running_nodes,['rabbit@cc01','rabbit@cc02',
'rabbit@cc03']},
{partitions,[]}]
...done
```

The last step will instruct RabbitMQ to use mirrored queues. By doing this, mirrored queues will enable both producers and consumers in each queue to connect to any RabbitMQ broker, so they can access the same message queues. The following command will sync all the queues across all cloud controller nodes by setting an HA policy:

```
# rabbitmqctl set_policy HA '^(?!amq.).*' '{"ha-mode":"all", "ha-sync-mode":"automatic" }'
```

 Note that the previous command line settles a policy where all queues are mirrored to all nodes in the cluster.

Edit in each RabbitMQ node its main configuration file /etc/rabbitmq/rabbitmq.config to instruct each node to join the cluster on restart as follows:

```
[{rabbit,
[{cluster_nodes, {['rabbit@cc01', 'rabbit@cc02', 'rabbit@cc03'], ram}}]}].
```

We can proceed to set up a load balancer for RabbitMQ. We need only add a new section in both haproxy1 and haproxy2 nodes and reload the configurations:

```
listen rabbitmqcluster 192.168.47.47:5670
  mode tcp
  balance roundrobin
    server cc01 192.168.47.100:5672 check inter 5s rise 2 fall 3
    server cc02 192.168.47.101:5672 check inter 5s rise 2 fall 3
    server cc03 192.168.47.102:5672 check inter 5s rise 2 fall 3
```

Notice that we are listening on the Virtual IP 192.168.47.47. Reload the configuration on both HAProxy nodes:

```
# service haproxy reload
```

Using the Virtual IP to manage both HAProxy as a proxy for RabbitMQ might require each OpenStack service to be configured to use the address `192.168.47.47` and port *5670*. Thus, you will need to reconfigure the RabbitMQ settings in each service running Virtual IP as follows:

- Nova : `/etc/nova/nova.conf`:

  ```
  # crudini --set /etc/nova/nova.conf DEFAULT rabbit_host
  192.168.47.47
  # crudini --set /etc/nova/nova.conf DEFAULT rabbit_port 5470
  rabbit_host=192.168.47.47
  rabbit_port=5470
  ```

- Glance: `/etc/glance/glance-api.conf`:

  ```
  # crudini --set /etc/glance/glance-api.conf DEFAULT rabbit_host
  192.168.47.47
  # crudini --set /etc/glance/glance-api.conf DEFAULT rabbit_port
  5470
  rabbit_host=192.168.47.47
  rabbit_port=5470
  ```

- Neutron : `/etc/neutron/neutron.conf`:

  ```
  # crudini --set /etc/neutron/neutron.conf DEFAULT rabbit_host
  192.168.47.47
  # crudini --set /etc/neutron/neutron.conf DEFAULT rabbit_port 5470
  rabbit_host=192.168.47.47
  rabbit_port=5470
  ```

- Cinder : `/etc/cinder/cinder.conf`:

  ```
  # crudini --set /etc/cinder/cinder.conf DEFAULT rabbit_host
  192.168.47.47
  # crudini --set /etc/cinder/cinder.conf DEFAULT rabbit_port 5470
  ```

Implementing HA on OpenStack cloud controllers

Moving on setting up of highly available OpenStack cloud controllers requires a way of managing the services running in the former nodes. Another alternative for the high

availabilitygame is using **Pacemaker** and **Corosync**. As a native high availability and load balancing stack solution for the Linux platform, Pacemaker depends on Corosync to maintain cluster communication based on the messaging layer. Corosync supports multicast as the default network configuration communication method. For some environments that do not support multicast, Corosync can be configured for unicast. In multicast networks, all the cluster nodes are connected to the same physical network device; it will be necessary to make sure that at least one multicast address is configured in the configuration file. Corosync can be considered as a message bus system that allows OpenStack services running across different cloud controller nodes to manage quorum and cluster membership to Pacemaker. But how does Pacemaker interact with these services? Simply put, Pacemaker uses **Resource Agents** (**RAs**) to expose the interface for resource clustering. Natively, Pacemaker supports over 70 RAs found at
`http://www.linux-ha.org/wiki/Resource_Agents`.

In our case, we will use native OpenStack RAs, including:

- OpenStack Compute service
- OpenStack Identity service
- OpenStack Image service

 There is a native Pacemaker RA to manage MySQL databases and the Virtual IP, which you can use as an alternative to the MySQL Galera replication solution.

In order to implement HA on OpenStack cloud controllers, go through the following steps:

1. Install and configure Pacemaker and Corosync on cloud controller nodes:

```
# yum update
# yum install pacemaker corosync
```

2. Corosync allows any server to join a cluster using active/active or active/passive fault-tolerant configurations. You will need to choose an unused multicast address and a port. Make a backup for the original `corosync` configuration file and edit `/etc/corosync/corosync.conf` as follows:

```
# cp /etc/corosync/corosync.conf.bak/etc/corosync/corosync.conf
# nano /etc/corosync/corosync.conf
  Interface {
      ringnumber: 0
  bindnetaddr: 192.168.47.0
  mcastaddr: 239.225.47.10
  mcastport: 4000
  ....}
```

In case of a unicast network, you might need to specify in the Corosync configuration file the addresses of all nodes that are allowed as members in the OpenStack cluster. There is no need to do this in a multicast cluster. A sample example template can be found at: `http://docs.openstack.or g/high-availability-guide/content/_set_up_corosync_unicast.htm l`.

3. Generate an authorization key on the cc01 node to enable communication between the cloud controller nodes:

```
# sudo corosync-keygen
```

4. We copy the generated `/etc/corosync/authkey` and `/etc/corosync/corosync.conf` to other nodes in the cluster:

```
# scp /etc/corosync/authkey /etc/corosync/corosync.conf
packpub@192.168.47.101:/etc/corosync/
# scp /etc/corosync/authkey /etc/corosync/corosync.conf
packpub@192.168.47.102:.etc/corosync/
```

5. Start the `pacemaker` and `corosync` services:

```
# service pacemaker start
# service corosync start
```

6. A good way to check the setup is by running the following command line:

```
# crm_mon -1
Online: [cc01 cc02 cc03]
First node (cc01)
```

By default, Corosync uses the **STONITH (Shoot the Other Node in the Head**) option. It is used to avoid a split-brain situation when each service node believes that the other(s) is (are) broken and it is the elected one. Thus, in the case of a STONITH death match, the second node, for example, shoots the first one to be sure there is only one primary node running. In a simple two-node `corosync` environment, it might be convenient to disable it by running the following:
crm configure property stonith-enabled= "false"

7. On `cc01`, we can set up a Virtual IP that will be shared between the three servers. We can use `192.168.47.48` as the Virtual IP with a 3 second monitoring interval:

```
# crm configure primitive VIP ocf:heartbeat:IPaddr2 params
ip=192.168.47.48 cidr_netmask=32 op monitor interval=3s
```

8. We can see that the Virtual IP has been assigned to the `cc01` node. Note that the VIP will be assigned to the next cloud controller if `cc01` does not show any response during 3 seconds:

```
# crm_mon -1
Online: [ cc01 cc02]
VIP     (ocf::heartbeat:IPaddr2):    Started cc01
```

9. Optionally, you can create a new directory to save all downloaded resource agent scripts under `/usr/lib/ocf/resource.d/openstack`.

Creating a new Virtual IP will require pointing OpenStack services to the new virtual address. You can overcome such repetitive reconfiguration by keeping both IP addresses of the cloud controller and the Virtual IP. In each cloud controller, be sure that you have exported the needed environment variables as the following:
export OS_AUTH_URL=http://192.168.47.48:5000/v2.0/

10. Set up RAs and configure Pacemaker for Nova. First, you download the resource agent in all three cloud controller nodes:

```
# cd /usr/lib/ocf/resource.d/openstack
# wget https://raw.github.com/leseb/OpenStack-ra/master/nova-api
# wget https://raw.github.com/leseb/OpenStack-ra/master/nova-cert
# wget https://raw.github.com/leseb/OpenStack-ra/master/
  nova-consoleauth
# wget https://raw.github.com/leseb/OpenStack-ra/
  master/nova-scheduler
# wget https://raw.github.com/leseb/OpenStack-ra/master/nova-vnc
# chmod a+rx *
```

11. You can check whether the Pacemaker is aware of new RAs or not by running the following:

```
# crm ra info ocf:openstack:nova-api
```

12. Now we can proceed to configure Pacemaker to use these agents to control our Nova service. The next configuration creates p_nova_api, a resource for managing the OpenStack nova-api:

```
# crm configure primitive p_nova-api ocf:openstack:nova-api
params config="/etc/nova/nova.conf" op monitor interval="5s"
timeout="5s"
```

13. Create p_cert, a resource for managing the OpenStack nova-cert:

```
# crm configure primitive p_cert ocf:openstack:nova-cert
params config="/etc/nova/nova.conf" op monitor interval="5s"
timeout="5s"
```

14. Create p_consoleauth, a resource for managing the OpenStack nova-consoleauth:

```
# crm configure primitive p_ consoleauth ocf:openstack:
nova-consoleauth params config="/etc/nova/nova.conf"
op monitor interval="5s" timeout="5s"
```

15. Create p_scheduler, a resource for managing the OpenStack nova-scheduler:

```
# crm configure primitive p_scheduler ocf:openstack:nova-
scheduler params config="/etc/nova/nova.conf" op monitor
interval="5s" timeout="5s"
```

16. Create `p_novnc`, a resource for managing the OpenStack `nova-vnc`:

```
# crm configure primitive p_ novnc ocf:openstack:nova-vnc
params config="/etc/nova/nova.conf" op monitor interval="5s"
timeout="5s"
```

17. Set up the RA and configure Pacemaker for Keystone. Download the resource agent in all three cloud controller nodes:

```
# cd /usr/lib/ocf/resource.d/openstack
# wget https://raw.github.com/madkiss/
openstack-resource-agents/master/ocf/keystone
```

18. Proceed to configure Pacemaker to use the downloaded resource agent to control the Keystone service. The next configuration creates `p_keystone`, a resource for managing the OpenStack Identity service:

```
# crm configure primitive p_keystone ocf:openstack:keystone
params config="/etc/keystone/keystone.conf" op monitor
interval="5s" timeout="5s"
```

Set up the RA and configure Pacemaker for Glance:

1. Download the resource agent in all three cloud controller nodes:

```
# cd /usr/lib/ocf/resource.d/openstack
# wget https://raw.github.com/madkiss/
openstack-resource-agents/master/ocf/glance-api
# wget https://raw.github.com/madkiss/
openstack-resource-agents/master/ocf/glance-registry
```

2. Proceed to configure Pacemaker to use the downloaded resource agent to control the Glance API service. The next configuration creates `p_glance-api`, a resource for managing the OpenStack Image API service:

```
# crm configure primitive p_glance-api ocf:openstack:glance-api
params config="/etc/glance/glance-api.conf" op monitor
interval="5s" timeout="5s"
```

3. Create `p_glance-registry`, a resource for managing the OpenStack `glance-registry`:

```
# crm configure primitive p_glance-registry
ocf:openstack:glance-registry params config="/etc/glance/
glance-registry.conf " op monitor interval="5s" timeout="5s"
```

Set up the RA and configure Pacemaker for the Neutron server:

1. Download the resource agent in all three cloud controller nodes:

```
# cd /usr/lib/ocf/resource.d/openstack
# wget https://raw.github.com/madkiss/openstack-resource-agents/
master/ocf/neutron-server
```

2. Now we can proceed to configure Pacemaker to use these agents to control our Neutron server service. The next configuration creates p_neutron-server, a resource for managing the OpenStack Networking server:

```
# crm configure primitive p_neutron-server ocf:openstack:
neutron-server params config="/etc/neutron/neutron.conf"
op monitor interval="5s" timeout="5s"
```

3. Check whether our Pacemaker is correctly handling our OpenStack services:

```
# crm_mon -1
Online: [ cc01 cc02 cc03 ]
VIP (ocf::heartbeat:IPaddr2): Started cc01
p_nova-api (ocf::openstack:nova-api):
Started cc01
p_cert (ocf::openstack:nova-cert):
Started cc01
p_consoleauth (ocf::openstack:nova-consoleauth):
Started cc01
p_scheduler (ocf::openstack:nova-scheduler):
Started cc01
p_nova-novnc (ocf::openstack:nova-vnc):
Started cc01
p_keystone (ocf::openstack:keystone):
Started cc01
p_glance-api (ocf::openstack:glance-api):
Started cc01
p_glance-registry (ocf::openstack:glance-registry):
Started cc01
p_neutron-server (ocf::openstack:neutron-server):
Started cc01
```

4. To use private and public IP addresses, you might need to create two different Virtual IPs. For example, you will have to define your endpoint as the following:

```
keystone endpoint-create --region $KEYSTONE_REGION
--service-id $service-id --publicurl  'http://PUBLIC_VIP:9292'
--adminurl 'http://192.168.47.48:9292'
--internalurl 'http://192.168.47.48:9292'
```

Implementing HA on network nodes

Networking in OpenStack has been empowered within the latest releases of OpenStack to tackle the concern of high availability. As discussed in previous chapters, a recommended design approach is to install the OpenStack network service in a dedicated node. The next challenge represents how to facilitate high availability and network redundancy for Neutron. The OpenStack network service involves the following agent composites:

- L2 agents
- DHCP agent
- L3 agent

L2 agents would sit on every compute node. That means layer 2 agents are inclusively separate and there is no need to maintain their high availability setup. Additionally, the DHCP agent can run across multiple nodes via its scheduler and it supports high availability by default.

The DHCP protocol permits the existence of several DHCP servers corresponding to the same pool of addresses per network. In Neutron, each new port created will be mapped within an IP and MAC assigned to it. This information will be held in a leases file in the dnsmasq server.

At this point, the L3 agent high availability setup presents a concern that needs to be addressed. Before bringing the L3 HA setup mode under the scope, let's refresh our memory of what L3 agents are responsible for:

- Scheduling virtual routers created by each tenant
- Providing external connectivity to instances
- Managing floating IPs to enable accessibility to virtual machines from an external network
- Interconnecting virtual machines within different private virtual networks in OpenStack

Obviously, losing a network node running an L3 agent will drop all connections initiated by its running scheduled routers that also will not exist anymore. Prior to the Icehouse release, there was not a built-in solution to answer the L3 agent HA issue. On the other hand, a few options could be used by means of an external cluster solution using Pacemaker and Corosync, as elaborated for the previous cloud controller services.

> Distribution of virtual routers across different L3 agent network nodes would help to scale by means of the scheduler, but does not present a direct solution for router HA.

Although the latter option would be a sufficient high available solution, demanding ever-higher levels of availability requires faster failover time. Considering a wide number of routers for different tenants, rescheduling all of them in a short time must go through a different alternative. To tackle such a challenge, new HA modes adopted for Neutron in OpenStack have been introduced since the **Juno** release using the following options:

- **Virtual Router Redundancy Protocol (VRRP)**
- **Distributed Virtual Routing (DVR)**

The next sections will look at how a redundant Neutron router setup can be achieved using the VRRP.

VRRP in Neutron

We have already briefly introduced earlier in this chapter the concept of the VRRP protocol. The OpenStack community has created from this protocol a new method to attain a high available routing setup for Neutron:

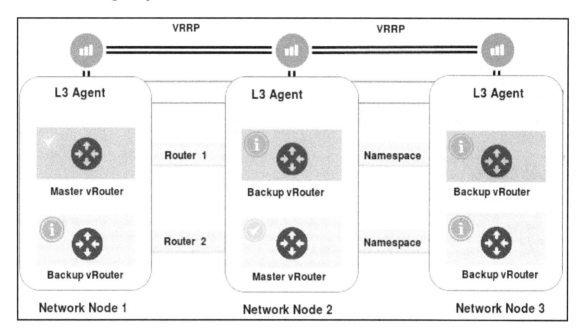

By using the same approach introduced earlier in this chapter, Neutron achieves a failed over router setup across several neutron nodes using **VRRP** as well as **Keepalived** for high availability. As shown in the previous diagram, routers can be seen in the form of groups, where each group presents an active router that is currently forwarding traffic to instances. Additionally, the load of instances traffic is spread among all network nodes based on the scheduling for the master and the rest of the backup routers. Based on the same concept of the Keepalived mechanism, the master router configures its **VIP** internally, and keeps informing the router group about its state and priority.

 The active router needs to periodically inform the standby ones about its state, noted as the advertisement interval timer. If a backup router does not receive such information, it will send a new master router election process based on the last advertised VRRP. The election is based on priority, where the router with the highest value will be elected as the master one. Priorities range from 0 to 255, 255 being the highest priority.

Every newly created HA router will add a new router namespace where its L3 agent starts **Keepalived**. Under the hood, routers configured in HA mode will be able to communicate via a specific **HA network** that is not visible to users. The HA network interface is denoted by **ha**.

Namespaces for each HA router support HA devices in which Keepalived traffic will flow.

By default, Neutron automatically creates an HA pool range network **169.254.192.0/18** used for given tenant routers with HA mode enabled. The next wizard will guide you through a few steps in order to check out the router resiliency setup in Neutron.

Considering our initial design, adding more Neutron nodes in which an L3 agent will be installed will enhance our OpenStack network performance and discard Neutron as a SPOF:

1. In a new network instance, nn02, install an additional Neutron L3 agent:

```
# yum install openstack-neutron openstack-neutron-ml2 openstack-
neutron-openvswitch -y
```

Make sure that any new network node will be connected to the network segments described in the network diagram in Chapter 1, *Designing OpenStack Cloud Architectural Consideration*.

2. Point the new Neutron agent to the running RabbitMQ IP address by editing the following parameter in the /etc/neutron/neutron.conf file:

```
...
rabbit_host = 192.168.47.47
...
```

3. Edit the Neutron L3 configuration file, `/etc/neutron/l3_agent.ini`, by specifying the interface driver that will be used. The preceding configuration in the cloud controller machine uses the Open vSwitch driver which supports HA for routers:

```
[Default]
interface_driver =
neutron.agent.linux.interface.OVSInterfaceDriver
```

 The `LinuxBridge` driver also supports HA and can be used as an L3 mechanism driver. This can be achieved by assigning the `interface_driver` directive to `neutron.agent.linux.interface.BridgeInterfaceDriver`.

4. Optionally, in `/etc/neutron/l3_agent.ini`, set the `router_delete_namespaces` directive to True:

```
...
router_delete_namespaces = True
...
```

This will enable all associated namespaces to be cleared when deleting a router.

5. Restart the L3 agent as follows:

```
# service neutron-l3-agent restart
```

6. The new L3 agent service should be running without errors, as indicated in the following:

```
# service neutron-l3-agent status
Redirecting to /bin/systemctl status neutron-l3-agent.service
neutron-l3-agent.service - OpenStack Neutron Layer 3 Agent
Loaded: loaded (/usr/lib/systemd/system/neutron-l3-agent.service;
disabled; vendor preset: disabled)
Active: active (running) since Sat 2016-11-26
...
```

7. The additional agents can be checked from any node running the Neutron command line as follows:

```
# neutron agent-list --agent-type="L3 Agent"
```

```
+-------------------------------------+------------+-----------+-------+----------------+-----------------+
| id                                  | agent_type | host      | alive | admin_state_up | binary          |
+-------------------------------------+------------+-----------+-------+----------------+-----------------+
| e7321c48-e967-4353-a319-a6074e089168 | L3 agent   | cloud     | :-)   | True           | neutron-l3-agent |
| b2a1ab35-f9e9-426b-ad5a-2bf73f538537 | L3 agent   | compute01 | :-)   | True           | neutron-l3-agent |
+-------------------------------------+------------+-----------+-------+----------------+-----------------+
```

8. The rest of the configuration will be performed on the cloud controller node. Neutron should be adjusted to enable the HA mode. This can be achieved by editing the l3_ha directive in the /etc/neutron/neutron.conf file:

```
l3_ha = True
```

   Any newly created router will be considered as HA and as not a legacy router.

9. In the same file, we will consider two other parameters to set the minimum and maximum number of L3 agents per router respectively, as follows:

```
...
max_l3_agents_per_router = 3
...
```

10. This will consider using two backup and one master router as the maximum number for L3 agents used per HA router:

```
...
min_l3_agents_per_router = 2
...
```

11. Restart the neutron-service process in the Cloud Controller node:

```
# service neutron-server restart
```

12. The last steps highlight how HA is effectively working for routers. To do so, an administrator can create a new router by setting the flag `--ha` to `true`. If it is a legacy router, the `--ha` flag can be overridden and set to false. Let's bring our first HA router up and running:

```
# neutron router-create Router_PP_HA --ha=true
```

```
Created a new router:
+------------------------+------------------------------------------+
| Field                  | Value                                    |
+------------------------+------------------------------------------+
| admin_state_up         | True                                     |
| distributed            | False                                    |
| external_gateway_info  |                                          |
| ha                     | True                                     |
| id                     | 2782ff83-15b0-4e92-83de-3b569d20cd09     |
| name                   | Router_PP_HA                             |
| routes                 |                                          |
| status                 | ACTIVE                                   |
| tenant_id              | 6fa47a2b492e48548c2c9596d1c2a5a2         |
+------------------------+------------------------------------------+
```

Bear in mind that only the administrator tenant can override the creation of legacy routers. The creation of routers can be performed using the previous command line as follows:
neutron router-create --ha=<True | False> name_router

13. Walking through different network nodes running an L3 agent, the newly created router can be observed by the means of its namespace as follows:

```
root@cc01 ~# ip netns
qrouter-2782ff83-15b0-4e92-83de-3b569d20cd09
qrouter-7151c4ca-336f-43ef-99bc-396a3329ac2f
qrouter-a029775e-204b-45b6-ad86-0ed2e507d5
root@nn01 ~# ip netns
qrouter-2782ff83-15b0-4e92-83de-3b569d20cd09
```

14. Checking the router namespace on the cloud controller demonstrates that the new router is a part of an HA setup. The IP address output shows the default IP assigned to the new router HA interface:

```
root@cc01 ~# ip netns exec qrouter-2782ff83-15b0-4e92-83de-
3b569d20cd09 ip address
202: ha-e72b5718-cd: <BROADCAST,MULTICAST,UP,LOWER_UP> mtu 1500
qdisc noqueue state UNKNOWN
```

```
link/ether fa:16:3e:a5:32:c0 brd ff:ff:ff:ff:ff:ff
inet 169.254.192.2/18 brd 169.254.255.255 scope global ha-e72b5718-
cd
valid_lft forever preferred_lft forever
inet6 fe80::f816:3eff:fea5:32c0/64 scope link
valid_lft forever preferred_lft forever
```
root@nn02 ~# ip netns exec qrouter-2782ff83-15b0-4e92-83de-3b569d20cd09 ip address
```
7: ha-3d3d639a-66: <BROADCAST,MULTICAST,UP,LOWER_UP> mtu 1500 qdisc
noqueue state UNKNOWN
link/ether fa:16:3e:71:0a:4b brd ff:ff:ff:ff:ff:ff
inet 169.254.192.1/18 brd 169.254.255.255 scope global ha-3d3d639a-
66
valid_lft forever preferred_lft forever
inet 169.254.0.1/24 scope global ha-3d3d639a-66
valid_lft forever preferred_lft forever
inet6 fe80::f816:3eff:fe71:a4b/64 scope link
valid_lft forever preferred_lft forever
```

Here, `169.254.0.1` is the VRRP IP.

HA CIDR is defined by the directive `l3_ha_net_cidr` in the `/etc/neutron/neutron.conf` file. By default, it is set to 169.254.192.0/18.

15. Additionally, once a new router in HA mode is created, Neutron automatically reserves a new dedicated HA network only visible to administrators:

 # neutron net-list

id	name	subnets
26adf398-409d-4f6e-9c44-918779d8f57f	private_network	d928d559-9f9c-4e1a-ab3f-139129babb71 10.15.15.0/24
e6c9e195-d2f9-4ee8-8412-cfc03079d5b5	HA network tenant 6fa47a2b492e48548c2c9596d1c2a5a2	d974b680-2d22-4cd5-b67e-8402af903f96 169.254.192.0/18
ac708df9-23b1-42dd-8bf1-458189db71c8	public_network	11b1015c-38bd-4a70-9315-d42552b3506e 10.0.2.0/24

To check which L3 agent nodes are hosting a given HA router, use the following command line:
 # neutron l3-agent-list-hosting-router Router_Name
Here, `Router_Name` is the name of the router configured in HA.

Another attractive feature provided by the VRRP in Neutron is the way given to check the state of a router namespace in which an L3 network node is active. In the latest releases, Keepalived is configured and runs in each namespace by using a persistent configuration file located at `/var/lib/neutron/ha_confs/ROUTER_NETNS/keepalived.conf`, where `ROUTER_NETNS` is the router namespace of the HA router.

Failover events are also logged in `neutron-keepalived-state-change.log` under the same directory. The following extract from a log shows a switch router during a failover event on the first network node:

```
...
DEBUG neutron.agent.l3.keepalived_state_change [-] Wrote router
2782ff83-15b0-4e92-83de-3b569d20cd09 state master write_state_change
...
```

More HA in Neutron

Like router HA, **Distributed Virtual Routers** (**DVR**) operate across multiple network nodes. Using DVR, network load can be distributed across operating routers. Unlike legacy routers, compute nodes run L2/L3 agents that eliminate SPOF for the network node.

External traffic flows through compute nodes for instances assigned floating IP addresses in each compute node. This can be very beneficial in terms of performance by removing bottlenecks compared to legacy router models. On the other hand, DVR requires routing traffic for instances with fixed IPs through a network node that also handles **Source Network Address Translation** (**SNAT**) traffic.

 It is possible to perform SNAT at the compute layer, but this may raise a compromise of adding more complexity and less loosely decoupled architecture

HA in Ansible:

There are several ways to implement a high available OpenStack cluster. As proven in the previous sections, HA can be achieved in each OpenStack layer by the means of many techniques including services redundancy, database replication, load balancing using HAProxy, and clustering methods such as Pacemaker and Corosync. HA setup in OpenStack should be also capable of automation. In this section, we will cover the last piece of our OpenStack: Ansible playbooks, offering an automated way of our previous HA implementation using Ansible.

As discussed in `Chapter 1`, *OpenStack Clustering the Cloud Controller and Common Services*, we have adjusted our initial deployment with three cloud controllers for running common services including databases and queuing messages. We need to describe our network ranges and our fleet of servers in the `/etc/openstack_deploy/openstack_user_config.yml` file. In the same file, we will need to adjust our `VIP` addresses for load balancing by pointing to the HAProxy endpoints. This can be achieved by updating the `global_overrides` section by setting the internal and external VIP addresses for the load balancer running HAProxy as follows:

```
...
global_overrides:
    internal_lb_vip_address: 172.47.0.47
    external_lb_vip_address: 192.168.47.47
```

Note that the previous directives can be also set by using both `haproxy_keepalived_internal_vip_cidr` and `haproxy_keepalived_external_vip_cidr` directives corresponding respectively to the internal and external VIP addresses. The default settings can be found in the `/etc/openstack_deploy/user_variables.yml` file.

The default `global_overrides` section denotes how different container networks can be configured. The `tunnel_bridge` and `management_bridge` directives are configured by default as `br-vxlan` and `br-mgmt` respectively. Make sure to have a networking setup correctly configured with the existing names of each of the network host interfaces. Naming conventions for bridges interfaces are referenced in the Ansible playbooks as follows:

- `br-mgmt`: used for inter-communication between containers that carry management OpenStack services traffic.
- `br-vxlan`: used for Neutron network traffic that carries **VXLAN** tunnel traffic.
- `br-vlan`: used for Neutron network of type **VLAN**. The untagged network interface is dropped into the `br-vlan` bridge.
- `br-storage`: used to provide block storage access between block storage and compute hosts.

As we have defined the different servers forming our OpenStack setup in `Chapter 1,` *OpenStack Clustering the Cloud Controller and Common Services*, we will need to point Ansible to where the HAProxy service will be installed. Running a load balancing software in dedicated nodes is highly recommended for better performance and service reliability. For the sake of simplicity, we can instruct Ansible to run HAProxy in our cloud controller nodes by adding the following section:

```
...
haproxy_hosts:
  cc-01:
    ip: 172.47.0.10
  cc-02:
    ip: 172.47.0.11
  cc-03:
    ip: 172.47.0.12
```

By default, the HAProxy playbook uses the variable file located under `/vars/configs/haproxy_config.yml,` to take care of different services including by default Galera, RabbitMQ, Glance, Keystone, Neutron, Nova, Cinder, Horizon, Aodh, Gnocchi, Ceilometer, and many other API services that are out of the scope of this book, such as **Sahara** and **Trove**. Each HAProxy entry is denoted with the **service** section, followed by the HAProxy service name, the backend nodes, SSL termination, port, and the balancing type. The following excerpt shows an example of the default HAProxy configuration for the Image API service:

```
....
  - service:
      haproxy_service_name: glance_api
      haproxy_backend_nodes: "{{ groups['glance_api'] | default([]) }}"
      haproxy_ssl: "{{ haproxy_ssl }}"
      haproxy_port: 9292
      haproxy_balance_type: http
      haproxy_backend_options:
        - "httpchk /healthcheck"
...
```

More services can be added or customized by adjusting the `haproxy_config.yml` file. The `user_variables.yml` file can be also used to customize each **HAProxy/Keepalived** instance by setting the priority of the **VRRP** value. By default, the master node is assigned a value of **100** whereas the slave is assigned a value of **20**. Setting the Keepalived configuration to use more than one backup node can be found in the `/vars/configs/keepalived_haproxy.yml` file. The default settings can be overwritten by setting priorities, for example, as follows:

```
haproxy_keepalived_priority_master: 101
haproxy_keepalived_priority_backup: 99
```

More additional settings can be configured to specify which interfaces on the cloud controller nodes Keepalived will bind both internal and external VIPs. The following excerpt sets the `br-mgmt` and `enp0s3` as the internal and external Keepalived interfaces respectively in the `user_variables.yml` file:

```
haproxy_keepalived_internal_interface: br-mgmt
haproxy_keepalived_external_interface: enp0s3
```

To install and update the HAProxy and Keepalived service configurations in the cloud controller nodes, run the `haproxy-install.yml` playbook as follows:

 # openstack-ansible haproxy-install.yml

The last piece of the HA setup from the playbooks is to update the OpenStack services by limiting the deployment of the updated nodes:

 # openstack-ansible setup-openstack.yml --limit haproxy_hosts

Summary

In this chapter, you have learned some of the most important concepts about high availability and failover. You have also learned the different options available to build a redundant OpenStack architecture within a robust resiliency. You now know how to diagnose your OpenStack design by eliminating any SPOF across all services. We have highlighted different open source solutions out of the box to arm our OpenStack infrastructure and make it as fault tolerant as possible. Different technologies have been introduced, such as HAProxy database replication using Galera, Keepalived, Pacemaker, and Corosync. New advanced built-in HA mechanisms for networks were introduced within the latest releases of OpenStack (**Juno** and **later**). HA routers using VRRP and DVR are very promising solutions that tackle the issue of network failure in an OpenStack environment. This presents a great step forward to architect a high available OpenStack platform and boost confidence to keep different environment layers up and running. By the end of this chapter, we highlighted briefly how to set up a high available OpenStack cluster using Ansible by going through the HAProxy playbook to load balance services and embrace their availability by enabling Keepalived with additional options.

Turning your IaaS into a highly available environment will also need more visibility. Preventive actions could save a lot of work and unnecessary *firefighting*. For that reason, any system running in production must be watched regularly by keeping an eye on each part of it and raising alerts when issues appear. In the next chapter, we will cover how monitoring OpenStack can be approached by implementing effective system checks for the cloud platform and troubleshooting materials.

10
Monitoring and Troubleshooting - Running a Healthy OpenStack Cluster

"To accept something on mere presumption and, likewise, to fail to investigate it may cover over, blind, and lead astray."

- Abu Nasr Al-Farabi

A functional OpenStack cloud environment cannot be achieved without having full control of every piece and component running in it. Being a proponent of keeping an eye on the resources and services running the OpenStack infrastructure is a step in the right direction. Monitoring is not limited to defining which problems can appear and how to react against them, but also is a pre-maintenance exercise where operators report the trend of resources usage and decide how the cloud architecture can be adjusted in terms of design and deployment. As you will learn in this chapter, the Telemetry module in OpenStack helps operators to gather information in the form of metering data and it provides pertinent functionalities including event and alerting handling. We will cover the following topics in the first part of this chapter:

- The growth of the Telemetry service in OpenStack
- The new design of the Ceilometer within the latest releases of OpenStack
- The new Alarming Service under the umbrella of Telemetry: Aodh
- The time series database as a Service sub-project: Gnocchi
- Installing and integrating the Telemetry service in OpenStack

The second part of the chapter will bring you to a new and extended monitoring layout by integrating an external monitoring tool in OpenStack; Nagios. Arming your infrastructure with advanced and customized monitoring corners will enhance the infrastructure stability. This part will cover:

- Introducing the Nagios server and installing it in the OpenStack environment
- Discovering the flexibility of the overwhelming Nagios plugins
- Starting to monitor your first OpenStack service node and getting your first alert

Monitoring will help to take preventive actions instead of firefighting. On the other hand, it might happen that alerts start shouting when an OpenStack host accidentally fails for any reason. Fighting against MTTR, an OpenStack operator should have a methodology that would help to alleviate a problem as soon as possible. The last part of this chapter will cover briefly the art of troubleshooting in OpenStack by going through:

- Presenting tools and simple methods to resolve incidents in OpenStack
- Learning in a nutshell how to check different OpenStack services and analyze them
- Demonstrating how to rescue instances when a compute node restarts or fails
- Resolving instances connectivity issues using OpenStack command line tools

Telemetry in OpenStack

The Telemetry service has been fully integrated in the OpenStack ecosystem since the launch of the Grizzly release. The Telemetry module was referred by one main project code named Ceilometer, which provides the users the ability to:

- Collect metering data of both physical and virtual resources deployed in OpenStack
- Store metrical data in a storage backend for further analysis
- Define and collect events for alarm evaluation
- Trigger alarms based on defined criteria

Starting from the Liberty release, the Telemetry module has changed the gears by enabling more features. This includes the introduction of two additional sub-projects working in tandem with Ceilometer as the core component of the Telemetry service:

- **Aodh service**: To handle alarm code functionality
- **Gnocchi service**: A dispatcher driver to Ceilometer for archiving metrics storage support

The Telemetry project in OpenStack has been changed since the Liberty release. In the following sections, we will dive into each Telemetry sub-project to understand how all the components work together in a typical production environment.

Rethinking Ceilometer

The Ceilometer project was originally intended (due to the Folsom release) to collect usage data and transform them into billable items so that the cloud operator would be able to create the customer's invoice. Due to its good modularity, Ceilometer has slowly grown to perform more monitoring and alarming for OpenStack. This has added more complexity to its core system components. Since the Liberty release, Ceilometer has been reorganized by splitting it into a few subsystems. That includes in a first iteration moving the alarm feature of Ceilometer to a new sub-project named Aodh.

Ceilometer glossary

It might be crucial to provide a basic understanding of the Ceilometer terminology before we take a closer look at its overall architecture within OpenStack's core integration:

- **Resource**: The Ceilometer resource can be any OpenStack entity that is being metered, such as instance, volume, and so on.
- **Meters**: A meter is a measurement tracked for a resource. It is also called a *counter*. Meters simply convert a particular resource usage to a human-readable value, such as CPU utilization per instance or overall bandwidth consumption in a particular host. Meters are defined as string values that have a unit of measurement and can be categorized essentially into three types:
  - **Cumulative**: This increases over a period of time
  - **Gauge**: The value is updated only when a change occurs in the current gauge or duration
  - **Delta**: This changes over a period of time when the previous value is updated

- **Samples**: Each meter is associated with a data sample compelling its attributes.
- **Agent**: This is a software service that is running on the OpenStack infrastructure and measuring the usage and sending the results to a collector.
- **Pipelines**: Ideally, a given metric data gathered by agents is pushed to the transformer for it to be manipulated and visualized via pipelines before delivering it to the publisher and emitted to the collector afterwards.
- **Archive policy**: A policy defining at which level measures will be captured during data aggregation. A policy defining the timespan that must be kept when aggregating data.

> Ceilometer can use the Gnocchi driver as a storage backend for metrics. It provides more granularity on configuring archives for metrics by the means of archive policies.

- **Retention**: Defines for how long a data source will be retained in the storage archive based on the archive policy.
- **Statistics**: This is like any other monitoring tool, collecting a set of values in certain laps of time and applying a defined function construct a statistical overview of a given metric. We find five functions in Ceilometer to perform different kinds of preliminary calculations, and they are as follows:
    - `avg`: This is the average value in the specified laps of time
    - `sum`: This is the sum of all values in the specified laps of time
    - `min`: This is the minimum value registered in the specified laps of time
    - `max`: This is the maximum value registered in the specified laps of time
    - `count`: This gives the number or values registered in the specified laps of time

> Since the Liberty release, the alarm code feature of Ceilometer was deprecated. It was forked and moved to a new sub-project under the Telemetry umbrella named Aodh. It was then completely removed in the Mitaka release from the Ceilometer core.

The Ceilometer architecture

The overall workflow of Ceilometer can be highlighted in four main phases that include:

- Data collection
- Data processing
- Data storage
- Data retrieval

At each stage of the precedent workflow, Ceilometer exposes different dedicated agents designed to facilitate the completion of the whole chain, which can be summarized as the following:

- **Polling agents**: These poll regularly each OpenStack infrastructure service to formulate measurements via API calls.

  A polling agent can be a wide term that may point to both a compute agent and a central agent. A compute agent specifically gathers statistics from instances running in a compute node and polls them to the message queue. The central agent could run in a central management server in OpenStack, such as a cloud controller. It polls statistics of resources other than instances.

- **Notification agents**: These listen periodically on the message queue bus, collect new notification messages set by different OpenStack services, and translate them to metrics before pushing them back to the appropriate message queue bus.
- **Collector agents**: These monitor the message queue, gather samples, and collect metering messages generated by either polling or notification agents. Therefore, the new metering messages will be recorded in a backend storage.
- **API service**: This exposes a standard API that provides access to the internal Ceilometer database if enabled to query metering data against it.

Data collected can be stored in an internal Ceilometer database. Ideally, MongoDB is the mostly used database for the Telemetry metric storage backend due to its capability of handling concurrent read/write operations. Nevertheless, the latest enhancements introduced to the Ceilometer design aim to provide more scalability to each of its core components. The data storage backend has raised a few major fundamental issues. First, firing a number of metric API requests at a large scale in a short period of time represents a big CPU eater and might lead to very poor performance. A famous example that crystallizes this problem is the usage of the orchestration service in OpenStack:

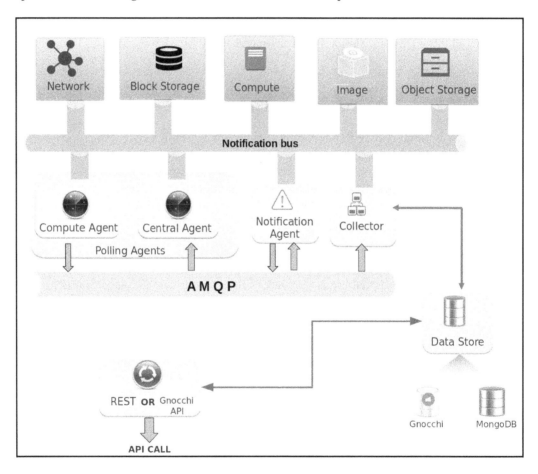

Gathering data is mainly performed by agents using a pipeline mechanism. Internally, they periodically send requests for sample objects, which reflect a certain meter. Every sample request will be forwarded to the pipeline. Once passed to the pipeline, meters can be manipulated by several transformer types:

- **Accumulator**: This accumulates multi-values and sends them in a batch
- **Aggregator**: This aggregates multi-values into one
- **Arithmetic**: This includes arithmetic functions to compute the percentage
- **Rate of change**: This identifies trends by deriving another meter from the previous data
- **Unit conversion**: This gives the type of unit conversion to be used

Once manipulated and transformed, a meter might follow its path via one of the multiple publisher types:

- **Notifier**: This is the meter data pushed over reliable AMQP messaging
- **rpc**: This is the synchronous RPC meter data publisher
- **udp**: This is the meter data sent over the UDP
- **file**: This is the meter data sent into a file

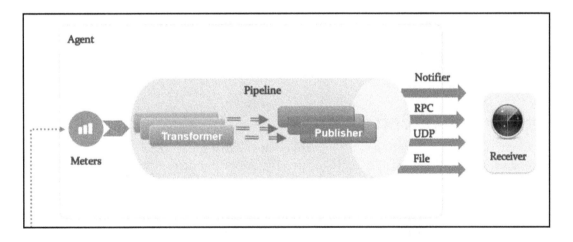

Eventually, launching several clusters from templates introduces a high compute load on the Telemetry service because of the evaluated alarms based on previous recorded sample sets, and hence, it makes it difficult to catch serial data metric points in time for storage. In addition, relying on a single MongoDB data store is a very limited solution that lacks scalability. The new trend comes with storing data on a scalable filesystem such as Swift or Ceph. These challenges have been addressed by a new Telemetry sub-project; Gnocchi. We will continue in the next section by adumbrating an overview about this new service time series database as a service Telemetry component in OpenStack.

Gnocchi - time series database as a service

The Gnocchi project aimed in the first place to store resource metrics at scale. Giving the Heat example, different resources can be spawned without the need to make additional metric computational operations on the fly. This drastically reduces any computing overhead.

Basically, samples are no longer written directly into a database, they are converted into Gnocchi elements and posted afterwards on its native API. Aggregated data is recorded in a time series. Each converted sample presents a data point that has a timestamp and measurement.

 More configuration details related to the performance topic will be addressed in `Chapter 12`, *OpenStack Benchmarking and Performance Tuning - Maintaining Cloud Performance.*

The Gnocchi architecture

As shown in the following diagram, Gnocchi comes with a great REST API to easily access metric data. Requesting data is usually tackled by Gnocchi indices from the database. Gnocchi is pluggable and supports several types of indexer drivers that include PostgreSQL and MySQL. The hallmark of data optimization using Gnocchi is about indexing resources and their associated attributes. This makes any data search a fast operation. As mentioned previously, Gnocchi introduces a scalable metric storage design by backing the metric data storage in a scalable storage system such as Swift and Ceph.

It is possible to configure Gnocchi to aggregate and store measures in Swift or Ceph as a storage backend by the means of its built-in storage drivers:

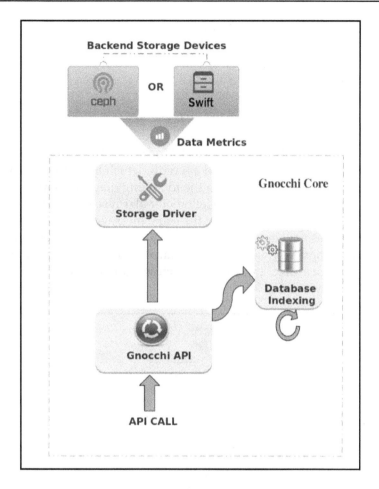

The Gnocchi project has joined the Telemetry service effort since the Kilo release. More information can be found at: `http://gnocchi.xyz/`.

Aodh - embracing alarms

Another brick added to the Telemetry service in OpenStack is the alarm handling mechanism, which was split from the Ceilometer core project after the Liberty release. The alarm subsystem has moved to a new sub-project named Aodh. The big win of such a redesign step is a loosely coupled architecture that leverages scalability.

Aodh is an old Irish word and it means fire. It was inspired from Irish mythology, which was borne by several kings.

The Aodh architecture

The alarm service becomes a standalone project. Since the Liberty release, the Ceilometer alarm feature has been forked and renamed as Aodh, which takes the lead of triggering alarms based on custom rules. As shown in the following diagram, a main difference can be noticed when compared to the preceding Ceilometer alarm service; the ability to scale horizontally when hitting more load. Using the same message queue, Aodh exposes an event listener that catches new notifications and provides an instant response time with zero latency. Aodh listeners rely on predefined alarms that will trigger instantly based on events and configured measures. In this case, reacting against auto-scaling conditions when using Heat becomes very useful:

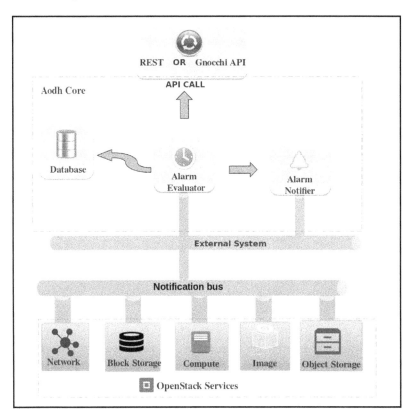

Additionally, the new design of storing alarms is more flexible, Aodh can use either the Ceilometer legacy database or the Gnocchi storage backend. As seen in the Gnocchi architecture, Aodh also supports an application programmable interface that can be accessed externally.

 The OpenStack Mitaka release includes a new performance enhancement in the Aodh core service that enables multiple workers support for alarm handling.

Installing Telemetry in OpenStack

In this section, we will include the Telemetry module in OpenStack. For the sake of simplicity, we will install the following Telemetry components using the command-line interface in the cloud controller node:

- Ceilometer with a legacy storage backend
- Aodh for alarm notification and evaluation

The Ceilometer installation

The next steps show how to install Ceilometer in our existing environment. We will first begin by configuring our controller node, cc01.packtpub:

1. Install the core components described previously:

    ```
    # yum install openstack-ceilometer-api openstack-ceilometer-
    collector openstack-ceilometer-central python-ceilometerclient
    ```

2. Install MongoDB, which Ceilometer needs for the backend database:

    ```
    # yum --enablerepo=epel -y install mongodb-server mongodb
    ```

3. Start the MongoDB server and make it autostart on machine boot:

    ```
    # service mongod start
    # chkonfig mongod on
    ```

4. Ensure that MongoDB binds to the management IP address of our cloud controller in the `/etc/mongodb.conf` file:

```
bind_ip = 172.47.0.10
```

5. By default, MongoDB creates a file of 1 GB to journal in the `/var/lib/mongodb/journal` directory. Optionally, you can reduce the size of the journaling space allocation, asserting a directive in `/etc/mongodb.conf` file: `smallfiles = true`. In order for the changes to take effect, follow your modification by restarting the mongodb service:

```
# service mongodb stop
# rm /var/lib/mongodb/journal/prealloc.*
# service mongodb start
```

6. Create a database for Ceilometer:

```
# mongo --host 172.47.0.10 --eval '
db = db.getSiblingDB("ceilometer");
db.createUser({user: "ceilometer",
pwd: "ceilometer_password",
roles: [ "readWrite", "dbAdmin" ]})'
```

7. After getting a successful configuration issued, you should see the output as follows:

```
MongoDB shell version: 2.6.11
connecting to: 172.47.0.10:27017/test
Successfully added user: { "user" : "ceilometer", "roles" : [
"readWrite", "dbAdmin" ] }
```

For the sake of simplicity, `MongoDB` has been installed in the controller node within one running database instance. Remember that we have created a single point of failure within the Ceilometer database, which might need a MongoDB cluster among other cloud controller nodes. Deploying Ceilometer with the MongoDB shared cluster is out of the scope of this book. Using Gnocchi is another alternative that directly removes any SPOF for the metric storage backend:

1. Point the Ceilometer service to use the created database:

```
# openstack-config --set /etc/ceilometer/ceilometer.conf
database connection mongodb://ceilometer: ceilometer_password
@cc01:27017/ceilometer
```

2. For a secure connection between the Ceilometer service and its agents running in other nodes in our OpenStack environment, define a secret key that can be generated using OpenSSL. We will need to install the rest of the agents in compute nodes later:

```
# ADMIN_TOKEN=$(openssl rand -hex 10)
```

3. Store the token generated in the Ceilometer configuration file:

```
# openstack-config --set /etc/ceilometer/ceilometer.conf
publisher_rpc metering_secret $ADMIN_TOKEN
```

4. Same as any other newly added service, we will always tell Keystone to authenticate against it. To do this, we create a new `ceilometer` user, which will have the role of admin:

```
# keystone user-create --name=ceilometer --pass=ceil_pass --
email=ceilometer@example.com
# keystone user-role-add --user=ceilometer --tenant=service --
role=admin
```

5. Register the Ceilometer service with the Keystone identity service by specifying its correspondent endpoint as follows:

```
# keystone service-create --name=ceilometer --type=metering
--description="Ceilometer Telemetry Service"
# keystone endpoint-create
--service-id $(keystone service-list | awk '/ metering / {print
$2}')
--publicurl http://cc01:8777
--internalurl http://cc01:8777
--adminurl http://cc01:8777
```

Edit the `/etc/ceilometer/ceilometer.conf` file and change the right directives in each section of the file as follows:

1. Change the following database connection information for MongoDB:

```
connection= mongodb://ceilometer: ceilometer_password
@cc01:27017/ceilometer
```

2. Change the following in the RabbitMQ section:

```
...
rabbit_host=172.47.0.10
rabbit_port=5672
rabbit_password=RABBIT_PASS
rpc_backend=rabbit
```

3. The authentication info for `Ceilometer` is as follows:

```
[service_credentials]
os_username=ceilometer
os_password=service_password
os_tenant_name=service
os_auth_url=http:// 172.47.0.10:35357/v2.0
```

4. The connection info for Keystone is as follows:

```
...
[keystone_authtoken]
auth_host=172.47.0.10
auth_port=35357
auth_protocol=http
auth_uri=http://172.47.0.10:5000/v2.0
admin_user=ceilometer
admin_password=service_password
admin_tenant_name=service
```

5. Change the shared secret key among nodes participating in the Telemetry service:

```
...
[publisher]
metering_secret=ceilo_secret
```

6. Finally, restart the Ceilometer services as follows:

```
# service ceilometer-agent-central ceilometer-agent-notification
ceilometer-api ceilometer-collector restart
```

The next stage will basically tell our compute nodes to run a set of agents to communicate via the API service to collect metrics' data and send them back to the database, where it will be stored and visualized. Remember that it is imperative that you install a Ceilometer agent in each compute node.

The **OpenStack-Ansible** (**OSA**) project provides a stable Ansible playbook for Ceilometer installation, which can be found at `https://github.com/openstack/openstack-ansible` `/blob/master/playbooks/os-ceilometer-install.yml`. Optionally, it is possible to automate the installation of the Ceilometer agents on compute hosts, for example, by creating a new role that specifies compute nodes that agents will be running on.
To install a Ceilometer agent in each compute node, perform the following steps:

1. Install the Ceilometer agent on the first compute node, `cn01.packtpub`:

   ```
   # yum install openstack-ceilometer-compute
   ```

2. Edit the `/etc/nova/nova.conf` file to enable the Ceilometer notification drivers in the default section:

   ```
   ...
   notification_driver = nova.openstack.common.notifier.rpc_notifier
   notification_driver = ceilometer.compute.nova_notifier
   instance_usage_audit = True
   instance_usage_audit_period = hour
   notify_on_state_change = vm_and_task_state
   ```

3. Keep updating the following sections in the `/etc/ceilometer/ceilometer.conf` file. Add the same `$ADMIN_TOKEN` shared secret key generated in our cloud controller node:

   ```
   ...
   [publisher_rpc]
   metering_secret= 47583f5423df27685ced
   Configure RabbitMQ access:
   ...
   [DEFAULT]
   rabbit_host = cc01
   rabbit_password = $RABBIT_PASS
   ```

4. Add identity service credentials:

   ```
   ...
   [keystone_authtoken]
   auth_host = cc01
   auth_port = 35357
   auth_protocol = http
   admin_tenant_name = service
   admin_user = ceilometer
   admin_password = service_password
   ```

5. Add service credentials:

```
...
[service_credentials]
os_auth_url = http://cc01.packtpub:5000/v2.0
os_username = ceilometer
os_tenant_name = service
os_password = service_password
```

6. For troubleshooting purposes, we will need to configure the log directory by commenting out the `log_dir` directive:

```
...
[DEFAULT]
log_dir = /var/log/ceilometer
```

7. Restart ceilometer-agent and nova-compute:

```
# service ceilometer-agent-compute nova-compute restart
```

Let's check out the Ceilometer service installation by logging in as the Admin account to the System Info section in Horizon. You can see the Ceilometer service enabled and running in the controller node:

Name	Service
nova	compute
neutron	network
cinderv2	volumev2
novav3	computev3
swift_s3	s3
glance	image
ceilometer	metering
cinder	volume

Configuring alarming

The next wizard will guide you through a few basic steps to install the Telemetry `alarmservice` in the cloud controller server as follows:

1. Access the node and create a new `aodh` openstack user:

    ```
    # keystone user-create --name=aodh --pass=aodh_pass --
    email=aodh@example.com
    ```

2. Assign the OpenStack admin role to the `aodh` to the managed services project:

    ```
    # keystone user-role-add --user=aodh -tenant=services --role=admin
    ```

3. Create a new OpenStack service called `aodh` to be attached later to a new endpoint in the OpenStack services list:

    ```
    # keystone service-create --name=aodh --type=alarming --
    description="Telemetry"
    ```

4. Once the new service is registered by Keystone, we can create its correspondent endpoints in the Cloud Controller node:

    ```
    # keystone endpoint-create
    --service-id $(keystone service-list | awk '/ alarming / {print
    $2}')  --publicurl http://cc01:8042
    --internalurl http://cc01:8042
    --adminurl http://cc01:8042
    ```

5. Create a new `aodh` database:

    ```
    MariaDB [(none)]> CREATE DATABASE aodh;
    ```

6. Grant privileges access to the `aodh` user to the `aodh` created database in the cloud controller node:

    ```
    MariaDB [(none)]> GRANT ALL PRIVILEGES ON aodh.* TO
    'aodh'@'localhost' IDENTIFIED BY 'AODH_PASSWORD';
    MariaDB [(none)]> GRANT ALL PRIVILEGES ON aodh.* TO  'aodh'@'%'
    IDENTIFIED BY 'AODH_PASSWORD';
    ```

Now that we have all the essential new service components in place, we proceed by installing the OpenStack Aodh packages in the cloud controller node:

```
# yum install python-ceilometerclient openstack-aodh-api  openstack-aodh-
listener openstack-aodh-notifier
openstack-aodh-expirer openstack-aodh-evaluator
```

Edit the /etc/aodh/aodh.conf file and change the rights directives in each section of the file as follows:

1. Change the following database connection information to point to the newly created Aodh database:

   ```
   . . .
   [database]
   connection=mysql+pymysql://aodh:AODH_PASSWORD@cc01/aodh
   Change the following in the RabbitMQ section:
   . . .
   [oslo_messaging_rabbit]
   rabbit_host=172.47.0.10
   rabbit_port=5672
   rabbit_password=RABBIT_PASS
   rpc_backend=rabbit
   ```

2. The authentication info for the Aodh service is as follows:

   ```
   . . .
   [service_credentials]
   auth_type = password
   auth_url = http://cc01:5000/v3
   project_name = services
   username = aodh
   password = aodh_pass
   interface = internalURL
   ```

3. The connection info for keystone is as follows:

   ```
   . . .
   [keystone_authtoken]
   auth_strategy = keystone
   auth_type=passowrd
   project_name = services
   username = aodh
   password = aodh_pass
   auth_uri=http://cc01:5000
   auth_url=http://cc01:35357
   memcached_servers = 172.47.0.10:11211
   ```

4. Before starting the new Aodh service, populate the new `aodh` database as the root:

```
# /bin/sh -c "aodh-dbsync" aodh
```

5. Finally, restart the Aodh services including the api, listener, evaluator, and the notifier service processes:

```
# service openstack-aodh-api.service openstack-aodh-
listener.service openstack-aodh-evaluator.service openstack-aodh-
notifier.service restart
```

Let's check out the Aodh service installation by logging in as the Admin account to the **System Information** section in Horizon. You can see the Aodh service enabled and running in the controller node:

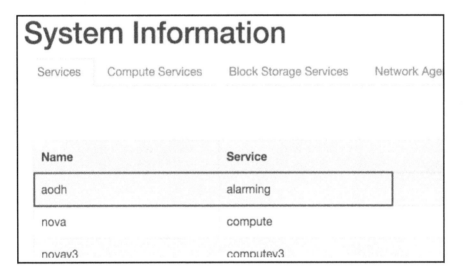

Arming OpenStack monitoring

There are several ways to keep an eye on and watch what is going on in your OpenStack private cloud. We have already discovered the expanding Telemetry module as an official monitoring service well integrated into OpenStack. It might be a very fruitful solution to facilitate customer billing as well. Although the former Telemetry module is expanding its metrics to cover the image, compute, block and object storage, and network service, it might be needed to bring more mature infrastructure monitoring tools for additional alerting. When dealing with large private cloud infrastructure, more hardware and virtual resources are added to the monitoring inventory list and keeping a close eye on any possible abnormal service activity is not an easy task. Dealing with such a challenge, an OpenStack operator should put in place a very sophisticated and complementary monitoring solution that covers not only the tenant cloud ecosystem, but also the hardware and OpenStack services. In the next section, we will introduce an additional great monitoring tool, Nagios to expand our monitoring area for the OpenStack ecosystem.

Running Nagios

You have most probably used and installed one or many monitoring tools in your infrastructure. Zabbix, Cacti, Munin, and StatsD are also good candidates to fulfill the monitoring position in our system. Feel free to bring any of the monitoring tools that you feel more comfortable or familiar with. In the next section, we will use a new installed Nagios server.

Placing Nagios

We will be configuring Nagios on a separate server that has access to all OpenStack servers. In addition, we will need Internet access to download the required packages for the Nagios server installation.

Our new monitoring server will eventually join:

- Administrative networks
- External networks

Installing the Nagios server

The next steps assume the installation of a Nagios server in a dedicated server running CentOS with enough CPU power, RAM, and disk space:

1. Install the required monitoring packages:

   ```
   # yum -y install nagios nagios-plugins-all nagios-plugins-nrpe nrpe
   php httpd
   ```

2. Enable the Nagios and web service to start on boot:

   ```
   # chkconfig httpd on && chkconfig nagios on
   ```

3. Start the web server and Nagios processes:

   ```
   # service httpd start && service nagios start
   ```

4. Protect the Nagios Admin panel by setting a password:

   ```
   # htpasswd -c /etc/nagios/passwd nagiosadmin
   ```

5. New password, adding password for user `nagiosadmin`.

> It is possible to change the admin username by editing the /etc/nagios/cgi.cfg configuration file and redefining the admin account.

Log in to the Nagios web interface by pointing via a browser to `http://NAGIOS_SERVER_IP/nagios`. Once successfully logged in, you are ready to start joining your OpenStack pieces to the monitoring server.

Configuring Nagios on OpenStack nodes

The Nagios server exposes a number of *plugins* (also called *checks*) that can run locally and enable agent-like checks on the OpenStack target nodes. The plugins can be easily installed and extended by the means of the *NRPE* (Nagios Remote Plugin Execution) plugin:

1. On each OpenStack service host, we will need to install NRPE and the Nagios plugins as follows:

   ```
   # yum install -y nagios nrpe nagios-plugins-all
   ```

2. The installed plugins are available under `/usr/lib/nagios/plugins` and enable the NRPE service to start on boot:

   ```
   # chkconfig nrpe on
   ```

3. Make sure to allow the Nagios server for check reports by editing the `/etc/nagios/nrpe.cfg` file:

   ```
   ...
   allowed_hosts = NAGIOS_SERVER_IP
   ...
   ```

The same file will be modified to specify commands used for running service checks:

- Allow port access from the Nagios server to the target nodes:

  ```
  # iptables -I INPUT -p tcp --dport 5666 -j ACCEPT
  # iptables-save > /etc/sysconfig/iptables
  ```

- Start the NRPE service:

  ```
  # service nrpe start
  ```

Considering a large sized OpenStack infrastructure, make sure to automate the last step by designing a common artifact that assembles common services including Nagios plugin installation. This can be achieved by running a specific common host service Chef cookbook, Ansible playbook, or Puppet manifest.

Watching OpenStack

One of the most powerful features provided by Nagios is the extensibility of defining checks using simple configuration files even for isolated cases. Additionally, plugins are very useful and can be reused. The Nagios community also offers several plugins that could fulfill an OpenStack operator's needs.

 An example of integrating ready-to-use Nagios plugins to monitor OpenStack can be found at: `https://github.com/cirrax/openstack-nagios-plugins`.

Before diving into a simple Nagios check configuration, let's shed some light on how checks could be defined ahead to cover most of the monitoring aspects in our OpenStack production environment. The following table is an example summary for Nagios check plugins for basic OpenStack services and components:

Infrastructure component	OpenStack service	Nagios check
keystone-api	Keystone	`check_http`
nova-api	Nova	`check_http`
glance-api	Glance	`check_http`
Glance-registry	Glance	`check_http`
neutron-api	Neutron	`check_http`
cinder-api	Cinder	`check_http`
nova-compute	Nova	`check_procs`
nova-scheduler	Nova	`check_procs`
neutron-server	Neutron	`check_procs`
mysql	Database	`check_mysql`
dnsmasq	DNS/DHCP	`check_dhcp`
rabbitmq-server	Messaging Queue	`check_rabbitmq_server`

There are a variety of available plugins that can be installed in the Nagios server to perform a few of the command checks elaborated in the previous table. These can be found at `https://www.monitoring-plugins.org/index.html`. Additionally, the official Nagios website exposes a very large set of plugins organized by category and they can be found at: `https://exchange.nagios.org/directory/Plugins`. The messaging queue checks can be performed using a great plugin available at `https://github.com/nagios-plugins-rabbitmq/nagios-plugins-rabbitmq`.

Let's take a step forward and define a new server object for the first compute node. To keep things well organized, we will create a new server directory where it will include all the server configuration files of our target OpenStack machines:

```
# mkdir /etc/nagios/servers
```

This will require updating the main Nagios configuration file when loading the host list. To do so, comment out the following line directive from `/etc/nagios/nagios.cfg`:

```
...
cfd_dir = /etc/nagios/servers
...
```

Now it is time to create our first host configuration file under the servers directory. The following example file defines a compute node with two main sections including the host description and service check run:

```
define host{
  use             linux-server
  host_name       cn01
  alias           compute01
  address         172.28.128.18
}

define service {
  use               generic-service
  host_name         cn01
  check_command     check_nrpe!check_nova_compute
  notification_period    24x7
  service_description    Compute Service
}
```

We can use a separate file to define command checks for all commands; this will include all `check_nrpe` checks for the remote hosts. Under the same `/etc/nagios` directory, create a new file called `nagios_commands_checks.cfg`. This should be followed by adjusting the Nagios configuration file in the server by adding the following directive:

```
...
cfg_file=/etc/nagios/nagios_command_checks.cfg
```

The new file will have the following content that defines a generic NRPE check in the command line including variables such as user, which runs the check in the remote host and its IP address:

```
define command{
  command_line    $USER1$/check_nrpe -H $HOSTADDRESS$ -c $ARG1$
  command_name    check_nrpe
}
```

Before moving to the compute node, restart the Nagios service:

```
# service nagios restart
```

 Check the correctness of the Nagios configuration file before every service restart by using the following command line:

```
# nagios -v /etc/nagios/nagios.cfg
```

The service section performs a simple check of the Nova compute process running on the compute node. The check command is not defined yet; we will need to adjust our NRPE configuration file in the compute node as follows:

```
...
command[compute]=/usr/lib64/nagios/plugins/check_procs -C nova-compute -u
nova -c 1:4
```

In the same file, add the Nagios IP address in the `allowed_hosts` directive as follows:

```
...
allowed_hosts=127.0.0.1,172.28.128.47
```

Before starting the NRPE service in each target monitored OpenStack host, make sure that the NRPE port is open by adding the following IP tables rule:

```
# iptables -I INPUT -p tcp --dport 5666 -j ACCEPT
# iptables-save > /etc/sysconfig/iptables
```

Restart the NRPE service to join the compute node to the Nagios host inventory list:

```
# service nrpe start
```

From the Nagios dashboard, the compute node will be automatically added to the Nagios inventory list within the monitored service named `Compute Service`:

Host ↑↓	Service ↑↓	Status ↑↓	Last Check ↑↓	Duration ↑↓	Attempt ↑↓	Status Information
172.28.128.18	Compute Service	OK	12-18-2016 20:34:43	0d 0h 1m 48s	1/3	PROCS OK: 1 process with command name 'nova-compute', UID = 162 (nova)

We can next run next a simple trigger check to raise an alert as CRITICAL by stopping the Nova compute service running in the compute node:

```
# service nova-compute stop
```

Eventually, the alarm will be raised based on our settings in the NRPE command line. In our example, `-c 1:4`, Nagios will fire up an alarm as `CRITICAL` if the number of Nova compute processes instances is 0 or above 4:

Host ⬆⬇	Service ⬆⬇	Status ⬆⬇	Last Check ⬆⬇	Duration ⬆⬇	Attempt ⬆⬇	Status Information
172.28.128.18	Compute Service	CRITICAL	12-18-2016 22:04:43	0d 0h 0m 28s	1/3	PROCS CRITICAL: 0 processes with command name 'nova-compute', UID = 162 (nova)

Troubleshooting - monitoring perspective

Gaining confidence in resolving issues when operating a large infrastructure based on OpenStack should be achieved in the first stage by an efficient monitoring and alerting system. The second round of troubleshooting tasks can be performed by digging into log files and debug messages thrown by the system or some parts of it. We have already set up a monitoring system that acts as a first watcher on our overall OpenStack installation. Reacting to escalated alerts generated by monitoring systems will first point to specific components of OpenStack that would help to start gathering valuable information for further investigation. Most importantly, the monitoring tool must be capable of triggering human readable notifications when operators and administrators configure a certain number of events that are highly customized. This will help quickly identify not only the affected part of the system, but also exactly what is causing the issue. For example, an alarm event firing a trigger that mentions *the number of messages in the queue is high*! can be a good trigger notification, but it is incomplete! Fixing threshold is not obvious. The best way to yield reasonable values is by learning the infrastructure behavior and its various limits.

Services up and running

Armed by useful Linux and OpenStack command-line tools, an OpenStack operator could start tracing the issue raised by the alerting agent. In general scenarios, first checking running services in OpenStack is a basic step to determine which process died or is not running. Some Linux commands such `ps` or `pgrep` are good friends to quickly resolve service issues. Likewise, we can also use numerous OpenStack commands to leverage process checks more efficiently.

For example, Nova can be a challenging OpenStack component to troubleshoot due to its overwhelming number of processes and composite dependencies. Checking the overall compute services can be performed by the following command line:

```
# nova-manage service list
```

Binary	Host	Zone	Status	State	Updated_At
nova-consoleauth	cloud	internal	enabled	:-)	2016-12-18 02:39:24
nova-scheduler	cloud	internal	enabled	:-)	2016-12-18 02:39:24
nova-conductor	cloud	internal	enabled	:-)	2016-12-18 02:39:23
nova-compute	cloud	AZ-1	enabled	:-)	2016-12-18 02:39:20
nova-cert	cloud	internal	enabled	:-)	2016-12-18 02:39:22
nova-cells	cloud	internal	enabled	XXX	2016-09-27 00:44:46
nova-console	cloud	internal	enabled	XXX	None
nova-compute	compute01	nova	enabled	:-)	2016-12-18 02:39:20

The example output identifies the status of each Nova service running across all the OpenStack clusters defined by:

- `Binary`: The Nova service name.
- `Host`: The server running the Nova service.
- `Zone` : The OpenStack zone in which a Nova service(s) is (are) running.
- `Status` : The administrative state of the Nova service.
- `State`: The current state of the Nova service. A smiley face refers to a running service and XXX points to a stopped service.
- `Updated_At`: A very time-informative column indicating the last change made to the Nova service.

Additionally, other Nova services such as `nova-scheduler` and `nova-api` cannot be shown using the `nova-manage` command line. This can be checked using a `ps` command line tool:

```
# ps -aux | grep nova-api
```

Failed services can be investigated from log files stated in `/var/log/nova*.log` files.

Chapter 11, *Keeping Track of Logs - ELK and OpenStack,* gives more details on how to interpret log entries for different OpenStack services.

Likewise, Cinder supports a dedicated command line to verify the health of all its process states using the following command line:

```
# cinder service-list
```

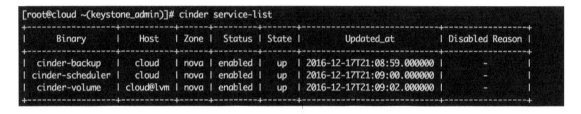

Where:

- `Binary`: The Cinder service name.
- `Host`: The server running the Cinder service.
- `Zone`: The OpenStack zone in which a Cinder service(s) is (are) running.
- `Status`: The administrative state of the Cinder service.
- `State`: The current state of the Cinder service. `up` refers to a running service and `down` points to a stopped service.
- `Updated_At`: A very time-informative column indicating the last change made to the Cinder service.
- `Disabled Reason`: An additional column to note a reason for disabling a Cinder process by the administrator.

Active Neutron services and agents across all the OpenStack setup can be listed using the `pgrep` command line tool:

```
# pgrep -l neutron
```

```
11303 neutron-dhcp-ag
20638 neutron-keepali
11274 neutron-l3-agen
11335 neutron-metadat
6348 neutron-ns-meta
4868 neutron-openvsw
5485 neutron-rootwra
11496 neutron-server
```

Similarly, Ceilometer and Aodh processes can be listed using `pgrep` or `ps` tools. However, it is important to check in each host whether the Ceilometer agent is running or not. Otherwise, the Horizon service usage tab will not be listing missed OpenStack hosts. As Glance at is not very complicated subject in terms of number of processes, a quick check of all Glance processes can be verified using the following command line:

```
# glance-control all status
```

```
glance-api (pid 19854) is running...
glance-registry (pid 19855) is running...
glance-scrubber (pid 19856) is running...
```

Likewise, the orchestration service exposes a few processes that can be checked including the `heat-engine` process that handles stacks. The Heat command line resembles the Cinder and Nova command lines by offering a `service-list` command that returns a list of engine process instances identified by engine IDs and which hosts are up and running:

```
# heat service-list
```

```
+----------+-------------+--------------------------------------+--------+--------+---------------------------+--------+
| hostname | binary      | engine_id                            | host   | topic  | updated_at                | status |
+----------+-------------+--------------------------------------+--------+--------+---------------------------+--------+
| cloud    | heat-engine | 1da90ffc-9b0f-4c95-a2ed-5e3e8c68cd99 | cloud  | engine | 2016-12-18T03:04:00.000000 | up     |
| cloud    | heat-engine | 37525c03-e113-4637-8769-1940b166e9fa | cloud  | engine | 2016-12-18T03:04:06.000000 | up     |
| cloud    | heat-engine | 43ff4ebc-c2d4-4a9a-82fe-c29495c2a8da | cloud  | engine | 2016-12-18T03:03:58.000000 | up     |
| cloud    | heat-engine | 6ef20f78-e7aa-4cce-9369-6915219f2bd8 | cloud  | engine | 2016-12-18T03:04:05.000000 | up     |
| cloud    | heat-engine | 8ac33a50-7745-47b7-a9a2-6631c3c0fb5c | cloud  | engine | 2016-12-18T03:04:00.000000 | up     |
```

Services should listen

Running services properly in OpenStack depends on which port each process should listen to. For example, starting the identity service can return the following error message:

```
keystone error: [Error 98] Address already in use
```

This error message refers to a misconfiguration in the Keystone service file and must be revised. In fact, the identity service socket listens by default on port `5000`, which can be occupied by another application or process. This typical issue can be tackled by checking which port is configured in each OpenStack configuration file and double-checked using friendly command line tools such as `lsof` or `netstat`. For example:

```
# lsof -i :5000
```

or:

```
# netstat -ant | grep 5000
tcp6 0 0 :::5000 :::* LISTEN
```

Another useful network tool for local testing is `telnet`. For example, checking if port 80 is listening for the web server running Horizon can be performed as follows:

```
# telnet localhost 80
Trying 127.0.0.1 ...
Connected to localhost.
Escape character is '^]'
```

Ports should be carefully managed by `IPtables` or an internal Linux `firewall`. Considering large OpenStack services, different processes need to reach other host services endpoints. If IPtables rules are not set correctly, ports will be not reachable and connections will stay dropped.

Ideally, preparing the IPtables rules per each OpenStack host in advance will reduce the troubleshooting time.

A great OpenStack reference for all services default ports can be found at: `http://docs.openstack.org/mitaka/config-reference/firewalls-default-ports.html`.

Rescuing instances

Due to a compute failure or reboot, there is a high chance of increasing the MTTR SLA value if this exercise is not handled with care. After an hypervisor crash or reboot, the instance state must be checked in the first place once it has been ensured that all OpenStack services are running as expected using the nova list command line:

```
# nova list
```

Where:

- `ID`: The instance ID running in the compute node
- `Name`: The name of the instance
- `Status`: The current state of the instance

 The complete list of state transitions for an OpenStack instance can be found at:

`http://docs.openstack.org/developer/nova/vmstates.html`.

- `Task State`: The transition state based on API calls to the instance
- `Power State`: The current hypervisor state
- `Networks`: The attached networks to the instance

Another great Nova OpenStack command line is `nova hypervisor-list`. It indicates an issue with the hypervisor running on a specific host resulting in instance failures. The following Nova check points to review the host configuration setup in terms of hypervisor support and Nova settings:

```
# nova hypervisor-list
```

```
+----+---------------------+-------+----------+
| ID | Hypervisor hostname | State | Status   |
+----+---------------------+-------+----------+
| 1  | cloud               | up    | enabled  |
| 2  | compute01           | up    | enabled  |
+----+---------------------+-------+----------+
```

Instances can be migrated from one host to another using the **live-migration** command line. This requires a shared storage of instances disks across the OpenStack cluster:

```
# nova live-migration --block-migrate b51498ca-
0a59-42bd-945a-18246668186d cc02.pp
```

```
)6d1c2a5a2 | MIGRATING | migrating | Running    | private_netv
```

In the worst case, when a compute node is no longer available, live migration won't help and we will need to relaunch the instances into a different compute node by adjusting the database set of the first host to be pointing to the second one:

```
MariaDB> use nova;
MariaDB [nova]> update instances set host='cc02.pp'
where host='cc01.pp';
```

Once record sets are updated, each instance requires a libvirt's XML file to boot properly, these can be located in /etc/libvirt/qemu/instance-*.xml. To start instances while creating the XML file, user reboot command line by adding the --hard option:

```
# nova reboot --hard b51498ca-0a59-42bd-945a-18246668186d
```

If the affected instances have attached volumes, you will need to detach and attach each volume UUID of the instance once updated to the database record sets for both Nova and Cinder databases to point to the new healthy compute node.

A quick check of the rebooting process of the instance can be verified via the console output either from **Log tab** in **Horizon** or by the means of the Nova command line tool:

```
# nova console-log b51498ca-0a59-42bd-945a-18246668186d
```

The complete console logs for each instance resides by default in the /var/lib/nova/instances/INSTANCE_UIID/console.log file, where INSTANCE_UIID is the instance UUID under question.

All green but unreachable

Covering all issues that might occur related to a networking service in OpenStack is a long exercise due to the complexity of such a service. Monitoring systems can trigger notifications when a Neutron process dies or restarts as seen previously. However, in some other cases, it might be more difficult to detect a network issue that prevent users from reaching instances or connecting them to the external network. In most cases, network issues appear when Neutron has been installed with the wrong configuration including plugins and drivers. Additionally, creating networks and routers are error prone operations that could result in a missing virtual tenant network setup. Neutron has reached a very good state of maturity by providing rich command line tools to help in tracing network reachability problems.

Understanding the basic network namespace concept is essential to visualize where exactly the traffic is manipulated. When creating L3 and DHCP agents in a network node, new namespaces will be created automatically to run each of them separately. This can be verified using the network utility command line:

```
# ip netns
```

```
qrouter-2782ff83-15b0-4e92-83de-3b569d20cd09
qrouter-7151c4ca-336f-43ef-99bc-396a3329ac2f
qrouter-a029775e-204b-45b6-ad86-0ed2e507d5bf
qdhcp-26adf398-409d-4f6e-9c44-918779d8f57f
```

The previous output shows two sorts of namespaces:

- `qrouter-UUID`: Represents the L3 agent router namespace and instance connected to the router UUID created in the network node
- `qdhcp-UUID`: Represents the DHCP agent namespace for a private network created in the network node

Delving deeper in to this network picture would bring more details in each namespace and show different IP addresses attached to active interfaces:

```
# ip netns exec qrouter-a029775e-204b-45b6-ad86-
0ed2507d5bf ip a
```

```
21: qr-c2902c14-3b: <BROADCAST,MULTICAST,UP,LOWER_UP> mtu 1500 qd
    link/ether fa:16:3e:df:7a:9d brd ff:ff:ff:ff:ff:ff
    inet 10.15.15.1/24 brd 10.15.15.255 scope global qr-c2902c14-
        valid_lft forever preferred_lft forever
    inet6 fe80::f816:3eff:fedf:7a9d/64 scope link
        valid_lft forever preferred_lft forever
22: qg-9de4d23f-70: <BROADCAST,MULTICAST,UP,LOWER_UP> mtu 1500 qd
    link/ether fa:16:3e:17:dd:26 brd ff:ff:ff:ff:ff:ff
    inet 10.0.2.51/24 brd 10.0.2.255 scope global qg-9de4d23f-70
        valid_lft forever preferred_lft forever
    inet 10.0.2.22/32 brd 10.0.2.22 scope global qg-9de4d23f-70
```

If you have many routers created in the network node, check the right UUID router by running the *neutron router-list* command line.

Attached routes to the same router namespace can be checked as follows:

```
# ip netns exec qrouter-a029775e-204b-45b6-ad86-0ed2507d5bf ip r
```

```
default via 10.0.2.2 dev qg-9de4d23f-70
10.0.2.0/24 dev qg-9de4d23f-70  proto kernel  scope link  src 10.0.2.51
10.15.15.0/24 dev qr-c2902c14-3b  proto kernel  scope link  src 10.15.15.1
```

Dedicated IPtables per each namespace are available by running the following:

```
# ip netns exec qrouter-a029775e-204b-45b6-ad86-0ed2507d5bf iptables -n
```

```
Chain INPUT (policy ACCEPT)
target     prot opt source               destination
neutron-l3-agent-INPUT  all  --  0.0.0.0/0            0.0.0.0/0

Chain FORWARD (policy ACCEPT)
target     prot opt source               destination
neutron-filter-top  all  --  0.0.0.0/0            0.0.0.0/0
neutron-l3-agent-FORWARD  all  --  0.0.0.0/0            0.0.0.0/0

Chain OUTPUT (policy ACCEPT)
target     prot opt source               destination
neutron-filter-top  all  --  0.0.0.0/0            0.0.0.0/0
neutron-l3-agent-OUTPUT  all  --  0.0.0.0/0            0.0.0.0/0
```

When routers are created in OpenStack, all required interfaces must be in an active state and attached to the defined subnets. If all basic requirements are set, we can start debugging the network traffic by following simple diagnosing points:

- Verify that the compute node is forwarding packets from the external interface to the bridged one

 Check the enabled kernel port forwarding by using the following command line:
# sysctl -A | grep ip_forward
net.ipv4.ip_forward = 1

- Verify the security groups assigned per each instance
- Verify the Egress and Ingress traffic

 Check security groups in detail by running:
neutron security-group-list

- Verify the association of a floating IP to the instance to connect to the external network
- Verify the network reachability within the same DHCP and router namespaces
- Use `tcpdump` to debug traffic on each virtual interface including bridge interfaces such as `br-int` and `br-ex`

If port forwarding is enabled on the compute node, we can add a security rule to the default one that is assigned to the instance:

```
# nova secgroup-add-rule default icmp -1 -1 0.0.0.0/0
```

Within the same namespaces, we can try to ping the instance using the `ip netns` utility:

```
# ip netns exec qrouter-a029775e-204b-45b6-ad86-
0ed2507d5bf  ping 10.15.15.5
```

Where `10.15.15.63` is an associated floating IP to the instance.

If reaching the instance outside of the namespace is still not successful, this will guide us to review the bridges and ports established by OpenvSwitch:

```
# ovs-vsctl show
```

The output mainly shows three categories of virtual switches and bridges: `br-int`, `br-tun`, and `br-ex`.

As we are intending to connect to the instance from an external network, br-ex should be connected to the physical network node interface. This will allow traffic to reach the OpenvSwitch. If it is not created, make sure to run the following command line:

```
# ovs-vsctl add-port br-ex enp0s3
```

Where `enp0s3` is the external network interface of the network node. Make sure to replace `enp0s3` by your network interface name.

 Verify that the `/etc/neutron/l3_agent.ini` file is properly configured and L3 agent restart with the following setting:

```
# external_network_bridge = br-ex
```

Using `tcpdump` on each bridge interface is very helpful to dig deeper on how traffic is flowing from/to hosts and ending up to instances. For example, from the router namespace, we can find the instance floating IP interface:

```
# ip netns exec qrouter-a029775e-204b-45b6-ad86-0ed2507d5bf ip a
```

```
        valid_lft forever preferred_lft forever
    inet 10.0.2.65/32 brd 10.0.2.65 scope global qg-9de4d23f-70
```

Then starting tcpdump on the **qg-9de4d23f-70** will look as follows:

```
# ip netns exec qrouter-a029775e-204b-45b6-ad86-
0ed2507d5bf  tcpdump -i  qg9de4d23f-70
```

```
tcpdump: verbose output suppressed, use -v or -vv for full protocol decode
listening on qg-9de4d23f-70, link-type EN10MB (Ethernet), capture size 65535 bytes
02:44:48.047321 IP 10.0.2.15 > cloud: ICMP echo request, id 24032, seq 1, length 64
02:44:48.048022 IP cloud.52770 > gateway.domain: 31916+ PTR? 22.2.0.10.in-addr.arpa. (40)
02:44:48.048822 IP gateway.domain > cloud.52770: 31916 NXDomain* 0/1/0 (99)
02:44:48.049688 IP cloud > 10.0.2.15: ICMP echo reply, id 24032, seq 1, length 64
02:44:48.050056 IP cloud.59070 > gateway.domain: 35800+ PTR? 15.2.0.10.in-addr.arpa. (40)
```

Summary

In this chapter, we have revisited the Telemetry service in OpenStack by scratching the surface of each sub-project including Ceilometer, Aodh, and Gnocchi. Although we did not cover all the available metrics within the latest releases of OpenStack, you should give more importance to understanding how the Telemetry module is being extended and works under the hood. We next expanded our monitoring vision by enforcing what was set up in the first part of the chapter with a sophisticated external monitoring solution: Nagios. You should be able to exploit its extreme benefits in terms of plugins and configuration flexibility. That opens the curtains to deliver a rich monitoring data where operators and administrators get more insight on the deployed OpenStack infrastructure. By the end of this chapter, we have looked at a few commons ways on how to take immediate actions and where to look once issues are raised and notified by the monitoring system. You should be keen on using a variety of tools that include OpenStack command lines and Linux useful utilities for troubleshooting.

But still, as mentioned earlier, monitoring is a necessity but not enough to dig deeper into issues when they appear. We could resolve an incident immediately by restarting an OpenStack service; for example, when Nagios reports it is down but ignoring what causes the downtime presents a risk to the infrastructure stability in the future. Additionally, more complex errors might be raised and relying on the monitoring alert message would be insufficient. For this matter, as the monitoring system gathers metrics to provide useful information, we will need to develop and organize efficiently that information history to track down the incident for deep analysis from other sources: Log files, which will be the topic of the next chapter.

11
Keeping Track of Logs - ELK and OpenStack

"Somewhere, something incredible is waiting to be known."
- Carl Sagan

You might be tempted to realize the importance of a complete suite of monitoring solutions for your private OpenStack cloud environment. In `Chapter 10`, *Monitoring and Troubleshooting OpenStack - Running a Healthy OpenStack Cluster* demonstrates a mixed approach by adopting an inbox telemetry solution to work in tandem with an external monitoring tool such as *Nagios* for more advanced monitoring purposes. On the other hand, we have mainly focused on the first part of the equation, namely exposing alerts and warnings. The second part of the equation involves how to react to issues. Monitoring systems cannot give you strong advice if they are not properly adjusted and alerts are not set carefully. Troubleshooting a complex suite of software such as OpenStack might not be an easy task for system and cloud administrators. Resolving them can be conducted by relying on logs that help to track down the root cause of the errors. Furthermore, if you attempt to upgrade your OpenStack packages, it can result in pressing fire on new bugs that are not fixed yet. Diving into logs will be a great way of encountering them. While logging is a standard refuge for system administrators to trace system errors, identifying the exact issue quickly and efficiently is highly required to minimize the downtime. Additionally, with the immense number of generated logs with different formats and versions, it becomes a sore spot among operators to fetch the exact information in a short time. Although many free and commercial logging tools exist that are able to serve complex IT infrastructure logging strategy, it is vital to learn how to deal logs information in OpenStack and bring them in highly customized logging system solutions.

This chapter opens the curtains of logging in OpenStack and accomplishes the mission of monitoring and troubleshooting tasks stated in the previous chapter. In this chapter, you will learn:

- Where OpenStack logs reside
- How to adjust your logging options by the OpenStack service
- Discover the ELK platform for log analysis and troubleshooting
- Centralize tones of OpenStack log files in one logging system
- Integrate the ELK platform in your OpenStack private cloud
- Start using ELK to serve logs of OpenStack services
- Build visualization graphs to learn about your OpenStack cloud system behavior
- Learn how to fire fast search query in ELK for fast troubleshooting experience

Tackling logging

Painful but crucial; this is what many system administrators and developers claim when they start debugging an error by consulting a huge log file. Depending on the system you try to fix, cutting down troubleshooting time is true if you do not realize where they live and how they are organized.

Demystifying logs in OpenStack

Most probably, you have installed new OpenStack versions prior to the **Mitaka** release and you might be tempted to start looking for logs in, their default location the Linux system `/var/log`. Eventually, their locations may vary depending on how you have deployed OpenStack. Since we have deployed our first OpenStack infrastructure using Ansible in the first chapter, you can check or modify the location of logs by service in each playbook file corresponding to each OpenStack service. For example, we can have a look at the Ansible `os-nova-install` playbook used in Chapter 2, *Deploying OpenStack - The DevOps Way*. In the `vars` attribute section of the YAML file, a directive attribute `log_dirs` describes the default settings of your Nova log files. For example, the next line from the playbook file code dictates the default location of Nova log files to be created in `/var/log/nova`:

```
...
  vars
    log_dirs:
      - src: "/openstack/log/{{ inventory_hostname }}--nova"
        dest: "/var/log/nova"
```

It is also possible to set the logging severity by default when installing OpenStack services from playbooks. Logs input can take different shapes depending on the increasing level of logging: DEBUG, INFO, AUDIT, WARNING, ERROR, CRITICAL and TRACE. By default, the debug level is disabled and the logging level is set to INFO.

Logs location

Most of the standard services in Linux/Unix systems write their logs under `/var/log` directory in subdirectories. Any node running any OpenStack service stores its log files under `/var/log/` directory. The following table depicts, in a nutshell, where logs reside by default:

Service name	Log location
Compute	`/var/log/nova/`
Image	`/var/log/glance/`
Identity	`/var/log/keystone/`
Dashboard	`/var/log/horizon/`
Block storage	`/var/log/cinder/`
Object storage	`/var/log/swift/` `/var/log/syslog/`
Shared File System	`/var/log/manila/`
Console	`/var/lib/nova/instances/instance-ID/`
Network	`/var/log/neutron/`
Monitoring	`/var/log/ceilometer/`
Alarming	`/var/log/aodh/`
Metering	`/var/log/gnocchi/`
Orchestration	`/var/log/heat/`

Note that, Horizon merges its log files depending on the Apache convention names. If you are using Fedora's distribution, log files will reside under `/var/log/httpd`. Operating systems based on Ubuntu or Debian distributions support Apache2 naming, where you can find log files by default under `/var/log/apache2`.

Additional non-native OpenStack services store their log files in the following locations:

Service name	Log location
HTTP server	`/var/log/apache2/` `/var/log/httpd/`
Database	`/var/log/mariadb/`
Messaging queue	`/var/log/rabbitmq/`
LibVirt	`/var/log/libvirt/`

Compute nodes generally merge log files for VM boot up messages that reside in the `console.log` file. Every instance within its ID will generate the same file in a different subdirectory `/var/lib/nova/instances/instance-ID`.

> Ceph is not a native OpenStack service. Since it is operating and well-integrated in our OpenStack private cloud setup, you can find all Ceph log files regardless of how OSD and monitors have been distributed in many nodes under `/var/log/ceph`.

Adjusting logs in OpenStack

It is possible to adjust the logging level in OpenStack for each running service. If you get an alert or message from your monitoring system telling you that one of the services has encountered a problem, you can always refer to your logs with different logging methods. For example, if you would like to troubleshoot your compute service, it is recommended to refer to its configuration file, `/etc/nova/nova.conf`, and increase the debug level by reverting its default value from `False` to `True`:

```
debug=True
```

Once you finish fixing the issue, it will be required to disable the debug directive by reverting `True` to `False`. Doing so will protect your node from being overloaded from a huge amount of debug messages that might not be necessary when your nodes are running without issues.

More advanced techniques have been elaborated to customize the logging output in each service in OpenStack by using a separate logging configuration file. This way will enable users to have more control on log information during analysis. For example, to leverage logging information for the Nova OpenStack service, add the following flag to the `/etc/nova/nova.conf` configuration file:

```
log_config_append = /etc/nova/logging.conf
```

Then create a simple file called `logging.conf` under `/etc/nova/` with the following content:

```
[loggers]
keys=nova

[handlers]
keys=consoleHandler

[formatters]
keys=simpleFormatter

[logger_nova]
level=DEBUG
handlers=consoleHandler
qualname=nova
propagate=0

[handler_consoleHandler]
class=StreamHandler
level=DEBUG
formatter=simpleFormatter
args=(sys.stdout,)

[formatter_simpleFormatter]
format=%(asctime)s - %(name)s - %(levelname)s - %(message)s
```

Restarting the Nova service will reshape the log output in the console with respect to the format and log level pointed in the nova logger section:

```
<DATE>    <TIME>  <LINE-ID> -  INFO - <DEBUG MESSAGE>
```

Example output:

```
2016-12-28 02:22:11,382 - nova.compute.resource_tarcker - INFO -
Compute_service record updated for cloud:cloud
```

To learn more about the supported logging module facility and configuration syntax, refer to the official Python module website documentation at: `https://docs.python.org/release/2.7/library/lo gging.html#configuration-file-format`

Two eyes are better than one eye

OpenStack produces tons of log files in a real production environment. It becomes harder for a cloud operating team to analyze and parse them by extracting data in each file using a combination of tail, grep, and perl tools. The more hosts you build, the more logs you have to manage. Growing a few paces should be companioned by a serious trace keeper. To overcome such a challenge, your log environment must evolve to become centralized. A good option can be by starting flowing logs in a dedicated *rsyslog* server. You may put in so much data and your log server start starving for larger storage capacity. Furthermore, archiving the former data will not be handy when you need to extract information for a particular context. Additionally, correlating logs data having different format (taking into consideration RabbitMQ and MySQL logs) with generated events might be even impossible. So, what we need at this point is a set of quality requirement points for a good OpenStack logging experience as follows:

- Efficient way for parsing logs
- More meaningful log searching
- Index processed log data
- Elegant logs exposure

Emerging as the spearhead of free logging, open source stack **ELK** is a complete log analysis suite solution that includes different components: **ElasticSearch**, **LogStash**, and **Kibana**.

Let's take a moment and see how this solution can be useful for logging tasks for our OpenStack production environment.

ELK under the hood

The ELK stack involves different components that work together to address the challenges cited previously. The core parts of the stack can be described in a nutshell as the following:

- **ElasticSearch**: Is a scalable and distributed document store. It allows to index data in real time by achieving fast search response. ElasticSearch is designed to scale horizontally and provides high availability capabilities.
- **LogStash**: This enables collecting and processing logs by defining a data pipeline. LogStash is able to parse different sets of structured and unstructured data. The hallmark of this component is the ability to centralize several input data source types and convert them to a standard format.

> LogStash supports a large number of plugins for input and output. Custom plugins can be also developed for specific data format. Examples of existing input plugins can be found here: `https://www.elastic.co/guide/en/logstash/current/input-plugins.h tml`

- **Kibana**: provides a great user experience for visualizing data stored in ElasticSearch indices. It exposes shipped and indexed logs through sophisticated graphs, charts, and many other different graphical layouts. The power of Kibana comes from its real-time capability to display understandable dashboards based on ElasticSearch queries.

The next illustration depicts an overview of the data log pipeline through the different ELK platform components:

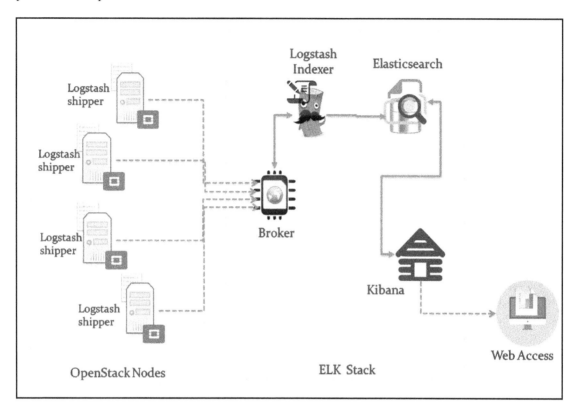

Additionally, to the core building blocks forming our ELK stack, other various component can enrich our logging pipeline which are depicted in the previous diagram as follows:

- **Filebeat**: serves as a LogStash agent shipper that transfers logs and events to Logstash

 A LogStash shipper can be any host running a LogStash agent or forwarder which sends log files to the LogStash server. The usage of Filebeat has more performance advantages compared to the traditional LogStash forwarder agent due to its utilization of a lightweight networking protocol called *'Lumberjack'*.

- **Broker**: Keeps receiving events logs from LogStash shippers

> Generally, LogStash uses Redis for performance wise as a broker to hold data received by the agent running in LogStash shipper.

- **LogStash indexer**: Indexes the events within the LogStash server

In our case, all functional OpenStack servers generate logs that will be shipped to the LogStash server. Received logs will be processed and filtered based on predefined filters. Any source of input is supported by LogStash such as TCP, UDP, files, Syslog, and so on. What you need is just to push logs to your LogStash server also known as *shipping*.

Once collected, LogStash gives you a hand to query any stored event and sort them the way you wish. The log event started by sending the collected logs by the LogStash agent to our central logging server. At this stage, where the LogStash server is running, the broker buffers the former collected logs which will be indexed next by the LogStash indexer. Now, it is the role of ElasticSearch engine to store the former log events and provides a full-text index so logs will be searchable. The final stage of a log event ends up at the LogStash dashboard or **Kibana** to execute log queries and build intuitive dashboards and are highly customizable.

> It is possible to run each component independently for scalability purposes.

Placing the ELK server

We will be configuring our first ELK server on a separate machine that has access to all OpenStack servers.

Our new monitoring server will join:

- Administrative network
- External network

Let's discover the different players that need to be installed in our logging server in order to ensure a successful installation:

- **Java**: Both ElasticSearch and LogStash require Java. Latest Java version is recommended while using OpenJDK is also an alternative for Java installation.
- **ElasticsSarch**: Powerful indexing and search engine for events shipped to the LogStash.
- **LogStash**: Defines the central log server that processes incoming logs.
- **Kibana**: Powerful web interface to query log events. It is highly customizable with several visualizations capabilities.
- **Nginx**: Kibana web interface will need a reverse proxy to access it externally. For that purpose, we will use Nginx.

Installing the ELK server

The next installation snippet will guide you through a package-based installation of the following LogStash components on a CentOS operation system:

- LogStash 5.1.1
- Elasticsearch 5.1.1
- Kibana 5.1.1
- Java 8
- Nginx

We intend to gather an important amount of log files from our OpenStack environment. It might be essential to plan for future resource consumption as your private cloud keeps growing gradually. Thus, a minimum set of specs will be required for the ELK server:

- Processor: 64-bit x86
- Memory: 8 GB RAM
- Disk space: 500 GB
- Network: Two 1 Gbps Network Interface Cards (NICs)

 Running CentOS with default configuration might prevent new services due to *SElinux* and *IPtables* restrictions. Make sure that SELinux is running at least in permissive mode or disabled and update your IPTables so packets can be forwarded to the ELK server.

Let's begin by installing the ElasticSearch component in the new ELK server.

Installing ElasticSearch

Both ElasticSearch and LogStash require the installation of Java. We will be installing a recent version of Java as follows:

1. Download and install Java 8:

   ```
   # wget http://download.oracle.com/otn-pub/java/jdk/8u111-b14/jdk-
   8u111-linux-x64.rpm
   # yum -y localinstall jdk-8u111-linux-x64.rpm
   ```

2. Add symbolic link in the /usr/bin directory to the java command:

   ```
   # alternatives --install /usr/bin/java java/usr/java
   /jre1.8.0_111/bin/
   ```

3. Check the correctness of the Java installation:

   ```
   # java -version
   java version "1.8.0_111"
   Java(TM) SE Runtime Environment (build 1.8.0_111-b14)
   Java HotSpot(TM) 64-Bit Server VM (build 25.111-b14, mixed mode)
   ```

4. Once Java is successfully installed, import the ElasticSearch public GPG key into yum:

   ```
   # rpm --import https://artifacts.elastic.co/GPG-KEY-elasticsearch
   ```

5. Next, create an ElasticSearch source list with the following content:

   ```
   # vim /etc/yum.repos.d/elasticsearch.repo
   [elasticsearch-5.x]
   name=Elasticsearch repository for 5.x packages
   baseurl=https://artifacts.elastic.co/packages/5.x/yum
   gpgcheck=1
   gpgkey=https://artifacts.elastic.co/GPG-KEY-elasticsearch
   enabled=1
   autorefresh=1
   type=rpm-md
   ```

6. Update the yum package database:

   ```
   # yum update -y
   ```

7. Initiate the following command to install elasticsearch:

   ```
   # yum install elasticsearch -y
   ```

8. Once installed, edit its main configuration file to enable access of the ElasticSearch server from external OpenStack services. By default, ElasticSearch uses port **9200**. For the sake of simplicity, the following line will allow any outside host to read data through HTTP API. Depending on your network setup, make sure to restrict access to a specific IP range within the OpenStack external network segment:

```
# vim /etc/elasticsearch/elasticsearch.yml
...
network.host: 0.0.0.0
...
```

9. Start the ElasticSearch service:

```
# systemctl start elasticsearch
```

10. Verify if the ElasticSearch service is listening on port 9200:

```
# netstat -ntpl | grep 9200
tcp6      0      0 :::9200      :::*      LISTEN      27956/java
```

Configuring ElasticSearch

We have a first instance of ElasticSearch up and running. In this section, we will highlight a few important topics related to the ElasticSearch configuration setup when dealing with a large amount of indexing operations. We have already mentioned a great capability of ElasticSearch: **Scalability**. OpenStack logs could go beyond dozens of Gigabytes per day, in this case, we face an indexing performance issue. Tuning ElasticSearch performance may expose several knobs you may twiddle, that is beyond the scope of this chapter. On the other hand, let's cover in a nutshell, a few interesting configuration directives that will guide us to prepare an ElasticSearch cluster capable of growing.

Defining ElasticSearch roles

An ElasticSearch node can be assigned the following roles:

- **Master Node**: The manager node that controls the state of the cluster
- **Data Node**: The core node that hold the data
- **Query Aggregator Node**: A load balancer node that responds to the client requests by initiating queries for results from Data Nodes.

In a large and heavily indexing ElasticSearch environment, it is recommended to dedicate three nodes as master to handle the cluster state fast enough.

By default, each ElasticSearch server can serve as a master, data, and perform as a query aggregator node at once. When dealing with a large environment, it is recommended to think in advance to designate more ElasticSearch servers with different roles.

To learn more on best practices for ElasticSearch scalability, the Elastic official website provides pertinent tips on how to plan for large environments that can be found here:
`https://www.elastic.co/guide/en/elasticsearch/guide/current/scal`
`e.html`

To make use of the node definitions in the ElasticSearch cluster, use the `elasticsearch.yml` configuration file to specify roles:

- The cluster name:

```
cluster:
...
name:    elk_pp_cluster
```

- The master node:

```
...
node.master: true
node.data: false
```

- The data node:

```
...
node.master: false
node.data: true
```

- The query aggregator node:

```
...
node.master: false
node.data: false
```

Extending ElasticSearch capabilities

The ElasticSearch module provides more advanced capabilities that facilitate different tasks which include indexing, sharding, and cluster management using **plugins**. ElasticSearch exposes, by default, a sophisticated RESTful API interface. Most of the developed plugins offer a REST client enabling communication, potentially with the ElasticSearch API in a much easier way. Mostly, plugins are **Kopf**, **Marvel,** and **Shield** to name a few. A full list of supported plugins for the latest version can be found here:
`https://www.elastic.co/guide/en/elasticsearch/plugins/master/index.html`

Since we have the latest stable version of ElasticSearch installed at the time of writing this book, we will introduce and install an amazing all-in-one plugin that comes with different extension plugins including: security, monitoring, internal alerting, and usage reporting. The new component extension called **x-pack**, enables graphs under Kibana without placing an extra dedicated endpoint dashboard.

 x-pack unifies the most used ElasticSearch plugins in the version prior to 5.0 in one extension that packages shield, watcher, and marvel.

The next wizard will guide you through a few steps on how to install x-pack using ElasticSearch plugin command-line tool:

1. Download the `x-pack zip` file into a temporary directory such as `/tmp` folder:

   ```
   [root@els001 tmp]# wget https://artifacts.elastic.co/
   downloads/packs/x-pack/x-pack-5.1.1.zip
   ```

2. Make sure that `elasticsearch` service is not running:

   ```
   # systemctl stop elasticsearch
   ```

3. Run the `elasticsearch-plugin` command-line tool from the ElasticSearch install directory by specifying the absolute path of the `x-pack` zip file:

   ```
   # cd /usr/share/elasticsearch
   # bin/elasticsearch-plugin install file:///tmp/x-pack-5.1.1.zip
   ```

4. Grant x-pack permissions to allow the Watcher add-on to send e-mail notifications:

   ```
   ...
   * javax.net.ssl.SSLPermission setHostnameVerifier
   ```

See `http://docs.oracle.com/javase/8/docs/technotes/guides/secur ity/permissions.html`for descriptions of what these permissions allow and the associated risks. Continue with installation? `[y/N]y`

This will unpack and install the x-pack plugin:

5. Start the ElasticSearch service:

```
# systemctl start elasticsearch
```

6. Verify that the new plugin is installed correctly by checking the plugin list as follows:

```
# bin/elasticsearch-plugin list
x-pack
```

Installing Kibana

Installing the latest version of Kibana at the time of writing can be performed as follows:

1. Create a new Kibana source list with the following content:

```
# vim /etc/yum.repos.d/kibana.repo
[kibana-5.x]
name=Kibana repository for 5.x packages
baseurl=https://artifacts.elastic.co/packages/5.x/yum
gpgcheck=1
gpgkey=https://artifacts.elastic.co/GPG-KEY-elasticsearch
enabled=1
autorefresh=1
type=rpm-md
```

2. Update the `yum` package database and install Kibana:

```
# yum update -y && yum install kibana -y
```

3. Run the following command-line to start `kibana` on boot up:

```
# chkconfig kibana on
```

Configuring Kibana

Kibana is now installed and we will need to adjust a few settings in its configuration file as follows:

1. Allow external connections to use Kibana by setting the `servers.host` directive in the `/etc/kibana/kibana.yml` configuration file as follows:

   ```
   # vim /etc/kibana/kibana.yml
   server.host: 0.0.0.0
   ```

 Make sure to restrict the allowed IP range in your external network.

2. Optionally, point Kibana at the ElasticSearch cluster instance. For the sake of simplicity, we are running Kibana in the same ElasticSearch server which is localhost by default:

   ```
   elasticsearch_url: http//localhost:9200
   ```

3. Start Kibana and check if it is running by checking its default port `5601`:

   ```
   # service kibana start
   # netstat -ntpl | grep kibana
   tcp        0    0.0.0.0:5601    0.0.0.0:*    LISTEN    5111/node
   ```

4. The next step will set up a reverse proxy so users can access Kibana externally. This can be achieved by installing Nginx and `httpd-tools`:

   ```
   # yum install nginx httpd-tools -y
   ```

5. Once installed, we will redirect HTTP traffic to our Kibana application listening on port 5601 locally. Create a new Kibana configuration file in Nginx under `/etc/nginx/conf.d/` as follows:

   ```
   # vim /etc/nginx/conf.d/kibana.conf
   server {
   listen 80;
   server_name els001.pp;
   auth_basic "Restricted Access";
   auth_basic_user_file /etc/nginx/htpasswd.users;
   location / {
       proxy_pass http://localhost:5601;
       proxy_http_version 1.1;
   ```

```
        proxy_set_header Upgrade $http_upgrade;
        proxy_set_header Connection 'upgrade';
        proxy_set_header Host $host;
        proxy_cache_bypass $http_upgrade;
    }
}
```

Where `server_name` is the `hostname` of our ELK instance running Kibana.

> If CentOS and SELinux are running, make sure to enable the HTTP
> daemon in the SELinux policies by setting
> `httpd_can_network_connect` to **1**:
> **# setsebool -P httpd_can_network_connect 1**

6. Before starting Nginx, let's install `x-pack` into Kibana. The new plugin will enable Kibana to exploit its security feature for login and dashboards:

    ```
    # cd /usr/share/kibana
    # bin/kibana-plugin install file:///tmp/x-pack-5.1.1.zip
    ```

7. This will extend the installed plugin list for Kibana that can be checked as follows:

    ```
    # bin/kibana-plugin list
    x-pack@5.1.1
    ```

8. Start the Nginx service:

    ```
    # service nginx start
    ```

9. Kibana can be accessible by using a browser and going to the FQDN or IP address of our ELK server. Once at the login page, use default username `elastic` and password `changeme` that comes with the x-pack module, which has super user privileges for the whole ELK stack. As the password requires changing, it can be performed via the command-line from the ELK server:

```
# curl -XPUT -u elastic 'localhost:9200/_xpack/security/user/
elastic/_password' -d {"password" : "AmazingPassword"}'
```

10. The first Kibana page will look empty since we have not configured any index patterns so far:

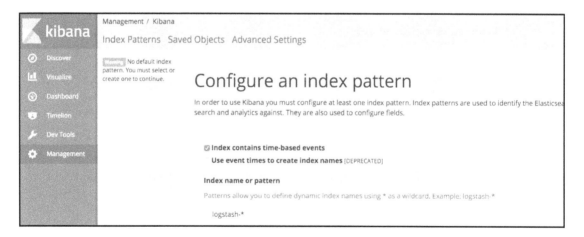

11. To speed up our Kibana setup, Elastic exposes sample Kibana dashboards including **Beats** index patterns as we intend to use **FileBeat** for shipping logs and indexing data. To download them, run the following command-line:

```
# curl -L -O https://download.elastic.co/beats/dashboards/
beats-dashboards-1.1.0.zip
# unzip beats-dashboards-*.zip
```

12. Load the downloaded dashboards and Beat index patterns into ElasticSearch:

```
# cd beats-dashboards-*
# ./load.sh
```

13. When accessing Kibana, the next index patterns will be available:

filebeat-*

packetbeat-*

topbeat-*

winlogbeat-*

Let's move to install LogStash and start configuring our first index pattern so OpenStack log files can be shipped and indexed by ElasticSearch.

Installing LogStash

Installing the latest version of LogStash at the time of writing this book can be accomplished as follows:

1. Create a new LogStash source list with the following content:

```
# vim /etc/yum.repos.d/logstash.repo
[logstash-5.x]
name=Elastic repository for 5.x packages
baseurl=https://artifacts.elastic.co/packages/5.x/yum
gpgcheck=1
gpgkey=https://artifacts.elastic.co/GPG-KEY-elasticsearch
enabled=1
autorefresh=1
type=rpm-md
```

2. Update the yum package database and install Kibana:

```
# yum update -y && yum install logstash -y
```

3. Run the following command-line to start Kibana on boot up:

```
# chkconfig logstash on
```

Configuring LogStash

As mentioned in a previous section, we will be using FileBeat to ship our OpenStack log entries in a secure way.

To verify the identity of our LogStash server, we will need to proceed as follows:

1. Edit the subjectAltName (**SAN**) directive located under the [v3_ca] section in the /etc/pki/tls/openssl.cnf file and locate the following:

```
...[v3_ca]
subjectAltName=IP: 172.28.128.19
```

This will resolve the private IP of the ELK server and allow you to gather logs from OpenStack servers.

2. The next step requires generating an SSL certificate and private key under /etc/pki/tls directory:

```
# cd /etc/pki/tls
# openssl req -config /etc/pki/tls/openssl.cnf -x509 -days 3650
-batch -nodes -newkey rsa:2048 -keyout private/logstash-
forwarder.key -out certs/logstash-forwarder.crt
```

 Notice that the outcome of this command is a logstash-forwarder.crt certificate file that will be copied to all our OpenStack production servers.

LogStash in action

Getting up to speed with LogStash involves getting to grips with a basic configuration. Basically, we find three main sections in any given LogStash configuration described as follows:

- **Input**: Defines how events are generated and get into LogStash
- **Filters**: Defines the way events are manipulated and customized
- **Outputs**: Defines how events can be sent from LogStash to an external system

An example of a LogStash configuration file is as follows:

```
input {
    stdin { }
    ...
}
filter {
    ...
}
output {
    stdout {
    .....
}
```

Input and Output blocks define events respectively from **STDIN** and to **STDOUT** standards streams in the I/O of the terminal. In LogStash, events entering via Input modified in filter and ending up via Output form a pipeline.

Like ElasticSearch, the LogStash processing pipeline can be enhanced by using plugins for each section described previously.

The most used LogStash plugins for the input section are *file, beats, stdin, lumberjack,* and *elasticsearch.* The filter section supports some powerful plugins such as *grok, mutate, dns,* and *multiline.* Lately, the Output section introduced the **Kafka** plugin for writing events to Kafka among other plugins such as *file, stdout, elasticsearch,* and *redis.* To learn more about the latest existing plugins for different LogStash sections, check out the following Elastic website link:
`www.elastic.co/support/matrix#show_logstash_plugins`

LogStash becomes very powerful with the latest versions thanks to the development of great plugins that resolve several challenges of processing complex entries.

Taking advantage of exploiting those plugins would generate a long configuration file. At some point, we will need to simplify our event processing pipeline by modularizing the LogStash configuration. A simple approach is to use three different files for each topic: inputs, filters, and outputs:

1. Create a new input file using the Beats plugin as follows:

```
# vim /etc/logstash/conf.d/02.beats-inputs.conf
  input {
  beats {
    port => 5044
    ssl => true
    ssl_certificate => "/etc/pki/tls/certs/logstash-
forwarder.crt"
      ssl_key => "/etc/pki/tls/private/logstash-forwarder.key"
    }
  }
```

   In this way, LogStash will use an SSL certificate and generate a private key to ship logs using beats input listening on port **5044**.

2. The second section can be described in a separate file under the same `/etc/logstash/conf.d/` directory. We will leave the implementation of our first filter for OpenStack messages in the next section:

```
# touch /etc/logstash/conf.d/15-openstack-filter.conf
```

3. The last output section is depicted in a new file using the `elasticsearch` plugin:

```
output {
  elasticsearch {
    hosts => ["localhost:9200"]
    sniffing => true
    manage_template => false
    index => "%{[@metadata][beat]}-%{+YYYY.MM.dd}"
    document_type => "%{[@metadata][type]}"
  }
}
```

   This will instruct LogStash to store data as beats in the ElasticSearch server running locally and listening on port `9200`. We will expect a new index with the format: `filebeat-YYYY.MM.dd`

4. Our first basic LogStash configuration is ready for testing. LogStash comes with a great test command-line tool to test the correctness of our LogStash configuration files. We will just need to specify the path of our configuration directory as follows:

```
# /usr/share/logstash/bin/logstash -t -f /etc/logstash/conf.d/
Configuration OK
```

> If you get a syntax error, the previous command-line will help to point directly to the misleading line in a specific configuration section file.

5. To make proper use of FileBeat, we will need to prepare a FileBeat index so that ElasticSearch will be able to analyze beats fields shipped by LogStash. We have already configured LogStash to output all inputs to our ElasticSearch instance. A very simple FileBeat index template can be downloaded as follows:

```
# curl -O https://gist.githubusercontent.com/thisismitch/
3429023e8438cc25b86c/raw/d8c479e2a1adcea8b1fe86570
e42abab0f10f364/filebeat-index-template.json
```

6. Loading the template can be performed using the ElasticSerach REST API:

```
# curl -XPUT 'http://localhost:9200/_template/filebeat?pretty'
-d@filebeat-index-template.json
Output:
  {
    "acknowledged" : true
  }
```

The message output indicates that our template was uploaded successfully.

> By default, `logstash-*` is assumed as the default index in Kibana. Using FileBeat would require a prior setup of the FileBeat index so data will be fed to ElasticSearch through FileBeat. Bear in mind that changing the name of the index mentioned in the LogStash output section should reflect the same name convention in the configured index.

To start shipping logs through LogStash we will need to set up our OpenStack servers.

Preparing LogStash clients

In the previous section, an SSL certificate has been generated to authenticate against the LogStash server and will be copied to the rest of the LogStash clients, which are, in our case, the different OpenStack servers. Let's start with our first cloud controller OpenStack server:

1. In the cloud controller server, create a new **cert** directory to stick to the same directory path setup for all servers and copy over the certificate file as follows:

```
@cc01 ~]# mkdir  /etc/pki/tls/certs
@cc01 ~]# scp packtpub@172.28.128.19:/etc/pki/tls/certs/
logstash-forwarder.crt   /etc/pki/tls/certs/
```

2. Let's move to install the FileBeat client package in the first OpenStack cloud controller server by creating a new yum database source package for FileBeat:

```
@cc01 ~]# vim /etc/yum.repos.d/elastic-beats.repo
[beats]
name=Elastic Beats Repository
baseurl=https://packages.elastic.co/beats/yum/el/$basearch
enabled=1
gpgkey=https://packages.elastic.co/GPG-KEY-elasticsearch
gpgcheck=1
```

3. Update the yum package database and install FileBeat:

```
# yum update -y && yum install filebeat -y
```

4. Instructing the LogStash client server is straightforward by editing one client's FileBeat configuration file /etc/filebeat/filebeat.yml. Let's start by adjusting lines from results and parameters collected from previous steps. The first excerpt points to the ELK host private IP address running LogStash. Check the *LogStash as output* section and change the default IP address to the one you have had configured:

```
...
### Logstash as output
logstash
    # The Logstash hosts
    hosts: ["172.47.0.10:5044"]
```

5. In the same section, define a window of maximum number of events that LogStash can process at one time:

```
...
bulk_max_size: 2048
```

6. The certificate copied to the LogStash client machine must be set in the FileBeat configuration file by pointing to the `tls` subsection:

```
...
    tls:
        certificate_authorities: ["/etc/pki/tls/certs/logstash-
forwarder.crt"]
```

7. Now we have the basic directives set and ready to check log files that we intend to ship. This can be addressed in the `prospectors` section by defining the path of the log source file. For example, the next excerpt will instruct the shipping of Keystone log files:

```
...
    prospectors:
            paths:
        - /var/log/keystone/keystone.log
```

8. Within the same `prospectors` section, it is possible to specify the type of each log file and optionally add a particular tag field. This way, searching entries for any type of OpenStack log files will be much easier via Kibana. The next excerpt will classify any keystone log as follows, a `Control Plane` document tagged as `keystone`:

```
...
    prospectors:
            paths:
        - /var/log/keystone/keystone.log
            document_type: Control Plane
            fields:
                tags: ["keystone"]
```

9. Start the `filebeat` service:

```
# servicectl start filebeat
```

Our filters are not accomplished yet. Let's check in the following section how OpenStack logs will be loaded using LogStash once shipped by Filebeat into ElasticSearch.

Filtering OpenStack logs

For instance, we will not be able to parse or browse any input log files in our graphical user interface. We have only prepared and established a connection between the client and the server. We will need to configure our LogStash to define a way of manipulating shipped files. File logs formats are not standard, sending logs as one blob of data will not be useful. Thus, we seek a way of identifying their type and drill down into events to extract their values. This constructs the main heart of LogStash contribution in log files management, filtering.

In our case, we have different log files generated either by the Linux system or by other services, most importantly OpenStack ones.

 Note that Syslog messages can be useful as well since they track down the internal system messages of the base operating system running your OpenStack node.

But what might be most interesting is how we can classify our logs by type in the first place. The filter plugin can achieve our requirements, by applying filter conditions based on chosen and specific fields.

The following code snippet depicts a new `filter` section in our central LogStash configuration file:

```
filter{
if [type] == "openstack" {
grok {
patterns_dir =>
"/usr/share/logstash/vendor/bundle/jruby/1.9/gems/logstash-
patterns-core-4.0.2/patterns/"
match=>[ "message","%{TIMESTAMP_ISO8601:timestamp} %
{NUMBER:response} %{AUDITLOGLEVEL:level} %{NOTSPACE:module} [%
{GREEDYDATA:program}] %{GREEDYDATA:content}"]
  add_field => ["openstask"]
  add_tag => ["openstackmetrics"]
}
multiline {
  negate => false
  pattern => "^%{TIMESTAMP_ISO8601}%{SPACE}%{NUMBER}?%
  {SPACE}?    TRACE"
  what => "previous"
  stream_identity => "%{host}.%{filename}"
}
mutate {
  gsub => ['logmessage', "" ," " ]
```

```
        }
    date {
        type    =>  "openstack"
        match => [ "timestamp", "yyyy-MM-dd HH:mm:ss.SSS" ]
            }
        }
    }
```

Let's take a closer look at the new filter plugin section: `grok`. The grok filter parses text and by the means of its patterns, it processes and structures it in a more elegant way.

> By default, LogStash includes several *grok* patterns that serve to tag specific fields and support customized regular expressions. To discover the available grok patterns, check out the `logstash-patterns-core` project in GitHub, which can be found at:
> `https://github.com/logstash-plugins/logstash-patterns-core/tree/master/patterns`.

The `grok` section defines the following options:

- `patterns_dir`: LogStash comes with a few patterns that can be found under `/usr/share/logstash/vendor/bundle/jruby/1.9/gems/logstash-patterns-core-X.X.X/patterns/where` *X.X.X* refers to the installed version of LogStash by default. Keep in mind that patterns are packaged regular expressions needed by the filter to parse the text and forward any match within the regular expression.
- `match`: The match option is the 'horse workers' of filtering events, which defines any matching of the grok expression within the log file format.
- `add_field`: If the filter matches the set condition, it will add an additional field to the processed event. This is useful to optimize queries for indexed events.
- `add_tag`: If the filter matches the set condition, it will add an additional tag to the processed event. The value type is an the array that enables several tags per event at once.

> All available plugin filters for grok can be found here:
> `https://www.elastic.co/guide/en/logstash/current/plugins-filters-grok.html`.

Of course, if you intend to run the LogStash service with a new filter plugin, it will throw an error showing that the matched pattern is not supported. More precisely, the tag `AUDITLOGLEVEL` is not defined and LogStash will need to know how its pattern should be. Thus, we will need to create a new `AUDITLOGLEVEL` file under the pattern directory and add the following regular expression package content as follows:

```
AUDITLOGLEVEL([C|c]ritical|CRITICAL[A|a]udit|AUDIT|[D|d]ebug|DEBUG|[N|n]oti
ce|NOTICE|[I|i]nfo|INFO|[W|w]arn?(?:ing)?|WARN?(?:ING)?|[E|e]rr?(?:or)?|ERR
?(?:OR)?|[C|c]rit?(?:ical)?|CRIT?(?:ICAL)?|[F|f]atal|FATAL|[S|s]evere|SEVER
E)
```

 Moreover, if you intend to create more patterns and test them, you can use `http://grokdebug.herokuapp.com/`.

The online grok syntax checker is very useful to verify the correctness of customized patterns. You can validate default patterns within conjunction of custom ones and test them by pasting an event line from your log file under scope. Our custom OpenStack grok filter pattern was tested first via the `gork` debug application and added later to our LogStash configuration file.

The next `multiline` block is very useful when we intend to combine disparate events into a single event. Let's grab the following pieces of events from the `ceilometer api` log file:

```
2015-04-07 20:51:42.833 2691 CRITICAL ceilometer [-] ConnectionFailure:
could not connect to 47.147.50.1:27017: [Errno 101] ENETUNREACH
2015-04-07 20:51:42.833 2691 TRACE ceilometer Traceback (most recent call
last):
2015-04-07 20:51:42.833 2691 TRACE ceilometer   File "/usr/bin/ceilometer-
api", line 10, in <module>
2015-04-07 20:51:42.833 2691 TRACE ceilometer     sys.exit(api())
2015-04-07 20:51:42.833 2691 TRACE ceilometer   File
"/usr/lib/python2.6/site-packages/ceilometer/cli.py", line 96, in api
```

The previous output shows a number of Python exception stack traces. Ceilometer was not able to find the IP address of the cloud controller to connect to and throws such exceptions from its native Python code. Imagine now that we will keep the default grok filter where LogStash will parse each line as a separate event. We won't be able to identify which line belongs to which exception. Moreover, such exception information treated in each line might hide the root cause of its generator. For example, we will need to point in the first place at the first line:

`CRITICAL ceilometer [-] ConnectionFailure: could not connect`. Then it comes in our dashboard: the exception in one line matching the same date. This way, you will be able to trace events and exceptions separately.

We can resume the multiline options as the following:

- **negate**: False by default. Any message matching the pattern will not be considered a match of the multiline filter. Vice versa when it is set to true.
- **pattern**: Any regular expression indicating that fields of a certain event constitute multiple lines of logs.
- **what**: If the line matches the regular expressions defined in the pattern, the LogStash will merge the current event either with the previous or next line. In the case of our Python stack traces, we want to merge the event with the one prior to it.
- **stream_identity**: Imagine that your LogStash forwarder has been restarted and needs to reconnect. In this case, LogStash will create a new TCP connection for the same stream. In this case, we will need to identify which stream belongs to which event by host '%{host}'. In addition, we are telling LogStash to differentiate events coming from multiple files in the same file input `%{filename}`.

> All available plugin filters for multiline can be found here: `https://www.elastic.co/guide/en/logstash/current/plugins-codecs-multiline.html`.

The next example is the `mutate` section that enables manipulating and modifying specific fields in the processed events: rename, remove, replace, merge and convert text, data type and so on Mutate supports a variety of configuration options. One of the most used ones is `gusb`, which takes an array of three elements and performs a conversion of a string field by a replacement operation. In our filter example, we instruct LogStash filter to replace all backslashes in any log field named as `logmessage` with a `space`.

> All available plugin filters for mutate can be found here: `https://www.elastic.co/guide/en/logstash/current/plugins-filters-mutate.html`.

The last filter `date` is the simplest plugin. Its main task is to parse dates and use them as LogStash timestamps. We would like to use the date format `yyyy-MM-dd HH:mm:ss.SSS` to parse the timestamps of the OpenStack log files, for example, `2015-04-07 20:51:42.833`.

We can see the date filter with a **type** of **openstack** specified to ensure it only matches our OpenStack events.

All available plugin filters for date can be found here: `https://www.elast ic.co/guide/en/logstash/current/plugins-filters-date.html`.

Our LogStash configuration file can be resumed in the next diagram. You may notice that filters are independent and a log file is being manipulated sequentially, starting with the first `grok` filter when the filter matches the type `openstack`, therefore manipulated by the `multiline` filter, then processed by the `mutate` filter, and ends up with the final filtering process by stamping the date of LogStash using the `date` filter.

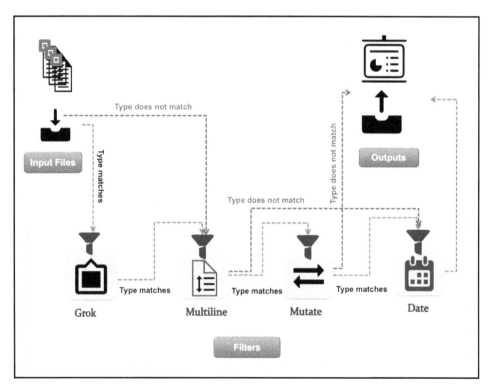

Extending the OpenStack-ELK pipeline

Our main LogStash configuration skeleton files are ready. A final step requires instructing every node in our OpenStack environment to start shipping their logs to our LogStash server. We will show a simple example that ships log files from a cloud controller for compute, identity, dashboard, and network services.

Let's extend our cloud controller FileBeat configuration file as performed in the **Preparing LogStach clients** section:

1. Specify multiple prospectors by including multiple paths and custom fields for each type of OpenStack service in the *prospectors* section:

```
...
    paths:
      - /var/log/horizon/*
    fields:
      tags: ["horizon", "dashboard", "openstack"]
   -
    paths:
      - /var/log/nova/*
    fields:
      tags: ["nova", "compute", "openstack"]
   -
    paths:
      - /var/log/neutron/*
     fields:
        tags: ["neutron", "network", "openstack"]
```

2. Additionally, we can specify the generic type for incoming logs from the cloud controller machine by editing the following directive:

```
document_type: Control Plane
```

This setting is very useful to understand which type of document indexed by ElasticSearch is visible in Kibana.

3. In the ELK server, modify the beats input configuration file by adding the path of each OpenStack file service using the `file` input plugin:

```
...
file {
  path => ['/var/log/keystone/*.log']
  tags => ['keystone', 'oslofmt']
  type => "openstack, identity"
}
file {
    path => ['/var/log/nova/*.log']
    tags => ['nova', 'oslofmt']
    type => "openstack, compute"
}
file {
    path => ['/var/log/horizon/*.log']
    tags => ['horizon', 'oslofmt']
    type => "openstack, dashboard"
}
file {
    path => ['/var/log/neutron/*.log']
    tags => ['neutron', 'oslofmt']
    type => "openstack, network"
}
```

4. The filter configuration file can be extended using a conditions set for each type of OpenStack log service. Each log service is tagged and associated with two possible types, which are `openstack` and an additional service OpenStack name: identity, compute, dashboard, or network. In this case, it is possible to perform a more granular filtering by each service type using condition sets and tags as follows:

```
...
if "nova" in [tags] {
    grok {
      match => { "logmessage" => "[-] %{NOTSPACE:requesterip}
    [%{NOTSPACE:req_date} %{NOTSPACE:req_time}] %
    {NOTSPACE:method}           %{NOTSPACE:url_path} %
    {NOTSPACE:http_ver} %{NUMBER:response} % {NUMBER:bytes}
    %{NUMBER:seconds}" } add_field => ["nova", "compute"]
      add_tag => ["novametrics"]
    }
    mutate {
    gsub => ['logmessage','""',""]
    }
}
```

Note that for each condition clause, it is possible to include a set of filters. The previous excerpt illustrates a filter, checks if the incoming log has a nova tag, if successful, the log events will be parsed by grok, and adds additional fields, nova and compute. During search, events will be showed with additional tags called **novametrics**. The mutate option will replace any backslash entry in the event log with a space:

1. The OpenStack filter log can also include a sophisticated way to detect failed events that cannot be processed by grok by tagging it, for example, as grok_error. This can be achieved by adding the following snippet:

```
. . .
if !("_grokparsefailure" in [tags]) {
    grok {
        add_tag => "grok_error"
    }
}
. . .
```

2. Restart the FileBeat process in the OpenStack cloud controller server to start shipping the new set of log data to the ELK server:

```
# systcemctl restart filebeat
```

LogStash can detect any new configuration changes automatically and does not require a restart of the service. If automatic configuration reload is not enabled, use the following command-line:
```
# bin/logastash -f /etc/logstash/conf.d/ --
config.reload.automatic
```

Visualizing OpenStack logs

Once we have verified that our imported logs are successfully indexed, we can start browsing the Kibana interface to obtain interesting results and perform useful analytics for the running OpenStack services. Since we have already defined our FileBeat index, we can jump to the first '**Discover**' tab in the upper left tool bar of the Kibana interface:

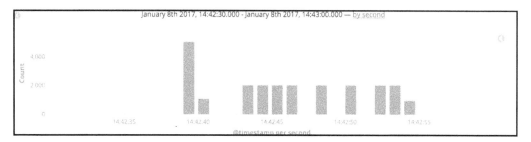

The following screenshot illustrates how nicely, lines for each log file are being indexed and parsed in different fields for a better visualization and user experience:

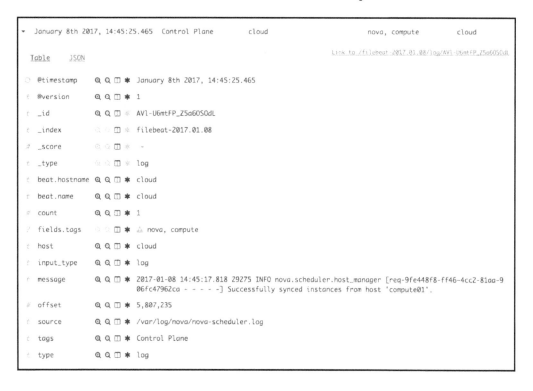

Additionally, it is possible to select fields from the upper left `filebeat-*` column for customization, for example, we are interested in lines with a data stamp, tagged log type, the hostname from which the logs are being shipped, and service OpenStack type by the means tagged option:

Time ⌄	tags	fields.tags	host
▸ January 8th 2017, 15:00:30.515	Control Plane	nova, compute, openstack	cloud
▸ January 8th 2017, 15:00:30.515	Control Plane	nova, compute, openstack	cloud
▸ January 8th 2017, 15:00:30.515	Control Plane	nova, compute, openstack	cloud
▸ January 8th 2017, 15:00:29.507	Control Plane	nova, compute, openstack	cloud
▸ January 8th 2017, 15:00:29.305	Control Plane	keystone, identity, openstack	cloud
▸ January 8th 2017, 15:00:27.645	Control Plane	neutron, network, openstack	cloud

Now we have properly indexed data, we can proceed by performing some searches to analyze our data and eventually discovering events that an OpenStack cloud operator could not find out without a centralized and efficient log solution as we have currently.

Use case 1, security analysis

A great first exercise is to highlight the number of failed and non-authorized attempts to log in to the Horizon dashboard. We can simply run a query search in the Kibana **Search Bar** for the last day, for example: `fields.tags: identity AND failed`

```
t  message    ⊕ ⊖ ▢ *  2017-01-08 15:04:37.347 26823 WARNING keystone.common.wsgi [req-9c9f313a-3969-4524-9657-f3ca5
                        10d1de1 - - - - -] Authorization failed. The request you have made requires authentication. f
                        rom 10.0.2.15
```

To make our last search reusable for further analysis and monitoring, it is more convenient to save the performed search in a simple and representable dashboard. Click on the second button in the upper-left tool bar of the Kibana interface named 'Visualize' and choose, for example, **Line Chart** to show the number of failed hits over time. Select 'From a new search' by specifying the used index `filebeat-*`. Now we can define the metrics of the data visualization for both the X and Y axis as follows:

- `Y-Axis`: Count by default
- `X-Axis`: **Date Histogram** from the drop-down list

Make sure to enter the previous search query in the new visualization dashboard and press the **play** button:

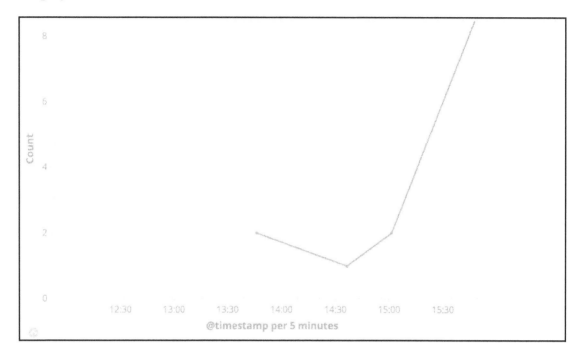

In the upper tool bar menu, select **Save** and give a meaningful name to the new visualization, such as **Failed Authentication**. All saved visualizations can be revisited by querying their names in the second column located in the Kibana **Visualize** section. Collecting data regarding authorization checks from Keystone log files presents a great exercise empowering the security of the OpenStack environment. As these types are continuously indexed and correctly parsed, cloud operators will have more insight and an easier way to properly monitor the OpenStack private cloud for any potential security threat. Based on the provided information by ELK, operators could take further actions by checking the validity of IP addresses for each keystone request, classify them according to mistaken password entry from eligible IP addresses and suspicious ones, and block them.

Use case 2, response code analysis

The second example can be used to expose graphically, the distribution of different 50x and 40x response codes generated by Horizon. Click on the second button in the upper-left tool bar of the Kibana interface named **Visualize** and choose **Pie Chart**.

Select **From a new search** by specifying the used index **filebeat-***. Now we can define the metrics of the data visualization as follows:

- **Split Slices**: Select Count from the Aggregation drop-down list.
- **Buckets**: Select **Filters** from the drop-down list and add two additional filters.
- **Filter 1**: Enter the search query `fields.tags: dashboard and 50?`. Change the name of the label to 5xx.
- **Filter 2**: Enter the search query `fields.tags: dashboard and 40?`. Change the name of the label to `4xx`.

Make sure to enter the previous search query in the new visualization dashboard and press the play button:

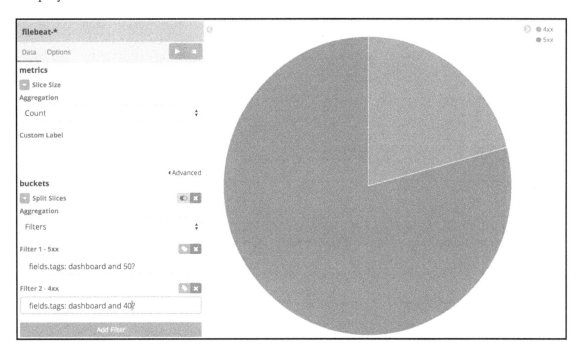

In the upper tool bar menu, select **Save** and give a meaningful name for the new visualization such as **Error Response Codes**. The previous graph gives a deeper insight into how the web server running the OpenStack dashboard is behaving based on the status error codes.

Troubleshooting from Kibana

As highlighted in Chapter 10, *Monitoring and Troubleshooting - Running a healthy OpenStack cluster*, log files construct the best place to find clues about root causes for any issue. As we now have a better way to collect and parse OpenStack log files, if the monitoring server raises an alert for a specific OpenStack service host, an administrator can quickly start a custom query in Kibana and check the correspondent event during that given time. If the same alert occurs on more than one occasion, the search query can be saved and operators could decide, based on the issue frequency, to make any further design or configuration changes for a specific OpenStack component.

As the OpenStack log data is being shipped and indexed in real time, an administrator could run as many queries as needed to detect specific, learned key words. Kibana keeps updating the dashboard with the latest data sorted by the timestamp of the processed events.

The following simple example queries log data in Kibana by filtering events generated by the OpenStack compute service and contains a string with a **failed** value:

```
fields.tags: compute and failed
```

```
message        Q Q ▯ ✳  2016-12-18 04:44:46.098 29502 WARNING nova.scheduler.utils [req-9e632bd4-2abc-4750-aee2-a1fe3
                        760d7cb 375ae5b3359a4a1ba835825fcc3fc8c3 6fa47a2b492e48548c2c9596d1c2a5a2 - - -] Failed to co
                        mpute_task_migrate_server: Unable to migrate instance (b51498ca-0a59-42bd-945a-18246668186d)
                        to current host (cloud).
```

The error event message shows that a migration operation initiated from the 'cloud' host of an instance having ID b51498ca-0a59-42bd-945a-18246668186d is failed. The next message line could help to mitigate the root cause of the issue:

```
6c7afbe 375ae5b3359a4a1ba835825fcc3fc8c3 6fa47a2b492e48548c2c9596d1c2a5a2 - - -] Failed to co
mpute_task_migrate_server: No valid host was found. There are not enough hosts available.
```

The last line acknowledges that the instance migration task could not be achieved due to unavailability of resources in the target host. Lack of resources could also refer to the unavailability of the target host which can be down or unreachable. This can be checked by running the following command-line in the cloud host:

```
# nova hypervisor-list
```

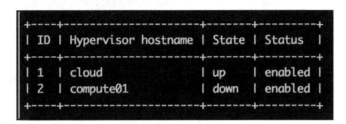

Further investigation can be performed by verifying if the compute01 in our example is physically down or only the compute service stopped running. Depending on how the monitoring system has been configured to trigger service alerts, the fast log query helped to react quickly to the latent problem. This can be resolved by bringing up the compute service running in the compute01 host and checking the resource availability allocated to the requested virtual machine.

Another useful log query to check the error state for the compute service and the messaging queue system can be achieved by an extended search string as follows:

```
fields.tags: (compute OR nova) AND AMQP AND error
```

This search query will show any errors detected in any nova component during the set period of search time in Kibana. The following message list a real-time error detection from the nova conductor that needs to contact the RabbitMQ service:

```
9-a087-267cb450796c - - - - -] AMQP server on 10.0.2.15:5672 is unreachable: [Errno 111] ECON
NREFUSED. Trying again in 2 seconds.
```

The nova-conductor is not able to reach the RabbitMQ server and a fast work around this issue is to check if the messaging queue service is up and running, by running, for example, `#rabbitmqctl status` from the command-line. Then, make sure that the specific compute node is able to establish a connection with the RabbitMQ server. This can be tested, for example, by issuing the an **lsof** from the command-line on the RabbitMQ server:

```
# lsof -i :5672 | grep Compute_IP_ADDR
```

A very common problem that might occur when adding a new compute node to the OpenStack cluster is the network configuration. Newly added compute nodes running a L3 agent service will need to contact the Neutron server running in the cloud controller nodes. You may have configured it properly but network configuration for an additional node in the OpenStack cluster can be an error prone process if it is not automated properly.

For example, an operator has added three new OpenStack compute nodes within a L3 agent. However, the created virtual machines were not networked properly so routing traffic to them was not possible. This can be seen from Kibana by running the following query for only new added compute nodes:

```
fields.tags: (neutron OR network) AND host: (compute02 OR compute03 OR
compute04) AND l3_agent AND ERROR
ERROR neutron.agent.l3_agent [-] The external network bridge 'br-ex' does
not exist
```

Our filtering result shows that one of the L3 agents running in the compute node 02 is not functioning properly. Obviously, the error points to wrong or absent bridge mapping configuration within the compute node. This type of network setting allows the network traffic within the host to reach the physical network via internal routing and ends up passing through the external bridge out to the physical network card. The error exposes the **br-ex** supposed to be our external bridge interface set in the **l3-agent** configuration file that will connect the virtual network managed by the **OpenvSwitch** and the external network. The agent will check the existence of the configured bridge from the OpenvSwitch list. To overcome such issues, you will need to create the **br-ex** interface on each OpenStack compute node. Adding the bridge is simple if using OVS:

```
[root@compute02 ~]# ovs-vsctl  --may-exist add-br br-ex
```

Check if the external bridge has been added successfully:

```
[root@compute02 ~]# ovs-vsctl show
8a7cc14f-5d97-43b9-9cc9-63db87e57ca0
...
    Bridge br-ex
        Port br-ex
            Interface br-ex
                type: internal
...
```

Summary

In this chapter, we have covered an efficient way of centralizing log files generated by different OpenStack components. Because your private cloud environment is most likely growing, this will add more load and will need more monitoring effort to piece events together. The chapter has demonstrated how to set up an ELK stack and integrate it into your existing OpenStack cluster. Logs provide valuable information on how an OpenStack setup is behaving and gives a great insight on debugging possible issues, analyzing performance degradation per OpenStack service, and helps to raise flags when a security threat comes along. The ELK platform provides a great and complete log analytics solution that empowers our OpenStack journey by addressing the challenges of dealing with an immense number of log entries and events. We have learned how to build a standard ELK pipeline ending up with a sophisticated solution enabling users to detect any OpenStack service event each time. The ELK stack becomes more mature and very overwhelmed with new features and plugins that users can take benefits of during a logging setup exercise. In the next part of the chapter, we have started exploiting the power of the ELK solution in OpenStack by visualizing specific topics as examples related to security and HTTP response codes. We learned at the end how to embrace troubleshooting tasks from simple search data queries which lead to verifying some of the chronic issues that might occur internally in your OpenStack installation.

Based on logging and monitoring results, you may conclude that some pieces of your OpenStack environment are facing performance degradation and need to be tuned. Thus, some advanced settings should be adjusted to keep your private cloud responsive to heavy workload which will be covered in the next chapter.

12
OpenStack Benchmarking and Performance Tuning - Maintaining Cloud Performance

"Geometry enlightens the intellect and sets one's mind right"
- Ibn Khaldun

The previous chapters have guided you through several topics to deploy and manage your first OpenStack infrastructure. Now you may intend to expose your environment and let users start creating and managing virtual resources in your private OpenStack cloud.

When it comes to troubleshooting issues related to system performance, you will most probably ask your team: *Why we did not expect that?* It was so fast that the server was suddenly overloaded and cannot handle any new requests to launch virtual machines. Such issues should be addressed on prior to exposing it to the masses.

Meeting the user expectations cannot be achieved without continuously testing the responsiveness, interoperability and scalability of the infrastructure running the cloud environment. Basically, to become more efficient as the user population grows, it is crucial to know your limits in advance; then you can go beyond and improve. A practical way is to measure your OpenStack cloud by simply generating workloads and watch what happens.

On the other hand, you will sooner or later have to proof your **Service Level Agreement** (**SLA**). This is can be done in different ways. We will choose the easiest one: Benchmarking our OpenStack environment! Our private cloud is a vast ecosystem, where each component of our OpenStack system has the potential to become a bottleneck if it is not chosen carefully. There are a variety of options to identify and adjust component that could present a source of bottlenecks and risk of failure. One of the most critical ones as is very potential: Databases. In the following, final pages of this book, you will learn how to:

- Improve the database performance in OpenStack
- Use caching to empower the database in OpenStack
- Plan and define acceptance criteria for benchmarking tests
- Benchmark OpenStack and identify source of performance bottlenecks
- Evaluate our cloud control and data plane using efficient testing tools
- Analyse results and reports of benchmarking and resolve performance issues.

Pushing the limits of the database

One of the most critical parts of OpenStack is the database. Usually, MySQL is used when there is no special configuration to prepare specifically for OpenStack to run smoothly and satisfy its multiple services. On the other hand, it becomes tough to maintain the MySQL databases when the cloud environment keeps growing. Database inconsistency constitutes one of the biggest challenges when running OpenStack in production. For example, it could happen that you have disassociated a network from an instance but the status in the database has not been changed. Nova claims that the network is associated within the instance, while Neutron claims the opposite. In this case, you will have to edit the database and change the start manually. In rare cases, manual intervention can be error-prone. Generally, it is much more difficult to keep consistency when other changes are being performed in each database table. All of this points to another database challenge-*concurrency*. For example, Nova keeps relying on a wrong status of a terminated instance that expects to de-associate the floating IP. At the same time, a new instance is being created, but it is not able to associate a floating IP (it is an extreme case when only one floating IP remains). Again, manual intervention can resolve the issue. However, you will need to enter many MySQL queries, and this might lead to another inconsistent state where you accidentally remove a table entry, using a wrong instance ID for example. We will consider that manual correction of an OpenStack database can be left as a last resort.

On the other hand, we first keep track of how to avoid such cases but taking care of our OpenStack databases. Of course, as your infrastructure grows, the risk of inconsistency in your data might increase. With a large number of tables for every OpenStack service, it recommended to plan in advance for preventive actions that can save your production day. Eventually, you should guarantee completion of the query in a shorter period of time from the database level. In other words, reduce the response time of database statements for a given workload. Several factors come into play if you aim to improve your OpenStack database's performance. Typically, there are these ways:

- Learn the OpenStack core software and start measuring performance when you get expertise in the internal system calls and database queries
- Keep improving the hardware capabilities and the configuration that is running in the databases

In our case, the second approach might be more convenient for the first OpenStack production cycle. For example, the database administrator can decide how the hardware should be configured to avoid any unexpected bottleneck in your environment. We have seen in `Chapter 9`, *OpenStack HA and Failover*, a few examples focusing on the use case of database architecture to reach a certain level of high availability and scalability. These concepts are vast and need deeper hacks and expertise to adjust to your needs. Eventually, from the alerts sent by your monitoring system, you can decide what kind of improvement should be done at the hardware level. For example, watching the CPU of your master database increasing slightly everyday during 2 weeks could be graded to a critical issue after a longer period. There are high chances that the CPU will be saturated when a huge amount of MySQL data in a short period of time fits in the memory and needs to be processed. I/O saturation is also considered a primary cause of bottlenecks affecting the performance of the MySQL database. This happens when the OpenStack environment generates much more data than they can fit in the memory.

Deciding the resources outfit

Investing in the input/output subsystem's performance is the best option when you consider adding more memory resources is necessary to fit your data. The nature of physical disks has a great influence on their capability to perform a certain number of operations. For example, a good option is to use **Solid State Devices** (**SSDs**) for database nodes. Depending on the type of database query, starting to play on the input/output wait factor can be very beneficial by improving the access time and transfer data speed. As we have stated previously, SSDs have evolved recently to forth many improvements to storage design. They are known as Flash storage devices and perform well by:

- Improving read and write operations
- Handling high operations rate concurrency well

Once the data is fitted into the memory, you should ensure that your memory-disk ratio is proper. On the other hand, such a goal cannot be achieved if you do not take into consideration the following challenge: avoid disk input/output. Increasing memory per MySQL node does not necessarily mean that you are improving the performance of your OpenStack databases. It still needs to find a good match to balance the memory and your disk's characteristics, such as size and speed.

Caching for OpenStack

Planning for the best outfit of hardware configuration to boost your OpenStack database's performance is strongly recommended. Even if you are not able to afford the right hardware specifications to handle the workload, you still have more options. You can shine brightly on an inexpensive solution that comes in the second place to tackle the database workload-**caching**. This technique is considered as a very powerful mechanism to handle high-load applications.

Caching happens at every step along the way, from the servers to the browsers of end users. In our case, Horizon, as an application level from the end user's perspective, can benefit from caching by minimizing any unresponsive status when passing queries all the way to the database. Moreover, caching might be very suitable to move a long queue of database queries entirely outside of the database server. In such cases, you are better off looking at an external caching solution, such as **memcached**. It can be used by OpenStack components to cache data. Then the database will appreciate it!

In a nutshell, **memcached** is a high-performance and distributed memory object caching system. By exposing a memory server, the OpenStack database servers can benefit from a caching layer for Horizon to store OpenStack services data. One important thing to be taken into consideration is that memcached does not store data. Once a memcached instance restarts, the data will be lost.

 memcached uses the least recently used cache. The oldest data will be replaced with new data when its memory capacity limit is reached.

You can run memcached in any type of configuration, unless you prefer to choose a dedicated server to run it. It can also run in a memcached cluster architecture, or even in multiple instances in the same server. A typical memcached setup requires only the usage hardware with less CPU specifications in contrast to database requirements. What you need is a set of instances providing memory. The next illustration depicts how memcached is used in a proposed OpenStack setup:

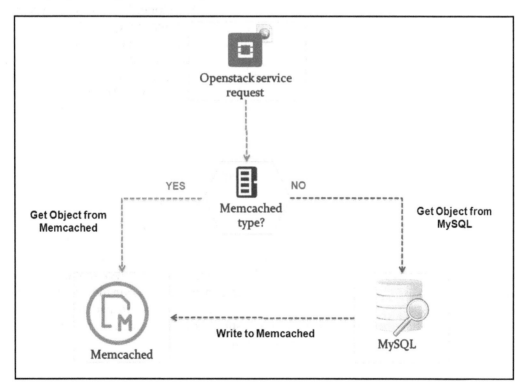

This workflow diagram exposes a write-through caching mechanism by getting data that is stored in memcached while it performs a read to the MySQL database.

Memcached in OpenStack

We will discuss in this section an example of a performance problem that might appear frequently, especially in an expanded OpenStack production environment. Basically, every service in OpenStack asks for a token while trying to execute command or to perform a specific task. A basic scenario could be the creation of a new instance. Several API requests are generated from different services:

- Horizon to Nova
- Nova to Glance to retrieve an image
- Nova to Cinder to attach a volume
- Nova to Neutron to assign network ports, bring up firewall rules, and so on

Such processes include internal token checks' validity by Keystone. The former Keystone process will have to check its records lying in the database at every request. Now imagine thousands of API requests being performed and forwarded by token checks at every call. This can affect your OpenStack's performance, since Keystone spends lots of CPU cycles to fetch tokens from large database tables. Furthermore, it can reach a point at which Keystone hangs and is not able to handle new incoming authorization requests. The end result is a long delay in lookup through the database table caused by expired tokens. So, this is what we can conclude from this scenario:

- Keystone keeps eating CPU
- Keystone's data layer becomes inconsistent

At the first glance, you may think of introducing a CPU upgrade. This can be useful unless you want to spend more time and budget. On the other hand, do you think expired tokens are still useful? Continuously expanding tables might generate unwanted database behavior at some workload, since it keeps running inefficient queries. Let's see how memcached can be part of a complementary solution to this problem. We make it simple: we tell Keystone to stop saving our tokens in the database and find our memcached layer. Keystone will save all its token records in a memcached server. This is also beneficial for speeding up authentication. The next section will show how to install a memcached instance and integrate it with your OpenStack environment.

Integrating memcached

As mentioned previously, it is up to you to decide whether to offer dedicated servers for memcached instances or not. The following example assumes a simple installation of memcached on cloud controller nodes running the Keystone service. So, do not forget to adjust your settings when installing memcached, including the IP addresses of cloud controllers:

1. Install memcached on your first cloud controller, as follows:

   ```
   # yum install -y memcached python-memcache
   ```

   The following steps can be performed on OpenStack Juno release and later. Make sure to check the appendix of the official OpenStack documentation if any module or directive is being deprecated or renamed http://docs.openstack.org/developer/keystone/configuration.html

2. Ensure that memcached starts automatically on system boot time:

   ```
   # chkconfig memcached on
   ```

   If you intend to set up a new memcached node, be sure that the time zone of the operating system is set properly by changing the ZONE parameter in your /etc/sysconfig/clock file. This is very important to verify because memcached determines the expiration date for Keystone according to **Coordinated Universal Time (UTC)**.

3. You can check the current statistics of your memcached instance:

   ```
   # memcached-tool 127.0.0.1:11211 stats
   ```

4. Optionally, you can adjust the cache size to 4 GB by editing the /etc/sysconfig/memcached file as follows:

   ```
   # vim /etc/sysconfig/memcached
   CACHESIZE=4096
   ```

5. Restart your memcached service:

   ```
   # service memcached restart
   ```

6. Adjust the Keystone configuration file to use the memcached driver in the **token** section to store the tokens as a persistence backend:

```
# vim /etc/keystone/keystone.conf
[token]
driver = keystone.token.persistence.backends.memcache.Token
caching = True
...
```

7. Enable cache capabilities in the **cache** section and specify memcached as the backend plugin for caching as follows:

```
[cache]
enabled = True
config_prefix = cache.keystone
backend = dogpile.cache.memcached
```

8. In the same **cache** section, set the backend plugin to use the memcached installed locally:

```
backend_argument = url:localhost:11211
```

9. Restart the keystone service:

```
# service keystone restart
```

10. Keystone should start connecting to the memcached instance that is running in our snippet example in the same machine. We can check the connection establishment within the 11211 default port used by memcached:

```
# lsof -i :11211
```

This command gives the following result:

```
     USER   FD   TYPE   DEVICE SIZE/OFF NODE NAME
memcached   46u  IPv4     6020      0t0  TCP *:memcache (LISTEN)
memcached   47u  IPv4     6021      0t0  UDP *:memcache
memcached   48u  IPv4    48171      0t0  TCP cloud:memcache->cloud:38801 (ESTABLISHED)
memcached   50u  IPv4 82732957      0t0  TCP cloud:memcache->cloud:41005 (ESTABLISHED)
memcached   51u  IPv4 82732973      0t0  TCP cloud:memcache->cloud:41007 (ESTABLISHED)
 keystone   14u  IPv4 82742444      0t0  TCP cloud:41005->cloud:memcache (ESTABLISHED)
 keystone   13u  IPv4 82738611      0t0  TCP cloud:41007->cloud:memcache (ESTABLISHED)
```

11. We can dynamically check every second the `get_hits` value increasing using the *watch* command line, as follows:

```
# watch -d -n 1 'memcached-tool 127.0.0.1:11211 stats'
```

```
Every 1.0s: memcached-tool 127.0.0.1:11

#127.0.0.1:11211    Field           Value
           accepting_conns             1
                auth_cmds              0
              auth_errors              0
                    bytes          30719
               bytes_read        1697108
            bytes_written         187184
                cas_badval             0
                 cas_hits              0
               cas_misses              0
                cmd_flush              0
                  cmd_get             29
                  cmd_set          10549
                cmd_touch              0
              conn_yields              0
    connection_structures             17
         curr_connections             16
               curr_items             11
                decr_hits              0
              decr_misses              0
              delete_hits              1
            delete_misses              0
         evicted_unfetched             0
                evictions              0
         expired_unfetched          5153
                 get_hits             3
               get_misses             26
               hash_bytes         524288
         hash_is_expanding             0
          hash_power_level            16
                incr_hits              0
              incr_misses              0
```

Few bounced usage statistics values are useful to verify the current behavior of the keystone caching mechanism in real time such as:

- `accepting_conns`: The number of accepted connections to the memcached server. Any newly added service configured to use memcached as a cache backend will increase its value by 1.
- `bytes`: The number of bytes used for caching items in real time.
- `bytes_read`: The number of incoming bytes to the memcached server.
- `bytes_written`: The number of outgoing bytes from the memcached server.
- `cmd_get`: The number of *get* commands received by the memcached server.
- `cmd_set`: The number of *set* commands processed by the memcached server.
- `get_hits`: The number of successful cache hits(*get requests*). The hit rate can be obtained by dividing *get_hits* by the *cmd_get* value in percentage.
- `get_misses`: The number of failed cache hits (get requests).

Nova services can also get benefits from the usage of memcached. In each compute and controller node, you will need to specify in each `nova.conf` file where memcached is running. It is important to bring under the scope how memcached can scale out easily. The deployment of a large OpenStack environment requires a scalable memcached setup if a single instance is not able to handle the current workload. For this purpose, you can use HAProxy to make use of multiple memcached instances in the TCP mode. The next snippet describes how HAProxy should be configured for a proper, scalable memcached setup. We assume in this setup the configuration elaborated in Chapter 9, *OpenStack HA and Failover*, for an HAProxy node. We will just add a new stanza at the end of both the `/etc/haproxy/haproxy.cfg` files, and reload both the HAProxy nodes, as follows:

```
...
listen memcached-cluster 192.168.47.47:11211
balance roundrobin
maxconn 10000
mode tcp
server cc01 192.168.47.100:11211 check inter 5s rise 2 fall 3
server cc02 192.168.47.101:11211 check inter 5s rise 2 fall 3
server cc03 192.168.47.102:11211 check inter 5s rise 2 fall 3
haproxy01# service haproxy reloadhaproxy02
# service haproxy reload
```

We will need to tell Nova services that we already have multiple memcached instances running in three different cloud controller nodes. When `cc01` becomes unavailable, `cc02` takes over, and so on. We set the following directive in each controller and compute node in the`/etc/nova/nova.conf` file:

```
...
memcached_servers = cc01:11211,cc02:11211,cc03:11211
...
```

Memcached can also be beneficial for our dashboard. We can tell Horizon to use memcached for the Django web caching. It just needs to point to the virtual IP, considering a scalable cloud controller setup. The dashboard includes the **CACHES** settings, which we need to edit/add. On your cloud controller nodes, edit the `/etc/openstack-dashboard/local_settings.py` file like this:

```
...
CACHES = {
'default': {
    'BACKEND' : 'django.core.cache.backends.memcached.
MemcachedCache',
        'LOCATION' : '192.168.47.47:11211',
    }
}
...
```

We can add the next stanza to each HAProxy instance to boost a scalable Django dashboard, which is now using a scalable memcached setup:

```
...
listen horizon 192.168.47.47:80
balance roundrobin
maxconn 10000
mode tcp
server cc01 192.168.47.100:80 cookie cc01 check inter 5s rise
2 fall 3
server cc02 192.168.47.101:80 cookie cc02 check inter 5s rise
2 fall 3
server cc03 192.168.47.102:80 cookie cc03 check inter 5s rise
2 fall 3
```

We finish our new, empowering caching setup with some scalability extension by reloading the newest configuration in each HAProxy node:

```
haproxy01# service haproxy reload
haproxy02# service haproxy reload
```

Benchmarking OpenStack at scale

Early better than late! This is what cloud operators should keep in mind when verifying the functional anomalies of the OpenStack private cloud at an early stage. In distributed computing systems, every circulated request incurs a performance hit. That represents obviously, several challenges to be able systematically to measure performance across all installed OpenStack components. Among those challenges is the inability to perform sophisticated tests in an easy and automated way to bring realistic and accurate measurement results. Additionally, with the continuous growth of the OpenStack ecosystem and the integration of more incubated projects, it will be hard to keep the initial setup up and running and prevent events of performance degradation without defining since the beginning a verification process which ensures that your cloud environment is in a good shape whatever workload it could face.

Performance measurement had been a complex task in a traditional infrastructure setup due to the lack of the right tools. With the evolution of network and hardware power and complexity, taking this art since the beginning of the journey is becoming a must. Specifically, for OpenStack, we will need to discover our performance limits, how much load our setup can handle and at which level our private cloud could meet the user expectations.

Bringing numbers and performance results under the scope is derived practically from the heart core of the networked underlying infrastructure running the private cloud. In OpenStack, we will define these architectural building blocks as follows:

- **Control plane**: it defines the component to a router that carries traffic. In OpenStack, the control plane represents the orchestration layer of the infrastructure. API operations are subset of this component.
- **Data plane**: it represents the network layer that carries traffic over network protocols and manages between remote peers. The data plane is served by the control plane which holds the network component to carry the traffic.

 Data plane can be also named **Forwarding Plane**.

- **Management plane**: it defines the component responsible for carrying the administrative and monitoring traffic. In OpenStack, the management plane can be treated as a subset of the control plane.

With the evolution of the **SDN** technology, the control, data and management planes are being moved and implemented in subsets of software. In OpenStack, this approach helps operators and administrators to have more flexible hands on shaping traffic with more control granularity level.

To address this gap of performance measurement, one key factor is to benchmark the private cloud setup under load at scale for each plane separately. It is heartening to be informed that with the great success of OpenStack, more benchmarking tools are being developed around its ecosystem and for each covered plane. In the next installment, we will cover benchmarking our Control Plane using Rally tool and for Data Plane, we will be using a very recent and promising tool called Shaker.

Testing the OpenStack API - Rally in a nutshell

Rally is simply a benchmarking tool designed to tell you more about how your OpenStack infrastructure performs under workload at scale. Originally, the OpenStack's official test suite is **Tempest**. It is built based on many python testing frameworks. Tempest basically accommodates several test scenarios against OpenStack service endpoints by executing API calls and ends up by response verification and validation from the endpoint.

You can read more about tempest and execute individual tests cited in Github `https://github.com/openstack/tempest`

Tempest is used by OpenStack community for continuous integration process covered in `Chapter 2`, *Deploying OpenStack - The DevOps Way*. Eventually, it is useful to report and publish relevant results based on Tempest execution which helps to identify what should be changed or improved in the OpenStack code. It is also crucial if you intend to adopt any system configuration tool such as Chef, Puppet or Ansible to deploy and manage your OpenStack infrastructure, which will help you to zero in what should be fixed from OpenStack code base in the first stage and reflect high level changes in the second stage to the artifacts for example.

Using the power of Tempest is very fruitful to test your OpenStack cluster environment. However, it might be more complicated and time consuming by diving into inline python code to start testing. Moreover, results should be collected and easily educed. To overcome such challenges, Rally can be a perfect solution. You should know that Rally is not an alternative of Tempest; however, it is a performance and benchmarking framework that installs, configures and uses Tempest tests during benchmarking process.

Eventually, Rally expands the Tempest use cases to:

- Verify and validate OpenStack deployment at scale
- Run with more flexibility tests in more than one OpenStack cloud site
- Compare benchmarking results by reposing on the historical data residing in Rally's database
- Execute more realistic test workloads within multiple simulated tenants and active users
- Extend test features by the means of plugins

Meeting OpenStack SLA

Service uptime, this is what your cloud user is concerned about. Eventually, SLA in the cloud still somehow silent on some points most importantly the variation of the cloud performance level during a certain period of time. With this brought in mind, performance awareness should be taken into consideration as early as possible where comes SLA into play to act for both parties (cloud provider and end user) as a roadmap for possible changes in the OpenStack cloud service. Running your OpenStack in production is not the end of the journey: We have just begun the fun!

The next target is to agree on the desired service level for your cloud end user and takes realistic measurements results. Bear in mind that SLA is something not to ignore. In some sense, end users would rather to be informed about the cloud limits and expectations. In other words, represent the workload performance metrics. Things like frequency of failures, mean time between failures and mean time to recover are some of the indicators that can be stated in a SLA for OpenStack cloud infrastructure. Submitting credible performance benchmarks might help you as provider to appear as a more trustworthy party while providing more confidence to the consumer cloud service. Growing cloud infrastructure will be accompanied by working on SLA improvement. To consistently put the headlines of our OpenStack SLA, we will use **Rally**.

Installing Rally

We will install Rally on a separate server that has access to all OpenStack servers. Rally node will join eventually the following OpenStack networks:

- Administrative network
- External Network

The next installation snippet will guide you through a package-based installation of Rally on a CentOS operation system with minimum hardware and software requirements as follows:

- Processor: 64-bit x86
- Memory: 2 GB RAM
- Disk space: 100 GB
- Network: Two 1 Gbps Network Interface Cards (NICs)
- Python 2.6 or higher version

Let's get hands on and install Rally:

1. Download Rally from the Github repository and run the installation script `install_rally.sh` as follows:

```
# wget -q -O-https://raw.githubusercontent.com/openstack/
rally/master/install_rally.sh | bash
# cd rally &&   ./install_rally.sh
```

```
Installation of Rally is done!

Rally is now installed in your system. Information about your Rally
installation:

 * Method: system
 * Database at: /var/lib/rally/database
 * Configuration file at: /etc/rally
 * Samples at: /usr/share/rally/samples
```

2. Register your OpenStack environment with Rally. This can be done via the local environment variables `keystone_admin` for example. You can copy it from your cloud controller to the Rally server and source it as follows:

```
# scp packtpub@cc01:/keystone_admin .
# source openrc admin admin
```

3. The next command will register your OpenStack cloud with Rally based on the environment variables:

```
# rally deployment create  --name existing --perf_cloud
```

4. A sample deployment create output may look as the following:

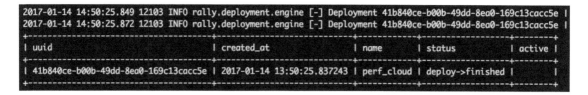

5. Verify the availability of your OpenStack deployment by the means of the `deployment check` command as the following:

```
# rally deployment check
```

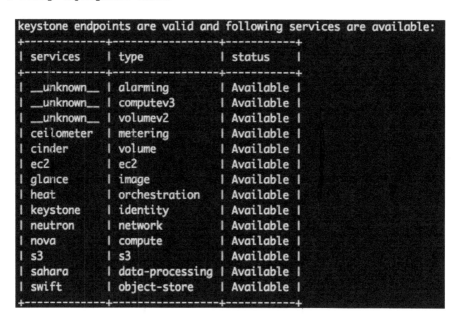

The previous output showed a proper Rally setup by listing the status of running services from an OpenStack environment.

> If the **deployment check** command throws the following error message:
> *Authentication Issue: wrong keystone credentials specified in your endpoint*
> *properties. (HTTP 401),* you will have to update your registration
> credentials in your *keystone_admin* file by including the right credentials.

Rally in action

Now that we have a Rally server installed and properly configured to talk to OpenStack
APIs, it is time for cloud benchmarking. By default, you may find numerous benchmarking
scenarios under `/rally/sample/tasks/scenarios` for all OpenStack services including
other incubated projects such as **Murano, Sahara,** and others. We will concentrate on
benchmarking our existing running OpenStack services. Before starting our first benchmark
test, it may be great to shine the spotlight on how Rally works in the first place. Scenarios in
Rally are being performed based on tasks. A task can include a set of running benchmarks
against the OpenStack cloud written in sample **JSON** or **YAML** file format. The former file
has generally the following structure:

```
ScenarioClass.scenario_method:
    -
        args:
...
        runner:
            ...
        context
            ...
        sla:
            ...
```

- `ScenarioClass.scenario_method`: Defines the name of the benchmark
  scenario
- `args`: Every method corresponding to a specific class scenario can be customized
  by passing parameters before launching the benchmark
- `runners`: Defines the workload frequency type and the order of the
  benchmarking scenarios. Runners stanza can support different types as the
  following:
    - `constant`: Running the scenario for a fixed number of times. For
      example, a scenario can be run for 10 times in total test period.

- `constant_for_duration`: Running the scenario for a fixed number of times until a certain point of time.
- `periodic`: Define a certain period [intervals] to run 2 consecutive benchmark scenarios.
- `serial`: Running the scenario for a fixed number of times in a single benchmark thread.

- `context`: Defines the environment type in which our benchmark scenario(s) can run. Usually, the concept of context defines how many tenants and active users will be associated with a given OpenStack project. It can also specify quota per tenant/user within a certain granted role.
- `sla`: is very useful to identify the overall scenario average success rate of the benchmark.

For those hoping to find a convenient benchmarking scenario that will reveal more significant results from your current OpenStack deployment, you'll have to keep looking for a real use case more specific for cloud operators. For example, Rally can help easily developers to run synthetic workloads such as VM provisioning and destroy for a limited period. However, the case with cloud operators seems to be more complicated. Such results generated from workloads are more high level but allow you to identify bottlenecks in the cloud. Let's encounter a real world example: companies have several applications needed to deploy in different usage patterns. If we have multiple concurrent instances application for QA/dev, they will be deployed in different version of this application on the cloud several times per day. Taking a use case of large deployment where there is a set number of teams running a bunch of standard stack applications and each application will contain a lot of VMs needed to be deployed certain times a day. Such workload requirements are translated to OpenStack terms as the following: We will have M amount of users provisioning N number of virtual machines within a specific flavor times every certain period of time in a concurrent way.

As we know, OpenStack is not a monolithic structure; it is distributed system within different daemons and services talking to each other. If we decompose a use case of provisioning of an instance to the primitives, it will be amazing to understand where we spend most of the time during the virtual machine provisioning phase. As soon as we get the baseline, our main goal is to provide some historical data. For example, running the same benchmark several times by changing each run time a certain number of parameters, in each run time, in the database configuration or by enabling glance caching for example.

Scenario example - Performing Keystone

Our scenario example is a benchmarking test based on Rally method named
`KeystoneBasic.authenticate_user_and_validate_token`. The scenario is intended
to measure the time of fetching and validating issued tokens by Keystone when
authenticating users under a specific load. Let's create a new file named
`perf_keystone_pp.yaml`.

The content of the file task looks as the following:

```
KeystoneBasic.authenticate_user_and_validate_token:
    -
    args: {}
    runner:
      type: "constant"
      times: 50
      concurrency: 50
    context:
        users:
            tenants: 5
            users_per_tenant: 10
    sla:
    failure_rate:
        max: 1
```

The sample scenario will create a constant load of a Keystone scenario *authenticating users
and validating tokens* **50** times without pausing by creating **5** different tenants with **10** users
in each. Note that in each single iteration, a number of **50** scenarios will be running at the
same time in a concurrency mode to simulate multiple users access. The *sla* section defines a
condition if one authentication attempt fails then the task will be aborted.

> Running similar scenarios with several authentication requests running
> simultaneously is very useful use case to test DDoS attack against the
> Keystone service.

Let's run the previous benchmark using rally command line as the following:

```
# rally task start --abort-on-sla-failure  perf_keystone_pp.yaml
```

Note that this time we add new option in our command `abort-on-sla-failure`. This is very useful argument if you are running such benchmark scenario in a real OpenStack production environment. Rally generates a heavy workload which might cause performance troubles to the existing cloud. Thus, we tell Rally to stop the load at a certain moment when the **sla** conditions are met. The output of our executed task is as follows:

```
+------------------------------------------------------------------------------------------------------------------------+
|                                            Response Times (sec)                                                        |
+--------------------------+-----------+--------------+--------------+--------------+-----------+-----------+----------+-------+
| Action                   | Min (sec) | Median (sec) | 90%ile (sec) | 95%ile (sec) | Max (sec) | Avg (sec) | Success  | Count |
+--------------------------+-----------+--------------+--------------+--------------+-----------+-----------+----------+-------+
| keystone_v2.fetch_token  | 5.379     | 25.036       | 41.745       | 48.185       | 57.831    | 24.286    | 100.0%   | 50    |
| keystone_v2.validate_token | 11.575  | 34.219       | 53.503       | 55.351       | 56.679    | 37.924    | 100.0%   | 50    |
| total                    | 35.014    | 57.384       | 88.948       | 92.12        | 100.932   | 62.211    | 100.0%   | 50    |
+--------------------------+-----------+--------------+--------------+--------------+-----------+-----------+----------+-------+

Load duration: 195.66706
Full duration: 405.882441
```

The rally benchmark results show that the scenario test has ran 50 times and completed at 100% success rate.

To dive into more details, we visualise the HTML report using the generated Rally task ID by running the following command:

```
# rally task report   c5493ee7-fba2-4290-b98c-36e47ed0fdb2 --out
/var/www/html/bench/keystone_report01.html
```

Our first test iteration benchmark involves a simple SLA condition that was met during the rally task:

Service-level agreement		
Criterion	Detail	Success
failure_rate	Failure rate criteria 0.00% <= 0.00% <= 1.00% - Passed	True

From the same report dashboard in the **Overview** tab, a second pertinent chart **Load Profile** illustrates how many iterations were running in parallel during the rally task:

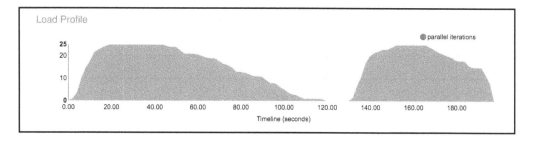

The **Load Profile** graph can be used to illustrate the variation of running iterations simultaneously over the workload time. This information is useful to learn about the system behavior at certain peaks and plan how much load can be supported at any given time.

More details are provided in the second tab **Details** where we can find **Atomic Action Durations** charts showing in our case two actions: keystone_v2.fetch_token and keystone_v2.validate_token:

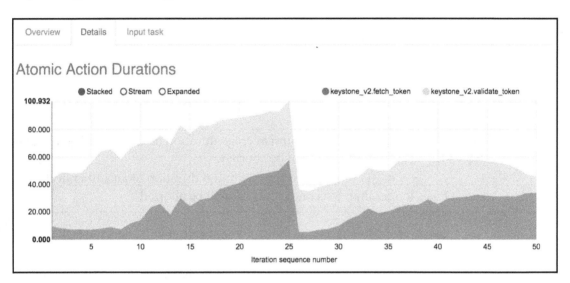

The chart helps to see the variation of the scenario for each action and how the duration is affected and changed throughout the execution of iterations. As we can see that both actions are not having same duration as fetching and validating tokens are two different operations. If our test case was failed in terms of SLA conditions such as very long duration for scenario execution, we can use this chart to drive a granular analysis on which action the bottleneck has been occurred.

We can adjust a bit our success criteria parameters in a second iteration for a stricter SLA to perform a more realistic scenario. For example, we can modify our *sla* section as the following:

```
...
sla:
      max_avg_duration: 5
      max_seconds_per_iteration: 5
      failure_rate:
         max: 0
      performance_degradation:
         max_degradation: 50
      outliers:
         max: 1
```

The new *sla* section defines five conditions:

- `max_avg_duration`: if the maximum average duration of an authentication takes longer than 5 seconds, the task will be aborted.
- `max_seconds_per_iteration`: if the maximum duration of an authentication request takes longer than 5 seconds, the task will be aborted
- `failure_rate`:
    - max: More than one failed authentication will abort the task.
- `performance_degradation`:
    - `max_degradation`: If the difference between the maximum and minimum duration of completed iterations is more than 50 percent, the task will be aborted
- `outlier`:
    - max: The outlier limits the number of long running iterations to a value of 1

Rerun the task as the following:

```
# rally task start --abort-on-sla-failure keystone_pp.yaml
```

Let's check our charts again by generating a new report with a different name so we can compare the difference of results with the previous iteration:

```
# rally task report  980957ef-4c4c-4e9b-a9c1-573839dcad80 --out
/var/www/html/bench/keystone_report02.html
```

Service-level agreement

Criterion	Detail	Success
performance_degradation	Current degradation: 4937.442268% - Passed	True
max_seconds_per_iteration	Maximum seconds per iteration 11.27s <= 5.00s - Failed	False
failure_rate	Failure rate criteria 0.00% <= 0.00% <= 1.00% - Passed	True
outliers	Maximum number of outliers 0 <= 1 - Passed	True
aborted_on_sla	Task was aborted due to SLA failure(s).	False

During the test, Rally detected a maximum value of iteration of **11.27 seconds** which does not comply with our SLA requirement:

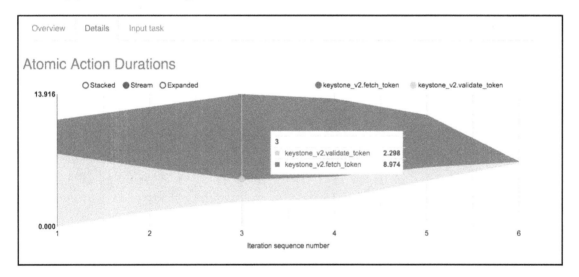

With the new SLA conditions, Rally execution stopped at the 6th iteration. The demanded average time of authenticating a user and validating the token was not met and hence this will affect the overall scenario execution duration time. The next goal is to compete against that value and decrease it below 5 seconds.

Our benchmark test showed that authenticating and validating user tokens at a certain peak of workload would not achieve our SLA requirements. Moreover, the time of authenticating one user increases and might be timed out as concurrency levels hits a specific threshold. This performance challenge can be tweaked by revisiting our Keystone setup. We can refer to an advanced Keystone design pattern that empowers our identity service performance within the OpenStack environment. As many OpenStack components are developed to support **eventlet-based** process, the Keystone component can run in different way by supporting **multi-threading** process at the price of our cloud controller CPU power. One recommendation is to deploy Keystone in a Nginx server under **WSGI** or Apache HTTPD server with `mod_wsgi` module enabled.

 Eventlet is a python library for concurrent network programming. It is designed to provide a networked environment with high performance due to its non- blocking I/O and operates handlers in a single thread. To learn more about Eventlet, check the following link: `http://eventlet.net/`

Fronting our Keystone instance by a web server will bring facilities on handling parallel HTTP connections and advanced features to proxy authentication requests to our identity instance in a multi-threaded based process mode.

The next wizard will guide us through a simple Keystone setup adjustment to utilize HTTPD server in our existing OpenStack environment:

1. In the cloud controller machine, install the WSGI module for the Apache web server:

    ```
    # yum install mod_wsgi
    ```

     Make sure to verify which Linux distribution you are using before installing Apache web server. Configuration file names and paths may differ between web server installation packages and versions.

2. Create the first Keystone Virtual Host file `/etc/httpd/conf.d/keystone_wsgi_main.conf` listening on port `5000` and pointing to the server name in which Keystone is running:

    ```
    <VirtualHost *:5000>
    ServerName cc01
    ```

3. Add the document `root` for the first *Virtual Host* and *Directory* options as follows:

```
DocumentRoot "/var/www/cgi-bin/keystone"
  <Directory "/var/www/cgi-bin/keystone">
    Options Indexes FollowSymLinks MultiViews
    AllowOverride None
    Require all granted
  </Directory>
```

4. Optionally, configure the *Virtual Host* directives to store logs under `/var/log/httpd`

```
ErrorLog "/var/log/httpd/keystone_wsgi_main_error.log"
CustomLog "/var/log/httpd/keystone_wsgi_main_access.log" combined
```

5. Set the WSGI process group name, number of processes per instance and number of threads to be ran by the keystone user. Note that we intend to increase the number of processed requests by adjusting the number for processes and threads in the `WSGIDaemonProcess` directive:

```
    WSGIApplicationGroup %{GLOBAL}
    WSGIDaemonProcess keystone_main display-name=keystone-main
group=keystone processes=4 threads=32 user=keystone
    WSGIProcessGroup keystone_main
```

6. Check the existence of the WSGI script by pointing the alias to the file path:

```
WSGIScriptAlias / "/var/www/cgi-bin/keystone/main"
```

Depending on which running OpenStack version. The default Keystone and web server installation might include the **WSGI** keystone scripts for both main and admin Virtual Hosts. Verify the path of each script file. Bear in mind that the `mod_wsgi` is used by default in freshly installed OpenStack **Mitaka** release and disables traditional Keystone by removing the usage of the **Eventlet**.

7. A basic WSGI script file is as the following:

```
import os
from keystone.server import wsgi as wsgi_server
name = os.path.basename(__file__)
application = wsgi_server.initialize_application(name)
```

8. Close the Keystone main *Virtual Host* instance:

```
</VirtualHost>
```

9. Repeat the previous steps by creating a second Keystone *Virtual Host* file `/etc/httpd/conf.d/keystone_wsgi_admin.conf` listening on port `35357` and pointing to the server name in which Keystone is running.:

```
<VirtualHost *:35357>
  ServerName cc01
```

10. Add the document root for the first *Virtual Host* and *Directory* options as follows:

```
DocumentRoot "/var/www/cgi-bin/keystone"
<Directory "/var/www/cgi-bin/keystone">
  Options Indexes FollowSymLinks MultiViews
  AllowOverride None
  Require all granted
</Directory>
```

11. Optionally, configure the Virtual Host directives to store logs under `/var/log/httpd`:

```
ErrorLog "/var/log/httpd/keystone_wsgi_admin_error.log"
CustomLog "/var/log/httpd/keystone_wsgi_admin_access.log" combined
```

12. Set the WSGI process group name, number of processes per instance and number of threads to be ran by the keystone user. Note that we intend to increase the number of the processed requests by adjusting the number for processes and threads in the `WSGIDaemonProcess` directive:

```
WSGIApplicationGroup %{GLOBAL}
WSGIDaemonProcess keystone_main display-name=keystone-admin
group=keystone processes=8 threads=32 user=keystone
WSGIProcessGroup keystone_admin
```

13. Check the existence of the WSGI script by pointing the alias to the file path:

```
WSGIScriptAlias / "/var/www/cgi-bin/keystone/admin"
```

14. A basic WSGI script file is as the following:

```
import os
from keystone.server import wsgi as wsgi_server
name = os.path.basename(__file__)
application = wsgi_server.initialize_application(name)
```

15. Close the Keystone main *Virtual Host* instance:

```
</VirtualHost>
```

16. Restart the web server:

```
# systemctl restart httpd.service
```

Now we have Keystone backed by a web server and empowered by *multi-threaded* process-mode by the means of **WSGI** module. We have already defined process daemons and threads that will help to trace the limit of our hardware and Keystone capabilities against the same scenario by running it once again:

```
# rally task start --abort-on-sla-failure keystone_pp.yaml
```

Demonstrating the last Keystone settings, our cloud controller should be running more **httpd** processes and hence more CPU power:

```
23552 keystone  20   0  986764  75248   6664 S 161.8  0.3   1:17.48 httpd
23554 keystone  20   0  986764  74456   6660 S 158.6  0.3   1:20.22 httpd
23553 keystone  20   0  986764  74800   6664 S  95.9  0.3   1:21.01 httpd
23551 keystone  20   0  986764  75236   6660 S  95.5  0.3   1:08.53 httpd
```

The new report should expose new performance results for authentication and validation duration change:

```
# rally task report  b36e4b72-0e86-4769-965d-cbe3662d647e --out
/var/www/html/bench/keystone_report03.html
```

Service-level agreement

Criterion	Detail	Success
performance_degradation	Current degradation: 806.294481% - Passed	True
max_seconds_per_iteration	Maximum seconds per iteration 4.19s <= 5.00s - Passed	True
failure_rate	Failure rate criteria 0.00% <= 0.00% <= 1.00% - Passed	True
outliers	Maximum number of outliers 1 <= 1 - Passed	True

That is first a great achievement! Now we have reached our goal by reducing the max of seconds per iteration below 5 seconds (4.19 seconds). As we have achieved a 'green' SLA as per set in our initial requirements, interpretations can be conducted from the **Load Profile** chart which reflects our new Keystone boost configuration:

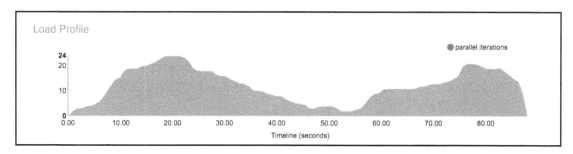

Compared to previous iterations, generated simultaneous requests can be handled by a pool of threads so Keystone was able to face concurrent iterations during the workload time line. Although the currency level was set higher, we can notice that the real concurrency performed during the test was only 24. That confirms that our thread and process settings for WSGI were in the right direction leaving more free slots for more concurrency and less time processing per iteration.

Shaking the OpenStack network - Shaker in a nutshell

Rally is a great tool to evaluate our OpenStack cloud control plane performance for API testing. On the other hand, we still need to collect more information on how our OpenStack infrastructure could handle data workload. Assuming that we have our OpenStack setup up and running, users would deploy their private environments and starting launching applications on top of the infrastructure layer. This means that a certain network workload is being generated and our network layer carrying that traffic should handle it in best effort.

It is necessary in this case to understand how the OpenStack data layer is behaving against specific network operation workload. From application layer, any event request between instances running within same network in OpenStack or interacting with Internet is considered as a network operation that should be accomplished successfully with zero error.

For this matter, a new incubated powerful benchmarking tool called **Shaker** joined recently the OpenStack effort and has been positioned to help cloud administrators testing the data plane performance of OpenStack.

Unlike Rally, Shaker focus on validating the OpenStack setup from application perspective. Basically, a cloud administrator intends to provide as best end user experience as he could by leveraging the capabilities of the OpenStack data plane. Shaker is designed in the first place to validate and test workloads across the network. The following points summarize the main characteristics of such benchmarking tool:

- Plan, verify and troubleshoot the OpenStack deployment
- Identify network anomalies under specific generated workload
- Package several network testing tools such as *iperf, flent* and *netperf*
- Automate test scenarios using OpenStack orchestration tool, Heat
- Provide customized and different user defined network topologies
- Generate detailed reports and statistics for better performance analysis.

 To read more about Shaker benchmarking tool for OpenStack, check the latest documentation website available at:
http://pyshaker.readthedocs.io/en/latest/index.html

Shaker architecture

The Shaker tool takes a different approach on running tests and deploy topologies in the OpenStack environment. Giving a succinct overview on its architecture would help us to understand how it works under the hood and start launching effective benchmarking scenarios:

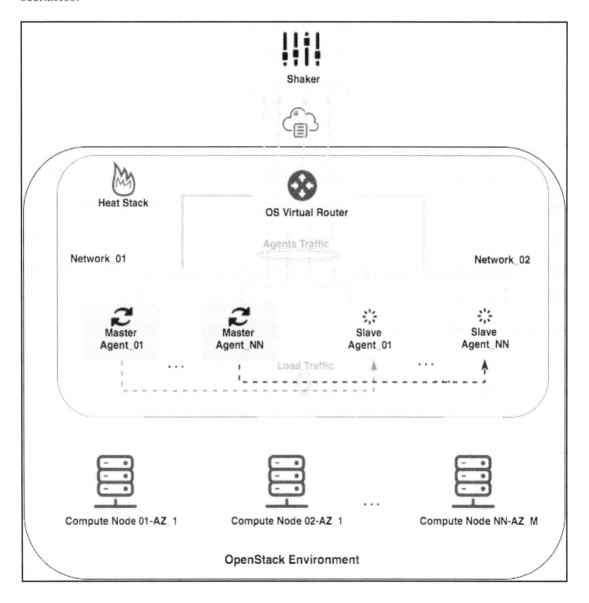

The previous diagram illustrates how Shaker server interacts with an OpenStack environment as follows:

1. Shaker instance runs workload scenarios by initiating connection to an OpenStack environment.
2. The Shaker process will deploy a predefined topology from the test scenario in OpenStack by the means of Heat orchestration tool.
3. Once the stack created, the Shaker process will execute tests after all pre-installed agents are set and joined the quorum in each deployed Heat instance in OpenStack.
4. The master agents are only involved in the case of network test scenario and slave ones will be serving only as back-end by receiving incoming traffic.
5. The execution will take part on all available agents in each instance deployed by Heat. The scenarios could be adjusted to execute a list of tests one by one within different compute nodes and across several networks.
6. When all tests are executed, all agents will send the test execution results to the Shaker server.
7. The Shaker server will generate a JSON format to store the collected results.
8. A Shaker command will be sent to the OpenStack API to destroy the Heat Stack.
9. Statistics and report will be generated based on the JSON input file in the Shaker server which creates a new HTML document providing detailed information regarding the benchmarking results.

The Shaker server requires an admin access to the OpenStack API to execute Shaker commands and run API requests. This can be achieved by sourcing the admin OpenStack environment variables in the Shaker machine. In addition, servers should be able to reach the Shaker server using routes to get results from the installed agents.

Installing Shaker

Like the Rally installation, we will setup a new Shaker server that needs access to the OpenStack environment. The Shaker server will join the following OpenStack networks:

- Administrative network
- External network

The next installation snippet will guide you through a package-based installation of Rally on a CentOS operation system with minimum hardware and software requirements as follows:

- Processor: 64-bit x86
- Memory: 4 GB RAM
- Disk space: 100 GB
- Network: Two 1 Gbps Network Interface Cards (NICs)
- Python 2.6 or higher version

Let's start by setting up our Shaker environment:

1. Start and activate a virtual environment where shaker will be running:

```
# virtualenv venv
# . venv/bin/activate
```

2. Using `pip` command line tool, install the shaker python binaries:

```
(venv) [root@shaker ~]# pip install pyshaker
```

3. Executing shaker scenarios will initiate the creation of Heat stacks in which each instance will be deployed from a base image stored in Glance. Make sure to build the proper image after sourcing the OpenStack admin credentials using the following command line:

```
(venv) [root@shaker ~]# source keystone_admin
[root@shaker(keystone_admin) ~]# shaker-image-builder
```

```
2017-01-15 15:53:02.694 17683 INFO shaker.engine.image_builder [-] Created image: shaker-image
```

By default the *shaker-image-builder* command line will download a base Ubuntu cloud image and execute predefined user data post scripts to install the needed shaker packages. Available base image templates are by default under `/venv//lib/python2.7/site-packages/shaker/resources/image_builder_templates/`. To use a different base image such as CentOS or Debian, point to `/venv/lib/python2.7/site-packages/shaker/engine/config.py` and edit the content of the `IMAGE_BUILDER_OPTS` by replacing the argument directive `ubuntu` by `centos` or `debian`.

4. The previous command line should create a new image and upload it to Glance in OpenStack:

```
# glance image-list
```

The **shaker-image-builder** command line will also create a new image flavor, a server deployed from the base image and create a snapshot to be stored in Glance after installing all required Shaker agent tools.

Shaker in action

Once our first image is successfully built and uploaded to Glance, we can start planning for test benchmarking scenarios and evaluate results. By default, a variety of scenario catalogs come along the installation of Shaker which can be found under /lib/python2.7/site-packages/shaker/scenarios/.

A Shaker scenario can be described in a YAML file in which few parameters will define what type of deployment and the list of tests that will be executed. Before starting our real benchmark scenario, let's summarize how a scenario file looks like:

```
title: ...
description:
  ...

deployment:
  template: ...
  accommodation: [..., ...]

execution:
  progression: ...
  tests:
  -
    title: ...
    class: ...
    method: ...
  -
...
```

Where the following sections are:

- **title**: Short name of the shaker scenario
- **description**: A summary describing which resources will be spawned and tested
- **deployment**: Custom configuration setup on how instances will be deployed across the OpenStack compute cluster nodes which consist of two main parts:
    - **template**: The Heat template name which the Shaker will be using
    - **accommodation**: Defines how instances will be placed and scheduled across the compute nodes by the means of following directives:
        - **pair**: Instructs the placement of the instances by two for shaker network traffic test by setting one instance as a load generator and the second one as receiver
        - **density**: Sets a multiplier digit for the number of instances per single compute node
        - **compute_nodes**: Sets the maximum number of compute nodes that will be used during the test
        - **single_room**: Instructs the Shaker test to provision one instance per compute node
        - **double_room**: Instructs the Shaker test to provision a pair of instances per compute node
        - **zones**: Instructs in which availability zones in OpenStack the test will be executed.

By default, if `compute_nodes` directive is not set, the shaker tool will use all the available compute nodes registered in the OpenStack environment.

- **execution**: the core of scenario will be described in this section in which Shaker executes the test suite at the same time across all available agents. The execution directive can be instructed by the following parameters:
    - **progression**: Controls the level of concurrency of running tests between agents with different run levels:
        - **linear**: Executes tests gradually by increasing the involvement of agents during the run by value of 1
        - **quadratic**: executes tests gradually by

increasing the involvement of agents during the run by doubling them in each test execution

- **no value set**: If none linear or quadratic not set, the execution will involve all available agents

    - **tests**: Each test section is separated by a '-' character, this will be executed in order as they described in the file. A test can be parameterized depending on its class definition. The next directives are common for all **test** in Shaker:

        - **title**: short name of the test step execution

        - **class**: the name of tool performing the network test

        - **sla**: an indicator of the overall scenario success rate of the test benchmark upon completion

Each test class provides specific attributes that can used to narrow the execution of the test. Test classes attributes vary from one tool to another, a complete section of each can be found here:
`http://pyshaker.readthedocs.io/en/latest/usage.html#test-classes`

A benchmarking scenario for OpenStack data plane should be performed by triggering workload in different OpenStack components while are operating in a steady state. In our case, testing the performance of our OpenStack network layer will help to verify the functionality of the applications that will run on top of the OpenStack infrastructure when it goes fully to production. As per discussed in the introductory chapter, OpenStack network service offers many networking capabilities by exposing Software Defined Network capabilities. This opens a variety of configuration options and topologies. But finding the best outfit for a custom OpenStack network setup cannot be collected without facing performance limitations.

Shaker will help to prevent such performance issues to happen before going to production. Operators then can decide how to rebuild or redesign a high-performance OpenStack networking installation based on the collected benchmarking results.

For this purpose, it is necessary to address the gap of the performance measurement at early stage specifically within Neutron by taking into account numerous network topologies which is offered by Shaker. Several benchmarking scenarios can be tested including:

- TCP/UDP throughput: Download and Upload performance
- Latency for instances built in OpenStack within same networks
- Latency for instances built in OpenStack in different networks
- Floating IP and NAT instances in the same L2 and L3
- External flows from external hosts

Scenario example - OpenStack L2

The next simple scenario, Shaker launches a couple of instances in the same tenant network. We intend to test the throughput between compute nodes where the traffic will go through the same L2 tenant domain network. We adjust it to place every instance in a different compute node. In our case, we will use two compute nodes where the master and slave belong to the same availability zone.

Make sure to include the **l2.hot** heat template in the deployment section. The test skeleton is derived from the predefined Shaker scenario available under `/lib/python2.7/site-packages/shaker/scenarios/openstack/`

```
title: OpenStack L2

description:
  Benchmark Layer 2 connectivity performance. The shaker scenario will
launch pairs of instances in separate compute node.
deployment:
  template: l2.hot
  accommodation: [pair, single_room, compute_nodes: 1]

execution:
  progression: quadratic
  tests:
  -
    title: Download
    class: flent
    method: tcp_download
  -
    title: Upload
    class: flent
    method: tcp_upload
  -
    title: Bi-directional
    class: flent
    method: tcp_bidirectional
  -
    title: UDP-Bursts
    class: flent
    method: bursts
```

The execution workflow of our scenario is **quadratic** summarized into three test steps running `flent` in order:

1. `tcp_download`: Download streaming TCP traffic
2. `tcp_upload`: Upload streaming TCP traffic
3. `tcp_biderctional`: Download and Upload streaming TCP traffic
4. `bursts`: Latency measurements for an intermittent bursting UDP traffic

To learn more about *flent* class tool, point to the the following URL:
`https://github.com/tohojo/flent/tree/master/flent/`

Running the previous scenario can be performed using the following command lines:

```
# cd  /lib/python2.7/site-packages/shaker/scenarios/openstack/
# shaker --server-endpoint 172.28.128.3:555 --scenario l2.yaml --
report /var/www/html/bench/l2_iteration01.html
```

```
2017-01-17 18:55:10.342 25161 INFO shaker.engine.utils [-] Logging enabled
2017-01-17 18:55:10.344 25161 INFO shaker.engine.messaging [-] Listening on *:555
2017-01-17 18:55:10.345 25161 INFO shaker.engine.server [-] Play scenario: /root/venv/lib/python2.7/site-packages
2017-01-17 18:55:10.347 25170 INFO shaker.agent.agent [-] Agent id is: __heartbeat
2017-01-17 18:55:10.348 25170 INFO shaker.agent.agent [-] Connecting to server: 172.28.128.3:555
2017-01-17 18:55:10.348 25170 INFO shaker.agent.agent [-] Agent config: {'polling_interval': 10}
2017-01-17 18:55:10.363 25161 INFO pykwalify.core [-] validation.valid
2017-01-17 18:55:10.577 25161 INFO shaker.openstack.clients.openstack [-] Connection to OpenStack is initialized
```

The previous shaker command line will run the scenario described in the *'l2.yaml'* file by contacting the OpenStack API endpoint on an available port. The shaker in this example uses port **555**. It instructs also to generate an output report file in **HTML** format that will be stored under `/var/www/html/bench/` folder.

Executing several scenarios would generate many reports HTML files. For a better report browsing, feel free to install in the shaker server any web server that could serve the HTML files from one single directory. In the previous example, `httpd` was installed and configured to serve reports generated by shaker from folder `bench`.

The execution of the scenario could take a while since Shaker will trigger OpenStack environment by APIs requests to set a complete stack using the OpenStack orchestration tool. The Heat stack is set in the scenario file. Each instance will be launched with pre-installed shaker agents. Before the execution of the series of tests take place, slave and master agents should wait and find each other so the quorum is required.

```
2017-01-16 01:41:00.076 20915 INFO shaker.engine.quorum [-] Waiting for quorum of agents: set(['shaker_uatdek_slave_1', 'shaker_uatdek_slave_
0', 'shaker_uatdek_master_1', 'shaker_uatdek_master_0'])
```

If you use an older Heat version in OpenStack, you might end up with a Heat error when launching the Shaker command line for the first time, make sure that `python-croniter` is installed and rerun the command line.

In the OpenStack cloud controller node, make sure that the Heat stack is successfully built:

The stack should be ready having a pair instance per each shaker master and slave roles:

```
# nova list | grep shaker
```

Once all agents joined the quorum in the created stack, shaker command line output will indicate that the test is accomplished and results written in row `json` file are exported to the HTML report file:

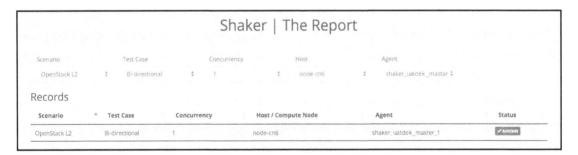

Similarly, to Rally, Shaker tool generates a pertinent report HTML file
`var/www/html/bench/l2_iteration01.html`. The report web page exposes different
options to navigate through different results per running test case: **Download**, **Upload** and
Bi-directional. Additionally, the test scenario includes available concurrency level against
specific hosts in the test benchmark. Note that the level of concurrency is relative to the
number of available nodes included in the benchmark. For the sake of simplicity, we keep
the concurrency level at 1 and derive result statistics from one node.Data Plane analysis can
be performed for each test case. We can take the **Bi-directional** one as our use case. The
results of sample stats can be shown in the following **Execution Summary**:

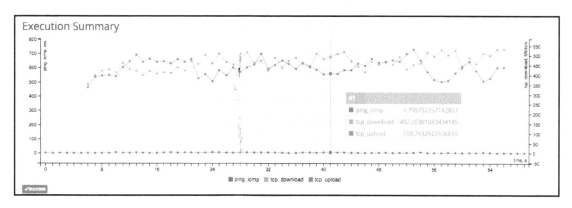

The test use case throughput for both tcp_download and tcp_upload stats as follows:

- **tcp_download:**
  - max: 530 MBits/sec
  - min: 350 MBits/sec
  - mean: 450 MBits/sec
- **tcp_upload:**
  - max: 730 MBits/sec
  - min: 460 MBits/sec
  - mean: 600 MBits/sec

Obviously, the obtained values may show a low throughput if considering a large-scale
environment demanding high traffic within private network. Building application setups on
top of OpenStack infrastructure could require higher throughput performance. This means
in our case we can achieve better network throughput between compute nodes residing in
the same L2 tenant domain network. As the packets are traveling through a private
network, we can consider adjusting the **MTU (Maximum Transfer Unit)** value as an
interesting point that deserves to look at.

Depending on the network hardware configuration and operating system settings running in the private cloud environment, the first executed test assumes a standard MTU with 1500-byte size. The goal of the next iteration of the Shaker benchmark test is to increase the value of MTU across the OpenStack test setup including the network physical interfaces of the OpenStack nodes: controller, compute and network. Changing the Neutron interfaces will be propagated to the virtual devices created by Nova and Neutron when booting a new virtual machine. All newly created VMs will be configured with the new MTU via DHCP ran by **dnsmasq** process. Note that this change requires adjustment of the physical devices including routers and switches in a production setup.

We will be adjusting our MTU value across the OpenStack benchmarking environment setup to **9000** to have larger packet payload sizes. This way we can run our test with less protocol overhead.

Ethernet frames with more than 1500 bytes of MTU are called **Jumbo frames**. In modern network devices and Linux distros, Jumbo frames are supported and can be used to improve network performance. Few hardware requirements are needed to support a larger MTU size including Network Interface Card compatibility. Another advantage of using Jumbo frames is the decrease of the server overhead by reducing the CPU load usage of the server when dealing with large payloads transfer.

The MTU size can be adjusted for all physical Network Interface Cards used by the tenant networks. That includes controller, compute and network nodes. To update the MTU size in each required OpenStack node, run the following command line:

```
# echo MTU=9000 >> /etc/sysconfig/network-scripts/ifcfg-eth0
```

Make sure to apply the previous command to the right network interface attached to the tenant network.

This change should comply with Neutron configuration as the new MTU will include additional overhead of the GRE and VXLAN network-based:

1. Set in the Neutron main configuration file the default physical network MTU size to 9000:

```
# vim /etc/neutron/neutron.conf
[DEFAULT]
...
global_physnet_mtu = 9000
```

2. To advertise the updated MTU size to instances, add the following directive to the default section in the same file:

```
...
advertise_mtu = True
```

3. Update the Neutron DHCP agent to support the new MTU size:

```
# vim /etc/neutron/dhcp_agent.ini
[DEFAULT]
...
network_device_mtu = 9000
```

4. Set the network_device_mtu directive for the L3 agent configuration file:

```
# vim /etc/neutron/l3_agent.ini
[DEFAULT]
...
network_device_mtu = 9000
```

5. Next, we will need to tell Nova to support the new MTU when creating network devices during the boot load of a new virtual machine:

```
# vim /etc/nova/nova.conf
[DEFAULT]
...
network_device_mtu = 9000
```

6. Update the ML2 plugin configuration to support the new MTU size:

```
# vim /etc/neutron/ml2_conf.ini
[ml2]
...
path_mtu = 9000
segment_mtu = 9000
```

After restarting the adjusted OpenStack and Linux network services, make sure that the new MTU value has been applied for each network interface. This can be checked simply by grepping MTU from ifconfig command line for example:

```
# ifconfig eth0 | grep MTU
UP BROADCAST MULTICAST MTU:9000 Metric:1
```

Additionally, we can verify the virtual interfaces in the network/compute nodes:

```
160: br-ex: <BROADCAST,MULTICAST,UP,LOWER_UP> mtu 9000 …
...
161: br-int: <BROADCAST,MULTICAST,UP,LOWER_UP> mtu 9000 …
...
162: br-tun: <BROADCAST,MULTICAST,UP,LOWER_UP> mtu 9000 …
```

Running the second iteration of our data plane benchmarking **Bi-directional** test case yields to the following result summary:

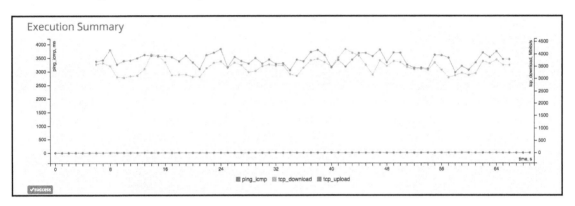

So far, our assumption was correct! Increasing the MTU size has increased the throughput performance as the following:

- **tcp_download**:
  - max: 4190 MBits/sec
  - min: 3030 MBits/sec
  - mean: 3470 MBits/sec

- **tcp_upload**:
  - max: 3800 MBits/sec
  - min: 2960 MBits/sec
  - mean: 3430 MBits/sec

Results could be different between environments depending on the network topology including network cards model, line speed, drivers, hardware capabilities, etc... This also depends on the installed software running in the OpenStack environment that includes the operating system, the used Neutron plugins and L2 segmentation types.

This great enhancement shows that there is always space to boost performance. Adjusting the OpenStack network configuration settings is a quite challenging task to achieve pertinent results. Particularly with network performance, there is no standard configuration that could be applied in any OpenStack setup to move the bits faster. In our previous example, our adjustment increased the throughput almost by 8 times, this can be applicable only to the showed benchmarked OpenStack network setup. Depending on the physical network, system configuration including the operating system and hardware capabilities, results could differ.

Summary

In this chapter, we brought our OpenStack setup to the next level by highlighting few advanced settings that leverage its performance such as the database. You should be able to understand the necessity of undergo rigorous and effective testing of the cloud platform. This should include the learning curve of the art of benchmarking that gives an insight on all facets of the running components in the OpenStack environment including system hardware and software resources. In addition, you should be able to correlate between performance testing and tuning based on benchmarking results. At this point, cloud operators should enjoy the plethora of benefits offered by existing and promising testing tools such as Rally and Shaker. We have conducted few benchmarking examples for both control and data planes. By the means of such example tools, you should be able to run more sophisticated scenarios based on your requirements and resources limits. This will give you more confidence on your setup and design decisions, help to improve, and strength the trust of users.

By this ending chapter, our journey of the second edition of mastering OpenStack has come to an end. During the course of this edition, we have revisited our initial cloud design patterns and built our OpenStack environment using different automation tool such as Ansible. The book was all enhanced by tackling the OpenStack control plane and discuss scalability and fault tolerance requirements. You also learned a new topic on compute power and hypervisor segregation for better scalability and reliability. You should be aware that containerization technology is being more and more involved in the OpenStack ecosystem. The new edition has covered few incubated projects such File Share service. Thus, OpenStack exposes more storage use cases and options that are making the cloud operator life easier to manage from one central and high available point. During our walkthrough, we have covered future and fast growing network useful features for the operational OpenStack cloud environment such as SDN and NVF technologies.

This journey also should give users the opportunity not only to run resources on top of OpenStack but also to orchestrate them whatever an application complex is.

With this edition, you should also notice the evolution of the telemetry service in OpenStack and how monitoring essential is. That reflects the overwhelming features of OpenStack incubated projects in each release. Monitoring helps us to troubleshoot and act proactively before incidents grow and become out of control. At this level, you should be self confident of how to troubleshoot issues in OpenStack and dig into root causes by improving the logging pipeline.

With this new updated edition, our great wish is that you have a clear vision on the trend of growth of the OpenStack platform in the cloud journey. By bringing shared experience update, we hope that you keep enjoying the cloud adventure brought by OpenStack and take yours to the next level where the journey of knowledge never ends.

Index

novncproxy 105

O

object storage device (OSD) 139
Ocata 105
Octavia
  configuring 228
Open Virtual Network (OVN) 215
  integrating, with OpenStack 220, 221
  virtual networks, implementing with 221, 222, 223
Open vSwitch (OVS) 22, 183
OpenID Connect 14
OpenStack Ansible (OSA)
  about 57, 126, 329
  deploying 91
  deployment node 92
  references 63
OpenStack API
  testing 407
OpenStack clustering
  about 74
  asymmetric clustering 75
  divide and conquer 75
  symmetric clustering 75
OpenStack community 132
OpenStack environment
  reference link 63
OpenStack logs
  response code analysis use case 388, 389
  security analysis use case 387
  visualizing 386
OpenStack Magnum project
  about 108
  Bay 110
  BayModel 110
  Pod 110
  reference link 110
OpenStack modules
  reference link 54
OpenStack monitoring
  arming 334
  Nagios, using 334
OpenStack Networking
  reference link 21

OpenStack orchestration
  about 244
  embracing 258
  HEAT, demystifying 244
  stacking in 246
  Terraform in 260, 261, 263, 265, 267
  Terraform, working 259
OpenStack playbooks
  executing 95
  Host Groups, configuring 96
  network configuration 95
  OpenStack Ansible (OSA), configuring 95
  playbooks 99
OpenStack provider
  reference link 258
OpenStack Resource Types
  reference link 247
OpenStack SLA
  meeting 408
OpenStack tenancy
  operating 234
  quotas, managing 237
  user capabilities, managing 235, 237
  users, managing 234
OpenStack, keystone
  reference link 401
OpenStack-ELK pipeline
  extending 383, 384, 385
  Kibana, troubleshooting from 390, 391, 392
  OpenStack logs, visualizing 386, 387
OpenStack
  about 11, 12, 48
  architecture, setting up 28
  benchmarking 406
  caching 398
  Ceph in 167
  Cinder 15
  conceptual model design 29
  continuous integration (CI) 51
  deployment 28
  Glance 17
  Keystone 14
  logical architecture 13
  Manila 16
  memcached in 400

W

X

Y

www.ingramcontent.com/pod-product-compliance
Lightning Source LLC
Chambersburg PA
CBHW081456050326
40690CB00015B/2825